A Tale of Two Teams, One City

Jerome Holtzman
George Vass

Copyright 2001 by Bonus Books, Inc.

05 04 03 02 01   5 4 3 2 1

Library of Congress Card Number: 2001093219
ISBN: 1-56625-170-2

Bonus Books, Inc.
160 East Illinois Street
Chicago, Illinois 60611

Photos courtesy of the Chicago Cubs, the Chicago White Sox and the authors.

Printed in the United States of America
Composition by Point West, Inc., Carol Stream, IL

THE BATTING ORDER

Introduction   x

CHAPTER 1
Black and Bleak Sox   1

CHAPTER 2
Off 'n' Running   21

CHAPTER 3
The Uncivil War   39

CHAPTER 4
Merkle's Boner   43

CHAPTER 5
Double Duty or Dubious Myth?   49

CHAPTER 6
Femmes Fatale   53

CHAPTER 7
The Grimm Silver Age   59

CHAPTER 8
Who Called What?   73

CHAPTER 9
Homer in the Gloamin'   81

CHAPTER 10
The Comiskeys' Iron Age   85

CHAPTER 11
All-Star of a Game   97

CHAPTER 12
Go-Go Sox, No-Go Cubs 103

CHAPTER 13
College of Confusion 125

CHAPTER 14
Klu to Winning 131

CHAPTER 15
Ill-Starred All-Stars 137

CHAPTER 16
The Iron Catcher 149

CHAPTER 17
Roller-Coaster White Sox 153

CHAPTER 18
Balls, Bats and Chicanery 167

CHAPTER 19
Spit and Follies 173

CHAPTER 20
Blustering 'New Tradition' 183

CHAPTER 21
Looking Good, Winning Ugly 195

CHAPTER 22
Pleasures, Pain, Big Hurt 201

CHAPTER 23
Ryno, Grace, Sammy Make 'em Run 213

CHAPTER 24
The Kids Really Can Play 229

CHAPTER 25
Character Development 239

CHAPTER 26
Ruling Dynasties 247

CHAPTER 27
Front Office Musical Chairs 259

CHAPTER 28
The Firing Line 279

CHAPTER 29
Wheelers, Dealers 293

CHAPTER 30
Hear It Now, See It Live 303

CHAPTER 31
Media Rare 313

CHAPTER 32
Dawn of Tradition 325

CHAPTER 33
Fields of Dreams 'n' Screams 341

CHAPTER 34
All-Time Chicago Team 353

CHAPTER 35
Top of the Charts 359

Index 369

INTRODUCTION

Chicago, the Second City? Ignore that arrogant dismissal of the capital of America's Heartland!

Second City, indeed!

Not at all, certainly not in the context of baseball, if in any association whatsoever. Rather when it comes to that incomparable, wondrous, exhilarating and exasperatingly unpredictable team sport it would be extremely appropriate and entirely just to proclaim Chicago either "First City" or more modestly "Fun City."

Nowhere in the entire realm of baseball has the sport produced for its fans more memorable players, games, feats, incidents and emotional outpourings, whether of rejoicing or lamentation, than in Chicago. The incredibly rich supply of unforgettable characters, teams and events that has contributed vitality, atmosphere and excitement to baseball for generations is unsurpassed elsewhere.

After all, while baseball is a business and has been from the time Harry Wright became its first professional by accepting a salary of $28.50 a week from the pioneering Cincinnati Red Stockings of the 1860s, at heart it's an amusement, an entertainment designed primarily for the enjoyment of rapt spectators paying for the privilege of looking on at an exhibition of athletic skill and pluck.

Keeping that in mind—which isn't always easy if you're a fervent, hot-blooded fan hungry for success on the playing field—most of the multitude of Chicagoans who revel in baseball's pleasures might echo onetime Chicago Cub manager Frankie Frisch's philosophy of how to play the game.

"Make fun, not war!" Frisch admonished his players.

While Frisch's reign as manager was brief, like that of many of his predecessors and successors, because his Cubs of 1949–51 were far more fun-loving than warlike, his dictum avows a deep, even comforting, truth about the way the game should be played.

So did one of the best-known poetic trifles about sports, the following lines written by fabled sportswriter Grantland Rice:

> *When the Great Scorer comes*
> *To mark against your name.*
> *He'll write not "won" or "lost"*
> *But how you played the game.*

Rice's noble sentiment obviously doesn't square with Vince Lombardi's alleged declaration, "Winning is not everything, it's the only thing," but the legendary football coach's harsh statement seems overly ruthless by Chicago sports standards judging from the results the city's teams have attained in recent decades.

At the very least, Rice's stanza provides comfort, if rather cold, for Chicago's baseball fans! During the last half-century or so the scorer has written "lost" far more often than "won." The Cubs last won a league pennant in 1945, the Chicago White Sox in 1959.

But even if Chicago's professional baseball teams have waged war by frequently marching to the rear since the White Sox brought the World Series to the city more than four decades ago they've never failed to "make fun." They've played and embellished the game with a gusto that belongs solely to **Baseball,** *Chicago Style*, which not so coincidentally is the title of this book.

And there was a time, though recalled from personal experience only by a dwindling handful of tottering survivors who have cashed Social Security checks for decades, during which the Cubs and White Sox rewarded their followers with that rare, gratifying combination of entertainment and success at decent intervals.

In fact, Chicago can lay a credible claim to being the First City of Baseball, the capital of what has been reverently hailed as "the national pastime." It still remains so to its legion of fervent supporters, if steady annual increases in major league attendance are a reliable criterion.

What's certain is that the Cubs are the oldest uninterrupted sports franchise in existence, never having skipped a season since their debut as a charter member of the newly-organized National League in 1876. Their record of continuous competition is a distinction to which no other baseball team—or for that matter any other professional athletic entity—can lay claim.

It's also undeniable that since the White Sox assumed major league status in 1901 with the elevation of the American League, Chicago has been the sole city in the nation to field teams without a break in both major leagues. The same can't be said of New York, Boston, Philadelphia and St. Louis, all abandoned by one or more teams between 1950 and 1960.

Although the partisan fans of each team might hotly deny it, the joint existence of the Cubs and White Sox in the same city for more than a century has formed an inseparable bond. Their histories and traditions are inextricably intertwined.

Significantly, White Sox is a compression of White Stockings, the original and abandoned former name of the Cubs, which the new team at the doorway into the 20th Century snapped up to form a familiar link with Chicago baseball tradition.

It's also noteworthy that the first manager and pitching ace of the White Sox was Clark Griffith, who led them to a pennant in 1901 after deserting the Cubs, for whom he had strung six consecutive 20-game winning seasons, a rare feat among pitchers.

The Cubs and White Sox have co-existed, if at times uneasily, for more than a century now in one city—or in one "market," as current jargon would have it. Neither team has always prospered, at times one or the other suffering downturns in success on the field or in public support, but they've endured and appear assured of doing so well into the foreseeable future.

As a result of this enviable durability and stability, Chicago's teams have provided generations of fans with an unmatched treasure trove of baseball memories. And memory above all sets baseball apart from all other sports because its past has struck more deeply into the national collective consciousness over a far longer period of time.

"Baseball," the poet Donald Hall remarked in a filmed interview for Geoffrey C. Ward's and Ken Burns' absorbing 1994 television documentary series on the game, "because of its continuity over the space of America and the time of America, is a place where memory gathers."

In the preface to their book, *Baseball*, published as a complement to their television series, Ward and Burns added the comment:

"Nothing in our daily life offers more of the comfort of continuity, the generational connection of belonging to a vast and complicated American family, the powerful sense of home, the freedom from time's constraints, and the great gift of accumulated memory than does our National Pastime."

"Accumulated memory" is a great portion of what baseball is about, providing endless material for the bragging rights, discussion, debate and argument that enhance enjoyment of the game for knowledgeable fans.

If baseball fans in general belong to what Ward and Burns call a "vast and complicated American family," those specifically of Chicago might be described as members of a "dysfunctional" household, given the traditional antagonism and ill-will toward each other's teams attributed to Cubs and White Sox loyalists.

While in most areas of life such unbridled and enduring animosity between partisans is generally deplored, in baseball it's a boon and a joy to those who treasure the competitiveness of the game. It also has been a reliable source of added income for the Cubs and White Sox franchises which from 1901 have capitalized on the antagonism.

Since the recent introduction of regular season inter-league competition the six annual games between the Cubs and White Sox have drawn capacity crowds and have been played with rare intensity. Preceding inter-league play, Cubs and White Sox fans in the early years expended their partisanship in an annual post-season City Series, generally of seven games, and later in a yearly mid-season charity exhibition game.

The zenith of this competitive enthusiasm was undoubtedly reached in what can only be termed as the ultimate confrontation between the Cubs and White Sox, the 1906 World Series. An encore has been ardently sought for almost a century but has painfully eluded Chicago's teams up to the present.

A newspaper headline the day after the opening game, won 2-1 by the White Sox (who went on to capture the Series) blared in large letters: "Partisan Feeling Runs High in Vast Throng of Exultant Fans, Whose Heated Arguments Counteract Icy Blasts at West Side Park."

An account of the game elaborated on the emotional outpouring of the fans, especially that centering on Nick Altrock, the winning pitcher: "The demonstration by White Sox rooters at the close of the game was wildly exciting. The players of the south side team were carried around on shoulders, Altrock especially had great difficulty in escaping the jubilant throng of fans."

Altrock! A good beginning if Chicago's cast of fascinating baseball characters is to be listed in alphabetical order of surnames.

After Altrock continue with Anson, Aparicio, Appling, Banks, Cavarretta, Chance, Durocher, Dykes and Evers, flow on to Grace, Grimm, Hartnett, Jackson, Jenkins, Jolley, Kelly, Lane, Lyons and Minoso, as well as many others preceding Sandberg, Santo, Shires, Spalding, Sosa, Tinker, Thomas, Veeck, Walsh, Williams, Wilson and Wood until a termination with Wrigley, Wynn, Zernial, Zimmer and Zimmerman.

If the list were complete, it would include the more than 4,000 players, managers, coaches, front office officials, owners and other personalities who have strutted, swaggered, staggered and skulked across Chicago's baseball stage. Such ancillary figures as radio and television sportstcasters, sportswriters, authors and even playwrights would be part of it.

All these thousands played a part in creating, participating in or merely observing with a critical, objective or overly-indulgent eye a stream of events, whether triumphs or disasters, memorable or deserving obscurity, that add up to a riveting panorama through many decades of **Baseball,** *Chicago Style.*

Not all of these people were associated with either the Cubs or White Sox because Chicago has had other, if short-lived, professional franchises, such as the Whales of the Federal League and teams in the Players' League, American Association and Union Association. They also deserve at least a smidgen of recall.

But the focus of **Baseball,** *Chicago Style* is inevitably on the Cubs and White Sox, past and present, though it rejects the deplorable current fashion of the media, and even of some otherwise loyal fans, to demean the current and recent teams as unworthy of their most successful predecessors.

It has become a stock cliché of sports writing and broadcasting, nationally as well as in Chicago, to belittle the Cubs as "lovable losers" and to point out, sometimes with malicious glee, that they haven't won a World Series since 1908, let alone a National League pennant since 1945.

Add to that such arrant nonsense as another slight, the one of the "ex-Cub factor," which suggests that a team engaged in post-season play that has more former Cubs on it than its opponent is doomed to failure. Or that the Cubs' chief attraction is the ambiance of Wrigley Field, or the engaging personality of a particular broadcaster, such as Harry Caray, or his predecessor on television, Jack Brickhouse.

Aspersions are also constantly cast on the White Sox. They are frequently censured for not keeping pace with the cross-town Cubs in attendance in recent seasons even when more successful on the field. The second Comiskey Park is regularly lambasted for falling short in fan enticement in comparison to storied Wrigley Field, or even to its predecessor, old Comiskey Park, opened in 1910 and replaced in 1991.

What's best known nationally about the White Sox is that they "threw" the 1919 World Series to the Cincinnati Reds. The dastardly act, celebrated in history, literature, film and television, transformed their previously innocuous nickname of Black Sox, based on the hue of their uniforms in preceding seasons, into an invidious epithet, which clings to them like a burr to corduroy.

Fair or foul enough! Yet put it into perspective.

The focus on the Black Sox scandal obscures the genuine achievements of the White Sox, both individually and as a team during an entire century. They won World Series in 1906 and 1917, celebrated additional American League pennants in 1959, 1919 and 1901, and fielded such Hall of Famers as Eddie Collins, Luke Appling, Ted Lyons, Carlton Fisk, Luis Aparicio, Nellie Fox, Ed Walsh and Ray Schalk, among others.

In 2000, the White Sox astonished the baseball world by running away with an American League division title, their young team led by one of the greatest hitters in baseball history, Frank Thomas. He also helped them to a division title in 1993, their second such modest achievement (having won in 1983) since each major league split like an amoeba after the 1968 season, the last to honor only pennant winners.

And to refute Lombardi's supposed declaration, winning is not the only thing, not in Chicago, not now, not ever.

Memorable losers also inspire affection, and few teams have been cherished more lovingly than the exhilarating Go-Go Sox of the 1950s that featured Nellie Fox, Minnie Minoso and Chico Carrasquel, as well as manager Jimmy Dykes' overachieving Depression Era squad of the 1930s and 1940s, paced by Appling and Lyons.

The same holds true of the Cubs, whose most unforgettable exploit of the last 55 seasons may have been to *not win the pennant* in 1969, the year of the Great Collapse. Not even division titles in 1984 and 1989, as well as a "wild-card" post-season excursion in 1998, all of which ended in tears, have displaced the sorrow of 1969 and all that from the collective grief of Cubs fans.

Those who scoff at Cub tradition conveniently ignore several glorious periods of their history. It's true they've won only two World Series (1907–08), but they've played in 10, far more than most teams. And their 1906 record of 116-36, for a percentage of .847, is unmatched in major league history.

What's more, they've enjoyed several stretches of great success. They captured four National League championships in five years (1906–08, 1910) and another four within 10 seasons (1929,

1932, 1935, 1938). They were a powerhouse in the early days of the National League, winning six pennants in 11 seasons from 1876 through 1886.

That all may have happened long ago, but those triumphant days are indelibly a part of the Cub record, and helped to build a tradition worthy of respect rather than derision.

Much the same can be said of individual achievements. Like the Sox, numerous Cubs have been elected to the Hall of Fame, among them Ernie Banks, Billy Williams, Fergie Jenkins, Gabby Hartnett, Frank Chance, Mordecai "Three-Finger" Brown, Hack Wilson, Billy Herman, and many more.

As for remarkable achievements by individuals, neither the Cubs nor White Sox need give way to the players of any other team. Their stars have shone just as brightly.

The most notable recent feat has been Cub outfielder Sammy Sosa's output of 66 home runs in 1998, second only to Mark McGwire's major league record 70, followed by 63 in 1999 and 50 in 2000, for a three-season total of 179, an average of almost 60 per campaign.

Sosa's cross-town slugging contemporary, first baseman/designated hitter Frank Thomas, through his first 11 major league seasons, all with the White Sox, kept pace with various offensive deeds of the greatest hitters in history. En route, Thomas twice won honors as the American League's Most Valuable Player (1993–94).

Sosa's and Thomas' exploits are merely among the latest accomplished by players clad in Chicago uniforms. Another of recent vintage was Cub pitcher Kerry Wood's record-tying 20-strikeout game in his rookie season of 1998.

Equally memorable among the more venerable achievements are Cub slugger Hack Wilson's still-unsurpassed 191 runs batted in 1930 as well as his 56 home runs the same year, which stood as a National League record until McGwire and Sosa smashed it in 1998.

Then there's White Sox shortstop Appling's league-leading batting average of .388 in 1936, rarely surpassed since then, and not at all by a right-handed batter.

Superlative achievements make up only part of the mystique of Chicago baseball. It also includes a wealth of unusually memorable incidents such as the "two balls in play" game, Gabby Hartnett's "homer in the gloamin'," Merkle's boner, Babe Ruth's alleged "called-shot" home run, Billy Goat's "curse," the Camp Ojibwa flap, "Disco Demolition Night," scoreboard shenanigans, and allegedly "frozen" baseballs and "corked" bats.

In addition, there's an amusing cast of colorful characters and "oddballs" who've left a mark, great or small yet always intriguing, on Chicago's baseball chronicles. Any roster of such eccentrics is sure to include Rabbit Maranville, Art Shires, Smead Jolley, Dizzy Dean, Andy Lotshaw, Don Rudolph, Bill Faul and Dave Kingman.

All the foregoing combines to make up the panoramic, fascinating excursion through all the eras of baseball in "Fun City" that we've chosen to call **Baseball, *Chicago Style*.**

A cautionary note! As someone once said, the past is a foreign country. The farther it recedes from the current time, the less accurately can its events and people be measured and evaluated for comparison with those of the present.

That insurmountable barrier may result in the perilous romanticizing of a bygone era and the people who lived in it, thus tending to make the legendary figures and feats seem greater than they really were. Nostalgia may make the past appear more pleasant and attractive than it actually was to those who lived in it.

Mr. Dooley, the newspaper folk philosopher invented by Chicago newspaper humorist Finley Peter Dunne, the equally talented precursor by a century of fabled columnist Mike Royko, mocked the sentimental souls who unrelentingly laud and long for "the good old days" with the shrewdly skeptical comment:

> *Th' past always looks better than it was.*
> *'Tis only pleasant because it isn't here.*

Mr. Dooley's couplet holds true when applied to professional baseball as practiced and malpracticed in Chicago for the last century and a half since it sank permanent roots as a popular entertainment during the Civil War era of the 1860s.

Nonetheless, the crowded stage of fascinating characters and episodes of the past is a delight to explore despite the mists of time by which it's shrouded. It provides the yardsticks with which to better measure the achievements of the fast-fleeting present.

It's the hope of its authors that **Baseball, *Chicago Style*** does so with full justice to those whose exploits and personalities have granted Chicago's multitude of fans the "great gift of accumulated memory" whether they follow the Cubs or White Sox.

And if that "gift" includes the dismal saga of the Black Sox, as it must, so be it. Even that criminal conspiracy sets Chicago apart for no affair in baseball history is so widely known even among those blighted souls whose interest in the game is non-existent. Thus it is fitting to have the tale of stinginess, greed and betrayal of "the faith of 50 million people" form the first chapter of this book, especially since it has never been told so fully and objectively without glib sentiment obscuring its uglier aspects.

Even when it comes to chicanery **Baseball, *Chicago Style*** need give way to no rival claimant to first rank.

Second City? Not by a "Homer in the Gloamin'"!

BLACK AND BLEAK SOX

1

"Who is he anyway, an actor?"

"No."

"A dentist?"

"No, he's a gambler." Gatsby hesitated, then added coolly: "He's the man who fixed the World Series back in 1919."

"Fixed the World Series?" I repeated.

The idea staggered me. I remembered, of course, that the World Series had been fixed in 1919, but if I had thought of it at all, I would have thought of it as a thing that merely happened, the end of some inevitable chain. It never occurred to me that one man could start to play with the faith of 50 million people—with the single-mindedness of a burglar blowing a safe.

"How did he happen to do that?"

"He just saw the opportunity."

"Why isn't he in jail?"

"They can't get him, old sport. He's a smart man."

—F. Scott Fitzgerald, in *The Great Gatsby*, describing gambler Arnold Rothstein who helped fund the fix.

No single event in modern sports has been exhumed as much as the 1919 Black Sox Scandal. There have been hundreds of newspaper and magazine articles and more than a dozen books, including Eliot Asinof's *Eight Men Out*, published in 1961 and 30 years later turned into a feature film.

Another well-known work is a sentimental biography, *Shoeless Joe Jackson, Say It Ain't So, Joe*, by Donald Gropman who campaigned for Jackson's election to the baseball Hall of Fame. Gropman insists Jackson, a functional illiterate, was duped as an innocent victim, and ignores much of the evidence that clearly demonstrates he participated in the swindle.

In addition to the eight alleged fixers, among the villains was White Sox owner Charles A. Comiskey, the so-called Old Roman, a highly-regarded baseball pioneer and co-founder of the American League who long ago was elected to the Hall of Fame. Comiskey knew the fix was in after the first game, possibly even before.

Also guilty, guilty as hell of unethical conduct, was Alfred Austrian, Comiskey's attorney, a Chicago legal powerhouse with crucial judicial connections. Austrian persuaded Jackson, Ed Cicotte and Lefty Williams that it would be in their best interest to admit their guilt and plead for mercy. Austrian said this would lessen the punishment. And, like a Dutch uncle, he told his three amigos, "Don't worry. We'll take care of you."

The players were bamboozled. Austrian was guarding Comiskey. The Austrian confessions, notes which have not been found, were the linchpins to the grand jury proceedings. He immediately informed the state's attorney of his cache and the state had its case.

According to James Kirby, a law professor at the University of Tennessee: "It was as rare in 1920 as it is today for a suspected felon to appear voluntarily before a grand jury and confess his crimes. It was even more peculiar that both Jackson and Eddie Cicotte waived immunity and paved the way for their confessions to be used against them in a criminal trial.

"The ultimate incredibility: Both players were acting on the advice of counsel, the elegant Alfred Austrian—Harvard graduate, arts connoisseur and senior partner in a prestigious Chicago law firm. But Austrian (contrary to the players' belief) was not their lawyer. He was in the service of Charles Comiskey. The Old Roman had fed his players to the grand jury to save his own skin."

Comiskey should have been awarded an Oscar for his performance. When he realized the Series had been rigged, he put on a furious game-face and vowed that, if the allegations were true, none of the crooked players would ever play for him again. He also offered a $10,000 reward and hired three detectives in an assumed effort to expose the scandal. In reality, it was the beginning of a massive cover-up.

Two petty gamblers, who had been on the fringes, sprinted to Chicago after the bounty: Joe Gideon, a 26-year-old second baseman for the St. Louis Browns, and Harry Redmon, St. Louis theater operator. Comiskey's offer of a reward was a "grandstand play." The Old Roman heard them out but decided the information was useless. No money changed hands.

Gideon revealed that on the advice of Swede Risberg, who had been among his teammates in the Pacific Coast League, he had bet on the Series and won $600. Redmon reported he had been in touch with Abe Attell, a small-fry gambler, and was aware of the fix. It was a costly admission for Gideon. Because he didn't reveal his knowledge of the betrayal, he was the ninth player banned in the scandal.

Hal Chase, a slick-fielding first baseman, also was on the inside and claimed he had won $40,000 betting on Cincinnati. Chase was baseball's leading serial fixer, repeatedly accused of selling games and corrupting teammates as well as opponents. Gideon said Chase had played an advisory role in the scandal.

Two of Chase's managers, George Stallings and Christy Mathewson, accused him of "laying down." Because of his knowledge of fixes—certainly no one knew more how games were thrown—Chase, who lived in California, refused extradition after being indicted by the Chicago grand jury, and never appeared in court. He eventually was suspended for life.

Generally, players were banned one at a time. In the four-year period from 1919–22, not including the Black Sox, there were five suspensions: Lee Magee of the Cubs; Chase and Heinie Zimmerman of the New York Giants; Gene Paulette of the Philadelphia Phillies; and Shufflin' Phil Douglas of the Giants.

Comiskey was confronted with the simultaneous loss of *seven* of his best players: his two best pitchers, two-thirds of the outfield and three-fourths of his infield. The only front-liners among the so-called "Clean Sox" were second baseman and team captain Eddie Collins, catcher Ray Schalk, pitchers Red Faber and Dickie Kerr, and Shano Collins and Norm Liebold who were platooned in right field.

To maintain silence and shield the conspiracy, Comiskey pacified the indicted players and offered them huge salary increases for the 1920 season. The Old Roman didn't want to lose them. They had an estimated combined market value of $300,000, big money in those days. In a companion move, Comiskey led the march for the election of baseball's first commissioner, Judge Kenesaw Mountain Landis, a Chicago jurist, in the apparent belief that he would not suspend the players.

Eight players were indicted. In addition to Jackson, they were pitchers Cicotte and Williams, first baseman Chick Gandil, shortstop Swede Risberg, third baseman Buck Weaver, outfielder Hap Felsch, and utility infielder Fred McMullin who had appeared in two Series games, both as a pinch hitter.

Three of the accused—Jackson, Cicotte and Williams—signed confessions of guilt. When the confessions were "lost," the Cook County Grand Jury dismissed the charges and the players were acquitted. Nevertheless, Landis banned the eight players for life, and declared: "Regardless of the verdict of juries, no player who throws a ball game, no player who entertains proposals or promises to throw a game, no player who sits in conference with a bunch of crooked players and does not promptly tell his club about it, will ever again play professional baseball."

The indications are that Comiskey's politically connected attorneys snatched the confessions (they may have stuffed them in a shoebox). The other possibility is that Rothstein, a notorious and wealthy New York gambler, with the apparent help of his attorney, William F. Fallon, bought them with a $10,000 bribe. More than likely, they pulled the heist in concert.

During the trial as Jackson emerged from the courtroom, a young boy, the obligatory urchin, approached Shoeless Joe and, according to a September 30, 1920 report in the *Chicago Herald-Examiner*, pleaded, "Say it ain't so, Joe?"

"Yes, kid, I'm afraid it is," Jackson supposedly replied.

Jackson's confession, in part, follows:

Hartley L. Reploge, the assistant state's attorney, is asking the questions.

Q. Did anybody pay you any money to help that Series in the favor of Cincinnati?

A. They did.

Q. How much did they pay?

A. They promised me $20,000 and paid me $5,000.

Q. Who promised to pay the $20,000?

A. Chick Gandil.

Q. Who was Chick Gandil?

A. He was the first baseman on the White Sox club.

Q. Who paid you the $5,000?

A. Lefty Williams brought it in my room and threw it down.

Q. Who is Lefty Williams?

A. A pitcher on the White Sox club.

Q. Where did he bring it, where is your room?

A. At that time I was staying at the Lexington Hotel, I believe it is.

Q. On 21st and Michigan?

A. 22nd and Michigan, yes.

Q. Who was in the room at the time?

A. Lefty and myself. I was there and he came in.

Q. Where was Mrs. Jackson?

A. Mrs. Jackson…let me see. I think she was in the bathroom. It was a suite. Yes, she was in the bathroom, I am pretty sure.

Q. Does she know that you got $5,000 for helping throw these games?

A. She did that night, yes.

Q. You say you told Mrs. Jackson that evening?

A. Did, yes.

Q. What did she say about it?

A. She said it was an awful thing to do.

Q. When was it that this money was brought to your room and that you talked to Mrs. Jackson?

A. It was the second trip to Cincinnati. That night we were leaving (for Cincinnati).

Q. That was after the fourth game?

A. I believe it was, yes.

Q. After the fourth game? Do you remember who won that game?

A. Dick Kerr, I believe.

Q. Cincinnati won that game, Cicotte pitched and Cincinnati won. Do you remember now? Cincinnati beat you 2-0.

A. Yes, sir.

Q. Were you in a conference of these men, these players on the Sox team at the Warner Hotel (in Cincinnati) sometime previous to this?

A. No, sir. I was not present but I knew they had a meeting, so I was told.

Q. Who told you?

A. Williams.

Q. Who else talked to you about this beside Claude Williams?

A. Claude didn't talk to me directly about it. He just told me things had been said.

Q. What did he tell you?

A. He told me about the meeting in particular. He said the gang was there and the fellow—Attell, Abe Attell, I believe—and Bill Burns, he was the man that gave him the double-crossing, so Gandil told me.

Q. Then you talked to Chick Gandil and Claude Williams both about this?

A. Talked to Claude Williams about it, yes, and Gandil more so, because he is the man who promised me this stuff.

Q. How much did he promise you?

A. $20,000 if I would take part.

Q. And you said you would?

A. Yes, sir.

Q. When did he promise you the $20,000?

A. It was to be paid after each game.

Q. How much?

A. Split it up some way. I don't know just how much it amounts to but during the Series it would amount to $20,000. Finally, Williams brought me this $5,000 and threw it down.

Q. What did you say to Williams when he threw down the $5,000?

A. I asked him what the hell had come off here.

Q. What did he say?

A. He said Gandil said we all got a screw through Abe Attell. Gandil said he got double-crossed through Abe Attell, he got the money and refused to turn it over to him. I don't think Gandil was crossed as much as he crossed us.

Q. You think Gandil may have gotten the money and held it from you, is that right?

A. That's what I think. I think he kept the majority of it.

Q. What did you do then?

A. I went to him and asked him what was the matter. He said Abe Attell gave him the jazzing. He said, "Take that or let it alone."

Q. At the end of the first game you didn't get any money, did you?

A. No, I did not. No, sir.

Q. What did you do then?

A. I asked Gandil, "What is the trouble?" He says, "Everything is all right." He had it.

Q. Then you went ahead and threw the second game, thinking you would get it then, is that right?

A. We went ahead and threw the second game. We went after him again. I said to him, "What are you going to do?" "Everything is all right," he says. "What the hell is the matter?"

Q. After the third game what did you say to him?

A. After the third game I says, "Somebody is getting a nice jazz, everybody is crossed." He said…Abe Attell and Bill Burns had crossed him. That is what he said to me.

Q. Didn't you think it was the right thing for you to go out and tell owner Charles A. Comiskey about it?

A. I did tell them once: "I am not going to be in on it. I will just get out of that altogether."

Q. Who did you tell that to?

A. Chick Gandil. He was the whole works of it, the instigator of it.

Q. What did he say?

A. He said I was into it already and I might as well stay in. I said, "I can go to the boss and have every damn one of you pulled out of the limelight." He said it wouldn't be well for me if I did that.

Q. What did you say?

A. Well, I told him anytime they wanted to have me knocked off, to have me knocked off.

Q. What did he say?

A. Just laughed.

Q. Weren't you in on the inner circle?

A. No, I was never with them. No, sir. It was mentioned to me in Boston. As I told you before, they asked me would I consider $10,000 and I said no. Then they offered me $20,000.

Q. What did he (Gandil) say?

A. Just walked away from me, and when I returned here to Chicago, he told me he would give me 20, and I said no again, and on the bridge where you go into the clubhouse, he told me I could either take it or let it alone, they were going through.

Q. What did you say?

A. They said, "You might as well say yes or no and play ball or anything you want." I told them I would take their word.

Q. What else did you say?

A. Nothing.

Q. After the fourth game, you went to Cincinnati and had the $5,000, is that right?

A. Yes, sir.

Q. Where did you put the $5,000. Did you put it into the bank or keep it on your person?

A. I put it in my pocket.

Q. What denominations, in silver or bills?

A. In bills.

Q. How big were some of the bills?

A. Some hundreds, mostly fifties.

Q. What did Mrs. Jackson say about it after she found out about it again?

A. She felt awful about it, cried about it for a while.

Four years later Jackson sued the White Sox for back pay and told a Milwaukee jury how he went to the ballpark the day after the Series ended and tried to give Comiskey the $5,000. The transcript of the Milwaukee trial runs 1,600 pages.

Page 72:

Q. What did you do when you got there?

A. I got to the office and the front office door was locked and they got a solid window there and when a ballplayer wants to talk to Grabiner (secretary-treasurer Harry Grabiner) or Comiskey you have to knock on the window.

Q. And did they raise it for you?

A. Yes, sir.

Q. Who came to the window?

A. Harry Grabiner.

Q. What did you say to Grabiner?

A. I told Grabiner I wanted to see Comiskey. He said Comiskey was busy and I couldn't see him, and I said, "It's important that I see him. I have some information that I got out of Williams in regard to the World Series." And he (Grabiner) slammed the window down in my face, and said, "Go home, we know what you want."

Like most former players (he was the first first baseman to play deep and off the bag), Comiskey was not a baseball romantic. It is the newer owners, particularly those who never wore a jockstrap, who are enthralled by the players, thrilled to be in their presence. A current example is Tom Hicks of the Texas Rangers, who after the 2000 season signed shortstop Alex Rodriguez for $25 million a year for 10 years.

Comiskey was in it for the money, a tight-fisted tyrant who kept his payroll to a minimum. It has often been charged that if his players had been adequately compensated, the rebellion could have been avoided. Low salaries are not an excuse, but do provide an explanation. Dropping the World Series, two weeks' work, had its appeal. The payoff would equal a year's pay.

Robert Burk, an American history professor at Muskingum College in Ohio, who researched comparative salaries, told Michael Hirsley of the *Chicago Tribune* that the average major league wage at the time was $4,000. "The White Sox salaries were comparable to other teams," Burk said. "But while they were an elite team in talent and revenue, they were in the middle echelon, not at the top."

The 1919 White Sox had a star at almost every position and are regarded as one of the best teams of all-time, the equivalent of the 1927 window-breaking New York Yankees. The Sox led the league in hitting and runs, were second defensively, and had the most effective starting pitching. The rotation included Cicotte, Williams, Kerr and Red Faber. Cicotte led the league with 29 victories. He and Williams were a combined 52-18.

Suddenly generous, possibly embarrassed by the public knowledge of his penury, Comiskey was anxious to show the troops he was now ready to share the wealth. After the scandal was exposed, he opened his vault at the Drovers National Bank and rewarded the eight players he knew were in on the swindle an aggregate 101 percent pay hike for the 1920 season.

Jackson, who had been playing for $6,000, at least half, possibly one-third of his true worth, was given a new three-year contract for $8,000 a year. Cicotte went from $5,000 to $10,000; Weaver from $6,000 to $7,250; Williams from $3,000 to $6,000; Risberg from $2,500 to $3,650; McMullin from $2,750 to $7,000; Felsch from $3,750 to $7,000; and Gandil from $4,000 to $6,000. Gandil was the only player who didn't sign. He retired after the 1919 season.

Jackson was born poor in Pickens County, South Carolina (near Greenville). When he was 12, Jackson followed his father into the cotton mills. He joined the Brandon Mill team the next year. His teammates, for the most part, were grown men. He made it to the big leagues with the Philadelphia Athletics in 1908 at 19, and batted .408 in 1911, his first full major league season.

There is no question Jackson was among baseball's greatest hitters. Ty Cobb repeatedly said Jackson was the best hitter he had ever seen. Jackson batted .395 in 1912; three more hits and he would have had a second consecutive .400 season. He finished with a .356 career average for 13 seasons, third only behind Cobb and Rogers Hornsby.

The White Sox bought Jackson from Cleveland midway in the 1915 season for $65,000, a princely sum, $15,000 more than the cost of second baseman Eddie Collins who the year before had been acquired from the A's. It was an indication of Jackson's value and Comiskey's determination to field a winning team. But there was a significant difference. Comiskey was willing to pick up Collins' $15,000 salary.

Following the 1915 season, *The Sporting News*, then not much more than a house organ, showered Jackson with surprising praise:

"Unlettered and unlearned in the ways of the world when he broke into the limelight a few years back, he is today a person in whose company one finds pleasure and profit, a gentleman of manners, at ease in any gathering, his homely wisdom a delight to those who meet him, and his sheer honesty and straight forwardness a relief in these sordid times."

Jackson's supporters claim he couldn't have been guilty of crooked play because he led all Series regulars with a .375 average, set a Series record with 12 hits and connected for the only home run. He was also errorless in the field and threw a runner out at the plate.

A breakdown of the play-by-play tells a different story. In the first five games Jackson came to bat with a total of 10 runners on base, six in scoring positions, but was inept in the clutch, failing to drive in a single run.

Jackson awoke in the last three games after the fix had been abandoned. He batted .462 in these last three games, drove in six runs, and was 5-for-8 with runners in scoring position. He delivered his home run and a two-run double in the eighth and final game when the Sox were hopelessly behind and within one loss of elimination.

Forgotten in the fog of time was Jackson's admission of guilt to reporters from the Associated Press and United Press. The AP and UP stories were identical and went out simultaneously on their national wires, available throughout the country. This was on September 19, 1920, the day before the Chicago grand jury launched its proceedings.

Jackson was quoted as saying, "When a Cincinnati player would bat a ball to my territory (left field) I'd muff it if I could. But if it would too much look like crooked work to do that, I'd be slow and would make a throw to the infield that would be too short. My work netted the Cincinnati team several runs that they never would have made if I'd been playing on the square."

Gambling was pervasive in that period. For more than two decades, gamblers consorted openly with players and owners. Fixed games were not uncommon. There had been so many rumors of scandal that a statute of limitations was imposed, setting five years as the period after which charges against ballplayers would be void.

There were other questionable practices that occurred without challenge. It was customary for contending teams to offer a suit of clothes to a non-contending pitcher for defeating a contender. In 1917, when the White Sox won the World Series, they awarded suits to two Detroit players for losing two doubleheaders.

On September 4, 1920, two weeks before the Black Sox were hauled before the Chicago grand jury, Bill Veeck, Sr., president of the Cubs, told reporters that prior to the August 31 Cub-Philadelphia game he had received two phone calls and several telegrams to the effect that a Detroit gambling ring had bet heavily on the Phillies to win.

Claude Hendrix was slated to make the start for the Cubs that day but manager Fred Mitchell, on orders from Veeck, lifted him. Hendrix was replaced by Grover Cleveland Alexander. Hendrix denied knowledge of a fix. No charges were filed but he was released the following February and was never re-engaged by a minor or major league club.

Three days later it was announced that the mystery game would be investigated by a special Cook County jury, with Judge

Charles McDonald presiding. The scope of the investigation soon was broadened to cover all possible phases of gambling in baseball, not just the Cub-Philly game. On September 22, subpoenas were issued to Hendrix and three of his teammates, pitcher Nick Carter, second baseman Buck Herzog and first baseman Fred Merkle.

But there was an unexpected reversal. Instead of going forward with the Cub-Philly game, the Cook County jury, at the suggestion of American League president Ban Johnson, began probing the rumors that the White Sox had taken a dive in the 1919 Series against Cincinnati. With bigger fish to fry, the investigation was dropped, never to reappear, and attention was transferred from the North Side to the South Side.

Jackson's grand jury testimony surfaced four years later, in 1924, when he sued Comiskey for $19,000 in back pay, the approximate residue of his 1922 and 1923 contracts and a Series share that had been withheld. The suit was filed in Milwaukee's Circuit Court, and was joined by Hap Felsch, a Milwaukee resident, and Swede Risberg.

According to the *Milwaukee Journal*, midway in the trial; "To the shock of the people in the courtroom and elsewhere, lawyers for Comiskey produced Jackson's signed Grand Jury confession in which Jackson admitted his role in the scheme to throw the World Series."

The jury found for the players 11-1 and awarded Jackson $16,711.04. But the verdict was set aside by Judge John J. Gregory who charged Jackson and Felsch with perjury. Gregory ordered Jackson's arrest. Jackson was then taken to jail where he was booked.

He was not placed in a cell and was permitted to remain in the jailer's office while an effort was made to raise the $5,000 bail that Judge Gregory had set. Raymond Cannon, Jackson's principal attorney, offered a check but it was refused. At 10 p.m. two other attorneys signed a real estate bond and Jackson was released and the charges were eventually dropped.

Felsch's bond was set at $2,000. According to the *Milwaukee Journal*, "Felsch deposited the $2,000 with the clerk of the court. The judge approved the bail and the undersheriff released the prisoners."

Judge Gregory insisted the jury's verdict was based on "flagrant" perjured testimony. Jackson had recanted and changed his story during the Milwaukee trial and denied the damaging dialogue in his grand jury confession. He insisted his confession was a falsehood and that he had played to win.

To many of the confessions, Jackson replied, "No, I didn't say that," or "I can't remember."

Judge Gregory wasn't buying.

"The actions of the jury can in no way interfere with the action of the court because on the record here, Jackson lied here or before the Grand Jury in Chicago, and in my opinion, he lied here."

"You say you started working in a cotton mill at the age of 12?" the judge asked Jackson.

"Yes, sir."

"Well, at that age I was a newsboy but that does not give me the right to commit perjury."

The judge granted minuscule financial settlements. Jackson was awarded $3,000, Felsch $1,166 and Risberg $400, minus $37 for court costs.

Hugh Fullerton was the first sportswriter who suspected— no, more than suspected. He may have been the first to know the fix was in. Fullerton had a national reputation and moved around. He worked on the *Cincinnati Enquirer, Philadelphia Enquirer, New York Evening World, Chicago Tribune* and for the Bell Syndicate in New York. He was generally regarded as the leading diamond Boswell of the day.

An example of Fullerton's influence:

In 1908 when he covered the Merkle playoff game at the Polo Grounds in New York, his seat in the press box was occupied by Louis Mann, an overweight actor and friend of Giants manager John McGraw. Mann refused to budge. Fullerton covered the game sitting on Mann's ample lap. A week later the Baseball Writers Association of America was born. Henceforth, no outsiders were allowed in the press box.

After prowling the headquarters Sinton Hotel in Cincinnati on the eve of the 1919 World Series, Fullerton wrote: "I don't like what I smell."

And when the heavily-favored White Sox lost the first two games, he reported, "Something is wrong."

When Cincinnati won the Series five games to three, Fullerton predicted, with uncanny accuracy, that seven of the White Sox players would not be back with the club the next season.

"There will be a great deal written about the World Series," Fullerton reported. "There will be a lot of inside stuff that never will be printed. The truth will remain that the team which was the hardest working...won. The team which had the individual ability was beaten. They spilled the dope terribly. So much so that an evil-minded person might believe the stories that have been circulated during the Series."

Fullerton closed with an ominous prediction.

"Yesterday's, in all probability, is the last game that will be played in any World Series. If the club owners and those who have the interest of the game at heart, have listened during the Series, they will call off the annual inter-league contest. Yesterday's game also means the disruption of the Chicago White Sox ballclub. There are seven men on the team who will not be there when the gong sounds next spring."

John H. Tennant, the managing editor of the *New York Evening Mail*, refused to approve one of Fullerton's subsequent stories unless Fullerton softened some of his charges. Even with the modifications, according to reports, Rothstein and his fellow gamblers were enraged and threatened to "rub him out."

Almost all of the baseball writers and columnists criticized Fullerton, claiming he was unnecessarily darkening baseball's image. *The Sporting News*, baseball's mouthpiece, responded with a vicious editorial:

"Because a lot of dirty, long-nosed, thick-lipped and strong smelling gamblers butted into the World Series...and some of the said gamblers got crossed, stories were peddled that there was something wrong with the games.... Comiskey has met that by offering $10,000 for any sort of clue that will bear out such a charge. But there will be no takers because there is no such evidence, except in the murky minds of the stinkers who—because they are crooked—think all the rest of the world can't play straight."

Convinced Fullerton's reports had the ring of truth, American League president Johnson, without advising Comiskey, had begun a separate investigation, using league funds and $10,000 from his personal account.

Comiskey and Johnson had been great pals and in 1901 were the co-founders of the American League. They later became enemies after Johnson had made several rulings against the White Sox. The big break occurred when Comiskey caught a trophy trout at his northern Wisconsin lodge. As a peace offering, Comiskey had the fish packed in ice and had it shipped to Johnson. The package was delayed. When it arrived, the stench was unbearable. Johnson interpreted it as a signal of impending doom.

Thereafter, Comiskey repeatedly accused Johnson of vengeance with the claim he was trying to run him out of baseball. But Johnson, not Comiskey, was the unfortunate loser. Comiskey walked away free. Johnson, previously baseball's dominant executive, went to his grave a broken man. His power was steadily and thoroughly diminished after Landis had been elected commissioner.

Forty years later, when the junior Bill Veeck was operating the White Sox, he discovered "Harry's Diary"—Grabiner's so-called journal which had been hidden under the Comiskey Park stands. Grabiner's notes are the ultimate insider's view of the 1919 season and revealed Comiskey knew the fix was in after the first game.

It was a clumsy fix, with a cast out of the musical *Guys and Dolls*, without the dolls. It was men only—cynical and hard-bitten gamblers a step ahead of the law.

Among them were "Sleepy" Bill Burns, a former player who sometimes fell asleep in the dugout; Bill Maharg (Graham spelled backward), a onetime Philadelphia prize fighter; Abe Attell, another boxer who a generation earlier won the world featherweight title and was known thereafter as "The Little Champ"; Arnold Rothstein, "King of the New York Underworld"; Nat Evans, a Rothstein associate who appeared under the name of Mr. Brown; Benjamin Franklin (real name), a St. Louis mule buyer; and Monk Eastman, the "enforcer."

Sport Sullivan, big in New England, was the first gambler to appear on the scene. Cicotte and Gandil told him a fix could be arranged. Sullivan brought Burns and Maharg into the den. The players wanted a total of $100,000, divided equally among 10 players, to be paid in increments of $20,000.

Short on funds, Sullivan went to New York to see Rothstein. According to what seem to be reliable reports, Rothstein refused to be involved. "I don't want any part of it," Rothstein has been quoted as saying. "You might be able to fix a single game, but not the Series. You'd get lynched if it ever came out."

At about the same time, Attell, "The Little Champ," had climbed into the ring. Though he was among Rothstein's principal couriers, Attell entered as an independent. When he realized big money was needed to swing the swindle, he appealed to Rothstein. According to Attell, Rothstein came in for the requested $100,000. Or so Attell told his co-conspirators.

The distribution began with $10,000 to Cicotte who was to pitch the opener. Cicotte insisted he wanted his share upfront or he would drop out. The night before the Series began he found $10,000 under his hotel room pillow. None of the other fixers was paid until after the fourth game: $5,000 each for Shoeless Joe, Williams and Felsch, for a total of $25,000 including Cicotte's $10,000.

Attell controlled the money. David Carlson, a Chicago attorney who spent four years exhuming the fix, estimated that Attell pocketed $40,000 of the $100,000. The indications are that Gandil, who parceled out the loot, is believed to have banked the remaining $35,000.

Carlson also insisted that the players were suspicious of Attell before the Series began. Fearful they would not be compensated, they attempted to double-up and sell the fix to a lesser gambling syndicate in St. Louis. More than likely, they were not successful. If they were, it can be assumed they would have swollen their take.

According to a Hollywood version, Cicotte had agreed to hit Morris Rath, the Cincinnati leadoff hitter, with a pitch. That would be the signal the fix was on. Cicotte later insisted the plan was for him to walk Rath. That he hit him was accidental.

The White Sox lost the first two games. Cicotte was knocked out in the fourth inning after he had given up five runs. The Reds won 9-1. Williams was the second game loser, 4-2. A control pitcher, Williams gave up six walks. "Honest" Dickie Kerr won the third game with a 3-0 shutout.

Cicotte made the fourth game start and lost again, 2-0. Ordinarily an excellent fielder, Cicotte committed two errors in the fifth inning. "He never pulled two like that in all his life," said Sox manager Kid Gleason. Williams lost the fifth game, 5-0. The Sox won the sixth and seventh games, 5-4 in 10 innings behind Kerr, 4-1 behind Cicotte. Williams lost for the third time the next day, 10-5, and the Series was over.

The *Chicago Tribune*, October 10, 1919:

"'The Reds beat the greatest ball team that ever went into a World Series.' That was the statement made by Boss Gleason of the White Sox when the show was over at Comiskey Park yesterday. Gleason's next statement was about like this: 'But it wasn't the real White Sox. They played baseball for me only a couple or three of the eight days.'"

Swede Risberg was the last survivor and died in 1975 at the age of 81.

OFF 'N' RUNNING

It may be small comfort to today's Cub and White Sox fans, who have suffered through interminable decades of frustration, dismay and disappointment, but there once was a Golden Age of major league baseball in Chicago.

Alas, hardly a soul is now alive to recall even the tail end of that wondrous period from 1901 through 1919 when Chicago's teams not only were almost invariably pennant contenders, but frequently won the prize. The Cubs and White Sox between them captured nine pennants and four World Series in those 19 seasons. In comparison, during the ensuing eight decades they've raised only six flags, none since the White Sox last won in 1959 and the Cubs in 1945. The World Series record is even drearier, the White Sox' final title coming in 1917, the Cubs' in 1908. How long ago it all seems—and is!

The first two decades of the 20th Century may appear as ancient to those living 100 years afterwards as are the days of Pocahontas yet they are an integral and glorious part of the traditions of the Cubs and White Sox.

Even now the names of many Cub and White Sox star players of that remote period rattle fluently off the tongues of ardent fans: Ed Walsh, Shoeless Joe Jackson, Frank Chance, Joe Tinker, Johnny Evers, Fielder Jones, Dickie Kerr, Three-Finger Brown,

Hippo Vaughn, Red Faber and Eddie Collins, to list a few. Their deeds—and the misdeeds of a few, including Black Sox conspirators Jackson, Eddie Cicotte and Chick Gandil—are not only recorded but well-remembered, such as pitcher Walsh's 40-game winning season of 1908 and the mythical double play skills of Tinkers to Evers to Chance.

Lost in the mists of time, however, are countless other aspects of baseball's earlier days. Among them is the memory of many prominent personalities other than players, as well as distinct differences in the game's rituals and practices.

While Charles "The Old Roman" Comiskey retains a solid grip on fan collective memory as co-founder of the American League and the White Sox, as well as a pivotal figure in the trauma of the Black Sox scandal of 1919–20, his peers are largely forgotten. Few recall Charles W. Murphy, the Cub owner from 1905 to 1914. Or Charles Weeghman, who in 1914 built the ballpark now called Wrigley Field for his Chicago Whales of the "outlaw" Federal League. Yet Murphy and Weeghman, if not so significant as Comiskey, also contributed in their ways to baseball in Chicago.

Comiskey and Murphy often got into each other's hair, and not only on the diamond as in the 1906 World Series, won by the Old Roman's Hitless Wonders, and the almost annual City Series between the White Sox and Cubs.

In a curious feature of early baseball, one condemned by the decorous as a "cheap circus act," it was customary to parade players in uniform through the streets in horse-drawn carriages from hotel to ballpark and back. Many parks had no dressing rooms for even home players, let alone visitors. To nullify any pretext for parades, the National League in 1906 decreed that all parks install locker rooms for visiting players. Ironically, while American Leaguer Comiskey applauded the move, Murphy of the N.L. defied it.

Comiskey explained he detested player parades because he wasn't in show business, an astounding position for a team owner. Murphy was less staid or more candid.

Murphy defiantly trumpeted he would transport his team any way he liked. Furthermore, he vowed to attach bells to the colorful and elaborate horse blankets so as to attract even more attention to his cavalcade of Cubs. He did bend enough to install a clubhouse at West Side Grounds, but visiting players derided it as a chicken coop. A $25 fine by the N.L. failed to bring Murphy to heel immediately, and it took the threat of far more severe penalties to ban carriage parades entirely by 1909.

More lasting was another Murphy contribution to Chicago baseball, the starting of games in mid-afternoon rather than early or late, a practice that lasted until World War II—and the advent of night baseball in the 1930s. Murphy decided his Cubs should start games at 3 p.m., virtually ensuring that in a era when most contests took less than two hours to play, fans would be able to get home for dinner.

Murphy explained: "We must cater to the wives and cooks...and try to get our patrons home in time to keep peace in the family." The ever-slick Murphy added that husbands would not even have to tell their wives that they were at the ball game.

Murphy was much maligned—often justly—and driven out of the game in 1914 for questionable financial practices. Nevertheless, it was on his watch that the Cubs won four pennants in five seasons (1906–08, 1910) and two World Series (1907–08), a record of success no later owner even approached.

Weeghman's tenure as chief owner was briefer than Murphy's, lasting only three seasons (1916–18), but left a major legacy. Wrigley Field may be considered his monument. When the Federal League folded after the 1915 season, Weeghman led a syndicate that purchased the Cubs from Murphy's successor and earlier financial backer Charles Taft, brother of William Howard Taft, 27th president of the United States. William Wrigley Jr., who built a fortune on chewing gum, joined Weeghman's group.

Weeghman moved the Cubs into the defunct Whales' park, where they've remained and flourished, for the 1916 season. Weeghman's policy of catering to the fans was exceptional for his day, setting the pattern for the similar course of the Wrigley family, his successors as Cubs owners from 1918 to 1981.

Weeghman installed the first permanent concession stand in any park to meet complaints that strolling vendors spoiled fans' view of action on the field. He also ended another nagging conflict between fans and owners. He was the first owner to let fans keep balls hit into the stands, a public relations move some of his colleagues were slow to copy. Park police had often harrassed fans to recover baseballs. Sometimes patrons even were searched, beaten and ejected from parks for "stealing" club property.

While it would be lax to ignore the contributions of Murphy and Weeghman to Chicago baseball tradition, Comiskey was indisputably more influential in his multiple roles in the game, at first as player, then as manager and finally as team owner and league builder. He was the major figure in Chicago baseball virtually from the ascent of the White Sox and the A.L. to major league status in 1901 until the 1919 World Series scandal dimmed his luster in the remaining decade of a life that ended in 1930.

It's unlikely that James A. Hart, Murphy's predecessor as the Cub owner, realized the full import and eventual impact of his reluctant assent to Comiskey's transfer of his then minor league team from St. Paul, Minnesota, to Chicago for the 1900 season. The result was a baseball "war" that has raged for more than 100 years and can never end, given the natural allegiance and antipathy of Cub and White Sox fans.

The early battles went to Comiskey's White Sox, as he renamed his team when it occupied the 39th Street Grounds, a renovated former cricket field.

The transplant was an immediate success both in attendance and on the field. The White Sox won the A.L. pennant in 1900 while it was still a minor league. For 1901, Comiskey, promoter Ban Johnson and their partners proclaimed the organization a major league, declared war on the established N.L. and raided it for players.

Comiskey's blows were the hardest and most fruitful. Among the players he lured from the Cubs were Clark Griffith, a 20-game winner in six consecutive seasons (1894–99) and reputed inventor of the screwball, pitcher/outfielder Nixey Callahan, and outfielder Sandow Mertes. Griffith was hired to manage the White Sox as well pitch. Two other major refugees from the N.L. were outfielder Fielder Jones and catcher Billy Sullivan, both future White Sox managers, as was Callahan.

Griffith led the White Sox to the first A.L. pennant with a 24-7 record, Fielder Jones furnishing much of the offensive fireworks by batting .350. Just as significantly, the White Sox drew more than 350,000 fans at home, almost doubling the attendance for Hart's Remnants, as his Cubs were derisively, if temporarily, renamed.

Hart took a dismissive attitude toward the A.L. and the players who jumped to the White Sox. He predicted that the new league, and certainly the White Sox, would fold quickly and that the "jumpers" would plead for reinstatement by the N.L.

"They may talk all they want about the city supporting two teams," Hart said."but they are mistaken. Chicago can only support one Chicago club."

He couldn't have been more wrong. Chicago has supported—though not always equally well—two teams for more than a century without a break. And for the first two decades with justification as both clubs often gave the fans plenty to cheer about.

Not that the White Sox followed up their initial success by establishing a dynasty. Through the next four years, 1902–05, both Chicago teams were also-rans as they competed for fan support. The White Sox missed Griffith, who left in 1902 after Comiskey denied his request to become part owner, a goal he achieved eventually with the Washington Senators.

When the N.L. and A.L. arrived at a settlement that produced the first World Series in 1903, the stage was set for the most memorable event in Chicago baseball history, the sole clash of the city's teams for the game's ultimate prize.

Heightening the drama and mythology of the 1906 World Series was the evident disparity of talent. The Cubs appeared vastly superior to the White Sox. They had great pitchers, famed fielders and outstanding hitters, while the White Sox were known as "The Hitless Wonders," a double-edged tag though meant to be complimentary when first used in a *Chicago Tribune* headline in July 1906.

Fielder Jones took over as White Sox manager during the 1904 season, and made the most of an outstanding pitching staff. The team came close to a pennant in 1905, finishing only two games behind Connie Mack's Philadelphia A's. Not one player batted .300, but the team earned run average of 1.99 was the best in the A.L. Nick Altrock's record was 22-12 and Frank Owen's 21-13. Doc White distinguished himself by pitching five consecutive shutouts en route to a 16-10 record in his second season.

If the White Sox were on the rise in 1905, so were the Cubs under Frank Chance. The players elected first baseman Chance as manager when owner Hart decided to leave the choice up to them after illness forced out Frank Selee in mid-season. The Cubs finished third with a 92-61 record, almost identical to the White Sox's 92-60. The standouts were Chance, second baseman Evers, shortstop Joe Tinker, catcher Johnny Kling and pitchers Ed Reulbach, Mordecai "Three-Finger" Brown and Jack Weimer, all 18-game winners.

Murphy hit the proverbial jackpot when he took over ownership of the Cubs from Hart prior to the 1906 season, Chance having assembled the powerhouse that was to dominate the N.L. for five campaigns. The chief newcomers for 1906 were third baseman Harry Steinfeldt, outfielder Jimmy Sheckard and pitcher Jack Pfiester.

The 1906 Cubs' mastery of the opposition is unequalled. They led the league in hitting, pitching and fielding. Their record of 116-36 represents the most wins in one season for any team and the highest winning percentage of .763. They finished 20 games ahead of the second place New York Giants. From May 31 on, they were 87-21 for a winning percentage of .806. They scored almost twice as many runs as the opposition, 704 to 381, while their team earned run average of 1.76 is incredible even for the "deadball" era. In fact, it was even better than the Hitless Wonders' 2.16 that season.

Steinfeldt's .319 was second on the team only to Chance's .327 and he led in RBI with 83. Sheckard's 90 runs were topped only by the manager's 103. Pfiester went 20-8 with an earned run average of 1.56, the second best performance among the pitchers to Brown's 26-6 and ERA of 1.04. Reulbach's 19-4 and 1.66 ERA almost obscured the incredible achievement of yielding merely five hits for every nine innings pitched over 33 games, 24 of them starts. Carl Lundgren, the No. 4 starter, was 17-6.

Such was the steamroller expected to easily flatten Comiskey's White Sox in the third World Series ever played. Though the White Sox pitching staff had produced a record 32 shutouts during the season, the dismal team batting average of .230, with just seven home runs, promised an easy time for Brown, Reulbach & Co.

However, the Cubs might have taken warning from the way the White Sox came to life after being nine games behind on August 2. A 19-game winning streak got them back in the running, with up-and-coming Ed Walsh contributing four shutouts, and they beat out the New York Highlanders, managed by Griffith, for the pennant.

Going against the Cubs, the White Sox obviously had to rely on their pitching, which featured two 20-game winners in Owen (22-13) and Altrock (20-13), as well as Doc White (18-6) and Walsh (17-13). And it was probably manager Jones' shrewd handling of his pitching staff that proved decisive.

Cub pitcher Reulbach gave Jones all the credit in an article in *Baseball Magazine* years after the White Sox upset the Cubs in the six-game World Series, which started with a 2-1 victory by Altrock over Brown on October 9, 1906, at West Side Grounds.

"In a 154-game season the best club is pretty certain to win, but there is no such certainty in a World Series," Brown said. "The Cubs in 1906 were in their prime. I think no person, however prejudiced, will claim the Sox were their equal.... Much credit has been given the generalship of Fielder Jones upon this occasion, and it is doubtful if the wisdom of a manager's policy ever proved a stronger factor in the final result.

"Miner (Three-Finger) Brown was going at a wonderful clip. It was certain that Chance would pitch him in the opening contest. Fielder Jones attacked the problem somewhat in this light: 'If I pitch Walsh, who is my best pitcher, I will probably lose, for Walsh is certainly not as good as Brown. Then I will have opened the Series with a defeat and temporarily used up my best man. On the other hand, if I used another pitcher and he loses, I am no worse off and I can bring Walsh into the second (or third) contest and probably win.'

"So he chose Altrock to pitch the opening game, feeling that if Altrock won (which he did) it would be a tremendous moral victory, while if he lost it would not be such a serious affair, since no one expected him to win."

By matching the White Sox' weakest points against the Cubs' strengths and his team's strengths against their weaker points, Jones "outled" Chance, the Peerless Leader, and captured the first crosstown World Series with Walsh winning both his starts. The White Sox hitting star of the Series was utility infielder George Rohe, who replaced injured shortstop George Davis in the lineup. Rohe delivered a decisive hit in Game 3, tripled and scored a run in the opening game 2-1 pitching duel, went three-for-four in the fifth game, and added two hits in Game 6, the concluding 8-3 White Sox victory.

The White Sox failed to build on their unexpected triumph. They dropped to third place in 1907 despite the efforts of three 20-game winners, Walsh (24-18), Frank Smith (22-11) and White (27-13), undermined by their lack of punch. The fiery Fielder Jones rasped in late season that it didn't matter where his team finished if it didn't win the pennant. "If we cannot be first we care not for second, which is but the anteroom to oblivion," he proclaimed.

Another third place finish in 1908, despite Walsh's 40-15 record, among the greatest pitching achievements of the 20th Century (though by current standards he would be credited with only 36 victories), ended Jones' tenure as manager, though he left voluntarily, unwilling to accept Comiskey's contract terms.

Another decade was to pass and several managers were to succeed Jones before the White Sox won another pennant. Nevertheless, they prospered sufficiently enough at the gate to induce Comiskey to abandon the dilapidated 39th Street Grounds. He built Comiskey Park, proclaimed the "Baseball Palace of the World" when it opened in 1910.

Even as the White Sox floundered after their great triumph, the Cubs emerged from the humiliation of the 1906 World Series with renewed determination. They captured their second successive pennant in 1907 almost as decisively as they had the first. Though their win total dropped from 116 to a still handsome 107 (45 losses), it was enough for a 17-game edge over second-place Pittsburgh.

The Cubs' hitting fell off, with Chance at .293 the only player to approach .300, but the pitching held up. Orval Overall, 23-8, emerged as the ace. Brown (20-6), Lundgren (18-7), Reulbach (17-4) and Pfiester (15-9) rounded out the top five.

This time the Cubs didn't disappoint their fans in the 1907 World Series, crushing a good Detroit Tigers' team led by 20-year-old sensation Ty Cobb, who had just won the first of his 12 A.L. batting championships with an average of .350.

After the first game, played before a crowd of 24,377 at West Side Grounds, ended as a 3-3 tie called because of darkness, the Cubs overwhelmed Detroit. They won the next four games 3-1, 3-1, 6-1 and 2-0 behind the pitching of Pfiester, Reulbach, Overall and Brown to capture their first World Series crown.

What was essentially a sweep of the Tigers proved that despite the upset by the White Sox in 1906, the Cubs were baseball's pre-eminent team. Their pitching held the Tigers scoreless in 43 of 48 innings, they stole 18 bases in five games, and their offense hit its stride. Steinfeldt batted .471 and Evers .350 while Cobb was held to .200.

Evers' jubilation equaled that of the Cub fans who had taken advantage of the $5.50 railroad round trip fare to witness the final game at Detroit's Bennett Field.

"Many of our Chicago admirers crowded about our bench, offering congratulations," he told a reporter, "and every one of the players was almost tickled to death, as we had at last reached the highest point in a ball player's life.... We returned to our hotels and were invited to drink a little toast by almost everybody we met, and by train-time most of the boys were looking for trains that were not on the schedule."

Unlike the previous two seasons, when the Cubs romped to pennants, they were fortunate to capture their third straight in 1908 when they won "only" 99 games. The celebrated Fred Merkle incident in a September 23 game in which the Giants' first baseman failed to touch second base while the apparent winning run was scoring enabled the Cubs to force a one-game postseason playoff in which they beat New York 4-2.

Evers batted .300 to lead the team, while Brown (29-9 with a 1.47 ERA) and Reulbach (24-7) paced the still solid pitching staff. Reulbach not only pitched four one-hitters, but for the third consecutive season led the N.L. in winning percentage.

The World Series was almost an encore of the previous year's. The Tigers won Game 3 by the score of 8-3 when Cobb came alive with four hits, but were outgunned or outpitched in the other four. The Cubs won the opener 10-6, Overall pitched a four-hitter for a 6-1 victory in Game 2, Brown shut the Tigers out 3-0 in Game 4 and Overall came back with a three-hitter and 10 strikeouts in the concluding 2-0 victory.

Reulbach credited catcher Kling's ability to contain the Tigers' running game, spearheaded by Cobb and Sam "Wahoo" Crawford, as key to his team's success.

"Much of the brilliant work of the Cubs against the Tigers was owing to John Kling, one of the greatest catchers who ever wore a mask," Reulbach said.

Sports writer Hugh Fullerton wrote of Kling: "He introduced brains to the art of catching."

With Kling behind the plate, their solid pitching, and an attack led by Chance (.421), Wildfire Schulte (.389) and Evers (.350) the Cubs became the first team to enjoy back-to-back World Series victories, and were the first team since 1900 to win three consecutive pennants.

They conceivably could have made it four in a row because they won 104 games in 1909, which in most seasons would have guaranteed first place, but the Pirates won 110 to finish ahead. Though the hitting fell off, leading one writer to attribute the failure to win to "a trifling diminution of force," the pitching was still exceptional. Brown (27-9, 1.31 ERA), Overall (20-11),

Reulbach (19-10) and Pfiester (17-6) continued to be highly effective. Brown's eight shutouts led the league.

Other than that their 104 victories failed to earn a pennant, the most noteworthy Cub happening of 1909 was the clash over hiring a hack (horse-drawn taxi) that triggered the notorious feud between second baseman Evers and shortstop Tinker, who angrily accused his teammate of riding off without him.

Tinker's explanation, in part, as to why they stopped talking to each other: "One word led to another and we had a fight. After we were pulled apart, I told Evers, 'If you and I talk to each other we're only going to be fighting. So don't talk to me and I won't talk to you. You play your position and I'll play mine and let it go at that.'"

They and the rest of the Cubs played their positions well enough for one more year to bounce back with 104 victories in 1910 and the team's fourth pennant in five seasons. This fourth 100-plus win season gave the Cubs a record of 530-235 for a percentage of .693 over five seasons, a winning pace no team has approached since during a similar stretch.

The offense perked up with center fielder Solly Hofman hitting .325, right fielder Schulte .301 with a league-leading 10 home runs, and manager Chance, though slowed by injuries, .293. Brown (25-13), and newcomer King Cole (20-4) led the pitching.

The Cubs were not at full strength for the World Series against Connie Mack's Philadelphia A's. Evers was out with a broken leg and was replaced by future star Heinie Zimmerman. Chance was able to play only part-time that year, as did catcher Kling, who had returned after skipping the 1909 season because of a contract dispute.

Mack also seemed hampered because pitcher Eddie Plank (16-10), his most reliable veteran, was sidelined by an arm ailment. Mack solved his dilemma by using just two pitchers, Jack Coombs (31-9) and Chief Bender (23-5) against the Cubs. They pitched every inning of the series, each winning two games, Bender losing only Game 2, a 4-3 victory in 10 innings for Brown in relief of Cole.

While Chance and Schulte each batted .353, and Tinker .333 as the veteran Cubs acquitted themselves with honor, the defeat was a landmark in Cub history. It was the first of seven consecutive World Series failures, a streak that remains unbroken more than 90 years later.

By 1911, not only were the Cubs' greatest days behind them, but also those of Chance and most of his stars. They finished second under Chance in 1911 and 1912. Schulte provided the highlights of the 1911 season by batting .300 and leading the N.L. in home runs with 21 and RBI with 105. In 1912, it was Zimmerman's turn to sparkle, as he won the rare Triple Crown. He batted .372, hit 14 home runs and batted in 103 runs.

By this time owner Murphy, with whom Chance was constantly at odds, was breaking up the team. Overall quit baseball for two years because of a salary dispute. Murphy traded away Kling, Tinker, Reulbach and other mainstays, and banished the fading Brown to the minor leagues. The culminating blow came on September 28, 1912, when he fired Chance while he was recovering from brain surgery.

Chance retaliated by charging that Murphy was interested solely in milking the team for profit. "In all the years I've been with this club," Chance said, "I've had to fight to get the players I wanted. Murphy has not spent one-third as much for players as have other magnates. How can he expect to win championships without players?"

After that parting shot, Chance departed to manage the New York Yankees, ending the most successful managerial tenure in Cub history with a record of 768-389 for a percentage of .664, four pennants and two World Series titles. He was replaced by Evers, who led the team to third place in 1913 before being fired in turn.

While the Cubs languished through the mid 1910s, so did the White Sox, though Comiskey was assembling the talent that was to carry them to two pennants in the latter part of the decade.

As White, Walsh and other veterans faded, a new pitching staff took shape with the arrival of Eddie Cicotte in 1912, Ewell

Russell in 1913, Urban Faber in 1914 and Claude Williams in 1916. Third baseman/shortstop Buck Weaver came in 1912, as did catcher Ray Schalk. Outfielder Happy Felsch was added in 1915. Comiskey's two most important acquisitions in deals, second baseman Eddie Collins from the A's in 1915 and outfielder Shoeless Joe Jackson from Cleveland the same year, rounded out the core of a fine team by 1916.

The usually perspicacious Fullerton earlier had written of the illiterate Jackson: "A man who can't read or write simply can't expect to meet the requirements of big-league baseball as it is played today." His evaluation was to have an unexpected application after the events of the 1919 World Series became known.

The Cubs and White Sox featured a constantly changing cast of managers and players during much of the period. They also suffered financially during the bitter battle with Weeghman's Federal League Whales in 1914–15. The Whales, managed by Tinker, cut deeply into both Cubs and White Sox attendance, especially in 1914 when they won the Federal League pennant.

Once the Federal League folded, and Weeghman took control of the Cubs in 1916, matters began to look up for both teams, especially for the White Sox with their wealth of superior young talent. Manager Clarence "Pants" Rowland led them to third place in 1915 as Collins batted .332 and Faber and veteran Jim Scott each won 24 games. They moved up to second the next year, Jackson's first full season with the team, when he batted .341, while Collins hit .308. Russell (17-11), Cicotte (16-9), Faber (16-7) and Williams (13-7) formed a solid starting rotation.

Comiskey had departed from the usual practice of hiring veterans to manage when he chose Rowland from Peoria, Illinois. Rowland was without major league experience as player or manager, so he was derided at first as a "busher" by some fans and press critics. Rowland retorted that it was no disgrace to be a bush leaguer, "But if you call me a bush leaguer at the end of 1916, I may regard it as a reflection."

Success quashes criticism, and Rowland's achievement of 1917 could not be topped. He not only directed the White Sox to a pennant but to a World Series title, the last won by a Chicago team in the 20th Century. Two key acquisitions by Comiskey solidified the team. They were first baseman Chick Gandil and third baseman Swede Risberg, whose arrival permitted Weaver to play shortstop, his best position.

The White Sox rolled to a record of 100-54 and won the pennant by nine games. Cicotte led the A.L.'s best pitching staff with a 28-12 record, Faber was 16-13 and Williams 17-8. Felsch batted .308 with 102 RBI, and Jackson .301 to lead the offense.

World War I was on, so 1917 produced the first wartime World Series. It opened in Chicago, and is remembered chiefly for the White Sox victory over the Giants and what was labeled, clearly unfairly, "Zim's boner," in the sixth and concluding game. "Zim" was former Cub Zimmerman, now the Giants third baseman.

The White Sox took three of the first five games in a rather sloppy set of contests, committing six errors in Game 5, though they won it. Game 6 in New York featured not only "Zim's boner," but also four errors, three by the Giants.

Game 6 was scoreless until the fourth inning when the White Sox pushed across three runs on their way to a 4-2 victory because Zimmerman allegedly compounded a physical error with a mental blunder to open the door.

Eddie Collins tapped a grounder to Zimmerman, who threw wild to first for an error, the runner reaching second. The right fielder dropped Jackson's fly ball, putting men on first and third. The next batter hit to Giants pitcher Rube Benton, who saw Collins halfway off third. Instead of throwing home, Benton threw to Zimmerman at third. Zimmerman tried to run down Collins while catcher Bill Rariden also advanced on him. Nobody covered home, and Collins beat Zimmerman in a foot race to the plate.

The Sox scored twice more before the inning ended, and Faber held the Giants to two runs and six hits to clinch the World Series. Press critics savaged Zimmerman.

"Who was I supposed to throw the ball to—myself?" he asked reasonably enough.

Such slurs and distortions were in keeping with the prevailing atmosphere of a rude and crude age as suggested by Giants manager John McGraw's reaction when Rowland approached him after the White Sox had beaten his team.

"Mr. McGraw, I'm glad we won, but I'm sorry you had to be the one to lose," Rowland said politely.

McGraw's harsh response: "Get away from me, you damned busher!"

It was on this brusque note that the first of three successive World Series to include games played at Comiskey Park terminated. Paradoxically, only two involved the White Sox.

While 1917 was a banner year for the White Sox, it was mostly just another campaign for the Cubs, but it did contribute a major achievement to the record book even as they meandered to fifth place under Fred Mitchell, their sixth manager in six years. That was the double no-hit game pitched by Hippo Vaughn of the Cubs and Fred Toney of Cincinnati through nine innings on May 2, with the Reds winning 1-0 as Toney held the Cubs hitless through 10 innings.

Weeghman was so frustrated by two mediocre campaigns as the Cub owner that he decided to try to spend his way to a pennant. Though his spending spree didn't work out quite as he expected, the Cubs did finish first in the war-curtailed 1918 season.

After failing to lure Rogers Hornsby from the St. Louis Cardinals for $50,000 and two front-line players, Weeghman obtained Grover Cleveland Alexander from the Philadelphia Phillies, for whom he had won 30 games in three successive seasons. Alexander and catcher Bill Killefer cost the Cubs $60,000 and two players. But Alexander was called into the U.S. Army in 1918 after only three starts.

Despite not adding Hornsby, Weeghman felt confident that 1918 was the Cubs' year. "We will try to get some other strong batter, but if we have to go into the pennant race with what we have I still think think we will be in the fight for the flag," he declared.

The 1918 Cubs not only were "in the fight for the flag" but won it, in part because unheralded players turned in unexpectedly good seasons, and also due to the wartime situation in which competitors lost key men to military service or "essential" jobs. It was a foreshadowing of the situation in 1945 when another Cub team of similarly questionable quality won a pennant during a war.

Because of the war the federal government ordered the major leagues to suspend the season by Labor Day, at which point the Cubs were solidly in first place with an 84-45 record. Their offensive star was rookie shortstop Charlie Hollocher, who batted .316. Vaughn (22-10), Lefty Tyler (19-9) and Claude Hendrix (19-7) formed the backbone of a hiighly effective pitching staff, which led the N.L. in least runs allowed.

The Cubs' home games in the 1918 World Series against the Boston Red Sox were played in Comiskey Park rather than their own field because of its greater capacity. Babe Ruth, still a pitcher, started the Red Sox out with a 1-0 victory over Vaughn. Boston also won two of the next three games, though in Game 4 the Cubs ended Ruth's record streak of 29⅔ shutout innings in World Series competition even as he won for the second time. Vaughn kept the Cubs alive with a 3-0 shutout in Game 5, but Carl Mays outdueled Tyler 2-1 to give the Red Sox the championship in six games.

Harder hit by the war effort than the Cubs, the White Sox lost many key players in 1918. Faber and Collins went into the military, Jackson and Williams took up draft-proof jobs, while Felsch deserted the team in mid-season because he couldn't get along with some of his fellow players. The decimated World Series champion White Sox slipped to sixth place and Comiskey fired Rowland.

By the opening of the 1919 season, much had changed for both the Cubs and White Sox. The war was over and the boys were back. Weeghman was almost broke, and sold out, Wrigley taking over as majority owner of the Cubs. Wrigley's effort to name Mitchell team president as well as manager violated league rules, so he handed the front office job to newspaperman William Veeck, Sr.

Mitchell stayed on as manager, but couldn't repeat his 1918 success though Vaughn went 21-14 and Alexander, back from the army, was 16-11. The Cubs finished in third place to round out their role in what we've called the Golden Era of Chicago baseball, the period from 1901 through 1919 in which they won five pennants and two World Series.

At least the Cub era ended quietly and with hope for the future rather than in the ignominious catastrophe that beset Comiskey's White Sox, and was all the more devastating because of the great expectations raised by his exceptional 1919 team.

On New Year's Eve, 1918, Comiskey handed the manager's job to Kid Gleason, who had been a White Sox coach off and on since 1912, and was extremely popular with the players, including star second baseman Collins.

"That's the best New Year's present I could think of," Collins rejoiced. "Mark it down: that in view of the fact that Gleason has been made chief skipper of the Sox, I would not change places with any one on any club in the American League. By this I mean to say that the White Sox look to me to be the best bet for 1919."

Collins was prescient, the White Sox winning their fourth A.L. pennant with one of the finest teams ever assembled. He batted .316 and Joe Jackson led the team with .351. The pitching, bolstered by newcomer Dickie Kerr (13-7) was paced by Cicotte (29-7) and Williams (23-11) and handled by an outstanding defensive catcher in Schalk.

As the White Sox prepared to face the Cincinnati Reds in the 1919 World Series, few doubted they would win. Gleason was supremely confident in the quality of his team, particularly that of his starting pitchers.

"It won't make any difference to them whether they're playing the Reds for the World's Championship or playing an exhibition game in a hick town," Gleason proclaimed, unaware of the impending gambling scheme that was to infect his team, destroy its chances in the World Series, and label it forever in history and legend as the infamous Black Sox.

The full extent of the conspiracy was not revealed until 1920, though there was no lack of rumor, suspicion and incisive reporting of manipulation by gamblers even while conspirators were throwing the World Series game by game in 1919.

It was a dismal ending to the White Sox's portion of the Golden Era, which might have shone as brightly as that of the Cubs whom they almost matched with four pennants and two World Series titles in 19 years, and surpassed in one respect—the winning of the ultimate crosstown conflict in 1906.

It's sobering to reflect that neither team has won a World Series since the first two decades of the 20th Century and that the White Sox have hoisted just one pennant. Furthermore, while the Cubs have won five pennants since 1919—though none for more than half a century—the World Series title eluded them even in what might be called their Silver Age of 1929 to 1945.

All the more reason to call the period 1901–1919 the Golden Era.

THE UNCIVIL WAR

Imagine this: The Cubs and White Sox winning the pennants and playing each other in the World Series. Impossible? It would seem so, but it did happen, almost a century ago in 1906. It was the first World Series matching teams from the same city.

The Cubs were runaway winners in the National League. They finished 20 games ahead of the second-place New York Giants. They won 116 games, a one-season record that has never been equaled despite the expanded schedule of eight more games.

They led the league in the three fundamental areas of play, batting, pitching and defense, and outscored their opponents 704-381, a remarkable differential. They had 31 shutouts and won 50 of their final 58 games. Going into the World Series they were regarded as the best team ever.

Mordecai "Three-Finger" Brown, their pitching ace, was 26-6, led both leagues in earned run average with 1.04 and the National League in shutouts with nine. First baseman Frank Chance, their player-manager, led in runs scored with 103. This was the team with the fabled Tinkers-to-Evers-to-Chance double play combination.

Statistically, the White Sox couldn't compare. Labeled the "Hitless Wonders," they had a team batting average of .230, lowest in the American League, and won the flag by only three games. From August 2 to 23 they had a 19-game winning streak, an A.L. record that wasn't equaled until 41 years later. There were eight shutouts in the streak, four by Big Ed Walsh who won seven of the 19 games.

Second baseman Frank Isbell hit .279, the highest batting average of any White Sox player. Three Cubs hit over .300: third baseman Harry Steinfeldt, who led the N.L. in hits (.327), Chance (.319) and catcher Johnny Kling (.301). In addition to Brown, the Cub rotation included Jack Pfiester (20-8) and Ed Reulbach (19-4).

Ominously, or so it seemed for the White Sox, shortstop George Davis was sidelined with a late-season injury. Manager Fielder Jones moved third baseman Lee Tannehill to shortstop and installed utility infielder George Rohe at third base. These moves proved to be a lucky stroke of genius.

According to Biart Williams, writing in *The White Sox Encyclopedia*, the Cubs won the coin toss for the home field advantage. Admission prices were doubled. There were two additional "viewing" sites, the Auditorium and the First Regimental Armory, both with approximately 5,000 seating capacity.

A 20-foot baseball diamond was erected on each stage. Balls and strikes and the batters' names were illuminated by light bulbs. An announcer, using a megaphone, described the play-by-play as it was received in Morse code by a Western Union telegrapher.

And the impossible happened. The Hitless Wonders won four games to two. It is often described as the greatest upset in World Series history.

Game 1

Snow flurries harried a crowd of 12,963 at the Cubs' West Side Grounds as Nick Altrock outpitched Brown, each allowing only four hits. Rohe's fifth-inning triple put the Sox ahead when Brown picked up an easy roller and threw poorly to Kling at the plate for an error. The Sox won 2-1.

Game 2

It was colder the next day at South Side Park, home of the Sox. Reulbach pitched a one-hitter, Steinfeldt went 3-for-3, and Joe Tinker collected two hits and scored three runs. The Cubs took the lead as early as the second inning against Doc White, an 18-game winner with a league-leading 1.31 ERA, and won 7-1.

Game 3

Walsh stopped the Cubs with a 12-strikeout, two-hit shutout. He gave up a single to Solly Hoffman and a double to Frank "Wildfire" Schulte in the first inning, then held the Cubs hitless. Rohe struck again with a bases-loaded triple that accounted for all of the Sox runs. The Sox won 3-0.

Game 4

Brown defeated Altrock 1-0 to square the Series at 2-2. Brown limited the Sox to two hits. The Cubs scored the only run in the seventh. Chance singled, went to second on Steinfeldt's sacrifice fly, and scored on Johnny Evers' single to left.

Game 5

The largest crowd of the Series, 23,257 at West Side Grounds, witnessed the Hitless Wonders assault Reulbach for 12 hits. Isbell paced the Sox with four doubles. George Davis drove in three runs with two doubles, one right-handed and another left-handed. Rohe was 3-for-4. The Sox won 8-6.

Game 6

The Sox wrapped up the Series with a controversial 8-5 victory. Just as Schulte prepared to haul in Davis' long drive in the third inning, a Sox fan reached over the outfield rope and pushed Schulte who dropped the ball, two runs scoring. Jiggs Donahue followed with another two-run double.

Cub manager Chance praised the Sox but insisted, "I will never believe the Sox have a better club. We did not play our game, and that's all there is to it."

The White Sox remained in character and hit only .198 as a team but their pitching held the Cubs to a .196 average. Chance failed to drive in a run. Left fielder Jimmy Sheckard was 0-for-21. Tinkers, Evers and Kling, combined, batted .164.

Utility man Rohe, who appeared in only 75 games and batted .258 during the regular season, was the Sox batting hero. He hit .333 and drove in four runs. His two triples helped win the first and third games. Donahue, the best fielding first baseman in the league, also hit .333, almost 100 points above his season's average. Neither team hit a home run.

It wasn't until 91 years later that the Cubs and White Sox again met in a championship game. Inter-league play brought them together in 1997 for a three-game series at the new Comiskey Park. The Cubs won the opener 8-3, but the Sox won the next two, 5-3 and 3-0. The scene shifted to Wrigley Field in 1998, the Cubs winning all three games.

For the fans it was Nirvana. The games counted in the standings and the ballparks were filled. Two of the games, on consecutive days in 1997, drew record-breaking crowds and so Commissioner Bud Selig expanded the annual series to six games, three home, three away.

The following year, in 1999, the Sox fans claimed the so-called "braggin' rights" as their heroes won four of the six games. The next year it was the Cubs' turn; they won four out of the six. After four years and 18 inter-league games it was a draw. The series was tied at nine victories for each club.

Prior to this there had been 203 Cubs–White Sox exhibition games under different designations, with the Sox holding a decisive edge, 123 victories against 75 losses and five ties. From 1902 through 1942 the teams played a City Series, often in a best-of-seven format, before or after the regular season. Thereafter one game was played annually for a variety of charitable causes.

MERKLE'S BONER

Whenever someone says the Cubs don't "get the breaks" they should be told of "Merkle's Boner." It occurred almost a century ago, on September 23, 1908, Cubs vs. New York Giants. It is the most controversial game in baseball history, forced an unprecedented pennant playoff, and enabled the Cubs to win the flag.

Here is the official report from umpire Bob Emslie, submitted to National League president Harry Pulliam:

"In the ninth inning of today's game at the Polo Grounds, with two men out and with New York baserunners on first and third bases, Bridwell made a clean safe line hit to the outfield. I had to fall to the ground to keep the ball from hitting me. When I got to my feet I watched to see if Bridwell ran his hit out to first which he did.

"Just after Bridwell had crossed first base Tinker of the Chicago Club made the claim to me that Merkle who was the baserunner on first when the hit was made had not run the hit out to second base. As my back was turned to that play watching Bridwell I did not know if Merkle had run to second or not, but as soon as my attention was called to it I looked out in right field and saw Merkle going towards the clubhouse and McGinnitty was down at second base scrambling with Evers to get the ball away from him.

"I had not seen the play at second base but I went to O'Day who was watching the plate, and he said the run did not count. As soon as the people seen (sic) Bridwell's hit was safe they all made for the playing field and O'Day and myself were jostled around by the people. Finally we got under the stand. It was rapidly growing dark and in my opinion could not have gone any further with the game. This is all in connection with the game."

An explanation is in order. According to the rule, never previously enforced, a baserunner or baserunners must proceed to the next base before a batter-runner is safe at first. This applies only on potential force plays, with a runner at first, runners at first and second, or with the bases loaded.

In this instance, Al Bridwell was not safe at first until Fred Merkle, the runner who had occupied first base, advanced to the next base. Merkle *had* to touch second base and until he did so the Cubs had a force play at second for the third out. If Merkle had touched second, Moose McCormick, the runner on third, would have scored for a 2-1 New York victory. Instead the game ended in a 1-1 tie.

Exactly what happened immediately thereafter never has been definitely established.

Charles Dryden of the *Chicago Tribune*, a premier baseball writer of the time, reported:

"Fred Hofman fielded Bridwell's knock and threw to second baseman Johnny Evers for the force play on the absent Merkle. But Joe McGinnity (a New York coach) cut in and grabbed the ball before it reached the eager Evers. Three Cubs landed on McGinnity and jolted the ball from his cruel grasp."

Gym Bagley of the *New York Evening Mail*: "Cub manager Frank Chance and third baseman Harry Steinfeldt got to second on the run, and those two, with Evers, surrounded McGinnity and began to wrestle him for possession of the ball. McGinnity threw it into the left field bleachers."

Evers' version:

"The ball had been hit to Hofman, our centerfielder. I yelled for him to throw me the ball. Because of the crowd swarming onto the field, Hofman couldn't see me and threw the ball over my head. Joe Tinker, our shortstop, headed toward first base, and became tangled in the crowd. The ball hit Tinker in the back.

"McGinnity, who was coaching third base and realized Merkle's mistake, started running for the ball, which was around the field being kicked by the crowd which didn't know what was going on. McGinnity picked up the ball but Tinker tried to pin his arms back and take the ball away. McGinnity snapped the ball with his wrist and it sailed into the crowd around the shortstop position.

"A spectator picked it up. Floyd Kroh, one of our pitchers (who was not in the game), asked the fan for the ball. The spectator refused, so Kroh took a swing at him, hitting the customer right on top of his bowler hat. The ball fell free, Kroh got it and walked over to me at second base, where I was parked, and handed me the ball.

"I couldn't find Emslie in the crowd, so I yelled to (Hank) O'Day who had been handling the plate. O'Day advanced as close to second as he could because of the crowd. I lifted my hand up to show him I had the ball.

"'Are you on the bag?' asked Hank. He couldn't see my legs.

"'Yes, right on it,' I answered.

"'And Hank said, 'The run doesn't count,' remembering the Pittsburgh game."

Three weeks earlier, on September 4 in Pittsburgh, there had been a similar incident when the Pirates beat the Cubs 1-0 on a ninth-inning run. The Pirates' Warren Gill was on first when the winning hit was delivered and he, too, broke for the clubhouse without touching second.

The brainy Evers called for the ball and stomped on second, claiming a forceout. To the Cubs' good fortune, O'Day was the base umpire. O'Day told Evers "he was off his rocker." But Evers was convinced he was correct and told Chance a protest should be filed with the league office. President Pulliam allowed the Pittsburgh victory to stand but conceded the protest had merit. Henceforth, the rule would be enforced.

After the Merkle game, the Giants were still in first place, a half game ahead of the Cubs. The Giants had 17 more games, the Cubs 11. From then on to the end of the regular season, the Cubs were 9-2, the Giants 11-6, both finishing with identical 98-55 records. Had the Giants won one more game, or had there been another Chicago loss, the Giants would have won the pennant and Merkle's Boner would have been lost in the fog of time.

According to the Giants' Christy Mathewson in his 1912 biography *Pitching in a Pinch*, the Giants were given the option of a five-game playoff or risking it all on one game. Because some of their front-line players were suffering with major or minor injuries, the Giants opted for one game.

"By this time," Mathewson wrote, "Merkle had lost 20 pounds, and his eyes were hollow and his cheeks sunken. The newspapers showed him no mercy, and the fans never failed to criticize and hiss him when he appeared on the field. He stuck to it and showed up at the ballpark every day, putting on his uniform and practicing. It was a game thing to do. A lot of men, under the same fire, would have quit cold."

The Great Matty wasn't alone. Many of the players sympathized with Merkle, a 19-year-old rookie, who in effect was an innocent victim appearing in the 53rd of his 1,637 major league games. He would not have been in the game, except possibly as a pinch hitter, if Fred Tenney, the Giants' regular first baseman, had not been on the sick list with lumbago. It was the only game the 33-year-old Tenney missed during the regular season.

Manager John McGraw repeatedly rushed to the defense of the forlorn Merkle, praising him for his skills and intelligence, absolving him of blame for merely following the practice of older players and pointing to a dozen games or more which the Giants should have won but didn't. Then, with his temperature at the boiling point, he roared, "We were robbed of the pennant and nobody can blame Merkle for that."

McGraw, because of his considerable influence in league affairs, dictated that the playoff game be played at the Polo Grounds, the Giants' home field. It was played on October 8 before an estimated 35,000 spectators, the largest baseball crowd to that time. The park was sold out, including standing room, three hours before the game. According to one account: "The bluffs overhanging the Polo Grounds were black with people, as were the housetops and the telegraph poles. The elevated lines couldn't run because people were sitting on the tracks."

The starting pitchers were Mathewson, a 37-game winner, and Jack Pfiester, called "Jack the Giant Killer," just as in the Merkle game. Three-Finger Brown, who helped in the winning of four pennants and two World Series, had started or relieved in 11 of the Cubs' previous 14 games. He was eager to make the start. Chance pacified him. If Pfiester faltered, he would come on in early relief.

Brown, in a subsequent interview, set the scene.

"I can still see Christy Mathewson making his lordly entrance," Brown recalled. "He'd always wait until about 10 minutes before game-time, then he'd come from the clubhouse across the field in a long linen duster like auto drivers wore in those days, and at every step the crowd would yell louder and louder. This day they split the air. I watched him enter as I went out to the bullpen, where I was to keep ready."

Pfiester didn't have his control, walking two batters, hitting another and giving up a double for a 1-0 Giant lead. Brown was summoned earlier than anticipated, with two outs and two on in the first inning, and struck out Art Devlin to retire the side without further cost.

The Cubs went ahead to stay with a four-run, third-inning rally. Tinker led off with a triple to deep center. Johnny Kling singled, Tinker scoring for a 1-1 tie. Brown sacrificed. Then with two outs, Wildfire Schulte and Chance, who had three hits, followed with RBI doubles and the Great Matty was doomed. He was lifted for a pinch hitter in the seventh. Merkle did not appear in the game.

Brown was never better. He went the rest of the way on a yield of seven hits and a harmless seventh-inning run in a 4-2 victory. It was the 29th win for Brown who also appeared in nine winning games in relief, and the third successive pennant for the Cubs. They went on to defeat Detroit in the World Series, their last World Series triumph in the 20th Century.

"We made it to the dressing room and barricaded the door," Brown said. "Outside wild men were yelling for our blood—really. As the mob got bigger, the police formed a line across the door. We read the next day that the cops had to pull their revolvers to hold them back. I couldn't say as to that. We weren't sticking our heads out to see.

"When it was safe, we rode to our hotel in a patrol wagon, with two cops on the inside and four riding the running boards and the rear step. That night when we left for Detroit we slipped out the back door and were escorted down the alley in back of our hotel by a swarm of policemen."

Double Duty or Dubious Myth?

There have been many storied double-play combinations but none more so than the Cubs' Tinker-to-Evers-to-Chance. And all because they were immortalized in a famous poem composed in 1910 by Franklin P. Adams, who was covering the New York Giants for the *New York Globe*.

These are the saddest of all possible words,
Tinker to Evers to Chance.
Trio of bear Cubs and fleeter than birds,
Tinker to Evers to Chance.
Thoughtlessly pricking our gonfalon bubble,
Making a Giant hit into a double,
Words that are weighty with nothing but trouble—
Tinker to Evers to Chance.

The poem is a wonderful example of myth making and the power of the pen. The full effect of Adams' poem, which was constantly reprinted, was realized 46 years later in the 1946 Hall of Fame voting. The trio of "bear Cubs" went in as a unit.

An explanation is necessary.

In the first balloting none of the candidates received the necessary 75 percent required for election. Frank Chance was named on 144 ballots, eight fewer than required. Johnny Evers was second with 130. Joe Tinker drew 55 and didn't finish among the top 10 candidates.

A runoff was held. Again, none of the candidates polled 75 percent. Confronted with the prospect of an empty Cooperstown stage, a special six-man committee was appointed and elected nine players, including Tinker, Evers and Chance. Nothing like that has happened before or since.

More than likely, the three Cubs were not much more than an average double-play combination. Curious about their ability, Warren Brown, who is among Chicago's Hall of Fame baseball writers, asked the National League office for a statistical accounting. Charles Segar, then the N.L. publicitor, exhumed the official fielding records from 1906 through 1909 when they were at their peak.

Segar's findings revealed a four-season *total* of only 29 Tinker-to-Evers-to-Chance twin killings (6-4-3 in scoring parlance). They completed eight in 1906, seven in 1907, eight in 1908 and six in 1909. Segar also checked the reverse (4-6-3) double plays, those started by second baseman Evers rather than shortstop Tinker. The numbers were essentially the same, 25. So in those four years the combined total was 54. They never led the league in double plays.

First baseman Chance, who was a strong player and a highly successful manager, was the most worthy Hall of Fame candidate. He would have been enshrined sooner or later. Evers, a heady player known as "The Crab," had a long and distinguished career, and was a prominent figure in the Merkle's Boner incident. Still, he was borderline. Tinker was just along for the ride.

In addition to the poem by Adams, Evers and Tinker are held up as an example to the contrary when team harmony is discussed. They were teammates for 10 seasons but for almost three years didn't speak to each other.

"We had a fight," Tinker said many years later. "We were in Bedford, Indiana, playing an exhibition game. We dressed in the hotel and went to the ballpark in hacks. Evers got into a hack by himself and drove off, leaving me and several others to wait until the hack returned.

"I was mad. As soon as I got to the park I went up to him and said, 'Who the hell are you that you've got to have a hack all to yourself? Now listen: If you and I talk to each other we're only going to be fighting all the time. So don't talk to me and I won't talk to you. You play your position and I'll play mine and let it go at that.'

"Evers said that suited him fine. We won two pennants after that, playing side by side, but we never spoke to each other again except in anger. Every time something went wrong on the field we would be at each other and there would be a fight in the club-house. But let anybody on another club pick on one of us and the two of us would jump him.

"He was a great player, a wonderful pivot man. But boy, how he could ride you. Chance used to say he wished Evers was an outfielder so he couldn't hear him."

The ice was broken many years later, in 1937, when they were invited to a broadcast for the Joe Louis–Jim Braddock heavy-weight championship fight.

"Neither of us knew the other would be in the studio," Evers recalled. "And when we met it looked as though we were going to start all over again. Then all of a sudden Joe threw his arms around me and I threw mine around him and we cried like a couple of babies."

Femmes Fatale

The Cubs lead the major leagues in *femmes fatale*, a pair of pistol-backing babes, one scorned, the other deranged and distraught with love. Their victims, almost a generation apart, were shortstop Billy Jurges and first baseman Eddie Waitkus, felled by so-called "romantic silver bullets."

Jurges was the first to fall. It was July 6, 1932, two months after his 24th birthday. He was in his second season with the Cubs, young and handsome, "single, running around and having a lot of fun." Among his lady friends was Violet Popovich, a pillow-soft, curvaceous brunette who had been around the baseball block.

"I'm staying around the Carlos Hotel, just a few blocks from Wrigley Field," Jurges said during a lengthy 1988 interview at his trailer home in Largo, Florida. "She called me from the lobby. It's early in the morning, about seven o'clock, and she said, 'I'd like to see you.'

"I said, 'C'mon up.'

"When she came to my room I told her. 'I'm not going to go out on any more dates. We've got a chance to win the pennant. I've got to get my rest.'

"And she pulled a gun out of her purse and started shooting. I was hit three times. In the right chest, once in the back on the right side. Then I grabbed the gun and it went off a third time. A bullet went through the palm of my left hand. Then she ran out.

"I ran into the hall and Marvin Gudat, a fellow on the club, a utility outfielder, was there, and he said, 'What happened? Were you shooting firecrackers?'

"And I said, 'Get a doctor!'

"I was bleeding like a pig, lying on the bed, and this young doctor, an intern who had come with the ambulance, was working on me. I could hardly breathe.

"I asked him, 'Doc, how am I?'

"'I'll give you 20 minutes to live. You've got it bad.'

"Dr. John Davis, the club doctor, came in and examined me and I said, 'What do you think?' He told me I'd be all right. And I said, 'That doctor over there gave me 20 minutes.'

"We went to court when I got out of the hospital. The judge was a baseball fan. He said, 'Bill, what's the story?' I told him and he said, 'What do you want me to do?'

"And I said, 'To hell with it, let's forget it.'

"So he let her go and that was the end of that. I never saw her again. Later I found out that three or four years before she shot me she had plugged another guy. I was screwing her. So were other ballplayers. She was a beautiful woman.

"I took the rap for it, but she had gone to Cuyler's room first. Kiki Cuyler was a big ladies' man. She had the key to his room but he wasn't there. She wrote a note and put it on the mirror: 'I'M GOING TO KILL YOU!'

"The police and the lawyer told me they found the note."

Jurges paused and stood up. He had been sitting on a large, cushioned chair. He crossed his heart and declared, "That's the absolute truth!"

But he may have left out a crucial part of the story. Al Lopez, the Hall of Fame manager, then a catcher with the Brooklyn Dodgers, said Jurges was engaged to Miss Popovich.

"I told him she had a bad reputation," Lopez revealed. "A lot of the National League players had been with her. When he heard that he said he would break off their engagement when he got back to Chicago. You know what they say—there's nothing worse than a woman scorned. That's probably why she shot him."

Popovich capitalized on the incident. She signed a 22-week contract to sing and dance at various night spots, billed as "Violet (I Did It for Love) Valli—The Most Talked Of Girl in Chicago."

Jurges was out for three weeks but was in the starting lineup for two of the Cubs' four World Series games against the New York Yankees. He had a long and distinguished major league playing career—17 years—and retired after the 1947 season. He was the fourth player to become a manager from the Cubs' 1932 infield, and directed the Boston Red Sox for parts of two seasons.

"*Femme fatale*" No. 2 wasn't a scorned woman. Ruth Anne Steinhagen, Waitkus' assailant, was with him only once, on June 8, 1949. Like Violet Popovich 17 years earlier, she called him at his room in Chicago's Edgewater Beach Hotel, an elegant, pink castle on Sheridan Road that backed into Lake Michigan.

Waitkus was out. She left a midnight message at the front desk, asking that he call her room on the 13th floor—1297A. "It's about something important."

Waitkus, 26, had been with the Cubs for the four previous seasons but had been traded to the Philadelphia Phillies. He returned the call. She was asleep. "What's so darn important?" he asked.

She told him she couldn't discuss it over the phone. "Can you come up tonight for a few minutes?"

Waitkus said he would be right up. Steinhagen told him she needed a half hour to get dressed.

The following is from an interview with Steinhagen made public by the chief of the Cook County Behavior Clinic:

"I remember when he knocked on the door I was scared stiff, but I thought to myself I will settle this thing once and for all. I had a knife in my skirt pocket and was going to use that on him.

"When I opened the door he came rushing in right past me. I expected him to stand there and wait until I asked him to come in and during that time I was going to stab him. He looked at me and said, 'What do you want to see me about?'

"I said, 'Wait a minute, I have a surprise for you.' I went to the closet and pulled out a .22 caliber rifle. I pointed it at him. He had a silly look on his face. I told him to get out of the chair and move over by the window.

"He got up right away and said, 'Baby, what is this all about?'

"He just stood there stuttering and stammering and asked me again, 'What's this all about? What have I done?'

"'For two years you have been bothering me and now you are going to die.'

"And then I shot him."

"For a minute I didn't think I shot him because he just stood there, and then he crashed against the wall. I knelt down next to him and put my hand over his. He said something to the effect, 'You like that, don't you?'

"I took my hand away and asked where he had been shot. I couldn't see a bullet hole or anything. He said I shot him in the guts. I thought, 'Well, now's the time to shoot myself.' I tried to find the bullets but I couldn't find them and then I lost my nerve."

Ruth Anne Steinhagen, 19, was a psychotic who had worked herself into a lovesick state after four years of worshipping Waitkus at Wrigley Field.

She talked about Waitkus constantly, dreamed about him, and built a shrine to him in her bedroom. She collected his pictures and press notices. Soon it became apparent it was not an ordinary teenage infatuation. When she discovered he came from Boston she developed an affinity for baked beans.

"As time went on I just became nuttier and nuttier about the guy," she said. "I knew I would never get to know him in a normal way, so I kept thinking I will never get him and if I can't have him nobody else can. And then I decided to kill him."

The shooting became a part of our national history. It was featured in *The Natural*, a novel by Bernard Malamud made into a major film, starring Robert Redford as an unsuspecting major league player who was shot in a hotel room by a woman wearing a dark veil.

A felony court found Steinhagen deranged. She was committed to a mental hospital. After extensive surgery, Waitkus accomplished a full recovery and the following year participated in the World Series with the Phillies. But he became paranoid when meeting new people and stopped drinking with his teammates.

Times have changed. Today the women don't shoot. They sue.

THE
GRIMM
SILVER AGE

He was called "Jolly Cholly," and prank-loving, banjo-twanging Charlie Grimm was often that, especially when the Cubs played well. He also could be justly regarded as the unifying thread in the warp and woof of the team for four decades, from 1925 well into the 1960s.

"Baseball to me is a lot of things," Grimm said in an autobiography written with *Chicago Tribune* writer Ed Prell. "It's winning pennants, and I'm way ahead in the game with four Cub jackpots, three as a manager...It's coming to the Cubs, playing on Joe McCarthy's 1929 flag winners in the electric atmosphere of Wrigley Field.

"It's succeeding the greatest right-handed hitter of all time, Rogers Hornsby, as manager in 1932 and coming down in front of the N.L. parade. It's winning the big prize three years later with a marvelous aggregation that won 21 in a row down the stretch. It's the let-down feeling of giving way in 1938 to Gabby Hartnett, who rallied the Cubs to win the championship. It's coming back to the old stand in 1944 and a year later the Cubs nailing down their last pennant."

Grimm's extended adventure with the Cubs as player, manager and even radio broadcaster encompassed every one of their last five pennants. It wouldn't be an exaggeration to term the period of his involvement the team's Silver Age—silver rather than gold because they failed to follow up regular season success with a single World Series title in five opportunities.

The "Grimm Era" didn't begin until 1925, when the Cubs obtained him in a trade with the Pittsburgh Pirates, for whom he had played first base since 1919. The preceding five seasons, 1919–1924, could just as appropriately be termed as a "grim era," with a parade of managers that marched into futility.

Fred Mitchell was fired after a fourth place finish in 1920 in favor of Johnny Evers, back for a second term. Evers didn't even complete the 1921 season, being replaced by Bill Killefer enroute to seventh place. Under Killefer the Cubs were fifth in 1922, fourth in 1923, fifth in 1924, and when they struggled again in 1925 he was supplanted in mid-season by Rabbit Maranville. The latter quickly gave way to George Gibson, who helped secure the Cubs' grip on last place for the first time in their history.

Despite the general team malaise, the Cubs achieved a few memorable moments and individual feats during the early 1920s. Among the players who distinguished themselves were Grover Cleveland Alexander, shortstop Charlie Hollocher, outfielder Lawrence "Hack" Miller and first baseman Ray Grimes.

Alexander shook off his World War I trauma from poison gas to regain the heights with a 27-14 record and 1.91 ERA in 1920, and remained a consistent winner. The slick-fielding Hollocher overrode stomach ailments to bat as high as .340 in 1922. Grimes hit .329 in four seasons as a Cub until a back injury cut short his career after 1924. Miller was a brief slugging sensation in 1922 and 1923.

Compact yet powerfully built, a noted weight lifter as well as a ballplayer, Miller caught the fans' fancy by batting .352 with 12 home runs and 78 RBI as a rookie. At a time when Babe Ruth had become a national hero, the Cubs hoped Miller might turn into a reasonable facsimile. Since owner Wrigley and team president Veeck were carrying out improvements for 1923 to what by now was called Cubs Park, they tried to help Miller, a right-handed batter, by installing temporary bleachers in left field to trim the distance.

Miller responded by hitting 20 home runs while batting .301 with 88 RBI in 1923, but fielding deficiencies reduced him to utility duty for two remaining seasons with the Cubs. His nickname "Hack" derived from his resemblance to a famous wrestler of his day, Hackenschmidt. Coincidentally, it anticipated a far more celebrated player with that nickname, Hack Wilson, who became a Cub in 1926, the season after Miller left.

Miller contributed a pair of three-run home runs to the most extraordinary event in this interval of the Cubs' long saga, a home game on August 25, 1922, with the Philadelphia Phillies. The Cubs won 26-23, and the total of 49 runs in one game has never been matched, while the 51 hits (26 by the Phillies) remain the most in a nine-inning game.

The Cubs scored a run in the first inning, the Phillies retaliated with three in the second. As if irritated, the Cubs exploded for 10 runs in the second, but the Phillies cut their lead to 11-6 by the bottom of the fourth. That's when the Cubs got serious, scoring 14 runs to take what seemed an insurmountable 25-6 lead.

If ever proof were needed that any "insurmountable" lead is illusory, this game provided it. The Phillies scored three runs in the fifth, eight in the eighth, and six in the ninth to cut the Cubs' edge to three runs before their fifth pitcher, Tiny Osborne, got the final out with the bases loaded and the score 26-23.

Cub center fielder Cliff Heathcote reached base seven times with three singles, two doubles and two walks for a perfect day at bat. Right fielder Marty Callaghan went to bat three times in the 14-run fourth, getting two hits before striking out.

In the long run, however, the most meaningful line in the grisly box score was provided by the name of a rookie catcher who relieved regular Bob O'Farrell late in the bizarre contest and had no official at-bat. He was Charles Leo "Gabby" Hartnett, who by 1925 was the regular receiver and an offensive force with 24 home runs.

With Grimm, Hartnett, pitchers Guy Bush and rookie Charlie Root, as well as a few other dependables already in place, Wrigley and Veeck resolved to build the team into a contender. The primary need was a competent manager.

In September 1925, Veeck met secretly with Joe McCarthy, then managing the Louisville, Kentucky, minor league team, and offered him the Cub job. McCarthy had never played a day in the major leagues and had turned to managing at the age of 26 in 1913. He had successfully developed young players and winning teams wherever he went. He was tough in an understated way, efficient, and extremely sharp in evaluating talent.

With Veeck's support, McCarthy began to restructure the Cubs in 1926. He got rid of Alexander, whose chronic alcoholism was a threat to team discipline, the transaction enabling the great pitcher to become a World Series hero for the St. Louis Cardinals that year. McCarthy persuaded Veeck to acquire minor league outfielders Hack Wilson and Riggs Stephenson. The Cubs moved up to fourth place, Wilson leading the league in home runs with 21 and Stephenson batting .338.

For 1927, McCarthy added shortstop Woody English. Wilson again led the league in home runs with 30 and Stephenson batted .344 as the Cubs again finished fourth. The next year, the Cubs made a deal for veteran outfielder Kiki Cuyler to round out an all-star outfield, brought up rookie pitcher Pat Malone and moved up to third place.

After the 1926 season, the fans responded to the resurgent Cubs by turning out in increasingly huge numbers, and Wrigley began a major renovation of the ballpark, now renamed for him. It was double-decked to give it much of its present aspect, and the seating capacity was increased to over 40,000. In 1927, the Cubs became the first Chicago team to surpass a million in attendance, drawing 1,163,347. For five consecutive years they topped a million, reaching a peak of 1,485,166 in 1929.

McCarthy was convinced that one more solid hitter, preferably an infielder, could give the Cubs a chance at the pennant in 1929. Wrigley and Veeck obliged by acquiring second baseman Rogers Hornsby for $200,000 plus five players from the Boston Braves.

Hornsby met McCarthy's expectations, batting .380 with 39 home runs and 149 RBI in 1929 to lead the Cubs to their first pennant in 11 years. Wilson matched Hornsby's home run output and drove in 159 runs. Malone led the pitching staff with a 22-10 record. Grimm batted .298 with 91 RBI as part of the supporting cast. The team batting average was .303.

Powerhouse though they were, the Cubs fell to the Philadelphia Athletics in the World Series, the opening game setting the pattern.

With an overflow crowd of 50,740 at Wrigley Field, A's manager Connie Mack passed up his ace pitchers to start Howard Ehmke, a 35-year-old veteran who had won just seven games all season. Ehmke struck out 13 Cubs for a World Series record, and scattered eight hits. A home run by Jimmie Foxx off Root in the seventh inning put the A's ahead to stay, and they added two runs in the ninth to win 3-1.

The Cubs' greatest humiliation came in Game 4 as they took an 8-0 lead into the seventh inning when the A's scored 10 runs to win 10-8.

Even Grimm was grim, recalling that after Foxx drove in the tie-breaking run for the A's he barked at the slugger, "Podner, the next time you come around first base, I'm going to trip you."

It was McCarthy who was tripped. Wrigley wasn't just the owner of the team, he was a fan. He took the World Series defeat to heart. He had hungered for a World Series championship and blamed McCarthy for having failed to win it.

Wrigley's disappointment grew during the 1930 season and was constantly stirred up by Hornsby, who considered McCarthy a "busher" because he had never played in the major leagues. Many of the other players felt the same. Hornsby, who had managed before in the N.L. at St. Louis, New York and Boston, was eager to supplant McCarthy.

Notwithstanding the greatest turnout of fans in Cubs history in 1929, with a virtual encore the following year, and despite Wilson's march to a major league record 191 RBI and a N.L. record 56 home runs, Wrigley fired McCarthy with four games left in the 1930 season and the team in second place. They missed another pennant partly because Hornsby was injured and able to play in only 42 games. Wrigley's stated reason: "McCarthy lacks enough desire for a world championship." Wrigley gave the job to Hornsby.

Impatient, outspoken and dictatorial, Hornsby was hardly an ideal manager for a team of veterans such as the Cubs. He took over with four games left in the 1930 season, and the pinnacle of his tenure might have been the four consecutive victories with which they closed the campaign.

While Hornsby was a great player who set the modern major league record with the .424 he batted in 1924 for the Cardinals, and posted a career batting average of .358, second only to Ty Cobb's record .367, he was his own worst enemy as manager. He led the Cardinals to a pennant in 1926, his first year as player-manager, but created havoc with his abrasive, arrogant manner in later stints with the Giants and Braves before Veeck gave him the Cub job.

He soon disenchanted Wrigley and Veeck in 1931 as the Cubs dropped to third place. His players, including Wilson whose home run output declined to 13, were driven to distraction by Hornsby's bluntness and impatience. He was intolerant of failure, whatever the circumstances, demanding perfection.

The situation festered during the 1932 season, despite changes over the winter, including the death of William Wrigley Jr. on Jan. 26. The new double-play combination of second baseman Billy Herman and shortstop Bill Jurges sparkled. Wilson had been traded to St. Louis and was replaced in center field by journeyman Joe Moore. Lon Warneke emerged as the ace of the pitching staff. Still, the Cubs treaded water with a record of 53-46 on August 1.

Adding to Hornsby's problems were allegations that he consorted with gamblers and bookmakers, originating in his obsession with horse racing. On August 2, Veeck and new owner Philip K. Wrigley fired Hornsby, replacing him with Grimm.

"I think it got down to Hornsby becoming bored with Veeck's championship claims," Grimm said, "and with Veeck finally getting tired of Hornsby emphasizing our shortcomings."

The Cubs responded quickly to Grimm's comparatively gentle and loose manner. They celebrated Charlie Grimm Day on August 16 at Wrigley Field by starting on a 14-game winning streak. They clinched the pennant on Sept. 20, and finished with a record of 37-18 under Grimm to round out the season at 90-64.

In his first full season with the Cubs, Warneke led the league with 22 victories, Bush was 19-11 and Root and Malone each won 15 games. The remarkable fielding range of Jurges and Herman made for a brilliant second base combination. Stephenson led the team in batting with .324, Herman hit .314, Grimm .307 and Moore .305.

Grimm's success did not carry over into the World Series against the New York Yankees, who won four straight games, the highlight being Babe Ruth's celebrated "called shot" home run, though Lou Gehrig also punished the Cubs.

The sweep got underway after the Cubs took a 2-0 lead in the first inning of the opening game in Yankee Stadium in which Bush faced Red Ruffing on the mound. Gehrig struck with a two-run homer in the fourth, and the rout was on. The Yankees scored five more in the sixth, and though the Cubs hit Ruffing hard, Stephenson driving in three runs with three hits, he weathered the storm. The Yankees won 12-6.

In Game 2, Lefty Gomez proved too tough for Warneke and the Cubs, Gehrig contributing three more hits and an RBI for a 5-2 Yankees victory.

Almost 50,000 overflowed Wrigley Field for Game 3, most apparently on hand to taunt Ruth, whose response was a three-run homer off Root in the first inning. With the game tied at 4 in the fourth, and the crowd and Cub players howling at Ruth, he allegedly pointed toward center field, then hit a home run to put the Yankees ahead 5-4. In the clamor over Ruth's "called shot" it was almost unnoticed that Gehrig also hit two home runs in the 7-5 Yankees victory.

The Yankees swept the Cubs with a 13-6 rout in Game 4 of a Series made memorable by Ruth's alleged gesture, a myth that overshadowed Gehrig's .529 batting average, eight RBI and three home runs.

Despite the World Series rout, Grimm solidified his standing with P.K. Wrigley, and for the rest of his life was a favorite of the owner, serving the team in many capacities, including that of manager for an unmatched three terms over entire and parts of 14 seasons.

Two third-place finishes followed the 1932 championship while Grimm replaced most of the veterans from the 1929 and 1932 pennant winners. When Veeck died in 1933, P.K. Wrigley turned to James "Boots" Weber as general manager, with Grimm combining an advisory role with his field job. By 1935 Weber and Grimm had rebuilt the team with such young stars as third baseman Stan Hack, first baseman Phil Cavarretta, outfielders Augie Galan and Frank Demaree and pitchers Bill Lee, Larry French and Tex Carleton in place.

Notwithstanding the fresh talent, the Cubs appeared to be falling out of the pennant race by Labor Day, but then put together a 21-game winning streak, their longest since 1880, to finish four games ahead of second-place St. Louis.

The second longest streak in major league history started with a doubleheader against Cincinnati on Labor Day, September 2, after Grimm held a clubhouse meeting to reinvigorate his team, just back from a road trip. "We're home for the next 20 games," Grimm told his players. "And either we do or we don't. But we are going to be loose."

During the season Grimm replaced himself at first base with 19-year-old Cavarretta (.275, eight home runs, 82 RBI) and Hack (.311, four home runs, 64 RBI) was in the early stage of his long run at third base, with Herman (.341) and Billy Jurges (.241) solidifying an exceptional infield.

Outfielders Chuck Klein (.293, 21 home runs, 73 RBI) and Galan (.314, 12 home runs, 79 RBI) and Hartnett (.344. 13 home runs, 91 RBI) provided much of the power. Veterans Warneke (20-13) and Root (15-8) and rising stars Bill Lee (20-6) and Larry French (17-10) led the pitchers. Hartnett won the N.L. Most Valuable Player Award.

With a 100-victory regular season behind them, the Cubs liked their chances in the 1935 World Series against the Tigers. Detroit's long suit was the hitting of Hank Greenberg (.328, 36 home runs, 170 RBI), Charlie Gehringer (.330, 19 home runs, 108 RBI) and Mickey Cochrane (.319, five home runs, 47 RBI) as well as a fine pitching rotation of Schoolboy Rowe (19-13), Tommy Bridges (21-10), Eldon Auker (18-7) and Alvin Crowder (16-10).

Once again, the Cubs failed, despite fine pitching by Warneke, who shut out the Tigers on three hits to defeat Rowe 3-0 in Game 1, and with help from Lee beat them for a second time, 3-1 in Game 5.

The height of Cub frustration came in Game 6 in Detroit, in which Herman drove in three runs. With the game tied at 3 in the top of the ninth, Hack tripled to lead off the inning, but was left stranded when Bridges retired the next three batters. Goose Goslin's single in the bottom of the ninth scored Cochrane from second base to win the Series for the Tigers.

Herman led the Cubs in hitting with .333 in the six games, and Warneke was 2-0, but the Cubs had lost their fifth consecutive World Series.

They finished second in both 1936 and 1937, and on July 26, 1938, they again seemed to be out of the running with a 45-38 record. Not even Wrigley's liberal spending, such as the $185,000 plus three players paid to the Cardinals for onetime 30-game winner Dizzy Dean, was helping. Dean had a lame arm, and it wasn't responding to treatment.

"I never had nothing," Dean admitted, though he finished the season 7-1 with a 1.81 ERA. "I couldn't break a pane of glass and I knew it."

Grimm turned the team over to Hartnett, hoping the managerial change would spark the players. The ploy worked, the Cubs winning 44 of their final 71 games. Hartnett himself provided the decisive moment with his famous "Homer in the Gloamin'" on September 28 to take the heart out of the Pittsburgh Pirates and propel the Cubs into first place and another pennant.

Much of the 1935 cast was still on hand, including Herman, Jurges, Cavarretta, (now in the outfield), Hack and Galan. What power the Cubs had was provided by veteran first baseman Rip Collins (.267, 13 home runs 61 RBI) and Hartnett (.299, 10 home runs, 59 RBI). Lee (22-9), Clay Bryant (19-11) and French (10-19) were the heart of a pitching staff bolstered by the damaged Dean (7-1).

The 1938 World Series was another disaster, the Yankees again sweeping the Cubs.

The Yankees had new stars, such as Joe DiMaggio (.324, 32 home runs, 140 RBI), Joe Gordon (.255, 25 home runs, 97 RBI) and Tommy Henrich (.270, 22 HR, 91 RBI) and veterans Gehrig (.295, 29 home runs, 114 RBI) and Bill Dickey (.313, 27 HR, 115 RBI) were still outstanding. So was their pitching, with Ruffing (20-12), Monte Pearson (19-7) and Gomez (13-7) leading the staff.

The Yankees achieved their third consecutive World Series triumph with humiliating ease, brushing the Cubs aside in four games. If there was a highlight for the Cubs, it was Dean's courageous effort in Game 2, in Wrigley Field on October 6, 1938.

Hartnett almost won his gamble in starting the lame-armed Dean. He held the Yankees for seven innings, giving up just three hits and nursing a 3-2 lead. But a two-run home run by Frank Crosetti in the eighth broke the trance and the Yankees went on to win 6-3, then finished off the Cubs with ease in the final two games in New York.

After the debacle, Wrigley decided to take the pressure off Grimm in 1939. Grimm was relieved of his duties as co-general manager with Weber, his place being taken by Clarence "Pants" Rowland, who had managed the White Sox to a World Series championship in 1917.'

For the next two years Grimm was a radio broadcaster of Cub games. He started 1941 as a coach, but in June left the Cubs to manage for Bill Veeck, Jr., who had just purchased the minor league Milwaukee Brewers. The younger Veeck was embarking on his spectacular entrepreneurial career after serving an apprenticeship with the Cubs during which he had installed the current scoreboard and planted the ivy at Wrigley Field.

It took a while for Wrigley to conclude that Hartnett was at best merely adequate as a manager. He seemed as lacking in tact as Hornsby. When angry, his face turned red, earning him the further nickname of "Tomato-Face."

Hartnett did have a sense of humor, though. When Commissioner Kenesaw M. Landis reprimanded him for a newspaper photograph that showed him leaning over a box seat to exchange pleasantries with gangster Al Capone, Hartnett replied, "If you don't want anybody to talk to the Big Guy, Judge, you tell him."

The precipitous decline of the Cubs after the 1938 pennant was hardly all Hartnett's fault. Ill-advised trades played a part. The most notorious was one with the Giants. The Cubs gave up brilliant shortstop Jurges, outfielder Demaree and catcher Ken O'Dea for outfielder Hank Leiber, shortstop Dick Bartell and catcher Ken Mancuso.

Early in the 1939 season, however, the Cubs made an outstanding deal for pitcher Claude Passeau who was to be a mainstay for years. Passeau (13-9) helped slow the Cubs' slide as they finished in fourth place. He also was a bright spot in 1940 with a 20-13 record as the Cubs slipped to fifth, ending Hartnett's term as manager. Wrigley and Weber fired him and hired Jimmie Wilson to replace Hartnett.

A fine defensive catcher, Wilson also was an experienced manager, having led the Phillies for five seasons (1934–38), though with little success, the team finishing in last place or seventh every season.

Wilson was a coach for Cincinnati in 1940 when he was pressed into service behind the plate again for the World Series against Detroit when Reds star Ernie Lombardi was injured. The 40-year-old Wilson helped the Reds win the Series, and also won himself a job as the new manager of the Cubs. Wrigley and Weber were impressed by his "guts" in the Series.

Wrigley also made a major change in the front office for 1941, replacing Weber and Rowland with Jim Gallagher, a sportswriter who had caught his attention by criticizing the team. (It was a reprise of the hiring of William Veeck, Sr., also a newspaper critic, by P.K.'s father two decades earlier.) Gallagher came in with a five-year plan to rebuild the Cubs.

New general manager Gallagher and manager Wilson united to dismantle the Cubs, trading away Herman, Galan and French. Among the newcomers were outfielders Bill "Swish" Nicholson, Lou Novikoff and Dominic Dallessandro, shortstop Len Merullo, catcher Clyde McCullough and pitcher Hi Bithorn. Nicholson was a genuine slugger who twice led the N.L. in home runs, with 29 in 1943 and 33 in 1944.

World War II, which the United States entered on December 7, 1941, complicated Gallagher's five-year plan because competent manpower became scarce. The Cubs, like other teams, scrambled for players who were not suited for military service.

The Cubs floundered, finishing sixth in 1941 and 1942, rising to fifth in 1943. After they started the 1944 season with a 1-9 record, Gallagher fired Wilson in May and recalled Grimm for his second term as manager.

Grimm took over a team that had possibilities despite the wartime manpower shortage. Among holdovers from the 1938 championship team were Hack and Cavarretta. New center fielder Andy Pafko was a standout, as were pitchers Passeau and Hank Wyse. Despite the poor start, Grimm lifted the Cubs up to fourth place in 1944.

And 1945 provided a "miracle" undoubtedly aided by the talent shortage that hit rivals harder than it did the Cubs. Among the newcomers were second baseman Don Johnson and the key mid-season acquisition, pitcher Hank Borowy, who finished the season 11-2 for the Cubs after a 10-5 start with the New York Yankees.

Cavarretta had a "career season," batting .355 to lead the league, and drove in 97 runs, earning him the Most Valuable Player Award for 1945. Pafko batted .302 and drove in 110 runs. Nicholson (.243, 13 home runs, 88 RBI) and Peanuts Lowrey (.283, seven home runs 89 RBI) rounded out a solid offense. Wyse was 22-10, Passeau was 17-9 and retread Paul Derringer was 16-11 as the Cubs won the pennant, aided hugely by taking 21 of 22 games from Cincinnati.

World War II had just ended when the Cubs and the Tigers met for the fourth time in a World Series. Like the Cubs, the Tigers relied on veterans, the most formidable being Greenberg, who had returned from military service for the last half of the season and batted .311 with 13 home runs and 60 RBI. Rudy York (.264, 18 HR, 87 RBI) and Roy Cullenbine (.277, 18 HR, 93 RBI) also were dangerous. Hal Newhouser (25-9), Dizzy Trout (18-15) and Al Benton (13-8) gave the Tigers three reliable starting pitchers, and Virgil Trucks, who had won 16 games in 1943, was back from the Navy.

Borowy pitched a six-hitter for a 9-0 Cub victory in the opener as Nicholson drove in three runs with a triple and a single. Cavarretta and Pafko each went 3-for-4, the former hitting a home run. After the Tigers won Game 2, Passeau came back with a one-hit, 3-0 victory, the first Series one-hitter since Ed Reulbach's in 1906.

The Tigers won the next two games to go ahead, three games to two, but the Cubs outlasted them in the 12-inning sixth game, winning 8-7 to even the Series when a line drive by Hack hopped over left fielder Greenberg's head to score a runner from first base. Grimm started a weary Borowy for the third time in Game 7, after he had also relieved in Game 6, and the Tigers manhandled him on the way to a 9-3 concluding victory.

It was hardly a classic World Series, most observers agreeing that the caliber of play by the wartime big leaguers was substandard.

"It was the fat men against the tall men in a game of picnic baseball," commented sportswriter Frank Graham, calling the fifth game "the worst game ever played." Columnist Warren Brown declared, "Neither team can win this Series."

Well played or not, the Cubs had lost their seventh consecutive World Series. They now were 2-8 in World Series competition.

Yet in winning another pennant, Grimm had reinforced his standing as Wrigley's favorite manager. He kept his job for almost four more seasons as the Cubs entered the most futile period of their history, a dark era that was to last two decades.

The downturn began slowly, the Cubs finishing third in 1946, then snowballed as they dropped to sixth in 1947 and to last in 1948. New players such as first baseman Eddie Waitkus, shortstop Roy Smalley, catcher Bob Scheffing and pitcher Johnny Schmitz didn't seem to make any difference. What's more, Gallagher and Grimm were at odds over how to rebuild the team.

The 1949 season started out like the 1948 campaign ended, the Cubs in last place with a 19-31 record when Wrigley decided Grimm needed another respite from the rigors of managing. Wrigley appointed him vice-president in charge of player personnel, commenting, "I think Charlie will live longer this way."

Grimm's major fault in Wrigley's view was that he was too nice. Wrigley said, "He's such a good guy that when you ask him whether such and such a player would be all right, he agrees, even though he doesn't mean it and regrets it later."

In an effort to change the tone, Wrigley's choice to manage the Cubs was a fiery veteran, Frankie Frisch, the former manager of the Cardinals' Gas House Gang of the mid-1930s, whose aggressive manner left no hint of being "nice."

Grimm remained a vice-president for a few months, then yielded to a renewed hunger to manage, first in the minor leagues, then for the Boston Braves in mid-season 1952, moving with them to Milwaukee in 1953. He kept that job into the 1956 season.

He wasn't through with the Cubs, though, with a swan song as their manager for a third time yet to come.

WHO CALLED WHAT?

Babe Ruth's "Called Shot" home run against the Cubs in the third game of the 1932 World Series is the biggest fairy tale in baseball history.

The following spring, Chicago's Hal Totten, a pioneer broadcaster, asked the Babe if he had pointed to the center field bleachers before he connected against Charlie Root.

"Hell, no!" Ruth replied. "Naw, keed, you know damn well I wasn't pointing anywhere. Only a damned fool would have done a thing like that. If I'd have done that, Root would have stuck the ball right in my ear. I never knew anybody who could tell you ahead of time where he was going to hit a baseball. When I get to be that kind of fool they'll put me in the booby hatch."

But the myth persists to this day. Sportswriters, of necessity, possess a flair for the dramatic and early on learn to gild the lily. More important, Ruth fell in love with the story.

It was another jewel in his crown. He assumed the role of a revisionist historian and began fueling the fable. In hundreds of subsequent interviews, including tapes for the Hall of Fame Library in Cooperstown, generally an impeccable source for researchers, the Babe insisted he had pointed. As he later told a questioning Ford Frick, then a New York newspaperman who was in his stable of ghostwriters, "It was in the papers, wasn't it?"

The centerpiece of the dispute was Mark Koenig, a veteran shortstop whom the Cubs had rescued from the minor leagues on August 17 as a replacement for Billy Jurges, their regular shortstop. Jurges was wounded: One slug in the chest, another in his back, the third on his right side, fired by a scorned female acquaintance, a *"femme fatale"* who packed a pistol. For several seasons thereafter the Chicago newspapers described him as "Bullet Bill."

Koenig had been among Ruth's teammates on the New York Yankees during three of their previous championship seasons. He played in only 33 games with the Cubs and had helped spark their pennant drive. He batted .353, exactly 100 points higher than the disabled Jurges. In their pre-Series meeting, when the Cubs divided their forthcoming players' pool, Koenig was voted a half share.

Woody English, the Cub third baseman/captain, presided at the meeting. "Only the players entitled to a full share were there," English revealed. "It had to be unanimous on every vote. Two players voted for a half share for Mark. The rest thought he should get a full cut. But the two held out. They said, 'He didn't get here until late in the season.'"

The Yankees regarded this as unfair treatment of an old pal and repeatedly badgered the Cubs as "cheapskates." It was the principal thrust of their bench-jockeying, orchestrated by Ruth.

More than likely as many as 100 baseball writers covered the Series but only one, Joe Williams of the *New York World Telegram*, reported in his game story, written on deadline, that Ruth had pointed to center field. But Williams later recanted. Why he changed his mind remains a mystery. Perhaps on second thought, he realized he was alone and may have been guilty of wishful thinking.

Herbert F. Simons, a Chicago baseball writer who later founded *Baseball Digest*, was on the scene and was adamant that Ruth didn't point. Obsessed, Simons exhumed the New York newspapers and reported that the first mention in print of a "called home run" was made simultaneously by Bill Corum and Tom Meany *three* days after the game.

The only explanation of how Simons missed Joe Williams' story was that it appeared on the day of the game, in the final Saturday afternoon edition, which may not have been on file. The *World Telegram* didn't have a Sunday paper.

In a column on "Men of the Series" for the *New York World Journal*, Corum rhapsodized:

"Words fail me. When he stood up there at the bat before 50,000 persons, calling the balls and strikes with gestures for the benefit of the Cubs in their dugout, and then with two strikes on him, pointed out where he was going to hit the next one and hit it there, I gave up. That fellow is not human."

Meany, on the same day, in the *New York World Telegram*:

"Babe's interviewer interrupted to point the hole in which Babe put himself Saturday when he pointed out the spot he intended hitting his home run and asked the Great Man if he realized how ridiculous he would have appeared if he had struck out?

"'I never thought of it,' said the Great Man. He simply had made up his mind to hit a home run and he did."

Paul Gallico of the *New York Daily News*, an amateur fencer and master of flamboyance, checked in: "He pointed like a duelist to the spot where he expected to send the rapier home."

Fifteen years later, in a book about Ruth, Meany conceded he "had changed his version several times...and had grown confused, uncertain whether he had picked out a spot in the bleachers to park the ball, or was merely pointing to the outfield, or was signaling that he still had one swing to go."

This was the setting:

The Yankees, managed by Joe McCarthy, had won the American League pennant in a breeze—their 107 victories during the regular season gave them a 13-game bulge over Connie Mack's Philadelphia Athletics, their closest pursuer. The Cubs were lagging behind the Pittsburgh Pirates until Charlie Grimm replaced Rogers Hornsby as their manager on August 2 and came with a furious stretch drive to win the National League flag by four games.

The Series opened in New York with the Yankees winning the first two games, 12-6 and 5-2. The Series then shifted to Chicago.

Thousands of people crammed into the LaSalle Street Station to see the Yankees arrive. Ruth, accompanied by his wife, Claire, fought his way through the hostile crowd to a freight elevator and then to a cab. Motorcycle police had to clear the way for the Yankee entourage. When Ruth and his wife entered their hotel, a woman spat on them.

Ruth complained a week or two later that the Chicago press had brought the fans down on him. "They wrote about me riding the Cubs for being tight and about me calling them cheapskates," Ruth said.

"Well, didn't you?" he was asked.

"Well, weren't they?" he replied. "They should have given Mark a full share."

In expectation of an overflow crowd, temporary stands were erected outside the ballpark in the streets behind the left and right field bleachers. Standing room only increased the crowd to 49,986, which included New York Governor Franklin Delano Roosevelt, who was running for president against Herbert Hoover, the incumbent, and Chicago Mayor Anton Cermak.

Whenever a ball was lofted Ruth's way in pre-game practice, lemons came flying out of the bleachers. The Babe was in a cheerful mood. He picked them up and threw them back. There was a strong wind blowing to right field and Ruth and Lou Gehrig put on an awesome batting show. Ruth hit nine balls into the stands, Gehrig seven.

Ruth shouted to the Cubs, "I'd pay half my salary if I could hit in this dump all the time."

The jockeying between the two teams, or, more accurately, between Ruth and the Cubs, became more intense as the game began. Guy Bush, Burleigh Grimes and Pat Malone were on the top step of the Cub dugout, leading the barrage. Andy Lotshaw, the grizzled trainer, yelled, "If I had you, I'd hitch you to a wagon, you potbelly."

Afterwards, Ruth said, "I didn't mind no players yelling at me but the trainer cutting in—that made me sore."

"The Cub fans simply couldn't believe how decisively their champions had been manhandled by the mighty Yankees in the

East," wrote John Drebinger in the *New York Times*. "The fans roared their approval on every good play made by the Cubs. They booed Babe Ruth thoroughly, even when he homered in his first time at bat. And they howled with glee as Ruth failed in a heroic attempt to make a shoestring catch on Billy Jurges' low liner in the fourth inning (a double that lifted the Cubs into a 4-4 tie). Good naturedly, the Babe doffed his cap to acknowledge the adverse plaudits."

Richard Vidmer of the *New York Herald Tribune*, who often sweetened his prose with wondrous jams, described the climactic fifth inning:

"As the Babe moved toward the plate with one out in the fifth inning, swinging three bats over his shoulder, a concerted shout of derision broke out in the stands, a bellowing of boos, hisses and jeers. There were cries of encouragement for the pitcher, and from the Cub dugout came a series of abuses leveled at the Babe.

"But Ruth grinned in the face of the hostile greeting. He laughed back at the Cubs and took his place, supremely confident. Charlie Root whistled a strike over the plate. Joyous outcries filled the air and the Babe held up one finger as though to say, 'That's only one. Just wait.'

"Root threw another strike and the stands rocked with delight. The Chicago players hurled their laughter at the great man but Ruth held up two fingers and still grinned, the super-showman. On the next pitch, the Babe swung. There was a resounding report like the explosion of a gun. Straight for the fence the ball soared on a line, clearing the farthest corner of the barrier, 436 feet from home plate.

"Before Ruth left the plate and started his swing around the bases, he paused to laugh at the Chicago players, suddenly silent in their dugout. As he rounded first, he flung a remark at Grimm; as he turned second, he tossed a jest at Billy Herman. His shoulders shook with satisfaction as he trotted in."

Beautiful descriptive stuff but not one word about a called shot.

The count was even at 2 balls and two strikes, not 0 and 2 as Vidmer indicated. Such fuzziness of detail is evident in several contemporary accounts. Westbrook Pegler, covering for the *Chicago Tribune*, reported the count went strike, strike, ball, ball. Pegler also was wrong. It was strike, ball, ball, strike. Bill Corum and the *New York Times* had the count 3 and 2. Tom Meany wrote it was no balls and 2 strikes. Years later, umpire George Magerkurth insisted he had worked the plate and said the count was 3 and 2. Magerkurth was wrong on the count and he didn't have the plate; he was at first base.

McCarthy, whose Yankees won the game 7-5, en route to a sweep, copped out when asked about the home run. "I'm not going to say he didn't do it," McCarthy said. "Maybe I didn't see it. Maybe I was looking the other way. Anyway, I'm not going to say he didn't do it."

The Cub players didn't see it either, not even catcher Gabby Hartnett, who was closest to Ruth. "If had pointed at the bleachers I would be the first to say so," said Hartnett. Like most players, Hartnett had great admiration for Ruth who had raised the salary level five years earlier when he signed a record $80,000 contract. "He didn't say a word when he crossed the plate."

English, 90 feet away at third base, had a clear view of the plate because Ruth batted left-handed. "He didn't point. He was looking directly into our dugout. He held two fingers above his head and said, 'That's only two strikes.'"

Pitcher Grimes, who was on the bench, concurred. "After two strikes he pointed a finger at our dugout. He never pointed to center. If he had done that, Root would have knocked him down."

Until he went to his grave, Root was repeatedly asked about the "called shot."

"If I thought he was trying to show me up, I would have knocked him on his tail. It's strange, I'm better known for that—for what never happened than for the things that did happen."

Koenig, Ruth's buddy, also punctured the balloon. "As far as pointing to center, no he didn't," Koenig said. "You know darn well a guy with two strikes isn't going to say he's going to hit a home run on the next pitch."

Ben Chapman, the Yankees' left fielder: "He was pointing at the pitcher. Someone asked him, 'Babe, did you call that home run?' Babe answered, 'No, but I called Root everything I could think of.'"

Shirley Povich of the *Washington Post* in his 1969 autobiography, *All These Mornings*, recalled a conversation years later with Yankee catcher Bill Dickey, who confessed that it didn't really happen that way.

"What did happen?" Povich asked.

"Ruth got mad at that quick pitch (for the second strike). He was pointing at Root, not at the center field stands. He called him a couple of names and said, 'Don't do that to me anymore, you —.'"

"How do you know?" Povich prodded.

"Because Ruth told us when he came back to the bench."

"How come you never told anybody?"

"All of us players could see it was a helluva story. So we just made an agreement not to bother straightening out the facts."

HOMER IN THE GLOAMIN'

It is known as "The Homer in the Gloamin'"—the most famous hit in Cub history. Darkness had descended at Wrigley Field and most of the fans in the crowd of 34,465 didn't see it. Gabby Hartnett also lost sight of the ball but he knew it was gone.

"I swung with everything I had," Hartnett said, "and then I got that feeling—the kind of feeling you get when the blood rushes out of your head and you get dizzy. A lot of people told me they didn't know the ball was in the bleachers. Well, I did. I knew the minute I hit it. When I got to second base, I couldn't see third because the players and fans were there. I don't think I walked another step. I was almost carried the rest of the way. But when I got to home plate I saw (umpire) George Barr taking a good look. He was making sure I touched the platter."

It was September 28, 1938, Cubs vs. Pittsburgh Pirates, score tied 5-5, two outs and the bases empty in the bottom of the ninth. Hartnett, then the Cubs playing-manager—he had succeeded Charlie Grimm on July 21—was aware that if he didn't get on base he would be the last batter. Play had begun at 3 p.m., heightening the possibility it would be finished in the twilight. The umpires had notified both benches the game would be called because of darkness after the ninth inning.

Mace Brown, the National League's premier closer, known for his curveball, was pitching for the Pirates. Phil Cavarretta, first up in the Cub ninth, flied to Lloyd Waner in deep center. Carl Reynolds grounded to second baseman Pep Young for the second out. Husky Hartnett, 6-feet-1, 220 pounds, was next, a low-ball hitter with a short stroke, unusual for a big man.

He swung and missed Brown's first pitch, a curve as expected. Brown threw another curve. Hartnett fouled it off for strike two. Instead of mixing it up, Brown risked another curve. It was high and inside, a "hanger." Hartnett, who subsequently said he didn't see the pitch, pulled it into the left field bleachers and the Cubs, for the first time since June 8, were in first place.

Twenty-five years later, Paul Waner, who was in right field for the Pirates, saw it all the way.

"I saw the ball land and I could hardly believe my eyes," Waner recalled. "I should have started for the clubhouse but I just stood there and watched Hartnett circle the bases. It took all the fight out of us. It broke our hearts.

"When I finally got to the clubhouse it was like a funeral parlor. Mace Brown was sitting in front of his locker, crying like a baby. I stayed with him all that night. I was afraid he would do something desperate."

While the Pirates mourned, the Cubs celebrated, just as they had the day before when Dizzy Dean, in a spectacular performance, beat the Pirates in the series opener. John P. Carmichael of the *Chicago Daily News*, seldom at a loss for words, was awestruck.

"We surrender to inadequacy," Carmichael wrote. "This Cub-Pirate pennant series has gone beyond our poor power to picture in words. When you squirm to fashion the pinnacle for Dizzy Dean, only to find you need at least its twin that a Gabby Hartnett may also brush the stars, word-painting becomes a magic art not given to the mine run of mortals to diffuse.

"So let this be, today, a confession of helplessness to treat an afternoon that beggars description; an afternoon in the life of a stout-hearted Irishman who, as darkness almost wrapped around him from the sight of 35,000 quaking fans, changed the map of the baseball world with one devastating blow. And that he is alive and in one piece at the moment, ready to carry on from that smash, is no fault of a Cub team and a Cub populace gone mad.

"For the second successive night, we stood in a clubhouse of crazed men in play suits. Only this time, they weren't even articulate. We can still see 'em fighting for words, staring at one another with glazed eyes. We can still see 'em pushing Hartnett from wall to wall with the irresistible force of robots gone wild. We can see Gabby trying vainly to free himself from his idolatrous teammates.

"We can still see Billy Herman standing in the middle of the floor, arms akimbo. When he could talk, it was first just a whisper of awe: 'Lord God Almighty.'

"Dawning consciousness of the moment brought it out again, louder, hoarser. 'Lord God Almighty.' Then the full realization of the terrific sight he had just watched in the twilight smote him: 'Lord God ALMIGHTY!' he suddenly screamed and threw his glove he knew not where.

"Sheer exhaustion and relief from the tension of what they'd gone through finally drove some players to their chairs where they slumped like marionettes whose guiding strings had let them down. Through the half-open door came the frenzied roar of the crowd from which only minutes before Andy Frain's ushers had barely saved Hartnett in his entirety."

The popular belief is that Hartnett's home run clinched the pennant. It didn't. But it lifted the Cubs into first place by .003 percentage points, a half-game ahead of the Pirates who had held the lead continuously since July 12. The Pirates went into the September home stretch with what appeared to be an insurmountable lead of 8½ games. Anticipating a World Series, construction had begun on a new press box in Pittsburgh. Souvenir press buttons had been ordered and delivered, ready for distribution. To this day, they are prized mementos.

The day after Hartnett's homer, on September 29, the Cubs completed their three-game sweep of the Pirates, 10-1, behind Big Bill Lee, a 22-game winner, to increase their lead to 1½ games. Two days later they clinched their third pennant in seven years with a 10-3 second-game win over the Cardinals in St. Louis. Charlie Root, a 39-year-old veteran of 13 campaigns, the victim of Babe Ruth's mythical "called shot" home run, went the distance for the victory. His exuberant teammates rushed to the mound and carried him on their shoulders into the clubhouse. Only six games separated the top four teams.

Leo "Gabby" Hartnett, his right index finger badly bruised by a foul tip, batted .091 in the World Series against the New York Yankees—one hit, a triple, in 11 at-bats. He hit .300 or better six times in his career and was the National League's Most Valuable Player in 1935. He was elected to the Hall of Fame in 1955, and had a career .297 batting average, with a club record, since surpassed, of 231 home runs. He died in Park Ridge, Illinois, a Chicago suburb, on December 20, 1972, his 72nd birthday.

THE COMISKEYS' IRON AGE

10

Nothing could more deeply emphasize the sorrow and pity of what befell the White Sox after the Black Sox scandal than the achievements of that mighty team and its great players in the 1920 season, though beset by rumors, allegations, revelations, evidence and final admission that the 1919 World Series had been fixed.

It might approach blasphemy to term the White Sox accomplishments of 1920 as the "Last Hurrah" of a great club, yet it would not be far wrong. The White Sox might well have—probably should have—won another pennant, leading the league as they did in late August before backing off with a suspect seven-game losing streak.

Even at that, they trailed the Cleveland Indians by only a half game with five games left until Sept. 29 when Comiskey no longer was able to disregard evidence and admissions of the World Series fix the year before. He suspended those implicated, including Eddie Cicotte, Joe Jackson, Buck Weaver and Happy Felsch. Manager Kid Gleason was forced to field a lineup of rookies and the innocent, now called the "Clean Sox" or "Square Sox," for the last three games, helping the Indians cling to first.

Yet despite well-founded allegations of also having "thrown" several games during the regular season, the 1920 White Sox registered remarkable achievements in addition to a creditable 96-58 record.

Half a century was to pass before the Baltimore Orioles of 1971 equaled the White Sox of 1920 in having four 20-game winning pitchers: Red Faber (23-11), Lefty Williams (22-14), Cicotte (21-16) and Dickie Kerr (21-9).

On the offensive side, only one other team (the St. Louis Browns of 1922) has had three batters produce 210 or more hits. Jackson (.382) had 218, Eddie Collins (.369) had 222 and Weaver (.333) banged out 210. Two other regulars, Felsch (.333) and Shano Collins (.303) batted over .300. The White Sox hit .295 as a team.

When their accused teammates were finally indicted, the Square Sox (square in those days meant honest) celebrated by dining together in a posh Chicago restaurant. One was quoted as saying, "Hardly any of us have talked with any of those fellows, except on the ball field, since the (1920) season opened.... We went along and gritted our teeth and played ball...and all the time felt that they had thrown us down. It was tough. Now the load has been lifted. No wonder we felt like celebrating."

He couldn't have suspected he was enjoying the last truly meaningful celebration by the White Sox for the next four decades. The White Sox, like the Biblical Israelites, were to wander in the desert of futility for 40 years, but without a Moses to lead them to the Promised Land. They were forced to rely on three generations of the Comiskey family, which often strayed off the right track.

The founding father, Charles Comiskey, the Old Roman, was hard-hit emotionally by his team's involvement in the most sensational scandal in the history of American professional sports. He also was stung by widespread charges that his tight-fistedness—well documented—had been partly responsible for the debacle.

In an effort to counter allegations of parsimony, he presented each of the Square Sox with a $1,500 check, designating the sum as "the difference between the winning and losing players' shares" of the 1919 World Series.

Comiskey's dividend on his investment came in the form of a letter to the team's fans signed by 10 players: "We, the undersigned players of the Chicago White Sox, want the world to know the generosity of our employer, who of his own free will, has reimbursed each and every member of our team the difference between the winning and losing share of last year's World Series, amounting approximately to $1,500."

Eddie Collins further pinned the blame squarely on the conspirators rather than on any failing of Comiskey's, unequivocally declaring, "They were old enough to know the difference between right and wrong."

His final verdict on the Black Sox was poignant. "It was really a great team. It even had a tough time losing on purpose."

No one could have said that of the White Sox during most of the thirty seasons after the Black Sox calamity. The problem became winning on purpose. No matter who managed or what players took the field, the White Sox finished in the bottom half of the standings for 15 consecutive seasons, 1921 through 1935, and in the top half only six times during the next 15 campaigns, 1936 through 1950. Seldom during those three decades was the team a serious pennant contender.

What made the White Sox's plight more humiliating as well as financially painful was that during most of the period they were overshadowed by the Cubs, who won pennants in 1929, 1932, 1935, 1938 and 1945. As a result, Cub attendance soared while the turnouts at Comiskey Park shrank, some years dropping to less than one third of that at Wrigley Field.

Not that the White Sox didn't have some fine players, including eventual Hall of Famers Eddie Collins, Ray Schalk, Red Faber, pitcher Ted Lyons and shortstop Luke Appling, as well as outfielders Johnny Mostil and Bibb Falk and first baseman Earl Sheely in the 1920s. They also rose to occasional heights of achievement such as the perfect game pitched in 1922 by rookie Charlie Robertson, the league-leading pitching of Faber and Lyons, and the batting championships won by Appling in 1936 and 1943.

Even as Comiskey smarted from the humiliation, pain and anger of the scandal, he and Harry Grabiner, the secretary/treasurer and virtual general manager, persevered throughout the 1920s to rebuild the White Sox. At times, it seemed as if Comiskey was determined to counter the charges that he was "cheap" by spending lavishly.

When the White Sox purchased third baseman Willie Kamm from San Francisco in 1922, the $100,000 price was the highest ever for a minor league player. Paradoxically, however, the same year Comiskey denied Kerr's demand for a modest $500 annual raise and a three-year contract after the left-hander won 19 games in 1921. Kerr angrily quit the team to play semi-pro baseball, and though he returned briefly to the White Sox in 1925 he was no longer effective.

Surprisingly, despite the Black Sox scandal, and perhaps largely because of the economic boom of the 1920s, attendance held up for the first half of the decade and so in 1926–27 Comiskey spent $600,000 on the renovation and expansion of Comiskey Park. It was double-decked, enlarging the capacity to 52,000, which proved excessive during the next 25 years because the park was seldom filled.

The White Sox gave fans little reason for great enthusiasm between 1922 and 1930 as a succession of managers strove in vain to lift the team into pennant contention. Kid Gleason left after five years on the job, his teams finishing seventh in 1921, fifth in 1922 and seventh in 1923. He was succeeded by Frank Chance for 1924.

Illness forced Chance, the former Peerless Leader of the Cubs, to resign before Opening Day (he died only four months later). Another former Cub star, Johnny Evers, took over, but an appendectomy sidelined him on May 14. After onetime pitching ace Ed Walsh failed a three-game test as interim manager, Comiskey let Eddie Collins run the team for a month until Evers returned to finish a campaign in which the Sox sank to the bottom for the first time. Not surprisingly, Evers was replaced by Collins, who had impressed Comiskey during his interim stint, for the 1925 season.

The outlook for 1925 wasn't as grim as the last place finish in 1924 might have suggested. Collins had some offensive weapons, including himself. He batted .349 in 1924 while Falk hit .352 with 99 RBI, and Sheely .320 with 103 RBI despite only three home runs. The pitching staff was promising with Sloppy Thurston (20-14), young Lyons (12-11) and veteran Faber (9-11) the key starters.

Collins was able to lead his troops to consecutive plus-.500 seasons in 1925 and 1926 with records of 79-75 and 81-72, but injuries began to cut his playing time (though he hit .346 in 118 games, then .344). Comiskey saw that Collins' double value as player manager was depreciating at the age of 39 and replaced him with Schalk for 1927.

Collins eventually finished his 25-year major league career with a batting average of .333 and 3,313 hits. He was possibly the best second baseman of all time, and certainly of the White Sox. Some people rated him as the best of all players at any position.

"That fellow Eddie Collins is the greatest player I ever seen in my long career, and I've seen a lot of them," said umpire Billy Evans in 1919.

As Collins' successor, Schalk inherited a team whose chief assets were Lyons, 18-16 with a no-hitter in 1926 after going 21-11 the previous year, superb fielding center fielder Mostil, who hit .328, and Falk, who batted .345 with 108 RBI. But Mostil's attempted suicide in spring training foreshadowed a dismal 1927 season, brightened only by the re-dedication of enlarged Comiskey Park and the pitching of Lyons (22-14), the league leader in wins as in 1925. The White Sox finished 70-83, to begin a string of nine consecutive seasons below .500.

Schalk survived as manager into the 1928 season until being replaced at mid-point by Lena Blackburne, a former White Sox shortstop who guided the team to its final 72-82 record. Blackburne staggered through 1929 with even less success than his predecessor, the team finishing 59-93. He gave way to Donie Bush, a manager who had just been fired by the Pittsburgh Pirates, and had a reputation as hard-driving.

Bush's two seasons of 1930 and 1931 at the helm were undistinguished with records of 62-92 and 56-97, though Lyons sparkled again during the first campaign by winning 22 games, better than one-third of the team's total victories. Even more significantly, rookie Appling played his first game for the White Sox on September 10, 1930. In 1931, he was fully launched on his 21-season career with the team, though he batted only .232 in 96 games, failing as yet to demonstrate his great hitting ability.

Frustrated, Bush quit in October 1931, and in his farewell address echoed the prevailing sentiment that the franchise was off course, with no clear sense of direction.

"I don't mind losing ballgames if there is a prospect of better days ahead," Bush explained, "but I feel that whatever reputation I possess as a manager would be jeopardized by remaining another year."

The most memorable event of 1931, however, was the death of Charles Comiskey on October 26, at the age of 72 after more than a half-century of playing a key role in baseball, the last 31 years as owner of the White Sox. In his final months the ailing Comiskey let Grabiner run the team, which he continued to do for the Old Roman's invalid son John Louis, and then the latter's widow, Grace, for another 15 years.

The White Sox of the elder Comiskey's final decade enjoyed little success in the standings, but in addition to producing two great players in Lyons and Appling, and some good ones such as Mostil, Falk and Sheely, they turned out several who became legendary for their idiosyncrasies rather than talent on the field. The three best-remembered are Moe Berg, Art Shires and Smead Jolley.

Casey Stengel once referred to Berg, a backup catcher-infielder who spent five seasons (1926–30) with the White Sox as "the strangest man to ever play baseball." He probably was also the most erudite, being a student of French Renaissance literature and other scholarly subjects as well as a remarkable linguist. The story of his enigmatic life, which included spying for the United States before and during World War II, has been explored in biographies and countless articles.

As mysterious as Berg's life was, he also was stumped by a mystery, the curveball pitch. It was of him that a scout reported laconically and memorably: "Good field, no hit." His career average of .243 with just six home runs in 1,812 at-bats confirms that, as does the quip: "He could speak 12 languages, but couldn't hit in any of them."

Unlike in the case of Berg, no one suspected Shires or Jolley of intellectual grandeur, and they were a definite contrast to him because while they both could hit, neither could field.

Shires, who gloried in his nickname of "The Great," distinguished himself even in the Roaring Twenties with his hard-drinking, violent life style after he joined the White Sox as a rookie third baseman in 1928. Blackburne named him team captain for 1929, and he hit .312 in 100 games, but his most telling blow came when he knocked out the manager with a punch in a hotel fracas. A foray into boxing didn't help, and after his average sank to .238 in 37 games in 1930, the White Sox dumped him.

Jolley was a highly-regarded hitter who had won six batting titles in the Pacific Coast League before Grabiner bought him for $50,000 in 1930. He measured up to his offensive reputation as a rookie, batting .313 in 152 games, but his fielding misadventures, which became legendary, reduced him to bench duty the next two seasons before the White Sox banished him. Jolley's ungainliness elicited a memorable line from national columnist Bugs Baer who wrote after he went 4-for-4 in a game: "He had the greatest day since Lizzie Borden went 2-for-2 in Fall River, Mass."

Lew Fonseca, the former hard-hitting outfielder who succeeded Bush as manager for 1932, finally gave up on Jolley, who was traded to the Boston Red Sox. It was the beginning of a series of deals engineered by a "triumvirate" consisting of Lou Comiskey, Grabiner and Fonseca, whose avowed policy was to strengthen the team by acquiring solid veterans rather than unproven minor leaguers as in the past decade.

The new course was as unproductive as the old, Fonseca's team plunging to a record of 49-102 in 1932. Even the payment of $150,000, a staggering sum during the Great Depression, for slugger Al Simmons, third baseman Jimmy Dykes and outfielder Mule Haas of the Philadelphia A's made little difference in 1933. The White Sox finished 67-83, though Simmons hit .331 with 14 home runs and 119 RBI, and Dykes and Haas also played well, while Appling came of age as a hitter with .322.

The most lasting benefit of the big deal with the A's turned out to be Dykes, who succeeded Fonseca early in the 1934 season and stayed on the job until 1946 for the longest managerial tenure in the team's history.

Lou Comiskey eventually realized he got his money's worth for the $150,000 he paid the A's even if Simmons and Haas failed to lift his team out of the doldrums.

"Well, I got the best manager in baseball, didn't I?" Comiskey claimed. "You can't pick up guys like Dykes out on street corners."

The aggressive, umpire-baiting yet whimsical Dykes was a shrewd judge of players who made the most even of those with limited talent. He had a gift for "bargain basement" shopping, enabling Comiskey and Grabiner to make useful acquisitions at minimal cost. During Dykes' 11 full seasons at the helm, the White Sox finished .500 or better six times despite financial and wartime constraints.

Dykes' best showing came in the late 1930s, despite struggling in the wake of manager Joe McCarthy's great New York Yankees, who won four consecutive World Series (1936–39). Eventual Hall of Famers Lou Gehrig, Joe DiMaggio, Bill Dickey, Red Ruffing and Lefty Gomez were merely the cream of McCarthy's crop of brilliant talent. Dykes is widely believed to have derided McCarthy as a "push-button manager," though he insisted his "quote" had been taken out of context.

"We got to talking about how great McCarthy was," Dykes explained. "Well, I'm a wisecracker at heart—always have been—and I said, 'What do you mean he's a great manager. All he's got to do is push a button and a better ballplayer comes off the bench.'"

Dykes made do with far lesser players than McCarthy, his only two standouts of Hall of Fame caliber being Appling and the aging Lyons, who continued to contribute into his forties as an "only on Sunday" starter. But Dykes extracted fine performances for a year or two or three from a succession of players of variable talent whose names became embedded in White Sox history and mythology.

Among them were outfielders Taft Wright, Rip Radcliff and Mike Kreevich, first basemen Zeke Bonura and Joe Kuhel, second baseman Jackie Hayes, pitchers Vern Thornton Lee, Edgar Smith, Clint Brown, Monty Stratton and Orval Grove.

Dykes finished out the 1934 season at 53-99, among the few pluses being rookie first baseman Zeke Bonura's team record 27 home runs, Simmons' .344 and Appling's .303. Improvement came in 1935 with a 74-78 record and the development of several young pitchers, including John Whitehead (13-13) and Vern Kennedy (11-11) who pitched a no-hitter, while the ever-dependable Lyons was 15-8. Bonura hit 21 home runs.

Bonura was a liability in the field, being almost immobile at first base. Dykes called him "my pet ox," and was exasperated beyond endurance by his lack of baseball sense. After Bonura was traded to Washington before the 1938 season, Dykes didn't bother to change signs for his team's first series against the Senators. "Why should we?" Dykes asked coach Bing Miller. "He couldn't remember them when he was with us."

Before Bonura left, he became an idol of the fans, who cherished him as "Banana Nose." He contributed heavily with his bat as Dykes lifted the team to an 81-70 record and third place in 1936, then to 86-68 and third again in 1937. Bonura batted .330 and drove in a team-record 138 runs in 1936 and followed that up with .345 and 100 RBI in 1937 before leaving for Washington in exchange for the fine fielding, solid hitting Kuhel.

Appling rose to even greater heights, becoming the first White Sox to lead the league in batting with .388 in 1936, while driving in 128 runs, remarkably with only six home runs. Kennedy (21-9) led the pitching staff. Appling hit .317 in 1937, and the entire outfield of Radcliff (.302), Kreevich (.302) and Dixie Walker (.325) topped .300. Young Stratton fulfilled his promise with a 15-5 record and appeared on his way to a brilliant career.

Major injuries to Appling and new first baseman Kuhel cast a pall during the 1938 season, the White Sox falling back to 65-83, though arm trouble failed to keep Stratton from again winning 15 games. It was after the season ended that the team suffered its most severe blow. Stratton accidentally shot himself while hunting on November 27, forcing amputation of his right leg. He subsequently attempted to pitch with a wooden leg—a struggle eventually depicted in a movie, *The Stratton Story*, starring Jimmy Stewart—but finally had to give up.

Dykes brought the White Sox back to respectability in 1939. They finished 85-69 but the most notable events were the first night games at Comiskey Park, and the unexpected death of Lou Comiskey at the age of 54 on July 18. Direction of the club passed to his widow Grace in custody for their son Charles, only 13, until the boy became old enough to take over. A daughter, Dorothy, who married pitcher Johnny Rigney in 1941, also shared in the team ownership.

"There must always be a Comiskey at the head of the White Sox," Mrs. Comiskey asserted. "My son, Charley, grandson of the founder of the White Sox, will be fully fitted to operate the franchise when he reaches the proper age."

The 1940 season started out spectacularly if negatively, Cleveland's Bob Feller pitching an Opening Day 1-0 no-hitter at Comiskey Park. The season ended more satisfactorily, the White Sox winning 82 games, and making the most of a pre-season deal that brought outfielder Taft Wright from Washington. He batted .337, Appling hit .348, Kuhel tied the team's home run record with 27 and Rigney won 14 games, as did Edgar Smith. Lyons, now 39, was 12-8.

Financial problems and the conservative policy of Grace Comiskey began to tell on the team's fortunes in 1941, even Dykes being unable to extract success from second-rate talent. A 77-77 finish was the result, though left-hander Thornton Lee distinguished himself with 22-11, Lyons went 12-10, Appling hit .314 and Wright batted .322.

With the United States involved in World War II from December 7, 1941 through most of 1945, the White Sox, like other teams, lost key players and had to make the most of men exempt from military service. The four seasons from 1942 through 1945 were among the most unmemorable in team history, with records of 66-82, 82-72, 71-83 and 71-78. There were some highlights, nevertheless.

In an extraordinary performance in 1942, Lyons, now 41, not only completed every one of his 20 starts with a 14-6 record for a poor team, but led the A.L. with a 2.10 ERA. In 1943, Appling won his second batting title with .328 before departing for two years in the military and outfielder Wally Moses stole a team record 56 bases. Orval Grove won his first nine decisions of 1943 on his way to a 15-9 record, and was a 14-game winner each of the next two seasons.

It was a period replete with retreads, aging and minor league caliber players pressed into service by all teams, the White Sox included. Two of them, veteran major league infielder Tony Cuccinello and career minor league outfielder Johnny Dickshot, provided a trivia note in 1945 by finishing second and third among A.L. batters. Cuccinello hit .308, and was just edged for the batting title by the .309 of Snuffy Stirnweiss of the Yankees. Dickshot batted .304. Both were gone by 1946.

So was Dykes a month after the 1946 season started. He was ill when it began, coach Mule Haas running the team until the manager returned on April 30. On May 24, with the White Sox 10-20, Mrs. Comiskey and new general manager Leslie O'Connor fired Dykes. He had lost support when Grabiner quit before the season started, Grabiner ended his 40-year association with the team because he could no longer go along with Mrs. Comiskey's policy

Lyons took over as manager by sounding the customary note of optimism: "Just tell the fans I'm going to do my best to give them the best White Sox team we ever had out there."

What he gave them after a promising 64-60 record to complete the 1946 campaign was two years of failure with 70-84 in 1947 and 51-101 in 1948 before he, too, went the way of all managers, though quitting rather than being fired. Not that he was so much to blame as were the financial problems of the White Sox and mismanagement by ownership and front office.

The few positive aspects of the almost three seasons under Lyons were the sustained hitting of Appling—.309, .306 and .314— and the emergence of "junkball" pitcher Ed Lopat (16-13) in 1947, as well as of second baseman Cass Kwietniewski (renamed Michaels). Journeyman outfielder Pat Seerey hit four home runs in an 11-inning game on July 18, 1948 to gain immortality in the record books.

Lyons' reign as manager was disastrous, but there was never any question of the pitching ability that enabled him to finish with a record of 260-230 during a career spent with mostly inept teams.

Yankee manager McCarthy's tribute: "If he'd been pitching for the Yankees, he would have won 400 games."

Lyons' philosophical attitude sustained him through many seasons of adversity. "According to some people," he said, "losing is the worst thing in the world. Well, it isn't. What's worse is allowing yourself to be eaten alive by it."

At her wit's end after Lyons quit, Grace Comiskey turned to son Charles, now 22, to find a new direction. In a stroke of genius, Charles, or "Chuck" as he became known, replaced O'Connor with Frank Lane, a dynamic and garrulous front office veteran, as general manager. In a stroke of feeble-mindedness, he elevated Jack Onslow, a baseball "lifer" as a minor league manager, to replace Lyons.

The whirlwind Lane era of the White Sox was at hand, though it reversed the usual course of matters by starting with a whimper rather than a bang. Yet the coming of Lane presaged the end of almost 30 years of mostly lackluster performances by the White Sox since the Black Sox scandal of 1919–20.

ALL-STAR OF A GAME 11

The All-Star Game is a Chicago invention. Arch Ward, sports editor of the *Chicago Tribune*, was the midwife who delivered baseball's annual mid-summer classic as a side-piece to the 1933 Chicago World's Fair.

According to Tom Littlewood, author of *Arch—A Promoter, Not a Poet*, it began when Chicago Mayor Edward J. Kelly approached Colonel Bertie McCormick, publisher of the *Tribune*. Kelly thought it might be appropriate if a sports event could be arranged in conjunction with the World's Fair.

"We've got the man you want right here," McCormick said.

Ten minutes later sports editor Ward was in McCormick's Tribune Tower office.

It was the year of the Chicago Centennial. The city was strangling in the grip of the Great Depression. Municipal governments were on the brink of bankruptcy. But a remarkable number of Chicago businessmen invested in a gala "Century of Progress" exhibition which evolved into the famous Chicago World's Fair.

Colonel McCormick had some doubts. "What if nobody shows up?"

Ward was certain he could fill old Comiskey Park, the home of the White Sox, and told McCormick, "You can take the losses out of my paycheck."

"If you're that confident, we'll underwrite it," McCormick said.

Six months later, on July 6, 1933, baseball's first All-Star game, matching the best players in the American and National leagues, was born.

"That's a grand show," said baseball Commissioner Kenesaw Mountain Landis, who immediately decreed that the All-Star game become an annual affair.

"Dad never thought the game would go beyond one year," recalled Tom Ward, Arch's son. "He felt it would be strictly a one-shot thing. He was very surprised."

Ward picked the managers, Connie Mack of the Philadelphia Athletics for the A.L. and John McGraw of the New York Giants for the N.L. The players were chosen by public ballot conducted by 55 newspapers throughout the country which relayed their tabulations to the *Tribune*.

Ward wasn't first with the idea of an All-Star game. As early as 1915, F.C. Lane, editor of *Baseball Magazine*, had made a similar proposal. Lane met with the league presidents and some of the club owners but failed to convince them an All-Star game would be beneficial.

On April 23, 1933, soon after his meeting with publisher McCormick, Ward went to see Will Harridge, president of the A.L. Harridge's headquarters were on Michigan Avenue, down the street from the *Tribune*.

Judge Landis' office was four blocks closer but Landis was an autocrat who ruled with an iron hand. Ward was in awe of Landis and like many ballplayers and owners was uncomfortable in his presence. Harridge was a kinder and considerably more agreeable soul.

The season had begun. Harridge brought the proposal up at the next league meeting. There were many details to overcome. If an open date was available, how would the players gather in Chicago on such short notice? Why should the clubs risk injury to their players for a meaningless exhibition game? If a precedent was established, wouldn't the other cities request future All-Star games? And the biggest problem: What if it rained on the day of the game?

Ward then went to work on the N.L. and contacted William L. Veeck, Sr., a former baseball writer who was president of the Cubs and as early as 1922 had campaigned, unsuccessfully, for inter-league play. Veeck was the ideal messenger and carried the proposition to owner Philip K. Wrigley.

Wrigley was opposed, arguing that a mid-summer inter-league game would diminish interest in the World Series. When Veeck reminded him of the potential harm in antagonizing the *Tribune*, Wrigley relented.

On May15, three weeks after he had seen Harridge, N.L. president John Heydler polled his owners. The St. Louis, New York and Boston clubs were opposed. Ward responded to the challenge with a blizzard of telegrams and phone calls. St. Louis and New York wilted under the pressure.

That left only the Boston Braves. Ward hammered them into submission. According to an unconfirmed report, he called the Boston owner and said, "We're going to announce the game the day after tomorrow and either we're going to announce that we almost had one and didn't because of you."

Ward was given a rain date but there was no need. The game was played in ideal weather and drew a paid crowd of 47,595. Babe Ruth hit the first All-Star home run, a two-run smash that gave the A.L. a 4-2 victory.

Ward's prose was pedestrian. He "covered" all the major events usually in the company of a *Tribune* staffer who wrote under his byline. Ward's column, "The Wake of the News," was written either by the talented Dave Condon or by rotating beat writers.

Ward often said, "You can buy a writer for $100 a week. It's the people with ideas who are hard to find."

In addition to the baseball All-Star game, Ward in the following year created the College All-Star football game, and later was architect of the All-America Football Conference, known in Chicago derisively as the "Arch All-American Conference," subsequently absorbed by the established National Football League.

Ward was of medium height, 5-foot-8 and about 160 pounds. He was without flamboyance, wore silver-rimmed spectacles and looked more like a bank president or a club owner than a news-paperman. He was among the highest-paid men in his profession and without doubt the most influential sports editor of the 20th Century.

Born on December 27, 1886 in Illinois' Kankakee County, Ward was orphaned when he was 12. He attended Loras (Iowa) College and, after two years there, transferred to the University of Notre Dame. He was closely associated with Knute Rockne, the legendary football coach, and was Rockne's first publicity director, in 1919 and 1920.

He was sports editor of the *Tribune* for 25 years. He died on July 9, 1955, and was buried on the morning of the 22nd All-Star game. The All-Star game's Most Valuable Player award is named in his memory.

The All-Star game has become one of baseball's major attractions and has been played annually since 1933 with the exception of 1945 when travel was curtailed because of World War II. Six games, including the inaugural, have been played in Chicago, three each at Wrigley Field and old Comiskey Park.

Babe Ruth, then in decline with the New York Yankees but still baseball's most popular player, didn't draw the most votes for the first mid-summer classic, which was billed as "The Game of the Century." Outfielder Al Simmons, then in his 11th major league season but his first with the White Sox, led with 346,291 votes. Chuck Klein of the Philadelphia Phillies was second with 342,283, Ruth third with 320,518. Gabby Hartnett, the Cubs' great catcher, topped the N.L.

Ever the showman, Ruth was the batting star with a decisive fourth inning home run and a single. The home run, a line drive to right center, was off Wild Bill Hallahan of the St. Louis Cardinals. Jimmy Dykes, also of the White Sox, had two hits for the Americans. Simmons had a single in four trips.

Fourteen years later, in 1947, Chicago hosted its second All-Star game, played before a capacity Wrigley Field crowd. Shortstop Luke Appling of the White Sox opened the sixth inning with a pinch-hit single and scored to lift the A.L. into a 1-1 tie. The Americans scored again in the eight for a 2-1 victory.

The third game, at Comiskey Park in 1950, was the longest and among the most controversial in history. Manager Burt Shotton of the Brooklyn Dodgers expressed dismay when power-hitting Hank Sauer of the Cubs was among the three leading out-fielders in the voting process.

None of Shotton's outfielders was a centerfielder, so he attempted to bench Sauer and replace him with the comparatively fleet Duke Snider of the Dodgers. Following an outburst from the fans, Commissioner Happy Chandler ordered Shotton to start the selected outfield. Sauer opened in right, Ralph Kiner of the Pittsburgh Pirates in left and Enos Slaughter of the Cardinals in center.

Shotton was also criticized for taking out Jackie Robinson of the Dodgers for a pinch batter in the 11th inning. Red Schoendienst of the Cardinals took over for Robinson at second base and won the game for the N.L., 4-3, with a towering, 14th inning home run that parachuted into the left field upper deck.

To accommodate the Players Association, which needed additional revenue for its pension fund, two games were played in 1962, the second at Wrigley Field. The A.L. won 9-4. Both teams knocked out 10 hits but the Americans had three home runs—by Pete Runnels of the Boston Red Sox, Leon Wagner of the Los Angeles Angels and Rocky Colavito of the Detroit Tigers. John Roseboro of the Los Angeles Dodgers connected for the Nationals.

The 50th anniversary game returned to Comiskey Park, the original site. The A.L. celebrated early with a record seven-run rally in the third inning and coasted to a 13-3 victory. Fred Lynn of the California Angels led the A.L. with the first grand slam home run in All-Star history.

Go-Go Sox, No-Go Cubs

12

I n a perverse way, 1948 was a "miracle season," the White Sox and Cubs accomplishing the unprecedented and uncomfortable feat of both finishing in last place in the same year. The Cubs, however, drew 1,237,972 fans, the White Sox far fewer, a total of 777,844, to witness what a wag dubbed the "Dungeon Derby."

Cub owner P.K. Wrigley reacted in typically eccentric fashion as his team struggled in the latter stages of the campaign by apologizing to the fans in a paid advertisement published in all the Chicago newspapers on August 30, 1948.

Wrigley's statement in part: "The Cub Management wants you to know we appreciate the wonderful support you are giving the ball club. We want to have a winning team that can be up at the top—the kind you deserve. This year's rebuilding job has been a flop. But we are not content to just go along with an eye to attendance. We want a winner just as you do and will do everything in our power to get one."

Unfortunately for Cub fans, notwithstanding Wrigley's promise of better times ahead, the team was merely in the early stages of the most grievous period of its history, two decades of confinement to the lower depths of the National League.

In contrast, the White Sox, after roving in the wilderness of non-contention for almost 30 years since the Black Sox scandal, were about to catch glimpses of the Promised Land. "Moses" was at hand in the form of energetic, even frenetic, new general manager Frank Lane, a minor league front office veteran.

Manager Ted Lyons' resignation on the final day of the disastrous 1948 season brought home to White Sox president Grace Comiskey the team's sad plight. Almost in despair, she gave son Charles "Chuck" Comiskey, only 22, authority to hire a new general manager and a manager. His choice of Lane for the first job was inspired. That of Jack Onslow, a manager in the White Sox farm system, to the latter post fell short.

Lane's "inaugural address" was blunt: "There are no sacred cows on this club!" There seldom were during his seven-year tenure as general manager from 1948–1955. He completed 241 deals involving 353 players in that stretch and even if many of the trades were insignificant, a few were blockbusters.

Especially his first one. On November 10, 1948, Lane sent catcher Aaron Robinson to the Detroit Tigers for left-handed pitcher Billy Pierce. The Tigers even threw in $10,000 to sweeten one of the most important acquisitions in White Sox history. The arrival of Pierce, 21, was the first step en route to the "Go-Go Sox" era of the 1950s. It was to arrive with Lane's further deals, especially those for Nellie Fox, Chico Carrasquel, Eddie Robinson and Minnie Minoso.

Not that Lane's first season of 1949 ended triumphantly. Or that Pierce was an immediate star. He was 7-15, and the Sox finished sixth at 63-91 under Onslow. Cass Michaels (.308) and Luke Appling (.301) led the offense, while Bill Wight (15-13) was the mainstay of the rotation. Rookie outfielder Gus Zernial, .318 in 73 games, was a sensation until he broke his collarbone on May 29.

The fans responded to the turnaround, attendance rising by 160,000, partly because of a record turnout of 53,325 for a doubleheader against the World Series champion Cleveland Indians on May 29. The crowd was rewarded with 10-0 and 2-0 shutouts of the Indians for one of the season's two highlights. The other came when Appling broke Rabbit Maranville's record of 2,153 games played at shortstop.

The Cubs again matched the Sox in one way in 1949 with an identical 61-93 record, but couldn't shed last place though Wrigley replaced Grimm with Frank Frisch as manager after 50 games. Frisch's chief contribution was to recommend a trade in which the Cubs acquired two outfielders, slugger Hank Sauer and speedster Frank Baumholtz, from the Cincinnati Reds. The deal was among the best in the team's uneven record of transactions.

Sauer quickly won the hearts of Cub fans, finishing the season with 31 home runs (27 for the Cubs), 83 RBI, and a team-leading .291. Third baseman/outfielder Andy Pafko completed a decent 1-2 punch by batting .281 with 18 homers and 69 RBI. But the pitching failed, staff leader Johnny Schmitz sinking from 18-13 in 1948 to 11-13.

Wrigley's reaction was to reshuffle his front office. Grimm had replaced Jim Gallagher as general manager during the 1949 season, but declaring, "These hands were never meant to carry a briefcase," quit the Cubs in January 1950 to return to the field in the minor leagues. Wrigley imported Wid Mathews, a Branch Rickey disciple, from Brooklyn to replace Grimm.

The trade for Sauer looked even better during the 1950 campaign but the Cubs didn't. They were last in fielding, last in hitting and next-to last in pitching as well as in the standings. Schmitz' sad record of 10-16 paled in negative comparison to Bob Rush's 13-20. Sauer, now hailed as the "Mayor of Wrigley Field," drove in 103 runs, hit 32 home runs and batted .274. Pafko led the team in batting at .304, hit 36 homers and drove in 93 runs.

Across town, the White Sox also continued to struggle despite Lane's ceaseless reshuffling. They finished sixth again in 1950, a season notable chiefly because it was Appling's last after 20 years in a White Sox uniform and Fox' first. Lane "stole" Fox, 21, a lightly-regarded utility infielder, from the Philadelphia A's in exchange for journeyman catcher Joe Tipton. Another major newcomer was rookie shortstop Carrasquel, plucked out of the Brookyn farm system.

After Lane persuaded the Comiskeys to fire Onslow, whom he called "a lousy manager" and "too dim" to win, early in the 1950 season and replace him with Red Corriden, a former Cub third base coach, he pulled off his most-heralded deal yet. Second baseman Michaels went to Washington on May 30 as the centerpiece of a three-for-three player swap in which the Sox got slugging first baseman Robinson.

Robinson's .311 led the team in 1950, and he hit 20 home runs. But the "big gun" was Zernial, who hit a team-record 29 homers, drove in 93 runs and batted .280. Pierce was still on the wrong side of .500 with 12-16, but the promise was clear.

Lane now was just two major moves away from the "Go-Go" era. The first was the hiring of manager Paul Richards, a former Detroit catcher and shrewd handler of players, after the 1950 season. The second was a daring and complex three-team deal early in the 1951 campaign in which Lane sent outfielders Zernial and Dave Philley to the A's via Cleveland for Cuban-born outfielder Minnie Minoso.

Actually, it was not Lane but Richards who wanted Minoso. Lane had been skeptical about his fielding ability, protesting, "But he can't play anything."

Richard persisted. "Don't you worry about him playing anything. I'll find a place for him. We'll just let him hit and run."

Minoso broke the team's color barrier with a bang, hitting a home run in his first at-bat on May 1, 1951. He hit nine more home runs, batted .326 and drove in 74 runs on the season. But it was his running (31 stolen bases) and that of rookie center fielder Jim Busby (26 stolen bases) that stirred the crowds to chants of "Go! Go! Go!" as the White Sox shed decades of dismay to stir excitement to a fever pitch at suddenly crowded Comiskey Park.

The Sox began a 14-game winning streak on May 15 and before it ended reached first place in the A.L. with a 32-11 record. Pitching in was right-hander Saul Rogovin, acquired by Lane from Detroit on May 16. He led the A.L. in ERA with 2.48 and finished 11-7. Though not even Rogovin or Pierce's coming of age with a 15-14 mark could keep the White Sox from fading to fourth place, they had served notice as a coming team.

New York Yankee manager Casey Stengel, wrapping up the third of five consecutive pennants in 1951, commented: "The Sox are gonna be up there a lot longer than most people figured."

Fox batted .313 and formed an expert double-play combination with slick-fielding Carrasquel while Robinson provided the power complement to the running game of Minoso, Busby and other speedsters with 29 home runs and 117 RBI. The fans responded with a record turnout of 1,328,234.

Robinson gave a great deal of credit to Richards' aggressive and astute managing. "We weren't that deep. Paul Richards had done a hell of a job with the team. He was getting top production from everybody, but we didn't have, really, that many great players. I mean, Rogovin was pitching like hell, and other guys too. They were not all that good, except they did good for Richards. Richards knew how to get it out of them."

Nobody could get much out of the Cub players in 1951 as the team finished last for the third time in four seasons. Phil Cavarretta replaced Frisch as manager in late July, but only after Mathews already had harmed the team in mid-June by trading Pafko to the player personnel director's old employers, the Dodgers, as part of a four-for-four deal Pafko starred for the Dodgers and Milwaukee Braves on three pennant winners. A sportswriter insisted the Cubs must have been "chloroformed."

Among the few bright spots for the Cubs were the play of center fielder Baumholtz who batted .284 and the slugging of Sauer (30 home runs, 89 RBI) and third baseman Randy Jackson (16 home runs, 76 RBI). Schmitz led the pitchers with 11-12.

The contrasting fortunes of the White Sox and Cubs made an impact on attendance in 1951. For the first time since 1944 the Cubs drew fewer than a million and topped that figure only once (1952) during the next 16 seasons. The pendulum swung to the White Sox, who surpassed the million mark with one exception (1958) from 1951 through 1965.

The A.L. in the 1950s was largely the preserve of the Yankees and Cleveland Indians (who won pennants in 1951 and 1954,

New York taking all the others through 1958), but the White Sox were often in the running. The rest of Richards' tenure brought records of 81-73 in 1952, 89-65 in 1953 and 91-54 until he resigned on September 10, 1954 to accept an offer from the Baltimore Orioles. Marty Marion, a former St. Louis Cardinal shortstop, took over as the Sox finished the season 94-60, their best record in 34 years.

Robinson, Minoso, Fox and Carrasquel continued to sparkle in 1952, first Robinson leading the team with .296, 22 home runs and 104 RBI. Pierce (15-12) and Rogovin (14-9) got boosts from other Lane pickups Joe Dobson (14-10) and Marv Grissom (12-10). Sherm Lollar, acquired from the St. Louis Browns, solved the catching dilemma for the rest of the decade.

Lane's deals for and during 1953 had mixed results. Robinson was sent to the A's for another first baseman, Ferris Fain, who proved a disappointment as well as a disruptive element. But acquiring right-hander Virgil "Fire" Trucks from the Browns in mid-June was a masterstroke. Trucks was 15-6 with the Sox (20-12 over all), teaming up with Pierce, 18-12, as pitching stalwarts. Minoso led the team in batting, home runs and RBI with .313, 15 and 104, and paced the league in steals (25) for the third consecutive season. Adding to the "Go-Go" was right fielder Jim Rivera, who stole 22.

Even though the Sox won 94 games in 1954, the season had its negatives with the departure of Richard and the disappointment of finishing third, 17 games behind the Indians who won a league record 111 games. Still, Fox batted .319 and Minoso again led the team with .320, 19 home runs and 116 RBI. Trucks (19-12) was steady even if Pierce (9-10) fell back, but the slack was picked up by Bob Keegan (16-9), Sandy Consuegra, (16-3) and Jack Harshman (14-8).

One of the more memorable, if less significant, developments of 1954 in Chicago baseball was the transfer of Phil Cavarretta to the White Sox after 20 years as Cub star player and manager. Cavarretta offended Wrigley in spring training by reporting that the Cubs had few first-rate players and would probably finish in the lower half of the standings. Wrigley charged Cavarretta with "negative thinking" and fired him. Lane seized on a public relations opportunity and signed Cavarretta, 37, as a utility player-pinch hitter. He responded by hitting .316 in 71 games.

Cavarretta's first full season as Cub manager in 1952 was a relative success, the team reaching .500 with a 77-77 record, the only time it did so in 16 seasons from 1947 through 1962. Sauer was voted the N.L.'s Most Valuable Player as he tied Pittsburgh slugger Ralph Kiner with 37 home runs, led the league with 121 RBI and batted .270. Baumholtz batted .325, second in the league. Rush led the pitchers with 17-13. Warren Hacker (15-9) and Paul Minner (14-9) also were effective.

The apparent promise faded in 1953, the Cubs sinking to 65-89 and seventh. Yet two major events highlighted an otherwise dreary campaign. The most significant came September 17 when the Cubs unveiled their first black player, 22-year-old, 160-pound shortstop Ernie Banks, purchased for $25,000 from the Kansas City Monarchs. Before that, on June 4, they acquired Kiner in a 10-player deal with the Pirates. Kiner in the previous seven seasons had led or tied for the N.L. home run title.

Sauer in right and Kiner in left flanked center fielder Baumholtz, who despite being constantly on the run between his slow "bookend" outfield colleagues batted .306. Kiner finished with 35 home runs (28 for the Cubs) but Sauer, hampered by injuries, dipped to 18. The pitchers suffered, Hacker at 12-19 leading the league in losses.

Columnist Warren Brown wrote: "Cavarretta should get a bonus for watching the Cubs every day."

In retrospect, the most important blow of 1953 was delivered by Banks when he hit the first of his 512 career home runs off Gerry Staley on September 20 in St. Louis. "Mr. Cub" was on hand, accompanied by another African-American, second baseman Gene Baker, who at first was considered the better prospect.

Wrigley dragged his feet on integration until Mathews pressed him to bring up Baker, a standout in the Cubs' minor league system. When Mathews casually mentioned that he had acquired another black player, Wrigley asked, "Who?"

"Fellow named Ernie Banks."

"Gee whiz!" Wrigley exclaimed. 'We are bringing up another Negro player this year. Why did you go out and get another one?"

"Well," Mathews replied, "we had to have a roomate for the one we've got."

It was thus, almost casually, that the Cubs acquired their most beloved and greatest player of the 20th Century who was to become the favorite not only of the fans as "Mr. Cub" but of Wrigley himself. It took a while, however, for Wrigley and Banks to adjust to a new situation.

"During my half month stay with the Cubs in September 1953 I met more white people than I had known in all my 22 years," Banks recalled.

Not even Banks and Baker, the new double-play combination, could do much for the Cubs of 1954 who were as bad as Cavarretta thought them to be in spring training. Manager Hack, the former star third baseman, couldn't keep from finishing seventh again with a 64-90 record. Banks batted .275 and hit 19 home runs, the most ever by a Cub rookie. Sauer's career-high 41 home runs topped the team and Kiner contributed 22. Rush was the only pitcher with more than 11 wins at 13-15.

The next four seasons, 1955 through 1958, continued to be frustrating for both the Cubs and White Sox, though in radically contrasting ways. While the Cubs were unable to even approach .500, the dilemma for the Sox was to get close to fielding a pennant-winner yet always falling short.

During 1955, the first of Marion's two full seasons as manager, the White Sox were in the race until they slumped in mid-September to finish third, just five games behind the Yankees at 94-60. Fox (.311) and Minoso (.288, 10 home runs, 70 RBI) fueled the offense with boosts from more recent acquisitions by Lane, first baseman Walt Dropo (19 home runs) and third baseman George Kell (.312). Pierce (15-10 and a league-leading 1.97 ERA), newcomer Dick Donovan (15-9) and Trucks (13-8) led the pitchers.

A nerve-wracking pennant race in which the White Sox were in a virtual dead heat with the Yankees and Indians as late as Labor Day told on Lane and Chuck Comiskey. The general manager resigned on September 21 after Comiskey publicly reprimanded him for a tirade against the umpires after a game. Lane complained, "Here I am sticking up for my club and players, and another official criticizes me for it." His seven-year run with the Sox over, Lane became general manager of the St. Louis Cardinals.

Lane's departure didn't faze Comiskey, who had come to detest Frantic Frankie's whirlwind style. He teamed up with brother-in-law John Rigney to run the team. They gave Marion a bonus for 1956 with a major trade, sending Carrasquel to Cleveland for Larry Doby, a power-hitting outfielder. The deal not only added power but it freed shortstop for Luis Aparicio, a spectacular fielder who won the Rookie of the Year award and began a string of nine consecutive seasons of leading the league in stolen bases.

Doby's 24 home runs and 102 RBI supported the customary offensive output of Minoso (.316, 21 home runs, 88 RBI) and Fox (.296) and Pierce turned in his best record yet with 20-8. A four-game sweep over the Yankees in which Doby hit three home runs and drove in seven runs in late June at Comiskey Park spiced a season ending in another third place finish at 85-69. Marion resigned when he discovered Comiskey and Rigney were courting Al Lopez, then managing the Indians.

Lopez had won a pennant in 1954 at Cleveland, and never finished lower than second in six seasons. Easy-going yet shrewd, Lopez believed the White Sox were on the verge of success.

"The Yankees are a good club, but they can be had, " Lopez forecast. "The White Sox have a chance to go all the way in '57."

In early season it looked as if they just might, the Sox winning 22 of their first 30 games. After that they slowed down but gave the Yankees a tussle before Lopez was forced to settle for his sixth second-place result in seven seasons with a 90-64 record. The offensive standouts as usual were Fox (.317) and Minoso (.310, 12 home runs, 103 RBI). Pierce was a 20-game winner with 20-12 for the second consecutive season, and Donovan (16-6) and newcomer Jim Wilson (15-6) were also highly successful.

Lopez couldn't shake the second place habit in 1958, though Frank Lane, back in the A.L. as Indians general manager, gave the White Sox a boost toward triumph the following year. Lane sent veteran right-handed starter Early Wynn and outfielder Al Smith to the Sox for Minoso and utility infielder Fred Hatfield. The Sox also opened center field for young and speedy Jim Landis by sending Doby to Baltimore along with Harshman, the chief return being third baseman Billy Goodman.

The immediate results of all this reshuffling were to make fans lament the departure of a favorite in "Minnie" and hasten the development of Landis, who was a greyhound in the field and hit a respectable .277 with 15 home runs. Fox again led the batters with .300, and Lollar was tops in home runs with 20 and RBI with 84. Pierce (17-11), Donovan (15-14) and Wynn (14-16) formed the solid pitching nucleus that enabled the Sox to linger in second again in 1958 with 82-72.

Tormented as the White Sox were by failing to overhaul the Yankees year after year, their problems paled beside those of the Cubs, who couldn't achieve even mediocrity. When journeyman pitcher Dave Cole was traded to the Phillies in 1955 after being 3-8 the previous year he complained, "They're the only club I can beat."

From 1955 through 1958 the Cubs were sixth with 72-81, eighth with 60-94, tied for seventh with 72-82 and tied for fifth with 72-82. Managerial changes were futile. Hack's three-year reign ended after the 1956 season when gruff former catcher Bob Scheffing began an identical term as his successor. The results were indistinguishable.

Similarly inconsequential was Wrigley's habit of changing general managers. He gave up on Mathews' "Five Year Plan" and relegated him to being a paid observer by anointing Clarence "Pants" Rowland, who had managed the 1917 White Sox to Chicago's last World Series title, as his successor. One of Rowland's earliest moves was to get rid of the fading Kiner.

But 1955 wasn't a totally "lost season" because of the feats of three players, one of them Banks. He exploded with 44 home runs, five of them grand slams, and the most ever hit by a shortstop. Catcher Clyde McCullough marveled, "He doesn't swing the bat around very far. But he is quick and has strong wrists. This way he can take a little more time to watch a pitch."

The other two Cubs to make a splash were rookies. They were Sam "Toothpick" Jones, who pitched a no-hitter and led the staff with 14 wins, and outfielder Bob Speake, who replaced the aging and declining Sauer in the lineup on May 2 and by the end of the month was batting .304 with 10 home runs, four doubles, two triples and 31 RBI. It was a brief, deceptive burst of glory. By season's end, Speake was down to .218 with only two more homers and five additional RBI.

Hack's final season, 1956, made 1955 look good. Before the campaign even began, Sauer was gone but the Cubs probably would have finished last for the fourth time in nine years with or without him. About the only positive aspects of the season were provided by Banks who led the team in batting average (.297), home runs (28) and RBI (85), and right fielder Walt "Moose" Moryn who was second in all three categories with .285, 23 home runs and 69 RBI. Rush's 13-10 topped an erratic pitching staff.

Wrigley decided to clean house for 1957 and fired Hack as well as Mathews and Gallagher. Cub minor league executive John Holland took over the personnel chores and Charlie Grimm returned again. The Cubs were deep in vice presidents with three in Rowland, Grimm and Holland even if shy of field talent in 1957, which produced another tail-end finish though it could charitably be called seventh place since they tied with the Pirates.

Not that all was bleak. Banks hit 43 home runs and drove in 102 runs, alternating between shortstop and third base. First baseman Dale Long was acquired in a trade by Holland that sent Banks' former double-play partner Baker to the Pirates. Long batted .305 with 21 home runs and 62 RBI in only 123 games. Rookie right-handers Dick Drott, 15-11, and Moe Drabowsky, 13-15, promised an upturn in pitching quality.

Alas, neither Drott nor Drabowsky could maintain their success in 1958 though the Cubs won a few more games (72) with raw power. Injuries reduced Drott to 7-11 and Drabowsky to 9-11, with rookie Glen Hobbie (10-6) the only pitcher to win 10 games. There was no shortage of punch, however, the Cubs breaking the N.L. home run record for a season with 182. Five players hit 20 or more.

Banks led the quintet of bombers with 47 home runs, 129 RBI, a slugging percentage of .619 and 379 total bases, four categories in which he topped the league while batting .313. The others with 20 or more home runs were outfielders Moryn, (26), Lee Walls (24) and Bobby Thompson (21), and first baseman Long (20).

Not surprisingly, Banks was the runaway winner of the Most Valuable Player award even though his team finished in a tie for fifth. He brushed off all enthusiastic comparisons with Babe Ruth as a home run hitter.

"You could put all my homers end to end and I wouldn't be able to match Ruth," Banks insisted.

Despite the cannonade, the Cubs made no actual headway under Holland's and Scheffing's obvious scheme to take advantage of Wrigley Field's reputation as a home run heaven. Their largely lead-footed players contrasted starkly with the speedsters favored by the White Sox, who finally proved in 1959 that the race goes to the swiftest.

Before the 1959 season began, control of the White Sox passed to a syndicate led by Bill Veeck, former chief owner of the Indians and Browns. When Grace Comiskey died in 1957 she left 54 percent of the stock to daughter Dorothy, leaving son Chuck a minority slice. On March 5, 1959, Dorothy Comiskey sold out to Veeck's group. Chuck Comiskey stayed on as an executive, but Veeck and Hank Greenberg, the former Detroit Tigers star acting as general manager, called the shots.

As it turned out, Veeck, who favored power and pitching over speed and defense, the major Sox ingredients, was skeptical about the chances of the team he took over. In his book, *Veeck—as in Wreck*, he revealed: "I should have listened to Al Lopez. Al told me from the beginning we were going to win it. 'This is my kind of team,' he kept telling me. I have always respected Al's ability and judgment.... But as far as I was concerned, it was his kind of team and he could have it."

To Veeck's astonishment, delight and profit, Lopez was right.

Yet while the Sox were good in 1959 they also were lucky. The Yankees were plagued by injuries and the only other viable contenders for the pennant were the Indians. Ironically, it was Cleveland general manager Lane who gave the Sox the edge by trading Wynn to them two years earlier.

Wynn went 22-11 to earn the Cy Young award for 1959 as the ace of a rotation including Bob Shaw (18-6), Pierce (14-15), Barry Latman (8 5) and Dick Donovan (9-10), with relief supplied by Gerry Staley (8-5, 14 saves) and Turk Lown (9-2, 15 saves). Staley and Lown accounted for 17 wins and 29 saves between them.

The pitchers got a huge lift from a brilliant defense down the middle with Fox and Aparicio around second base, Landis in center and Lollar behind the plate. Third base was a collaborative effort with Goodman, Bubba Phillips and Sammy Esposito, but first base was a problem, particularly offensively, until veteran slugger Ted Kluszewski arrived in a waiver deal on August 29 to fill the final piece of the pennant puzzle. Kluszewski satisfied Veeck's urge for a power hitter and hit .297 in 31 games down the stretch though he contributed only two home runs.

A season that began auspiciously on April 10 in Detroit when Fox hit his first home run in two years in the 14th inning to beat the Tigers reached its climax on September 22. That's when Staley's first pitch in relief induced Vic Power to hit into a game-ending double play to give the White Sox a 4-2 victory at Cleveland and the A.L. pennant for the first time since 1919.

In Chicago that night the air-raid sirens blared triumphantly—if in violation of the rules regulating their use—for five minutes to celebrate what turned out to be the lone White Sox pennant during a stretch of 81 seasons. It was also the only one for either Chicago team in the second half of the 20th Century.

A crowd estimated at 100,000 greeted the team at Midway Airport when it returned to Chicago at 1:30 in the morning. Mayor Richard J. Daley rejoiced, "A Chicago pennant! Now for the World Series. We'll win it in four straight."

Speed, defense and pitching were the weapons that prevailed. Fox led the team in batting with .306, but his chief contribution might have been as the team's "spiritual" leader. His overall play earned him the Most Valuable Player award in a vote in which Aparicio and Wynn finished second and third. Aparicio's 56 stolen bases led the team, with Landis next at 20. Home runs were scarce, Lollar leading with 22 and in RBI with 84. Left fielder Al Smith added 17 home runs.

The 1959 World Series against the Los Angeles Dodgers began uncharacteristically at Comiskey Park on October 1 with the White Sox exploding for a 11-0 victory behind Wynn and Staley. Kluszewski drove in five runs with a pair of two-run home runs and a run-scoring single.

It was a good start, but the Go-Go Sox had shot their bolt. They lost the next three games of the Series, 4-3 at Comiskey Park and 3-1 and 8-4 in the huge Los Angeles Coliseum. They managed to stay alive with a 1-0 victory in Game 5 behind Shaw, Pierce and Donovan before the largest crowd ever to see a major league game, 92,706 in the Dodgers' temporary home. The Dodgers wrapped it up 8-3 in Game 6 in Chicago.

If the Sox went down, it was not without distinction. Kluszewski drove in 10 runs, a record for a six-game Series, hit three homers and batted .391. Fox batted .375. But the Series hero was Dodger reliever Larry Sherry who won two games and saved two others.

Veeck's final assessment: "Two guys beat us really: Maury Wills and Larry Sherry. We thought we would have by far the best shortstopping with Aparico, but it turned out that Wills had a re-markably fine Series in the field. And Sherry, of course, never pitched as well before that and never pitched as well after that."

As for the White Sox, they never succeeded as well after 1959, though they later won three division titles. But pennants and the World Series remained out of reach.

What were the Cubs doing in 1959 while the Sox were tri-umphant? Not much, except for Banks. Scheffing served out his three-year sentence with a 74-80 record for a fifth place tie. Banks drove in a career-high 143 runs, hit 45 home runs (his third consecutive season of 40 or more), and broke two shortstop records with fewest errors (12) and highest fielding percentage (.985). He won his second Most Valuable Player award.

Second baseman Tony Taylor, Baker's replacement, was about the only other standout, batting .280 and leading the unhurried team in runs scored, 96, and stolen bases, 23 out of the entire team total of 32. Only Hobbie (16-13) and rookie Bob Anderson (12-13) were adequate among the starting pitchers, though relievers Don Elston and Bill Henry, a right-lefty duo, combined for 19 victories and 25 saves.

In what was widely regarded as a ploy to steal attention from the triumphant White Sox who were about to open the 1959 World Series, Wrigley fired Scheffing immediately after the season. Incongruously, Wrigley congratulated Scheffing on "a helluva fine job."

Scheffing was shocked. He thought he had done well to finish just six games under .500, considering the mediocre talent at his disposal. "I figured I'd get both a new contract and a raise. When I got to his office, Mr. Wrigley said they had decided to make a change and would bring Charlie Grimm back in an effort to loosen up the club."

Wrigley brought Grimm back for a third term, but also foreshadowed what was to come. "Managers are expendable," he said. "I believe there should be relief managers like relief pitchers."

The most expendable apparently was Grimm, who after a 6-11 start in 1960, was transferred to the radio booth in exchange for Lou Boudreau, former manager of the Indians, Boston Red Sox and Kansas City A's. It didn't help. Players came and went. So did Boudreau, going back to radio after the Cubs finished seventh with 60-94.

Banks was the sole star in a clouded firmanent, with 41 home runs and 117 RBI. It was his fourth 40-plus home run season in five years. Hobbie led the club in victories with 16 but also in losses with 20. Don Cardwell, obtained in an ill-advised trade with the Phillies that cost the Cubs Tony Taylor, pitched a no-hitter on May 15 but didn't do much to enhance a poor pitching staff.

Only one newcomer was significant for the future. Rookie third baseman Ron Santo, just 20, made his debut on June 26 at Pittsburgh and drove in five runs with three hits in a double-header sweep. Third base was his through 1973.

The rookie crop was even better in 1961, with outfielder Billy Wiliams and left-handed pitcher Dick Ellsworth the main prizes, but their virtues were almost ignored in the shadow of Wrigley's latest eccentricity. On January 19 he declared managers to be passé and instituted the so-called College of Coaches. Instead of a manager, the Cubs would have a platoon of coaches, all equal and interchangeable who would rotate through the whole Cub system. A head coach would run the team for a designated period, then be replaced by a colleague, also temporarily.

The scheme was in operation during 1961 and 1962 with Vedie Himsl, Harry Craft, Elvin Tappe and Lou Klein head coaches the first season, Tappe, Klein and Charlie Metro the second. The results: 64-90 and seventh place in 1961 and 59-103 and ninth (in the now 10-team league) in 1962.

Even Banks had an off year in 1961, though this was due to a knee-injury. He dropped to 29 home runs and 80 RBI, yielding the club lead in the latter category to outfielder George Altman's 96. Altman hit .303 with 27 home runs. Cardwell was the sole starting pitcher with a plus record at 15-14.

Most encouraging, however, were two young players, Santo, who batted .284 with 23 home runs and 84 RBI in his first full season, and outfielder Billy Williams, Rookie of the Year after batting .278 with 25 homers and 75 RBI.

While the specifics of the 1962 season are best forgotten, including Metro's tenure as head coach (43-69 from June 3 on), several products of the Cub farm system eased the sting of failure as did Banks' permanent and succcessful shift to first base after knee problems reduced his range at shortstop.

"Those ground balls aren't much different and now I've got a bigger glove," Banks said of his new position. He made himself comfortable with 37 home runs and 104 RBI.

For the second successive year the Cubs paraded a Rookie of the Year in second baseman Ken Hubbs, who was the first rookie to also win a Gold Glove award. Less impressive at this point was outfielder Lou Brock, who batted only .263 with nine home runs, but was destined for the Hall of Fame. Because of the most reviled trade in the team's history, Brock didn't enter in a Cub uniform.

Not even veteran Bob Buhl, acquired in an April trade from the Milwaukee Braves, could lift Cub pitching over-all. He led with 12 wins, but the most notable record was Ellsworth's 9-20.

Wrigley surrendered for 1963, abolishing the College of Coaches. He hired Bob Kennedy as "permanent head coach" but told the press "you can call him manager." Nonetheless, he developed a new quirk, appointing Robert Whitlow, a retired Air Force colonel, as athletic director in command of the entire organization, even over general manager Holland and Kennedy.

Despite the circus atmosphere and frequent, if ineffective, interference by Whitlow, the Cubs finished 82-80 in 1963, topping .500 for the first time since 1946 though seventh in the now 10-team league. They might have done even better if eye troubles, mumps and other problems hadn't hampered Banks, who slipped to .227 with just 18 home runs and 64 RBI. Not even fine seasons by Santo (.295, 25 home runs, 99 RBI) and Williams (.286, 25 home runs, 95 RBI) could make up the deficit. Brock stole 24 bases, the most since Kiki Cuyler's 37 in 1930.

Most surprising was the pitching turnabout, especially that of Ellsworth, who went 22-10. Larry Jackson (14-8) and Lindy McDaniel (13-7, 22 saves), obtained in a trade from the Cardinals, were also outstanding.

The promise of 1963 was blighted early in 1964, the first blow being tragic, the death of Hubbs in an airplane accident on February 13. Yet the Cubs got off to a good start and on June 14 Holland completed a six-player trade with the Cardinals to enhance their chances. "We're taking a shot at the pennant," Holland proclaimed. "The race is wide open.'"

It was, but to the Cardinals not the Cubs, and it was the trade that helped them slam it shut. The key players of the six-man deal were Cub outfielder Brock and Cardinal pitcher Ernie Broglio.

While Broglio finished the season 4-7, Brock hit .348 in 105 games for St. Louis to spark his new team to a pennant.

Even Jackson's record of 24-11, best in the major leagues, couldn't lift the Cubs higher than eighth. Nor did a partial recovery by Banks, with 23 home runs and 95 RBI, and great showings by Santo (.313, 30 home runs, 114 RBI) and Williams (.312, 33 home runs, 98 RBI).

Kennedy lost his job after 56 games (24-32) in 1965, and was replaced by Klein, the former head coach, but the end result was no better, eighth again with a 72-90 record. Banks (.265, 28 HR, 108 RBI), Santo (.285, 33 home runs, 101 RBI) and Williams (.315, 34 home runs and 108 RBI) continued to pound, giving the Cubs three 100 RBI men for the first time in 35 years. Jackson (14-21), Ellsworth (14-15) and Buhl (13-11) paced an erratic rotation.

In the long run, more memorable was the advent of two rookies, second baseman Glenn Beckert and shortstop Don Kessinger who were to form an outstanding combination for nine seasons. And a feat by journeyman left-hander Bob Hendley (4-4), who on September 9 pitched a one-hitter at Los Angeles against Dodger Sandy Koufax' perfect game, almost matching the famous double no-hitter of 1917.

With Kennedy gone—as well as Whitlow, who resigned before the 1965 season started finally having figured out he was superfluous—and having little confidence in Klein, Wrigley pondered his next move. It was to be as unexpected as the earlier ones.

While the Cubs stumbled from one failed experiment to another during the first half of the 1960s the White Sox were far better, always winning more often than they lost. But they weren't wholly successful though Lopez guided them skillfully through the 1965 season. Perhaps their most exciting move of six frustrating years was Veeck's installation of the exploding scoreboard at Comiskey Park in the winter of 1959–60.

Veeck's obsession with power hitters dictated a series of ill-advised trades after the 1959 season in which the White Sox disposed of a wealth of young talent for veterans in decline. Minoso,

38, returned from Cleveland essentially in exchange for first baseman Norm Cash, who was to star for Detroit, and catcher John Romano. Another future standout was outfielder Johnny Callison, who went to the Phillies for slow-footed, erratic fielding third baseman Gene Freese. Catcher Earl Battey and first baseman Don Mincher, both to have solid careers, brought aging slugger Roy Sievers from Washington.

According to Lopez, "Bill (Veeck) made the remark, 'If Lopez could win the pennant with that club, I'm gonna get some hitters in here and he'll win the pennant next year easy.'"

Years later, Landis told Bob Vanderberg, author of the book *'59 Summer of the Sox*, he couldn't understand what was happening.

"When you win a pennant and are in a World Series, why do you want to change a ballclub that much?" Landis asked. "I'll never forget that. It was a shame. And all those guys—Cash, Callison, Battey, Romano and Latman—were All-Stars within three years. So it did come back to haunt them."

With the trades, the "Go-Go" Sox turned into the "Go Slow" Sox in 1960 even if Aparicio stole 51 bases. Lopez kept them respectable with an 87-67 record, and third place. Despite the new emphasis on sluggers, the Sox hit just 15 more home runs than in 1959, first baseman Sievers leading with 28 and Minoso next with 20. Minoso led in RBI with 105 and Al Smith's .315 was also tops. Wynn (13-12) and Pierce (14-7) paced a decaying pitching staff.

Veeck's illness, requiring a prolonged rest, cast a pall over the 1961 season and he decided to sell. White Sox majority ownership passed to former Veeck-associate Arthur Allyn in June. Greenberg followed Veeck out the door, Allyn's surprising choice for his successor as general manager being Ed Short, the team publicist. The Sox almost repeated the record of 1960 with 86-76 but sank to fourth. Two newcomers, pitcher Juan Pizarro (14-7) and outfielder Floyd Robinson (.310) stood out and Smith led the team in home runs with 28 and RBI with 93, in each category just one more than Sievers.

Leaning on Lopez for advice, Short embarked on a rebuilding program, trading away Pierce, Sievers and Minoso for younger blood. The most notable acquisition for 1962 was first baseman Joe Cunningham, whose .295 helped keep the Sox above .500 at 85-77 though they finished fifth. Robinson led the team in batting (.312) and RBI (109) but no one reached 20 home runs. Ray Herbert (20-9) was the pitching ace.

In 1963 it seemed as if Short's repairs, which continued with the dispatch of Aparicio to Baltimore for shortstop Ron Hansen, outfielder Dave Nicholson and third baseman Pete Ward, were succeeding. The Sox rose to second, winning 94 games though finishing far behind the Yankees. Right-hander Gary Peters won Rookie of the Year honors with 19-8 and Ward finished second in the voting. Ward led in batting (.295) and RBI (84) and tied Nicholson in home runs (22). Pizarro (16-8) again was outstanding.

Short's "ruthlessness" reached its apex in December 1963 when he traded Fox, the very personification of the "Go-Go" era, for two nonentities from Houston. Fan outrage simmered despite one of the most heated pennant races in the team's history. The White Sox, winning 98 games, pursued the Yankees to a bitter end, winning their last nine regular season games of 1964. But the Yankees won 13 of their final 14 to finish one game ahead for their fifth consecutive pennant.

Pitching kept the Sox in the running with a sparkling Big Four rotation of Peters (20-8), Pizarro (19-9), Joel Horlen (13-8) and John Buzhardt (10-8) and outstanding relief from old Hoyt Wilhelm (12-9, 27 saves) and Eddie Fisher (6-3, 9 saves). Ward's 23 home runs and 93 RBI led the club and Robinson batted .301, but there just wasn't enough offensive depth, Nicholson's power was undeniable, but he struck out far too much.

Lopez and Short tried to reinforce the offense for 1965 by turning first base over to veteran Bill Skowron, the former Yankee star, regaining catcher Romano and starting speedy rookie Ken Berry in center field. When the White Sox won 23 of their first 31 games it looked as if they were on the right track. But injuries, especially a torn muscle that ended Pizzaro's season, set in and they were forced to settle once more for second place. They won

95 games even though not a single player batted .300, reached 20 home runs or drove in 100 runs (Skowron topping the team with 78).

Even more unusual, reliever Fisher (15-7, 24 saves) led the staff in wins, with the best record among the starters being newcomer Tommy John's 14-7.

In its way the remarkable achievement of 1965 in leading a punchless team to second place was a fitting conclusion to Lopez's nine-season (1957–65) run as manager, a stretch during which the Sox never won fewer than 85 games, raised one pennant and finished second five times.

The results validated Lopez's view: "A manager's main job is inspiring his players and handling the pitchers."

Health problems were plaguing Lopez in 1965 and he decided to retire as manager though he remained an advisor to owner Allyn, helping to choose fiery Eddie Stanky as his successor.

No one suspected at the time that Lopez would return, if only briefly, as manager. But in actuality the Lopez period of White Sox history ended in 1965, at the same time as the Cubs' futile College of Coaches scheme exhaled its final gasp with the dismissal of Lou Klein, the last survivor of Wrigley's folly.

It was a watershed year for both teams and as usual they were headed in different directions. The Cubs would eventually enter the "Up" elevator while the Sox would stumble into the one marked "Down."

COLLEGE OF CONFUSION

13

Philip K. Wrigley, ever the pioneer, was weary of firing managers and so he came up with another of his startling innovations. Instead of giving the ax to his managers, which he had done at acceptable intervals, he decided on an unprecedented system of employing rotating head coaches.

"I looked up the word 'manager' in the dictionary and the definition was 'dictator,'" Wrigley announced at the Cubs' winter press conference on January 12, 1961 at the Wrigley Building. "Heavens, we don't need a dictator."

Minutes later he elaborated.

"It's like hiring a man to operate a bulldozer. If the man gets sick that doesn't mean the bulldozer has broken down. Not at all. You have another driver ready and he steps in. That isn't a bad simile, is it?" he asked, as if surprised himself.

Wrigley then realized he had forgotten something and he called for his son Bill and asked him to go to his 16th floor office and bring it down for the benefit of the photographers. It was a sign prepared by the art department of the William Wrigley Co., but obviously intended for the Cubs. The sign read:

Anyone who remains calm
In the midst of all this
CONFUSION
Simply does not understand
The situation

Wrigley hung the sign around his neck, either unaware or re-fusing to acknowledge it was the bulldozer that needed repair. It was also another example of Wrigley's passion for divided authority. The Cubs led the league in vice presidents, all jockeying and competing for his approval.

Baseball's top three administrators were unimpressed with Wrigley's folly but were careful not to spank him in public and expressed reluctant approval. There was nothing they could do. There is no rule stipulating a manager is required.

National League president Warren Giles was the first to check in. "Certainly, Mr. Wrigley knows what he wants to do," Giles said. "But I've never heard of a team without a manager."

Asked if he thought it was a good idea, Giles replied, "I'd rather not be quoted on that."

Joe Cronin, American League president: "I'd feel a lot better with one chief and more Indians."

Said Commissioner Ford Frick: "If Mr. Wrigley wants eight coaches and no manager that is strictly his business. My only concern is that nine men must be on the field and it doesn't make any difference if Mr. Wrigley has a manager or a head coach."

Bill Veeck, baseball's leading entrepeneur and president of the crosstown White Sox, said he had long since ceased being surprised at Wrigley's ideas. Asked if he would follow suit, Veeck laughed up his sleeve: "No, I'll go along with tradition. I guess I'm just an old stick-in-the-mud."

The Cubs opened the 1961 season with 11 potential head coaches. In alphabetical order they were Bobby Adams, Dick Cole, James "Rip" Collins, Harry Craft, Charlie Grimm (who was also a vice president who had served three terms as the Cub manager), Vedie Himsl, Goldie Holt, Lou Klein, Fred Martin, Elvin Tappe and Verlon Walker.

An advisory board was appointed and included general manager John Holland, farm director Gene Lawing and center fielder Richie Ashburn, the team's player representative, listed as an ex-officio member. This group, Wrigley said, would elect the head coach. But when it came time to choose the first head coach, typically, it was Wrigley who made the decision.

After everyone had assembled at the Cubs' Mesa, Arizona, training camp, catcher Sammy Taylor observed: "I can't even fart without one of the coaches hearing it."

As could be expected, the reporters jumped on the story with glee. The *Chicago Sun-Times* ran a chart, in the manner of a Kentucky Derby line, complete with odds and a few words of racetrack comment. Himsl, the least known of the entries, was the long shot at 100-1.

And so Wrigley, who delighted in tweaking the press, awarded the assignment to Himsl. The announcement was made on the final weekend of the exhibition season, at 30,000 feet in the aisle of the Cubs' chartered DC-6 en route to Houston.

Ed Prell of the *Chicago Tribune* observed: "It was the first time a manager and/or head coach has been hired and at the same time given two weeks' notice."

"Do you think the other coaches wanted Vedie to win nine straight?" veteran third baseman Don Zimmer asked many years later. "They were jealous of each other."

Himsl was in charge for the first 11 games, five wins, six losses. Don Elston, the bullpen star, kept Himsl afloat. Elston won three of these games, all in relief, and saved another.

"Being human, I'd prefer to stay," Himsl said when his term was up and he was rotated to the Cubs' minor league affiliates, San Antonio of the Texas League and then to Wenatchee, Washington, of the Northwest League.

Craft took over for the next 12 games and was succeeded by the returning Himsl who remained for 17 games. Then it was Tappe's turn. Tappe was in charge for a two-game series in Philadelphia. It was then announced there would be a new head coach for every series. Craft handled the team for a four-game series in Cincinnati, Himsl for another four-game series in St. Louis.

By this time even Wrigley was becoming confused and on June 9 announced Tappe would be in charge "for an indefinite period." Tappe, who was Wrigley's favorite, had the longest consecutive run, 85 games, including a 7-7 tie. Lou Klein was "knighted" on September 7, managed five games, and passed the baton back to Tappe for the last 16 games of the season.

The final won-loss tally was Himsl 10-21, Craft 7-9, Tappe 45-57 and Klein 2-3 (a cumulative 64-90). There was no improvement. The Cubs finished seventh, their 15th consecutive season in the second division. The head coaches were in constant competition and juggled the lineup and batting order to their preference. As the season progressed, the effect of the so-called advisory board diminished.

When the season ended, team leaders Ashburn and Zimmer spoke up:

"It was a nutty idea," Ashburn said.

"I can't play under that many bosses," declared Zimmer who asked to be traded.

They never played for the Cubs again.

The chaos continued in 1962, as did the Cubs' lack of success—a 59-103 season, in ninth place (the N.L. had just expanded to 10 teams), 42½ games out of first place, with the most losses and fewest victories in the club's history since 1901. But unlike the previous season when there were eight head-coach changes, there were only three. Tappe opened, went 4-16, and was rescued by Lou Klein, 12-19. Charlie Metro, a grizzled veteran who had been added to the mix, replaced Klein on June 5 and finished the season. He was 43-68.

A disciplinarian, Metro had managed in the minors 15 years in the Detroit organization, winning three pennants, only once finishing out of the first division. He refused to be rotated and told Holland, "I've done my stint in the minors." Metro was fired at the end of the season.

A quarter of a century later, in a 1988 interview, Metro conceded he was constantly feuding with the Tappe camp and revealed an incident typical of the infighting:

"All of the coaches were supposed to get together and decide the lineup. It was the second game of doubleheader. Some of the recommendations were ridiculous. I just put my lineup on the table and said, 'If there are any objections, speak up.' Nobody said anything.

"I go out to the bench and there's another lineup. And it wasn't mine. I tacked up my lineup and threw the other one in

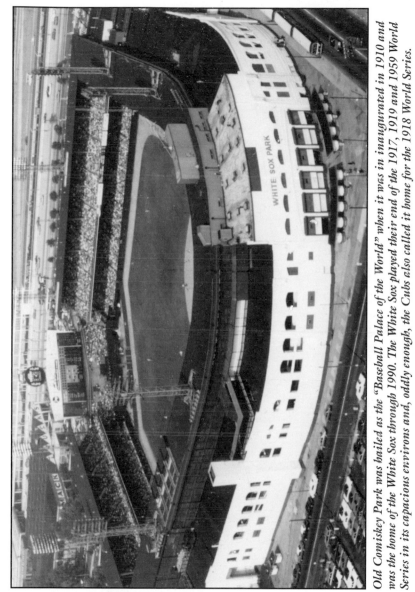

Old Comiskey Park was hailed as the "Baseball Palace of the World" when it was in inaugurated in 1910 and was the home of the White Sox through 1990. The White Sox played their end of the 1917, 1919 and 1959 World Series in its capacious environs and, oddly enough, the Cubs also called it home for the 1918 World Series.

Old Comiskey Park

Photos courtesy of the Chicago White Sox

Sleek, modern Comiskey Park II has housed the White Sox since 1991. It twice hosted the American League Division Series, in 1993 and 2000. Critics deplore the steep upper deck but the park was modified for the 2001 season and further changes are planned.

New Comiskey Park

Charles Comiskey

Charles Comiskey, the "Old Roman," was one of baseball's most celebrated pioneers and a founding father of the American League as well as of the White Sox. Comiskey's reputation suffered as a result of the Black Sox scandal of 1919–1920 which darkened the last decade of his life until his death in 1931.

Jerry Reinsdorf

Jerry Reinsdorf has been the major figure in the ownership of the White Sox since 1981 when he led a group of investors that purchased the franchise from the colorful Bill Veeck and his partners. During Reinsdorf's reign, the White Sox have won three A.L. Division titles (1983, 1993 and 2000) and moved into Comiskey Park II in 1991.

Ron Schueler

Ron Schueler, a former major league pitcher, coach and scout, took over as general manager of the White Sox in 1990. Through trades, free agent signings and farm system development, Schueler assembled the talent that won division titles in 1993 nd 2000. He stepped down after the 2000 season.

Bob Elson

Bob Elson was the laid back voice of the White Sox for almost 40 years until the conclusion of the 1970 season. His broadcasting career began in radio's early days in the 1920s and for a time including Cubs games, World Series and a wide range of celebrity interviews and programs.

Hawk Harrelson

Ken "Hawk"Harrelson, a colorful former major league outfielder, became a White Sox broadcaster in 1982. He served briefly (1985–86) as the team's general manager but the results were mixed and he returned to television broadcasting, teaming up at first with Tom Paciorek and later with Darrin Jackson.

Chuck Connors

Chuck Connors didn't hit much (.239 in 66 games) for the Cubs during his brief stint at first base for them in 1951, but hit it big as the popular star of The Rifleman television show a few years later.

Pants Rowland

Clarence "Pants" Rowland, at first ridiculed as a "Busher," managed the White Sox to their last World Series title in 1917. Rowland later became a Cubs vice president.

Al Lopez

Al Lopez led the White Sox to their last pennant in 1959 during his first tenure as their manager (1957–65). He returned briefly (1968–69) but health problems forced the retirement of one of the most respected baseball men.

Tony La Russa

Tony La Russa managed the "Winning Ugly" team to the A.L Division title in 1983 during his tenure as the team's field boss (1979–86) and went on to even greater success with the Oakland A's and St. Louis Cardinals.

Jerry Manuel

Jerry Manuel, a former backup in-fielder and minor league manager, took over the White Sox in 1998 and directed his players to the A.L. Central Division title in 2000.

Ed Walsh

*Ed Walsh was a pitching mainstay
of the 1906 "Hitless Wonder" White
Sox who upset the highly-favored
Cubs in the World Series. Walsh
beat the Cubs twice. Walsh's greatest
season came with a 40-15 record in
1908.*

Eddie Collins

*Eddie Collins, among the greatest
second basemen and players of all
time, denounced his guilty Black
Sox teammates for throwing the
1919 World Series. A .333 career
hitter, Collins managed the White
Sox for two seasons in the mid-1920s.*

Shoeless Joe Jackson

*Shoeless Joe Jackson batted .375 in
the 1919 World Series but there can
be no doubt of his guilty role in the
Black Sox scandal. Jackson was one
of the greatest hitters of all time with
a .356 lifetime batting average.*

Red Faber

Urban "Red" Faber was a 20-game winner four times during his 20-season (1914–33) career, all with the White Sox. His 254 victories are the second most in team history, surpassed only by Ted Lyons.

Ted Lyons

Ted Lyons won 260 games pitching for mostly poor or mediocre White Sox teams from 1923 through 1946, and also managed the team (1946–48). His most remarkable feat may have come when at the age of 41 he completed every one of his 20 starts in 1942, went 14-6, and led the A.L. with a 2.10 earned run average.

Al Simmons

Al Simmons was among the A.L.'s premier sluggers in the 1920s and 1930s, batting .381 and .390 in successive seasons for the Philadelphia A's to lead the league both times. He batted .331 for the White Sox in 1933 and .344 the following year.

Luke Appling

Luke Appling was known as "Old Aches and Pains" during his 21-season (1930–50) career, all with the White Sox. The Hall of Fame shortstop twice led A.L. in batting (.388 in 1936 and .328 in 1943) and finished with a .310 career average.

Paul Richards

Paul Richards, former Detroit Tigers catcher, twice managed the White Sox, most memorably during the "Go-Go" period of 1951–54 when he brought them to life after decades of stagnation.

Billy Pierce

Billy Pierce was one of the finest left-handers of his day, a 20-game winner for the White Sox in 1956 and 1957. He was the A.L.' starting pitcher in three All-Star Games. Pierce led the league in earned run average with 1.97 in 1955, losing four 1-0 decisions.

Ted Kluszewski

Ted Kluszewski, a powerfully built first baseman, helped propel the White Sox to the pennant in 1959 and hit two home runs in the first game of the World Series against the Los Angeles Dodgers.

Nellie Fox

Nellie Fox reached the zenith of his career at second base as the sparkplug of the White Sox in the pennant winning year of 1959 and won the A.L. Most Valuable Player award.

Minnie Minoso

Minnie Minoso frequently led the White Sox in batting average, home runs, runs batted in and stolen bases to become a fan favorite in the 1950s and 1960s.

Luis Aparicio

Luis Aparicio may have been the greatest fielding shortstop of all time. He was also a pesky hitter and outstanding baserunner, leading the A.L. in stolen bases nine consecutive seasons (1956–64).

Jim Landis

Jim Landis was the prototypical "greyhound" center fielder during his eight seasons (1957–64) with the White Sox. Landis also displayed some power at bat with a high of 22 home runs in 1961 when he batted .283.

Gary Peters

Gary Peters, a 20-game winner for the White Sox in 1964, was among the outstanding left-handed starting pitchers in baseball throughout the 1960s.

Joel Horlen

Joel Horlen as a "hard luck" pitcher for the White Sox, often losing 2-1 or 3-2 because of weak offensive support during the 1960s. But he reached a peak in 1967 with a 19-7 record, a no-hitter and a league-leading earned run average of 2.06.

Dick Allen

Dick Allen spent only three seasons (1972–74) with the White Sox, but made a huge impact. He was called the "savior of the franchise" after the 1972 season in which he batted .308, hit 37 home runs and drove in 113 runs and won the A.L. Most Valuable Player award.

Bill Melton

Bill Melton took over third base in 1968 and remained a White Sox mainstay through the 1975 season. In 1971 he became the first White Sox player ever to lead the league in home runs when he hit 33. He hit the same number the next season.

Carlton Fisk

Carlton Fisk spent half of his long and distinguished career with the Boston Red Sox before solidifying his status as a Hall of Fame catcher with the White Sox from 1981 through 1993.

Frank Thomas

Frank Thomas emerged as one of the game's all-time greatest hitters during the 1990s, winning the A.L. batting title with .347 in 1997 and driving in 100 runs in eight consecutive seasons.

the crapper. Either Ron Santo or Ernie Banks, I don't remember who it was, said, 'Which lineup are we going to use?' And I said, 'The one that's got my name on it.'"

The record books show the no-manager experiment was in force for four seasons, but Wrigley threw in the towel after the second year. Bob Kennedy ran the club without interruption in 1963 and 1964.

Kennedy climbed aboard on February 20, 1963. A week earlier a disillusioned Wrigley told reporters, "We are trying to sign another man and if we get him he'll be our permanent head coach. Or if you fellows wish, you can call him a manager."

Kennedy was dismissed in the middle of the 1965 season, Klein finishing out the campaign. Leo Durocher arrived the next year and made his famous comment, "This isn't an eighth place club." He was right. The Cubs finished 10th.

KLU TO WINNING

The White Sox were in first place, 4½ games in front, but owner Bill Veeck was restless. He didn't want to take any chances and was convinced the club needed a power hitter, a big slugger who could reach the fences.

So he acquired aging Ted Kluszewski from the Pittsburgh Pirates in a waiver deal. When Klu reported on August 25, Barnum Bill was delighted. "We have so many little guys," Veeck said. "At least we now have someone big enough to scare somebody."

Kluszewski, who had been an All–Big Ten fullback at Indiana, was in his 13th major league season and had awesome credentials: Five seasons, 100 or more runs batted in and four, 40 or more home runs. In 1954 he led the N.L. with 49 home runs and 141 RBI.

And for those days he was big—6-feet-2 and 240 pounds. His uniform blouse didn't have sleeves. To display his huge biceps the sleeves were snipped to the top of the shoulder. He was the Samson of the baseball world.

But once he joined the White Sox he was shorn of his power. His first 14 hits were singles. Klu joked about it later, "I was just trying to be one of the guys."

It was 1959, the year of Chicago's last pennant. The Sox were a throwback to the 1906 Hitless Wonders. They had a pitch-and-putt attack and were last in the A.L. in home runs with 97, but lapped the league in stolen bases with 113 and 35-15 in one-run games. There was a stretch of 70 innings, the equivalent of eight games, without two extra base hits in the same inning. On April 22 they routed Kansas City 20-6 wih an 11-run rally on 10 walks, three errors, a hit batsman and a lonesome hit, a single by Johnny Callison.

They held an edge over every club in the league except Baltimore, which also relied on pitching and defense—teams as identical as two peas in a pod. They tied the Orioles 11-11 on the season. There were six extra-inning games—one 18-inning marathon, two 17s, one 16 and two 10s.

Al Lopez, then in his third season as White Sox manager, seldom expressed dismay over the club's lack of power. Unlike Veeck, Lopez believed pitching, defense and speed are the ingredients essential for victory. Especially speed, the only weapon that comes into play both on offense and defense. Lopez was right. He guided the Sox to their first pennant in 40 years.

The defense, particularly up the middle, was spectacular. Looie Aparicio, brilliant in the field, was at short, Nellie Fox at second, and Jim Landis in center field. More than likely, Aparicio was the best shortstop in the 20th Century. So claimed Donie Bush, an ancient baseball lifer and former White Sox manager who was among Ty Cobb's teammates.

Aparicio was 5-feet-8, Fox 5-feet-6. A typical rally: Aparicio led off with a single. Fox, who batted second, had outstanding bat control. He would take a pitch or two, allowing Aparicio to steal second. Then Fox would advance him to third with a bunt or a grounder to the right side. Jim Landis or Sherm Lollar would bring Looie across with a sacrifice fly.

Aparicio, who led the league in stolen bases in his first nine seasons (1956–64), tied Wally Moses' club record with 56 and could have had 80, maybe 100, if he ran when there was no need. Landis had 20 steals but was faster than Aparicio going from first to third. Landis took a bigger lead and drew more pickoff throws; he took two bases seven times on wild throws. Once in Boston, he scored from first on a single to Red Sox right fielder Jackie Jensen who had a strong arm.

Burly Early Wynn, Bob Shaw, Dick Donovan and Billy Pierce were the rotation starters, supported by relievers Gerry Staley and Turk Lown who, together, had 17 victories and 29 saves. Wynn led the staff with 22 wins, Shaw, a rookie, was next with 18.

Big Klu had been hitting for an average—.350, 14-for-40, with two RBI—when he regained his power in a Comiskey Park Labor Day doubleheader sweep against the Kansas City Athletics. He connected for a pair of three-run home runs, one in each game. Even then, he had to share batting honors. Landis had six line drive hits to center; two singles, two doubles and two triples.

Three days later, on September 10, the White Sox were in Washington for a series with the Senators. Vice President Richard Nixon, a genuine baseball fan (whose original ambition, he said, was to be a sportswriter) invited the club to a luncheon. Coach Don Gutteridge shepherded seven players, including Pierce, to the Capitol Building.

Nixon praised the players, telling them, "You certainly have captured everyone's fancy around the country and everyone seems pleased that you have put the Yankees in their place. It isn't that people are against the Yankees," Nixon added, laughing, "But it's just like politics. They've been in power too long."

Asked if he thought the Sox would finish ahead of Cleveland, Nixon replied, "That's one controversial issue I must stay out of."

The Sox, never lower than second, were two games behind the Indians at the All-Star game break and went into first place to stay on July 28. They never led by more than 6½ games and clinched on September 22 with a 4-2 win at Cleveland. The Indians had 70 more home runs than the Sox during the regular season and out-hit them in this game 11-9 but all their hits were singles.

Often ridiculed for their lack of power, on this night it was the White Sox who played long-ball. Al Smith and Jungle Jim

Rivera broke a 2-2 tie with consecutive sixth-inning home runs off Mudcat Grant who took the loss. Wynn, who made the start and was relieved in the sixth, got the win.

Bullpen star Staley was the pitching hero. He inherited a perilous situation, one out with the bases loaded in the ninth. He sealed the victory with one pitch, a sinker low and away. Vic Power grounded to Aparicio who stepped on second and threw to first baseman Kluszewski for a game-ending double play.

The Sox finished five games ahead of Cleveland and, better yet, 15 ahead of the third-place Yankees who had won the four previous pennants. The Sox were 13-9 against the Bronx Bombers who were held to a cumulative .243 batting average. It was a pleasure, the first time in 34 years, when Babe Ruth had his famous stomachache in 1925, that the Yankees had lost a season series to the Sox.

The Sox swept the board in the Most Valuable Player voting. Fox finished first, Aparicio was second and Wynn third, an achievement matched only by the 1941 Brooklyn Dodgers. Landis was seventh and catcher Lollar, who led the club with 22 home runs and 84 RBI, was ninth. Five players from the same team were in the top 10, a rare testimonial to team play.

Fox led the club in batting with a .306 average and, though 78 percent of his hits were singles, he also led in total bases. In addition, he topped the league with fewest strikeouts (13). Other league leaders were Shaw in wining percentage (18-6 for .750) and the 39-year-old Wynn in victories (22-11) and innings pitched (255). The Sox also had a club record home gate of 1,423,144.

They played the Los Angeles Dodgers in the World Series and opened with a bang, an 11-0 first game victory at Comiskey Park that tied the Series record for the most one-sided shutout. Kluszewski led the assault with a first-inning RBI single and a pair of three-run home runs, in the third and fourth innings.

Charlie Neal, the Dodgers' 160-pound second baseman, responded with two home runs in the second game. Chuck Essegian also hit a pinch home run in the Dodgers' 4-3 victory.

The Sox rallied for a run in the eighth on Al Smith's double off the left field wall. Earl Torgeson, on at second, scored easily but the slow-footed Lollar, who was the tying run, tried to come in from first and was thrown out at the plate, Smitty taking third. There was only one out but Billy Goodman fanned and Rivera fouled out.

Another record crowd of 92,650 witnessed the fourth game. Again the Dodgers won by one run, 5-4, widening their Series lead to three wins against one loss. Roger Craig got the victory and was the beneficiary of four third-inning runs. The Sox rallied for a 4-4 tie on Lollar's three-run, seventh-inning home run but the Dodgers regained the lead in the eighth on Gil Hodges' home run.

The Sox stayed alive and won the fifth game, 1-0. Lopez used three pitchers, the most ever in a Series shutout. Shaw worked $7\frac{1}{3}$ innings, was relieved by Billy Pierce who gave way to Donovan. Pierce faced only one batter who, with first base open, was given an intentional pass. Donovan finished with $1\frac{2}{3}$ hitless innings. The Sox scored the only run in the fourth. Fox singled, went to third on Landis' single and came across when Lollar grounded into a double play.

The Series returned to Chicago for the sixth and final game. The Dodgers won cruising, 9-3. They led 8-0 in the fourth when they bombed Wynn and Donovan for six runs. Sherry relieved Johnny Podres in the bottom of the fourth and worked $5\frac{2}{3}$ scoreless innings, becoming the first pitcher to participate in all of his club's four Series victories—two wins and two saves.

Kluszewski and Hodges, the rival first basemen, led the hitters with identical .391 averages. Fox was next with .375. Klu drove in 10 runs, a record for a six-game series, and tied Ruth's record with three home runs in a six-game set. It was the last Series appearance for a Chicago team in the 20th Century.

It was a brief honeymoon. Veeck, still searching for power, in the off-season acquired Roy Sievers from Washington for catcher Earl Battey and first baseman Don Mincher. Outfielder Callison was dealt to the Philadelphia Phillies for third baseman Gene

Freese and catcher John Romano and first baseman Norm Cash went to Cleveland to retrieve Minnie Minoso.

The result: The White Sox raised the team batting average to .270 in 1960 from .250 the year before, hit 112 home runs compared to 97 and finished third, 10 games out.

ILL-
STARRED
ALL-STARS

Philip K. Wrigley's capacity for astounding Cub fans and the baseball world in general with unexpected moves was inexhaustible. A few weeks after the deplorable 1965 season ended under Lou Klein with a 72-90 record, the Cub owner hired fiery, unpredictable, irascible and often disagreeable Leo Durocher.

Durocher's self-made "job description" tossed the final lingering vestiges of Wrigley's futile College of Coaches scheme into the dumpster.

"If no announcement has been made of what my title is, I'm making it here and now," Durocher declared. "I'm the manager. I'm not a head coach. You can't have two or three coaches running a ball club. One man has to be in complete authority. There can be only one boss."

No one could envision Durocher, 60, and a 40-year veteran as player, coach and manager, as Wrigley's kind of man. The genteel if candid owner stepped completely out of character in hiring "Leo the Lip," a hustler with a record of antagonizing almost everyone who dealt with him—players, umpires, rival managers, general managers, owners and the media. But Durocher was a proven winner, having led three teams to pennants, and one of them, the New York Giants, to the 1954 World Series title.

Wrigley said he hired Durocher because he was tired of losing. The financial drain—and by 1965 it was considerable—didn't bother him. He often said he didn't care whether the Cubs made money or not. But the seemingly endless parade of non-contending seasons was irritating and humiliating.

"Losses at the gate don't worry me," he explained, "but losses on the field do, and that's why we got Durocher. I felt that the team just wasn't putting out.... I decided that what we needed was somebody with the drive, the toughness and the leadership of Durocher to get their best out of them. Somebody to wake them up."

"Wake them up" the authoritative, combative, outspoken, yet often deceptively charming Durocher certainly did. Not only did he arouse Cub players but also the fans during his almost seven-season run as field boss and virtual general manager. While Holland faded submissively into the background, Wrigley let Durocher make the final decisions on all trades and roster moves. The result was one of the most exciting Cub teams in history, perhaps the best that never won a pennant though it came heartachingly close two or three times, most memorably and excruciatingly in 1969.

First, however, Durocher had to swallow one of his early declarations about the Cubs: "This is definitely not an eighth place ball club." It wasn't in 1966, starting out by losing eight of the first nine games and eventually plunging to 10th place with 59-103 to tie the team's 1962 record for worst ever. It was the Cubs' 20th consecutive season of failing to finish in the top half.

Nonetheless, though Durocher mumbled he would "back up the truck," progress was made. A trade brought two rookies, catcher Randy Hundley and pitcher Bill Hands, from the San Francisco Giants. Two more youngsters, pitcher Ferguson Jenkins and outfielder Adolfo Phillips, arrived from the Philadelphia Phillies. While Phillips was only a "shooting star," Hundley, Hands and Jenkins were to become standouts. Rookie left-handed pitcher Ken Holtzman, signed out of the University of Illinois, also was a future star though his first year record was 11-16.

Indicative of how bad things were in 1966, Holtzman had the best record on the staff, with Dick Ellsworth's 8-22 the most painful and Hands finishing 8-13. Jenkins was 6-8, mostly in relief, but Durocher in an inspired move gave him his first start on September 6. He beat the Los Angeles Dodgers 2-0, with ninth inning help, and *Chicago Sun-Times* writer Edgar Munzel accurately proclaimed, "A star was born..."

Center fielder Phillips hit .262 with 16 home runs but stole 32 bases. Second baseman Glenn Beckert "arrived" by batting .287 and combining with rookie shortstop Don Kessinger (.274) to give the Cubs outstanding mid-infield play. Ron Santo overcame a fractured cheekbone to pace the team at .312 while producing 30 home runs and 94 RBI. Billy Williams hit .276 with 29 home runs and 100 RBI. Hundley's chief distinction, in addition to 19 home runs, was catching 149 games, including 31 in a row as Durocher's confidence in his handling of pitchers became absolute.

Durocher's spirited leadership brought tangible results in 1967 with "CUB POWER" becoming a rallying cry among fans as the team finished third, out of the bottom half of the league for the first time in 21 years and at 87-74 with its best record since the pennant season of 1945. During one stretch, from mid-June into early July, the Cubs won 17 of 19 games to surge into first place, if only briefly.

Phillips was Durocher's darling, if briefly, winning a game with a steal of home, then going wild on June 11 with six hits, four of them homers, eight RBI, and two spectacular catches in a doubleheader sweep of the New York Mets. It was Phillips' apotheosis. His average slid later in the season as pitchers "worked inside" on him and his tendency to bail out cost him Durocher's respect. Yet he finished with .268, 17 home runs, 68 RBI and again led the team with 24 stolen bases.

While the fans responded to Phillips' heroics with chants of "Ole! Adolfo! Ole!" better-grounded performances came from Santo (.300, 31 home runs, 107 RBI), Williams (.278, 28 home runs, 92 RBI) and a revived Banks (.276, 23 home runs, 95 RBI), now 36. Jealousy of Banks' popularity nevertheless dismayed Durocher, who scathingly referred to him as "Mr. Cub, my ass," and insisted his increasing immobility was detrimental. Banks had lost much of his speed and never took more than a minimal lead when on base. Durocher further embarrassed him by telling him in front of his teammates he would give him $100 each time he was picked off.

Durocher's attitude toward Banks approached the absurd. After the first game of a doubleheader in Philadelphia in which Banks hit two home runs and drove in five runs a reporter sought Durocher's comment and was told, "Beckert had a helluva game." Perhaps because the second baseman's playing style resembled his own, Beckert was Durocher's favorite player.

Not that Durocher didn't have other favorites, temporarily cozying up to whoever was playing well, then discarding him in a downturn. A sure sign of esteem was the manager's invitation to play gin rummy on airplane flights or in the clubhouse. Among those "honored' were Phillips, Holtzman and Santo but all eventually lost favor. If Durocher warmed up to them again, they were astute enough to see through his "game" and rejected further invitations.

The most important development of 1967 as a pivotal season was in the pitching. Jenkins went 20-13 in the first of his six consecutive 20-victory years and broke the team's 59-year-old strikeout record with 236. Holtzman, his season often interrupted by military service, went 9-0. Hands both as a starter and in relief was only 7-8, but two rookies, Rich Nye (13-10) and Joe Niekro (10-7) were highly effective.

Banks' slogan for 1968 was "Don't Fear, This Is the Year!" but he was wrong. The Cubs never won more than five successive games, and despite leading the league in home runs with 130, contrived to go scoreless for 48 consecutive innings to tie a major league record for futility. Yet they finished third with an 84-78 record, helped greatly by reliever Phil Regan's 10 victories and 25 saves after he was acquired on April 24.

Among the highlights of the season were Beckert's 27-game hitting streak (he batted .294), a team-leading 32 home runs by

Banks, and continued punch from Santo (26 home runs, 98 RBI and Williams (30 home runs, 91 RBI). Jenkins (20-15) became the first Cub pitcher since Lon Warneke in 1934–35 with back-to-back 20-game seasons despite losing five games 1-0 and again set a strikeout record with 260. Hands (16-10), Niekro (14-10) and Holtzman (11-14) completed the rotation.

The fans were paying attention. Attendance in 1968 surpassed a million for the first time since 1952 at 1,043,409, and Durocher was riding high, wide and confident for 1969.

"The Cubs now are ready to go for all the marbles," he proclaimed. "We have sound hitting, the best defense in the league, and pitching that is constantly improving."

Even after a fractured hand sidelined center fielder Phillips in spring training—in any case, Durocher had lost faith in him—the Cubs for the first time in decades were looked on as genuine title contenders. (Each major league split into two divisions in 1969 with the Cubs in the East.)

Pitching ace Jenkins was among the few who had at least slight reservations: "The Cubs are two players away from being a pennant winner. All we need is another good outfielder and a starting pitcher who can win about 15 games."

Durocher thought he had the "good outfielder" in rookie Don Young, who started in center field in place of the injured Phillips. The need for another starting pitcher was addressed in a late April deal that sent Niekro to the San Diego Padres for Dick Selma.

By that time the Cubs were on their way, to echo the theme song of one of the most exciting seasons in team history, "Hey, Hey, Holy Mackerel! No Doubt About It. The Cubs Are on the Way."

A spectacular Opening Day victory over the Phillies was a happy omen. Banks hit two home runs and drove in five runs and pinch hitter Willie Smith's two-run homer in the bottom of the 11th drove 40,796 fans wild as they left Wrigley Field. The Cubs were "for real." They won 11 of their first 12 games, were 15-6 in April, won 16 more games in May, and began to pull away from their division rivals.

At this point no one could have suspected it was to be the year of the Great Flop, the most disappointing season in Cub annals.

The Cubs held first place for 155 days without interruption, had the N.L. All-Star game starting infield of Banks, Beckert, Kessinger and Santo, as well as catcher Hundley. They also had a pair of 20-game winners in Jenkins (21-15) and Hands (20-14) and a long ball triumvirate in Banks, Williams and Santo. Combined, the three batted .279 with an average of 24 home runs and 108 RBI, Santo leading the team in the latter category with 123.

The Cubs broke the Chicago attendance record with 1,674,993, surpassing the 1,644,460 drawn by the White Sox in 1960, the year after they won the A.L. pennant. The Cub players were lionized daily by a deluge of newspaper and broadcast publicity, and were in constant demand for personal appearances and testimonials. But at the bitter finish there was no doubt the '69 Cubs were among the storied failures in diamond history.

At the agonizing end they staggered home in second place in the East Division, eight games behind New York's "Miracle Mets," who mauled them head-to-head and won 38 of their last 49 games. "I never saw anything like it," Durocher lamented as his team slid. "Our offense went down the toilet, the defense went down the drain, and I'm still looking for a pitching staff."

While riding high, the players were certain of success and agreed to divide the spoils. Jack Childers, a Chicago business agent, had free run of the clubhouse and was constantly returning with endorsement deals. Player representative Regan revealed in May that $30,000 was already in the till, in a special bank account, to be divided equally, similar to World Series shares. Prior to the collapse, the pot had grown to $125,000.

Failure seemed out of the question when things were going as well as they did from May 11 to 13 when Holtzman, Jenkins and Selma pitched consecutive shutouts, 8-0 over the Giants, and 2-0 and 19-0 against the Padres. The following week the Cubs launched an eight-game winning streak. They were 21 over .500 with an 8½ game lead after sweeping a June 15 doubleheader from Cincinnati.

With Young playing well in center field, Durocher sought to shore up the bench and at the same time dispose of Phillips. He complained he hadn't been able "to wake him up" in three years. The Cubs got utility infielder Paul Popovich from the Montreal Expos in exchange for Phillips and pitcher Jack Lamabe on June 11. Durocher's public criticism of Phillips, who was popular with his teammates, might have been the first chink in the team's armor.

What happened in late June was even more disturbing to the players. In the third inning of a game with the Los Angeles Dodgers on June 26, Durocher complained of a stomach ache and left the club. But instead of going to his hotel he boarded a chartered plane and went to see his stepson at Camp Ojibwa in Eagle River, Wisconsin, 400 miles away. When he returned three days later, his "secret mission" was discovered. Wrigley was among the severe critics of Durocher's "desertion" of the team.

"The players have been showing wonderful spirit," Wrigley said. "Leo owes them an apology."

More dissension followed. On July 8 against the Mets in Shea Stadium, center fielder Young misplayed two ninth-inning fly balls, both falling for doubles, which led to a 4-3 defeat. Durocher and Santo mercilessly berated Young. "He had a bad day at the plate," Santo said, "so he's got his head down. He's worried about his batting average, not the team." The next day, however, the always emotional Santo called a press conference to say he was sorry, that he didn't mean to jump on Young.

When play began on August 14 the Cubs still had a commanding lead, 8½ games ahead of the second-place Cardinals, 9½ ahead of the Mets. Holtzman added to the general confidence by pitching a no-hitter against the Atlanta Braves on August 19, and the Cubs ended the month with four straight victories.

There seemed no reason for great concern going into September but the Cubs began to stumble. A 5½-game lead on September 2 shrank to 2½ by the time they opened a two-game series with the Mets in New York six days later. But a split would protect that edge.

It wasn't to be. The pivotal game was the opener, a 3-2 loss in Shea Stadium. Tommie Agee, who had hit a two-run home run in the third inning, scored the winning run from second on a single to right in the sixth. The throw came in on one bounce. A quarter of a century later Hundley was still insisting, "I made the bloomin' tag."

The Mets won again the next night, 7-1 behind their ace, Tom Seaver, to trim the Cub lead to a half game, then took over first place with a doubleheader sweep against Montreal on September 10 and led the rest of the way. During one stretch, they won 20 of 25 games. The Cubs finally ended an eight-game losing streak on September 12, but by season's end were 92-70 while the Mets finished 100-62.

The Cub players were crushed, forever fated to bear the scars of their frustrating experience, though they could always point out that the Mets were a good team which went on to beat Atlanta in the playoff for the N.L. pennant and stun the Baltimore Orioles in a World Series upset.

Santo admitted, "Those three weeks were a nightmare."

Some critics blamed Durocher for the failure, suggesting he had not given his regulars enough rest, that he had tired them out. All the same, Hundley, who was obviously worn down from catching a record 160 games at Durocher's insistence in 1968 and 151 in 1969, many years later said he was proud of the 1969 team. He avoided recrimination.

"To me, that '69 team was made up of guys who gave it every stinking thing they had," Hundley said. "And I think we can all be comfortable with that. We did everything we could. It didn't work out, but when you fill that bucket up and you put one more drop in it, and it overflows, that's 100 percent. That's not 110. It's a 100 percent, and I feel that's what the Sam Hill we gave them."

Wrigley's reaction was typically low-keyed and analytical:

"I think all the TV appearances, the speaking engagements, the columns the players wrote in the newspapers, the recording sessions, the autograph signing parties, and other activities took the players' minds off the game. They're all young and our

Chicago players aren't used to being celebrities. They didn't know how to handle it. They got overconfident, and that had a lot to do with the way they played.

"Naturally, I'm disappointed, but after so many years of disappointment, I'm used to it."

A Chicago psychiatrist offered the final word on the cause of the team's failure, and it was certainly unorthodox. The reason the Cubs lost, said Dr. Harvey Mandel, was they had "an unconscious desire to lose the pennant."

Nevertheless, they seemed very eager to redeem themselves in 1970 when they made another stab at the prize. Trades before and during the season brought veteran reinforcements, among them outfielder Johnny Callison, first baseman Joe Pepitone, starting pitcher Milt Pappas and reliever Hoyt Wilhelm, but all for naught.

As they had in 1969, they started out fast, with an 11-game winning streak in April catapulting them into first place. But a doubleheader loss to the Mets in early June dropped them to second and they never led again, finishing second with a 84-78 record five games behind the triumphant Pittsburgh Pirates.

There was no shortage of individual achievements on this ill-fated team of all-stars. Though Durocher finally got his way, relegating Banks, now 39, to part-time duty, the veteran still had a spark left, and on May 12, 1970, hit the 500th home run of his career off Pat Jarvis of the Braves. He finished the season with 12 home runs.

Banks' first base replacement, Jim Hickman, erupted with a career season, batting .315 with 32 home runs and 115 RBI. Williams hit .322 with 42 home runs and 129 RBI and Santo contributed 26 home runs and 114 RBI, to make the Cubs the only N.L. team with three sluggers with more than 25 home runs and 100 RBI.

Jenkins (21-15), Hands (18-15) and Holtzman (17-11) also made the Cubs the only team to have three pitchers with 15 or more wins. It was probably the bullpen failure that doomed them, with Regan slipping and Durocher unable to find a reliable replacement.

The most memorable events of the season were Banks' 500th home run, the end of a 1,117 consecutive game playing streak by Williams, a plea by Santo not to break up the team by trades, and increasingly vituperative criticism by Durocher of the media and players. Wrigley's reaction was to extend Durocher's contract, and permit him to hire an old friend, former major league manager Herman Franks, as a coach.

Wrigley's realistic comment about complaints of Durocher's hostility and verbiage: "Well, Mr. Durocher is Mr. Durocher. This is like the cigarette commercial: what do you want, a good manager or good taste?"

Wrigley's loyalty to Durocher, or stubbornness, was demonstrated even more forcefully in 1971, another trying season, the Cubs finishing in a third-place tie with an 85-79 record after occasional stabs at first place.

A player rebellion on August 23 was touched off by Durocher's criticism of Pappas' failure to "waste" a pitch on a 0-2 count. After first baseman Pepitone came to Pappas' defense, Durocher turned on Santo, accusing him of malingering and front-office politics, saying, "Ron, the only reason we're having a 'Ron Santo Day' is because Billy (Williams) and Ernie (Banks) had one and *you* asked John Holland for one." Santo had to be restrained from attacking Durocher. Player discontent festered.

In the aftermath of the incident, Wrigley took out paid advertisements again in the major newspapers. The sixth and final paragraph: "Leo is the team manager and the 'Dump Durocher Clique' might as well give up. He is running the team, and if some of the players don't like it and lie down on the job, during the off-season we will see what we can do to find them happier homes."

If the player revolt was the most notable event of the season, the next was surely the retirement of Banks after his 19th campaign. He hit his final home run, No. 512, on August 24 against Cincinnati's Jim McGlothlin to tie Eddie Mathews on the all-time list.

Second baseman Beckert, a career .283 hitter, had an exceptional season, batting .342 to lead the club. Williams batted .301

and led with 28 home runs and 93 RBI. Jenkins led the league in wins at 24-13, complete games (30) and 325 innings. It was his fifth consecutive 20-win season. Pappas was 17-13 and Hands 12-18, but Holtzman slipped to 9-15 although he pitched the second no-hitter of his career on June 3 against Cincinnati. The relief corps, with only 13 saves, was the Achilles' heel.

Despite Wrigley's threat to exile players, the only major figure to depart was Holtzman, who went to the Oakland A's after the season for center fielder Rick Monday. In another deal, the Cubs obtained outfielder Jose Cardenal for 1972, and Durocher filled out the rotation with a couple of promising rookies, Rick Reuschel and Burt Hooton.

By mid-season it was clear that the holdover players and Durocher hadn't kissed and made up. While the team lingered around .500, it lacked verve and obviously wasn't going anywhere.

On July 24, 1972, Wrigley joined the "Dump Durocher Clique" by dismissing the manager with the team's record 46-44. A few days later the owner explained that the change was made because of "friction between Leo and the players…and the team as a whole had not been playing up to its full potential."

During Durocher's six and a half seasons as manager the Cubs had a record of 535-526, a .504 percentage. Other than his first year when they plummeted to 10th place in 1966, they were never lower than third, including two second-place finishes. A month after he left the Cubs, he became manager of the Houston Astros.

Durocher was succeeded by Whitey Lockman, 46, who played for him when he managed the Giants. It was Lockman whose double prolonged the Giants' rally that was climaxed by Bobby Thomson's heroic home run in the 1951 playoff game against Brooklyn. Lockman batted ahead of Thomson in the order. Had he grounded into a double play to end the game, Thomson would not have come to bat.

When Durocher arrived in Chicago for the 1966 season, Lockman was managing the Cubs' farm team in the Texas League. Durocher then installed Lockman as his third base coach but as the season progressed became aware that many of the players were going to Lockman for advice. This didn't sit well with Durocher and the next season Lockman was returned to the minor leagues to manage the Cubs' Tacoma (Wash.) club in the Triple A Pacific Coast League. Lockman later served as the Cubs' vice president in charge of player development.

Under Lockman, the Cubs played at a .600 pace the rest of the 1972 season, winning 39 games and losing 26. They finished second, 11 games out with an 85-70 record, and had responded to Lockman's congenial personality, much more relaxed than that of Durocher.

Jenkins and Williams again were standouts. With a 20-12 record Jenkins became the fourth pitcher since 1920 with six consecutive 20-victory seasons, the others being Lefty Grove, Warren Spahn and Robin Roberts. Williams came close to winning the Triple Crown. He led the league with a .333 average, but was second to Cincinnati's Johnny Bench in home runs, 40 to 37, and RBI, 125 to 122.

Among the starting pitchers, Pappas was second to Jenkins with a 17-7 record and on September 9 came within an out of a perfect game against San Diego. He walked the 27th batter, but completed a no-hitter. Hooton also pitched a no-hitter, against the Phillies on April 16 in his fourth major league start, and at 11-14 had a respectable rookie season as did Reuschel with 10-8.

With Durocher gone, and the more cordial Lockman in place, the Cubs appeared poised for a new thrust in 1973 even if many of the key players were aging. Williams voiced the general feeling.

"It is now or never for us," Williams admitted. "We've got an old club. There's no tomorrow for us. We have to win today."

But there was to be neither "tomorrow" nor "today" in the sense of a redeeming pennant-winning season for the Cub veterans of the 1969 collapse, the ill-fated all stars whose era for all practical purposes ended in 1972.

THE IRON CATCHER

In 1968, Randy Hundley, the Cubs' "iron man" catcher, set the major league record for most games caught in one season with 160. And, as often happens, there is a story behind the story.

When Hundley was eight years old and playing Little League, he told his father, "Dad, I don't like shortstop. There isn't enough action."

Randy's father Cecil had been a semipro catcher in and around the family home in Martinsville, Virginia. Recalled Randy many years later, "His hand was messed, mangled, from all those bloomin' foul tips."

"C'mon, I'll show you where the action is," Cecil said to his son.

And as they walked into the backyard, the father pointed his finger between Randy's eyes and told him, "I'm going to teach you to be a catcher. But you're going to be a one-handed catcher. And if I ever see you catching two-handed, I'm going to take you out of the game."

"He never took me out because I never forgot," Randy said. "Even when I got to the big leagues and was on national television I knew my father was watching. I worried about getting my bare hand too close to where I was catching the ball."

From the beginning of his professional career in 1960, Hundley encountered opposition. Catchers caught with two hands, not one. Hundley prevailed. He explained to his managers and coaches that by keeping his bare (throwing) hand behind his back he was minimizing the risk of injury and increasing his value because he wasn't as likely to be on the shelf with a broken finger.

When the bases were empty, he kept his bare hand behind his back where it was protected from foul tips. With men on, he brought the bare hand forward near the glove to present a target but the instant the pitch was thrown the hand was withdrawn and positioned adjacent to the right shoulder, a foot or more away from where the pitch was received.

Though the bare hand is exposed, there is almost no risk of injury. This is because a foul tip comes off the top or bottom of the bat. Off the bottom, it drops down. Off the top, it bends neither to the right nor left but always comes straight back.

There is still another advantage. By keeping the bare hand away from the pitch, there is less likelihood of being hit by the pitched ball. Previously, many injuries were caused when the catcher was too quick covering the ball with the bare hand. When this happens, the pitch nicks the bare hand before it hits the glove.

Or to put it another way: The old-timers moved their throwing hand into the mitt. Hundley reversed the procedure. He moved the mitt into the bare hand to load it. The disadvantage: The one-handed catcher usually snares the ball instead of catching it.

Soon, other catchers began adopting Hundley's style. Foremost among them was Johnny Bench, the Cincinnati Reds' Hall of Famer. Probably, because of Bench's prominence, he is sometimes credited with being the first one-handed catcher.

Bench's conversion came after he was struck on the thumb by a foul tip on September 29, 1967, in a game against the Cubs. Because of a quirk in the schedule, the Reds in 1967 played the Cubs in six of their final seven games. It was then that Bench saw Hundley for the first time. When Bench returned for the '68 season, he was catching one-handed, with a slight variation. He kept his hand behind his right leg.

Hundley had a 14-year major league career, which included eight seasons with the Cubs. In three of those seasons he caught more than 150 games. When he retired he had the hands of a pianist. Never as much as a fractured finger. He had only one hand injury, a broken right thumb on a tag play at the plate.

Randy's son Todd has since also become an All-Star catcher. A one-handed catcher, of course.

ROLLER-COASTER WHITE SOX

17

The alliance of Eddie Stanky and the White Sox was brief, tempestuous and while it featured a burst of near-glory it signaled the approach of another lengthy period of frustration. During 17 roller-coaster seasons from 1966 through 1982 the White Sox more than once nearly left Chicago, changed ownership three times, managers often, and entirely avoided post-season competition.

When owner Arthur Allyn and general manager Ed Short chose Stanky to replace the ailing Al Lopez after the 1965 season, it was a stunning reversal of managerial styles and personalities. The successor to the gentlemanly and calm, if tough, Lopez was nicknamed "The Brat" for his fractious playing style as an infielder. His belligerent style earned him the admiration of Leo Durocher who in late 1965 coincidentally became the Cub manager. Stanky had played second base on Durocher's pennant-winning 1951 New York Giants.

Durocher once said of Stanky: "He can't hit, can't run, can't field. He's no nice guy, but all the SOB can do is win." Rudy Schaefer, a long-time White Sox executive, characterized Stanky as "a pup out of Durocher," though the latter was far more sophisticated in dealing with people.

Stanky was actually a nice guy off the field, but a driven, obsessive terror on it, always to the opposition, often to the umpires, frequently to the media, and sometimes to his own players. For a time his abrasive, confrontational approach produced results for the Sox. His 1966 team was last in the league in hitting but made the most of speed and pitching to finish fourth with an 83-79 record.

The White Sox stole 153 bases, their most since 1943, with second baseman Don Buford leading the pack with 51. Next with 44 was center fielder Tommie Agee, who won the A.L. Rookie of the Year award with an impressive debut, leading the team in batting at .273 and with 22 home runs and 86 RBI. Tommy John (14-11), Gary Peters (12-10 and a league-leading 1.98 earned run average) and Joel Horlen (10-13) were the key men on a sound pitching staff.

A ceaseless stream of temperamental outbursts by Stanky may have been the highlight of the '66 season. The most absurd was a "striptease" in which he tore off his uniform and scattered it around his office upon being annoyed by a sportswriter's question. He went out of his way to offend fellow managers, most notably Charlie Dressen of the Detroit Tigers whom he called "bush." He openly ordered his pitchers to throw at opposing batters and proudly labeled himself as "the retaliation manager."

Stanky's frenetic managerial career reached its pinnacle in 1967 when a team that batted only .225 almost matched the achievements of the "Hitless Wonders" of 1906 who batted five points higher. With a lineup in which the top batters, Buford and center fielder Ken Berry, reached only .241, and third baseman Pete Ward led in home runs with merely 18 and RBI with 62, the White Sox stayed in the pennant race to the last day of the season, losing out to the "Impossible Dream" Boston Red Sox.

With five games left, the Sox held first place statistically but lost a doubleheader on September 27 to the puny A's in Kansas City, then dropped the next three games to finish the season with a five-game losing streak and in fourth place at 89-73.

Even Stanky called his over-achievers the "dullest ball club he had ever seen," but it overcame controversy and managerial harassment largely because of superlative pitching, both starting and relief. Ace of the staff Horlen (19-7), Peters (16-11) and John (10-13), and relievers Hoyt Wilhelm (8-3, 12 saves) and Bob Locker (7-5, 20 saves) kept the team in contention.

It's indicative of the antipathy Stanky aroused that when the White Sox lost the first nine games of the 1968 season, Casey Stengel, now retired from baseball, was quick to point out to a reporter: "It's not a nine-game losing streak, it's a 14-game losing streak." The Sox also lost the next game so if Stengel had waited another day he could have spoken of a 15-game losing streak. While managing the New York Mets in the early 1960s, Stengel had clashed with Stanky and revenged himself by combining the sad finish of '67 with the futile start of '68.

Short tried to build on the near-success of 1967 with a series of trades which were counter-productive, other than one that regained shortstop Luis Aparicio from Baltimore. Among those sent away were Agee and infielder Al Weis, who were to become pivotal for the "Miracle Mets" of 1969.

The 10-game opening dive condemned both the White Sox and Stanky, the former to their first sub-.500 and second division finish since 1950, the latter to a suggested resignation on July 12. Even more alarming, with attendance falling off and attempts to secure a new stadium failing, Arthur Allyn shifted nine "home games" to Milwaukee, abandoned by the Braves, as a test-run for a possible move.

"Stanky nearly took the South Side franchise down the drain with him," commented columnist Brent Musburger, later a noted television sportscaster, in the *Chicago American* after the manager quit.

In an attempt to regain footing, Allyn and Short turned to Lopez. But less than two weeks after Lopez, the new and former manager, replaced Stanky he underwent an emergency appendectomy and was sidelined a month. Neither coach Les Moss, who filled in during the interval, nor Lopez, after he recovered, could save a season in which the Sox finished 67-95 and tied for eighth place.

Among the few positive aspects of 1968 were the continued brilliant play of Aparicio, the emergence of right-handed reliever Wilbur Wood (13-12, 16 saves), who appeared in a major league record 88 games, and the promise shown by rookie third baseman Bill Melton. Injuries hampered the "Big Three" starters Horlen (12-14), John (10-5) and Peters (4-12).

The next season was horrendous for the Sox, who again played part of their schedule, this time 11 games, as the home team in Milwaukee's County Stadium. Attendance fell to a 25-year low of 589,546, the 70 games in Comiskey Park drawing only 392,862, the situation exacerbated by the Cubs' exciting, if futile, bid for a division title.

Renewed health problems forced Lopez to retire for good on May 3, 1969. First base coach Don Gutteridge took over as the Sox finished fifth with a 68-94 record in the new six-team West Division created when each major league split into two parts for 1969. Melton stood out with 23 home runs and 87 RBI and outfielders Walt "No Neck" Williams (.304) and rookie Carlos May (.281, 18 home runs, 62 RBI), hit well. May, however, suffered a major mishap on August 11 when a mortar misfired at a U.S. Marine camp and blew off a portion of his right thumb. Horlen (13-16) again led the starters but reliever Wood (10-11, 15 saves) was the sole pitching standout.

Being forced into the West Division, which meant late-night West Coast games reduced television ratings and morning newspaper coverage, was almost the last straw for owner Arthur Allyn. He seriously entertained a bid from a group led by Bud Selig, the future commissioner of baseball, to buy the team and move it to Milwaukee for the 1970 season. Eventually, Allyn sold his half interest to his brother John, who declared the "White Sox are in Chicago to stay."

John Allyn went into 1970 without illusions about a sudden turnabout, predicting that it would "be the poorest we can envision—worse than this year." He was right on target, the Sox losing a team-record 106 games. Paradoxically, Aparicio, now 36, had his finest season, batting a career-high .313, and by playing game No. 2,219 broke Appling's major league record for most games at shortstop. Melton set a club record for home runs with 33. Wood (9-11, 21 saves) again led the league in most appearances with 77.

Before season's end, Gutteridge and Short were gone. Allyn delegated Stu Holcomb, a former football coach whom he named vice president and general manager, to take command in early September. Roland Hemond, farm director of the California Angels, replaced Short—though called director of player personnel – and Chuck Tanner, a former journeyman outfielder, took over as manager on September 13, coach Bill Adair running the team in the interim after Gutteridge's dismissal 10 days earlier.

Hemond and Tanner represented a new departure, the former soft-spoken yet energetic, the latter an eternal optimist, cheerful and friendly to outsiders, but a tough disciplinarian in the clubhouse and a strongman who might have been the first Chicago manager since Frank Chance able to impose his will physically on his players.

Hemond and Tanner immediately swung into action. Such veterans as Aparicio, Ken Berry and outfielder Tom McCraw were sent away in trades. Nine separate deals, involving 31 players, were consummated prior to opening day of 1971. Only seven holdovers remained from the 25-man roster of 1970. Among the newcomers were outfielders Jay Johnstone and Rick Reichardt and starting pitcher Tom Bradley.

"We decided to trade value just to change things around," Hemond explained. "After you lose 106 games, you need new personnel—you need new faces."

The new faces, and some of the old, responded to the new leadership. The Sox improved to 79-83 and third place in the West in 1971, and celebrated their first-ever A.L. home run champion when Melton again hit 33. Tanner's most significant move was the conversion of reliever Wood to a starter. Wood went 22-13 with a 1.91 ERA to begin a string of four successive 20-game winning seasons. Bradley was 15-15 and Tommy John was 13-16.

The team was not truly in contention in 1971 but the foundation was laid for a breakout campaign the next year. Hemond's most controversial trade, that of John and a utility infielder to the Los Angeles Dodgers for slugger Richie "Dick" Allen, spearheaded a revival in both the standings and attendance in 1972. The acquisition of right-handed starter Stan Bahnsen from the New York Yankees also helped.

"He was the savior of our franchise," Hemond later said of Allen, and it's true that the first baseman's bat almost carried the team to second place and an 87-67 record in 1972. His 37 home runs and 113 RBI led the A.L. and he hit .308 to earn the Most Valuable Player award. His presence in the lineup also lifted May (.308) as well as Melton until the latter was lost for the season with a ruptured disc in late June.

Allen was comfortable, a rarity in his turbulent career, to be playing for the White Sox and Tanner, whom he had known from youth. He said, "I feel like I've found a home here. The fans have been wonderful. Can you imagine them giving me a standing ovation at the end of the season in my final appearance at the plate— when I struck out?"

Allen might have been the major reason attendance rose over a million for the first time since 1965, but solid pitching, tutored by coach Johnny Sain, played a big role. Knuckleballer Wood, sometimes working every second or third day, was 24-17 and pitched a staggering 376⅓ innings while Bahnsen contributed a record of 21-16 and Bradley went 15-14. Reliever Terry Forster (6-5, 29 saves) led the bullpen.

What appeared to be great promise for 1973, especially after a 27-15 start, evaporated on June 28 when Allen fractured his kneecap and was sidelined for all but five at-bats the rest of the season. It was the most damaging of 38 injuries that condemned the team to a final 77-85 record and fifth place.

Melton (.276, 20 home runs, 87 RBI) and May (.268, 20 home runs, 96 RBI) stood out among the hitters and Allen finished with .316, 16 home runs and 41 RBI for 72 games. Wood (24-20) and Bahnsen (18-21) started 90 games between them and achieved the rare feat of giving a team two 20-game losers in one season. On July 23, Wood started both ends of a double-header against the Yankees, but was pounded twice, becoming the first pitcher in four decades to lose two starts on the same day.

Disharmony also dragged down the Sox, particularly after Holcomb made Allen the game's highest-paid player with a three-year contract calling for $250,000 a season. The resulting furor, in which Tanner joined, led to Holcomb's resignation in mid-campaign, with Hemond taking over his title of general manager. Still, the Sox drew 1,316,527, their best attendance since 1960.

Stagnation continued in 1974, Tanner seemingly having lost both his touch and his luck as the Sox staggered to 80-80 and fourth place. A late-season deal in 1973 paid off handsomely as Jim Kaat, thought to be fading at Minnesota, went 21-13 to join Wood (20-19) at the top of the rotation. But a trade on December 11, 1973, which brought former star third baseman Ron Santo from the Cubs in exchange for pitcher Steve Stone and three others, was irrelevant. Santo hit only .221 in his final year as a player.

There were better results from second baseman Jorge Orta, whose .316 was second in the league, outfielder Ken Henderson who had career highs of 20 home runs and 95 RBI while batting .292 and rookie shortstop Bucky Dent who hit .274.

Allen again led the league in home runs with 32, batted .301 and drove in 88 runs, but struck his biggest blow on September 14, 1974 by announcing his retirement. He changed his mind later, and played three more years, but not for the Sox. His departure foreshadowed the end of Tanner's tenure because it weakened prospects for 1975.

And 1975 was no bargain, things going from bad to worse not only for Tanner, but also for owner Allyn. The Sox retreated to 75-86 and fifth place. What hurt even more was a precipitous drop in attendance to 770,880 as well a decline in Allyn's non-baseball financial interests. This was more important in the long run than a few strong player performances such as Kaat's second consecutive 20-win season at 20-14, Orta's .304 and Dent's solid play in the field, or a deal in which the Sox got fine outfield prospect Chet Lemon in exchange for Bahnsen.

Adding to the turbulence was a running feud between Harry Caray, the team's principal broadcaster, and Melton and Henderson who insisted he was constantly belittling the players' efforts and contributed to the poor performance. Tanner supported the players. Allyn fired Caray after the season ended.

Caray counter-attacked by calling the owner "stupid" and added, "The best thing that could happen for the White Sox would be if John Allyn sold the team."

Allyn did do just that, but not in obedience to Caray. He sought a buyer for the Sox and found at least two, one a Seattle syndicate that would have moved the Sox out of Chicago, the other Bill Veeck, eager to reprise his 1959 triumph. While several A.L. owners hated Veeck and tried to block his return to Chicago, he won out as Allyn preferred not to be a party to the team's abandonment of the city. Veeck, as head of a large group, took command of the Sox for the second time on December 16, 1975.

He immediately began to revamp the team, with six trades in the next 53 hours. Veterans Melton, Henderson and Kaat departed. So did manager Tanner who was replaced by Paul Richards, now 67, who had managed the Go-Go Sox from 1951 through most of 1954. Among the newcomers Veeck and Hemond, who stayed on as general manager, gave Richards to work with were infielder Alan Bannister, first baseman Jim Spencer, outfield veteran Ralph Garr and reliever Clay Carroll. Veeck, perhaps reluctantly, also restored the team's most severe critic, Caray, to the broadcast booth.

An early 10-game winning streak raised hopes, but the 1976 season turned into a disaster on May 9 when a line drive to the mound broke Wood's kneecap. The White Sox finished 64-97, last in the West. Garr batted .300, the sole regular to reach that plateau. The only pitcher to win 10 games was Ken Brett (10-12) acquired for Carlos May from the Yankees on May 18 to replace Wood. Veeck's many and often outlandish promotions such as beer-stacking contests and gimmicks such as attiring his players in shorts failed to lift attendance over a million.

"You can't ballyhoo a funeral," scoffed rival A's owner Charlie Finley.

Veeck not only kept ballyhooing, but came up with a new plan for 1977 which succeeded beyond all expectations. Financial problems prohibited the signing of expensive free agents to long-term contracts so Veeck hit upon a "rent-a-player" scheme. He would acquire players with minimal time left on their contracts, then let them depart when their asking price became too costly.

The first deal under the new system brought hard-hitting outfielder Richie Zisk from Pittsburgh for relievers Rich Gossage and Terry Forster after the 1976 disaster. A couple of "bargain" free agents, third baseman Eric Soderholm and pitcher Steve Stone, also were signed, the latter for a second term with the Sox. Just before the 1977 season opened, Hemond traded shortstop Dent to the Yankees for outfielder Oscar Gamble and pitchers LaMarr Hoyt and Bob Polinsky.

With the laid-back Bob Lemon replacing Richards as manager, Zisk, Gamble and Soderholm led a furious White Sox offensive attack throughout the 1977 season. The Sox clubbed 192 home runs, a team record, to earn the label "South Side Hit Men," and Stone led the pitching staff with a 15-12 record. Fan enthusiasm was unprecedented, attendance zooming to a record 1,657,136, with 20 crowds in excess of 30,000, compared to only four in 1976 and just one in 1975.

The Sox held first place from July 1 until August 12, then stumbled but finished with a 90-72 record and third place in the West. Lemon was voted Manager of the Year, Veeck Executive of the Year and Soderholm, who hit 25 home runs, Comeback Player of the Year. Zisk (.290, 30 home runs, 101 RBI) and Gamble (.297, 31 home runs, 83 RBI) were supported on offense by center fielder Chet Lemon, one of the few defensive standouts on the team, who hit 19 home runs, and first basemen/designated hitters Spencer and Lamar Johnson, who each hit 18. In addition to Stone, the pitching standouts were Francisco Barrios (14-7) and reliever Lerrin LaGrow (7-3, 25 saves).

In the aftermath, it's clear the "South Side Hit Men" campaign of 1977 was Veeck's "Last Hurrah." He couldn't afford to retain expensive free agents Zisk and Gamble after the season and the signings and trades for 1978 didn't do much good. Among the newcomers were such shopworn articles as former Cub shortstop Don Kessinger, designated hitter Ron Blomberg, outfielders Bobby Bonds and Claudell Washington. A stretch of 17 victories in 19 games between May 28 and June 15 raised false hopes, the team soon reverting to indifferent play.

Veeck replaced 1977 Manager of the Year Lemon on June 30, 1978, with Larry Doby, the team's batting coach, in what was an effort to revive fan interest by making baseball's second African-American player also its second black manager. But Doby failed to arouse the Sox and they declined to fifth place with a 72-90 record.

Amidst the ruins of a forgettable season, Lemon's defensive play, though limited to 105 games by injuries, and average of .300 were among the few positive aspects. Soderholm led the team with 20 home runs. Stone's 12-12 paced the starters. A few rookie pitchers, notably left-hander Steve Trout, who was 3-0 after being called up from the minors in September, looked promising.

It's almost sufficient to note that a horrendous promotion called "Disco Demolition Night" became the most remembered event of the 1979 campaign in which Veeck, Kessinger— who had replaced Doby by becoming a player-manager—and the White Sox could never find their way. The promotion arranged by a radio disc jockey between games of a doubleheader on July 12 resulted in a cluttering of the field by "anti-disco" enthusiasts so the second game had to be forfeited to Detroit.

Among Veeck's other projects to go wrong, including the team which went 73-87 to finish fifth again, was the "hype" of 5-foot-3 rookie shortstop Harry Chappas, who fell short of being an adequate replacement for Kessinger. Actually, with the team going nowhere, the replacement for Kessinger turned out to be Tony La Russa, who took his job as manager on August 2.

Chet Lemon, however, had another outstanding season, batting .317 with 17 home runs and 86 RBI to lead the team in all three categories. Lamar Johnson also stood out as he hit .309 and shortstop Alan Bannister batted .285. Developing starters Trout

(11-8), Ross Baumgarten (13-8) and Tex Wortham (14-14) joined veteran Ken Kravec (15-13) in a fair rotation

Veeck's selection of La Russa, a former fringe player, to manage the White Sox was one of the superior decisions of his swan-song years as owner. "I think we're going to find out that he is one of the really outstanding managers before he's through," Veeck predicted, adding, "...when you're a scuffler, like Tony was—up and down, trying to stick with limited talent—then you have to learn the nuances and that gives you a little bit of an advantage."

And so it proved, because 1980 was a significant turning point for the White Sox on the field as La Russa showed a sure managerial touch in developing promising youngsters, including rookie outfielder Harold Baines, who batted .255 in 141 games. It also brought an end to Veeck's striking career as baseball's preeminent showman.

As the team struggled to a 70-90 record and a third consecutive fifth place finish, Veeck spent much of the year trying to sell the club. Two deals, one of which might have moved the White Sox to Denver, the other to New Orleans, fell through, the second because the baseball establishment twice vetoed a sale to Edward DeBartolo, partly because of his horse-racing interests. Veeck eventually found an acceptable buyer in a group headed by Chicago area businessman Jerry Reinsdorf. The papers were signed on January 29, 1981.

By that time, the Sox were preparing for spring training and the prospect of building on the promising points of 1980. Chief among those was the progress in pitching, with Britt Burns (15-13), Richard Dotson (12-10), Lamarr Hoyt (9-3) and Trout, despite 9-16, in the forefront. Closer Ed Farmer (7-9) had a team-record 30 saves. In addition to Baines, first baseman Mike Squires (.283) made a good impression.

The new ownership plunged into the free agent market for 1981 and came up with three strong acquisitions, veteran star catcher Carlton Fisk, slugging outfielder Greg Luzinski and second baseman Tony Bernazard. Though the player strike from

June 10 to August 12 resulted in a split-season format, the White Sox showed progress in their 106 games, winning 54 of them. Burns led the pitching staff with 10-6. Luzinski's 21 home runs and 65 RBI topped the hitters.

Harry Caray and his broadcasting sidekick, former outfielder Jimmy Piersall had plenty to criticize the Sox about in 1981 and often did. Their running feud with La Russa became increasingly vociferous and notorious. But Caray was set adrift when the Reinsdorf group turned to new broadcast ventures after the season, and went on to even greater fame and popularity by airing Cub games for the rest of his life.

Hemond made two major deals for 1982. Lemon went to Detroit for outfielder Steve Kemp, who hit 19 home runs, drove in 98 runs and batted .286. Outfielder/first baseman Tom Paciorek, who hit .312, was acquired from Seattle. The transactions paid off, the '82 Sox enjoying their finest season since 1977, ending up with an 87-75 record and third place in the West.

"Good team, but not great," remarked La Russa, somewhat disappointed after having predicted a division title. He appeared prescient when his team went 8-0 to start the 1982 season, but they relapsed to 49-49 by late July before recovering. Hoyt won his first nine decisions but was 11-7 by the All-Star break and finished with 19-11.

The inconsistent play continued to the very end, but over-all there was much about 1982 to hearten the fans and management. In addition to Kemp and Paciorek, Baines (.271, 25 home runs, 101 RBI), Luzinski (.292, 18 home runs, 102 RBI) and Fisk (.267, 14 home runs and 65 RBI) contributed to a heavy offense. Baines and Luzinski gave the Sox two 100 RBI men for the first time in 46 years. Center fielder Rudy Law, who batted .318, added the ingredient of speed, stealing 36 bases.

Hoyt, Burns (13-5), Dotson (11-15) and veterans Dennis Lamp (11-8) and Jerry Koosman (11-7) were inconsistent over the season yet formed a solid basis for 1983, as did the roster over-all.

A couple of minor league prospects who made brief late-season appearances also fanned hopes for the future. Outfielder

Ron Kittle hit 50 home runs in the Pacific Coast League in 1982 and first baseman Greg Walker, who missed most of the year with a broken wrist, had two home runs and seven RBI while going 7-for-17 for the White Sox in a September call-up.

If 1982 had been a roller-coaster season for the White Sox, as indeed had been the entire 17-season stretch since 1966, it hadn't been entirely ugly because of the progress made since Veeck's final years as owner.

What's more, ugliness was about to come into fashion in 1983, the year of "Winning Ugly."

BALLS, BATS AND CHICANERY

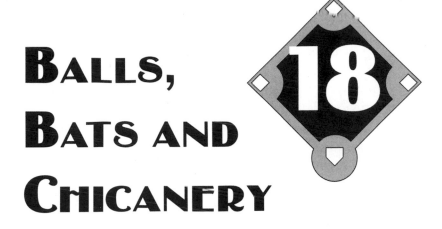

G ary Peters, the former White Sox pitching star, and Jim Fregosi were participating in a charity golf tournament in Tampa, Florida. And Fregosi, as he had done many times before, voiced his usual complaint.

"I hit one off you and it should have been on the roof, or at least in the upper deck," Fregosi declared, still beefing about an at-bat in the 1960s, more than a quarter of a century earlier. "And Tommie Agee caught it in front of the warning track."

"What's the difference?" Peters asked. "You couldn't hit anyway. I always tell you that."

Fregosi insisted, "I never hit a ball harder than that."

Fregosi, who later managed four major league clubs, was playing shortstop for the California Angels. He has an excellent memory. Under ordinary circumstances it would have been a home run but these were unusual times. The White Sox were short on power hitters. To overcome this deficiency they deadened the ball.

It began two years before, in 1965 when the Sox were in Detroit for a four-game series. Tommy John was pitching for the Sox and noticed the baseballs had been tampered with.

"All the balls I got that day were like cue balls, hard and slick," John recalled. "And the seams were so low, almost non-existent. When you're a sinkerballer you can't sink the ball without seams."

John relayed the information to manager Al Lopez who told him to bring a ball into the dugout after every inning. According to John's recollections, Lopez said, "That's okay. We'll get them when we get back to Comiskey Park."

Lopez summoned Gene Bossard, a second-generation groundskeeper who knew all the tricks. Bossard understood what had to be done and began storing boxes of balls in a small, windowless brick-walled room. He installed a humidifier. In two weeks the balls were soaking wet, moist from the humidity.

Before the balls were put into play, Bossard, like a mad scientist, carried them to the upper deck along with a supply of balls taken from an unopened cache. He operated in secrecy, in the early morning when the ballpark was empty. The regulation balls were lighter and bounced about four feet higher.

But this was a rush job. The Tigers would be returning to Chicago the following weekend. "Doctor" Bossard didn't have time for extensive experimentation. Still, the results were truly remarkable. In the four-game series at Detroit, the Tigers had hit 13 home runs, three each by Don Demeter and Norm Cash, two apiece by Bill Freehan and Don Wert and solos by Al Kaline, Dick McAuliffe and Jerry Lumpe.

In the ensuing four-game series at Comiskey Park from July 30 through August 2 the Tigers were swinging at the doctored balls. Suddenly, they were shorn of their power. Their longest hit in the entire series was a double.

Roger Bossard, Gene's son, now the White Sox groundskeeper, would wipe the balls dry. He discarded the rotted boxes which were swollen with mildew. The balls were placed in fresh containers and brought into the umpires' room three hours before game-time. He said the umpires didn't notice the difference.

The elder Bossard was not a pioneer. Connie Mack's Philadelphia Athletics, who won three consecutive A.L. pennants from 1929 to 1931, and the 1920 Pittsburgh Pirates froze balls in an ice box. Remember, Mack was baseball's "Grand Old Man."

The 1925 Philadelphia Phillies did the same. It was not an unknown practice.

"I could tell the difference," said White Sox catcher Jerry McNertney. "When I got the new ball I had a habit of smelling the ball. Most balls have a leathery smell. These balls smelled rusty. But once the ball was put in play the feel was the same."

Shortstop Ron Hansen disagreed. "We weren't privy to what was going on," Hansen said. "But you could feel the ball was harder. The skin wasn't soft." Hansen remembers a series with the New York Yankees. "They lit up the stadium in batting practice but didn't do much when the game started."

The White Sox hitters were confronted with the same ball but there were no complaints. They relied on pitching and defense. In 1967, a typical year, their leading hitters were Ken Berry and Don Buford, with identical .241 averages. Pete Ward led with 18 home runs. The strength was in their pitching rotation of Gary Peters, Joe Horlen and Tommy John, who had a career total of 288 victories and is a perennial Hall of Fame candidate.

It wasn't long before opposing players began hollering. First base coach Don Gutteridge still chuckles when he tells of Yogi Berra's frustration: "Yogi was rounding first base thinking he had hit one out. He said, 'I hit the hell out of that ball and it didn't go anywhere.'"

The American League investigated. According to Roger Bossard, the league office sent two detectives to Chicago. "They knew Dad was in charge of the baseballs but they didn't know where he stored them," Roger recalled. "They followed him around for three or four days. And, of course, he took them to the 'dry' room. It was on the other side of the stadium."

The elder Bossard also created what was known as "Bossard's Swamp." After the lights were turned off, Bossard had his helpers dig into the dirt, about four or five inches in front of the plate, and soaked it. The next day the top soil appeared to be dry. Down below it was a marsh.

It was another clever deception that helped White Sox pitchers. Horlen, John and John Buzhardt, particularly, were sinkerballers. Sixty-five percent of the balls hit off them were grounders. It was a double-whammy. The batters were not only hitting a dead ball but pounding it into the mud.

When Minnesota came into town, Roger Bossard recalled that Harmon Killebrew and Bob Allison, the Twins' big sluggers, would go to the plate and stomp on the dirt to pack it in, make it harder.

Horlen recalled the day Detroit's Freehan went berserk. It was during batting practice. "He hit a couple of groundballs in the sod and they just rolled over. Freehan began screaming at Bossard and picked up some of the sod and threw it away."

When Eddie Stanky succeeded Lopez as manager after the 1965 season he began a give-away program. Any pitcher who went the distance and got 20 groundballs—base hits included— in a winning performance was rewarded with a $300 suit.

"I killed Stanky," Horlen recalled. "One year I got five suits. Tommy John got two or three. We were regulars at Hart, Schaffner & Marx."

And all the while third base coaches Tony Cuccinello and Grover Reisinger, his successor, were stealing signs.

One common illegal stratagem escaped them. So far as is known, the White Sox didn't "cork" their bats. Probably because they couldn't hit anyway. But they were the victims of a celebrated corked-bat incident during the 1994 A.L. Central Division race, subsequently known as "Bat-Gate."

The culprit was Albert Belle of the Cleveland Indians.

Corked bats, like deadened balls and soaked fields, are not uncommon. There are variations. In 1974 during a Yankee-Detroit skirmish at Yankee Stadium, New York's Graig Nettles swung at a Woody Fryman pitch and "singled" to left field. As Nettles made contact, his bat splintered and four or five "super-balls" dropped out.

Catcher Freehan pounced on them as he would a bunt and handed them to plate umpire Lou DiMuro. The bat had been sawed off at the top and the inside had been chiseled out. The super-balls were inserted into the hollow. DiMuro called Nettles out but there was no ejection.

In the Albert Belle caper there was no visible evidence of chicanery. Belle had had an outstanding first half and was among the league leaders in home runs and runs batted in. Gene Lamont, the White Sox manager, was suspicious and told his players he would have Belle's bat inspected in his first plate appearance.

The umpire immediately impounded the "magic wand." For safekeeping, the bat was taken to their quarters which during the games was always under lock and key. It would be shipped to the A.L. office in New York the next morning for X-rays.

But someone slipped into their room and lifted the confiscated lumber. It was replaced with a model used by Paul Sorrento who was among Belle's teammates.

"It was definitely a break-in," umpire Dave Phillips announced. It was Phillips who had taken Belle's bat and given it to Vince Fresso, the umpires' caretaker. Fresso put the bat behind Phillips' equipment suitcase and covered it with Phillips' civilian clothes.

Fresso returned to the umpires' room in the sixth inning and noticed clumps of the ceiling insulation on the floor. Ceiling tiles in two locations were askew. The metal support strips that held the false tiles were twisted.

"This is a serious crime," observed White Sox chairman Jerry Reinsdorf. His view was subsequently endorsed by acting Commissioner Bud Selig. An avid reader of mystery novels, Selig said, "We're going to get to the bottom of this."

An investigation began at noon the following day. The umpires' room was dusted for fingerprints. Kevin Hallinan, a former FBI agent and baseball's chief security officer, flew in from New York. A.L. president Bobby Brown was awakened in his New York hotel room and advised of the theft. The Chicago police were also alerted.

"This is bizarre," A.L. umpire supervisor Marty Springstead declared in a telephone interview from his New Jersey home. "In 31 years of baseball you think you've seen it all but you haven't."

Umpire Phillips said, "Usually what they do is drill a hole through the top of the bat and put in a long tubular piece of cork. When the cork is inserted they put the top back on, glue it and sand it down. Sometimes they paint it. I'm not sure if it was painted black or brown. It looked like a shiny new bat."

Chicago baseball writers put the finger on an unidentified "fervent Cleveland fan" who made the trip to Comiskey Park from his home in Shaker Heights, Ohio.

It became a running crime story. Daily accounts, with fresh quotes and diagrams, were reported by the press to an eager public, the biggest Chicago heist since the days of Al Capone and Bugs Moran. One young sportswriter, who had played semi-pro ball in Montana, stuffed a bat with cork, swung at a dozen balls and confirmed they traveled as much as 20 to 30 feet farther. The bat was lighter and had a better whip action. Newspaper circulation increased.

With each clue more details were uncovered. It was determined that the thief gained entry through the office of Cleveland manager Mike Hargrove. Standing on a chair, he opened the false ceiling. Clutching Sorrento's bat, he crawled 40 feet to the umpires' room, dropped down and switched the bats. Using the same route, he made it back to Hargrove's office.

Six years later, in 2000, Jason Grimsley confessed. In an interview with Dave van Dyck of the *Chicago Sun-Times*, Grimsley, who had been a fringe pitcher with the Indians and now was with the Yankees, said he didn't take another of Belle's bats because he knew they were all corked. As suspected, he had crawled through the ceiling.

"It was hairy," Grimsley said. He wasn't sure where he would land. "Most of my teammates knew what I had done but didn't tell anyone.

"I'll tell you what was funny. The next day, before the game, I was in the outfield, and Mike LaValliere (White Sox catcher) came up to me and said, 'Hey, I hear you guys had a mission impossible last night.'"

SPIT AND FOLLIES

U nlike Phil Cavarretta, the manager whom P.K. Wrigley had fired during spring training two decades earlier for gloom about the Cubs' chances, Whitey Lockman brought tidings of comfort and joy to the team owner before the outset of the 1973 season.

"We've got the best team we've had for many years," proclaimed Lockman, who had succeeded Leo Durocher as manager during the previous campaign. "I don't see a weakness anywhere. We've got the best pitching staff in the league with five starters and a much improved bullpen."

Lockman had been director of player development and knew the quality of Cub farm system prospects. Unfortunately, he rated most of them far too highly. Only a few met expectations and the post-Durocher Cubs plunged back into a period of depression for 11 years during which they reached .500 (exactly) just once.

No one could have foreseen this midway through the 1973 season when Lockman's affable but firm handling of his players was getting the most out of them. With the five starters (Ferguson Jenkins, Burt Hooton, Rich Reuschel, Milt Pappas and Bill Bonham) in fine form, the Cubs took first place on May 9 and reigned until July 21.

The offense kept pace into mid-season. Ron Santo led the league in batting at .360, Glenn Beckert ran up a 26-game hitting streak and Rick Monday had 21 home runs in early July, twice as many as his previous season total.

The Cubs' high point was reached on June 29 when they were 46-31 and eight games in front. Then the axle broke on the triumphal cart. Within three weeks they slid to second place, then added to their discomfiture with an 11-game losing streak in August, part of a horrendous free-fall during which they dropped 14 of 15.

Yet because no team in the N.L. East was playing well they remained "alive" in the title race until September 30, the next-to-last day of the season, which ended with the New York Mets winning the championship with an anemic 82-79 record. The Cubs sank to fifth place at 77-84.

The result of this latest misfortune was to convince Wrigley, general manager John Holland and Lockman it was time to re-build, get rid of fading veterans and go with youngsters. "We'll probably suffer for a year or two," Wrigley admitted, "but at least we will have some younger players who will work hard to make places for themselves."

Only the outfield distinguished itself in '73, Jose Cardenal pacing the team in batting with .303. Monday's 26 home runs also led as did Billy Williams' 88 RBI. Third baseman Santo, despite his hot start, slid to .267. Injuries made the future usefulness of second baseman Beckert and catcher Randy Hundley questionable.

The pitching was also in disarray despite Lockman's early optimism. After six consecutive 20-game winning seasons, Jenkins slipped to 14-16 and demanded to be traded. Only Reuschel (14-15) stood out with a 3.00 earned run average, while Hooton (14-17), Pappas (7-12) and Bonham (7-5), new to the rotation, were at best adequate, as was reliever Bob Locker, with 10 wins and 18 saves.

A historic footnote to 1973: Ernie Banks, now a coach, became the first African-American to manage a major league team, filling in for an inning and a half on May 8 after Lockman had been ejected.

At Wrigley's urging, Holland unloaded four of the club's long-time heroes in preparation for 1974. Jenkins went to Texas, Beckert to San Diego, Hundley to Minnesota and Santo to the White Sox. The only infield survivor was shortstop Don Kessinger who lamented, "This is the first time I'll be going to spring training not knowing what to expect." He should have expected misery.

Among the newcomers on an opening day roster with nine rookies were third baseman Bill Madlock, who came in the deal for Jenkins, outfielder Jerry Morales, first baseman Andre Thornton, and starting pitchers Steve Stone and Ken Frailing who joined the rotation with Reuschel, Bonham and Hooton.

As Wrigley forecast, the Cubs were in for a period of anguish. No one suffered more than Lockman, who quit as manager at mid-season to return to his role as Holland's assistant. Third base coach Jim Marshall took over. When asked why he hadn't named Banks, Wrigley explained it was out of consideration for Mr. Cub's welfare. "Becoming a major league manager is like being a Kamikaze pilot," Wrigley said. "It's suicide."

Neither Lockman nor Marshall went to that extreme in '74, but the Cubs declined to 66-96 and last place. Among the few bright spots were the play of Madlock, who batted .313 (helping justify the departure of Jenkins, who went 25-12 at Texas), Monday (.294), Cardenal (.293) and Reuschel (13-12), now the ace of the pitching staff.

The disappointments were many, including Bonham, 11-22, and a number of players who failed to impress as second basemen, Vic Harris, Rob Sperring and Dave Rosello, and as catchers, Steve Swisher and George Mitterwald.

The only significant change for 1975 was the departure of another hero of the Durocher era. Billy Williams was traded to Oakland for Manny Trillo, who was to plug the hole at second which he did in fine fashion for the next four seasons.

The fans were vociferously upset when Holland traded Williams, among the greatest of Cub players. He defended the deal philosophically: "Our primary interest was in getting Trillo, and when you get a young player not known to the public, you don't expect a good reaction."

In spite of the misery of 1974, Marshall, a friendly sort though more hard-edged than Lockman, remained in charge for two more seasons, neither of which provided much cheer for Cub fans. In both 1975 and 1976 the Cubs were 75-87, finishing in a tie for fifth the first year, in fourth place the second.

The most memorable event during the two years was Monday's blocking of an attempt by a demonstrator on April 26, 1976 to burn an American flag in the Dodger Stadium outfield. Monday briefly became a national hero, hailed by *The Sporting News* as "Francis Scott Key, Betsy Ross, Verdun, and Iwo Jima— all wrapped up in a fleeting moment of patriotism."

More to the point, Monday played a strong center field and hit well with 17 home runs and 89 runs batted in for 1975 and a career-high 32 home runs the next year. Cardenal hit .317 then .319, but the standout was Madlock, who won consecutive N.L. batting titles with .354 and .339. His three consecutive seasons over .300 are often ignored in statements that the Cubs had no outstanding third baseman after Santo. The best starting pitching during the two seasons was provided by newcomer Ray Burris (15-10 and 15-13) and Reuschel (11-17 and 14-12), with Bonham (13-15 and 9-13) failing to progress. A dissatisfied Hooton was deported to Los Angeles early in the '75 campaign, and provided the Dodgers with a front-line starter for the next decade, the Cubs getting little in return. But there was hope in the bullpen, split-fingered pitch (forkball) specialist Bruce Sutter breaking in with a 6-3 record and 10 saves in 1976.

The final survivors of the '69 collapse faded from the scene after the 1975 season. Kessinger went to the St. Louis Cardinals for next to nothing and Holland, plagued by ill-health, retired to a consultant's role, giving up the general manager's post he had held for two decades to E.R. "Salty" Saltwell, who had been in charge of park operations and knew little about baseball talent. Wrigley's command to Saltwell: "Get tough with the players." It was Saltwell who sent Kessinger to St. Louis.

With the advent of free agency at this point, dramatized when Catfish Hunter signed with the New York Yankees for $3 million for five years, Wrigley's dismay at rising player salaries became intense. "Baseball might have to be subsidized like grand opera," he warned, "if we can't get these astronomic salaries under control."

This concern was to lead to what might be called Wrigley's final folly, eclipsing even the naming of Saltwell as general manager. He realized his mistake after one season, and after failing to lure Durocher back in a major role, settled on Bob Kennedy, who had managed the Cubs during the 1960s, to replace Saltwell. Kennedy's first move was to fire Marshall and bring in Herman Franks, Durocher's buddy and a former Cub coach, as the manager.

The brusque, no-nonsense and candid Kennedy, a former U.S. Marine Corps pilot, had his hands full from the start. Monday and Madlock demanded major pay raises after their fine 1976 showings, the latter having become the only 20th Century Cub to win back-to-back batting titles. Madlock asked for a long-term million-dollar contract, far more than Banks had ever earned.

"No ball player is worth more than $100,000 and I'm not sure they're worth that much," Wrigley complained. "We'll just have to field the best team we possibly can." He added that Madlock had the kind of body that was likely to become too fat for him to play well for more than a year or two.

Kennedy got the message and struck. Madlock was traded to San Francisco, the Cubs' chief gains being center fielder Bobby Murcer and third baseman Steve Ontiveros. Monday was shipped to the Dodgers, the Cubs getting outfielder/first baseman Bill Buckner and shortstop Ivan DeJesus. Ironically, Murcer was paid about what Madlock sought. And Madlock won two more batting titles for four altogether in an impressive 15-year career that ended with a .305 lifetime average.

If trading Madlock was a folly, it was Wrigley's last. The eccentric owner, who had run the team since 1934, died at the age of 82 on April 12, 1977. The scepter passed to son William, whose interest in baseball was minimal. Bill Wrigley preferred to leave all but the most vital matters up to Kennedy and Franks.

Franks, 63, was a baseball lifer whose uniform was usually spattered with chewing tobacco juice by game-time. Kennedy was the spit and polish of the new regime while Franks could be regarded as the "spit" without the polish. Yet he was a canny manager, an old catcher, capable of extracting performance, particularly from pitchers.

On noticing people flinch as he sprayed tobacco juice on his uniform while talking in the dugout, Franks barked, "Hey, I ain't here to look pretty."

He certainly proved his tactical skill in 1977, a virtual encore of 1973 as well as other seasons in which the Cubs fanned their fans' ardor to white-hot heat with a fast start before the customary ice-cold bath of reality. This time, however, injuries played a far greater role in the team's eventual failure than in similar campaigns.

As long as the joy lasted, the '77 season was a rousing reenactment of the scenario of four years earlier. At one point the Cubs led the division by eight and a half games. They soared 25 games above .500. For 69 days nobody was ahead of them. They were in first place the entire months of May and June.

Their collapse, however, was so swift and complete that they relinquished first place on August 4 and completed the season by losing eight of their final nine games to finish at .500 (81-81) and fourth.

What happened? A series of injuries, the most damaging being to Sutter and Reuschel. Buckner, now the first baseman, and Morales and Cardenal also went down for various periods.

Sutter's forkball had been virtually unhittable. By July 26, he had made 45 appearances with 24 saves, five wins, an 1.11 earned run average and 94 strikeouts in 81⅓ innings. But overwork caused a swelling beneath his right shoulder and forced him to the disabled list for three weeks. He finished the season with 31 saves, a 7-3 record and an ERA of 1.35. Meanwhile, back trouble plagued Reuschel who was 15-3 by July 30 and he slumped, closing the season at 20-10.

It was evident neither the pitching nor offense had been deep enough. Burris (14-16) was the only dependable starting pitcher other than Reuschel, Bonham (10-13) continuing to disappoint. Young Mike Krukow (8-14) mostly showed potential. Murcer with 27 home runs was the only player to hit more than

11 and no regular reached .300, Ontiveros coming closest at .299. Such puny power was atypical for a Cub team.

To add punch, Kennedy signed the Cubs' first free agent, Dave Kingman, who also happened to be a "free spirit" as well as an atrocious outfielder, to a five-year deal for $1.3 million after the season. Kingman, an unpredictable personality, had a habit of wearing out his welcome quickly. He accomplished the rare feat of playing for four teams in four divisions in 1977, and batted a cumulative .221 with 26 home runs.

Kingman was moody and undisciplined but had supporters, among them Sutter.

"He wasn't the most graceful outfielder," Sutter said, "but Dave gave you what he had. He'd run through a wall trying to catch the ball. He came to play every day.... He just played, and he hit a lot of long home runs. He had a big swing, and he'd strike out a bunch, too. If you wanted those three-run homers, you had to live with those strikeouts, and that's the way it goes."

Not even the most charitably-minded could describe Kennedy's other deals for 1978 as other than appalling. He disposed of Cardenal, Morales and Bonham and none of the players he got in return, including veteran pitcher Woody Fryman, was of much use.

After an early season prance in first place, the '78 Cubs sank beneath the weight of general mediocrity though they finished a decent 79-83, in third place. There were a few outstanding performances even if Kingman, hampered by injuries, was held to only 119 games in which he hit 28 home runs. That was 19 more than the fading Murcer, who was second on the team with nine after hitting 27 the previous year.

The sole offensive standout was Buckner who batted .323 despite severe ankle problems. Among the pitchers, Reuschel (14-15) was the only one with more than nine victories. Sutter earned 27 saves and was 8-10. A nostalgic, if ineffective, mid-season pick-up was onetime left-handed ace Ken Holtzman (0-3) rescued from the Yankees.

It was an unmemorable campaign yet the Cubs drew 1,523,311 fans, their best attendance since 1971. Among the attendant trivia was a running feud between Franks and Kingman and the sprouting of beards by several players, including Sutter.

Kennedy's brusque response to the hirsute outbreak among his players: "If they want to look like idiots that's all right with me."

Franks was more accommodating: "I'll try to grow one myself if we're in first place in September."

He didn't have an incentive to do so in 1978. Nor for that matter in '79. In fact, he didn't even finish the latter campaign as manager.

Not that the 1979 campaign lacked interest even though the team finished 80-82 and in fifth place. The Cubs drew their third largest attendance ever, 1,648,887. The huge turnout was inspired by Kingman's heroics. The big man led the N.L. in home runs with 48, drove in 115 runs and batted a respectable (for him) .288. For one brief shining moment he was the idol of Cub fandom.

The apex of his career came on May 17, 1979, in one of the most unusual games ever. The Cubs trailed the Phillies 17-6 in the fourth inning but gained a tie at 22-22 in the eighth inning before losing 23-22 on Mike Schmidt's home run in the10th for Philadelphia. Kingman hit three of 11 home runs in the game and drove in six runs. Buckner went 4-for-7, including a home run, and drove in seven runs.

While Kingman was performing his pyrotechnics, Sutter also had a career year with 37 saves, a 6-6 record and a 2.23 earned run average to win the Cy Young award. Reuschel was 18-12 to lead the starters, with veteran pickup Lynn McGlothlen next at 13-14. Other than that of Kingman and Buckner (.284, 14 home runs and 66 RBI) the hitting was undistinguished.

Franks quit a week before the season ended, on his way out blasting some players as "selfish." Coach Joey Amalfitano finished the campaign as interim manager.

Kennedy's choice to manage the Cubs in 1980 was Preston Gomez, soft-spoken but a strong disciplinarian in stints with the San Diego Padres and Houston Astros. Gomez' brief reign was eminently undistinguished not because of his lack of ability but due to a shortage of talent among the players.

The 1980 season started out farcical—or ominous—when Kingman dumped a bucket of ice water on a sportswriter. He later compounded his eccentricities by going AWOL to fish, missing a game in which fans were given a T-shirt in his honor. Prior to the All-Star break, he was mocked with a proliferation of bumper stickers announcing, "Hey! Hey! The Cubs Are on Their Way! Ding Dong Went Fishing Today!"

Kingman played only 81 games, often being benched for failing to hit or because he was hurt. He finished with 18 home runs in 255 at-bats. He was also finished with the Cubs, who dumped him on the New York Mets after the season.

Not much went right in 1980 other than for Buckner, who led the league in batting with .324, and DeJesus, who stole 44 bases, the most since Johnny Evers' 46 in 1907. Sutter led the league with 28 saves, but the starters suffered, Reuschel going 11-13, Krukow 10-15, McGlothlen 12-14 and Dennis Lamp 10-14. The most significant rookie was reliever Lee Smith who checked in at 2-0.

Gomez' troubles started early and ceased only when he was fired on July 25 with the team's record 38-52.

"Firing Preston is not the answer," Sutter insisted. "What this club needs is a major overhaul."

The Cubs proved Sutter correct by going 26-46 the rest of the season under Amalfitano, Gomez' successor for a final 1980 record of 64-98 and a grip on last place.

The "overhaul" for 1981 was far more encompassing than Sutter could have suspected, involving not only himself—he was traded to the Cardinals-but also Reuschel, Kingman and lesser players, as well as even general manager Kennedy and to cap it all, the Cub franchise itself.

The deaths of P.K. Wrigley and his wife just a few months apart in 1977 created inheritance tax problems for Cub owner Bill Wrigley who was financially strapped by 1981. Reuschel was sold to the Yankees for $400,000 to meet the immediate cash shortage. That was a mere band-aid and Wrigley decided to sell the team. The Tribune Co., a huge media conglomerate whose radio and television stations broadcast Cub games, jumped on a chance to profit from also owning the team.

Kennedy left his post on May 22 while the sale of the Cubs for $18.5 million was being arranged. Wrigley recalled Franks to act as a "caretaker" general manager during the transfer of the franchise to the Tribune Co., which was announced June 16, 1981, ending more than 60 years of Cub ownership by three generations of the Wrigley family.

As if this was not turbulent enough, the 1981 season provided a bitter labor relations confrontation between the players and major league owners. A 50-day player strike beginning on June 12 resulted in a split-season. The Cubs flopped in both halves, going 15-37 before June 11 and 23-28 after play resumed August 10. Their combined 38-65 record was the worst in the league.

Buckner's .311 in 108 games stood out on a team that was last in the league in batting as well as most other categories. His 10 home runs were matched by promising outfielder-first baseman Leon Durham, obtained from the Cardinals in the Sutter trade. Krukow (9-9) was the only pitcher to win more than five games.

Soon after the team staggered to its sorry finish, Franks and manager Amalfitano resigned to clear the way for the Tribune Co. to take charge. The new Cub executive vice president and general manager was large and blustering Dallas Green, an import from Philadelphia who promised to start a "new tradition" without being aware the Cubs already had a great one.

BLUSTERING 'NEW TRADITION'

20

ndrew J. McKenna, a Chicago dynamo who sits on the boards of a dozen corporations and presides over three or four local annual charity banquets, was confronted with a difficult assignment. After brokering the sale of the Cubs to the Tribune Co. he was asked to hire a general manager. A veteran of many executive searches, McKenna listed the requirements:

Experience as a farm director; a former player and/or manager; age between 40 and 50; and it would be his "maiden run" as a general manager. This was crucial. If he failed, he couldn't hide behind an earlier success and, in effect, claim that "winning with the Cubs is impossible."

McKenna had a modest baseball background. As a boy he was twice stricken with rheumatic fever. He was the sports editor of his high school paper and the student baseball manager at the University of Notre Dame. In 1959 he operated the Michigan City, Indiana, franchise in the Class D Midwest League.

McKenna devoured baseball's Blue Book which lists the executive table of organization of the big league clubs. Within 48 hours he had fingered his man: Dallas Green of the Philadelphia Phillies. Green met the qualifications. He had been in charge of the Phillies' farm system, had been a player and manager, was 43, and had never been a general manager.

Green had the manner of a Marine drill sergeant, proud and stubborn and incapable of compromise, which was to be a fatal flaw. He descended to the clubhouse much more often than most general managers and bludgeoned the troops with bluff and bluster. Gruff, he usually closed his press conferences with the announcement, "And you know I'm a baseball man!" as if there was no other.

He also had a sense of humor and was able to joke about his failures, certainly an endearing characteristic. He often said he was a 20-game winner, referring to his 20-22 career record. "But it took me eight years." He never won more than six games in any season.

McKenna reported his findings to Stanton Cook, president of the Tribune Co., which had purchased the club five months earlier, on June 15, ending three-quarters of a century of ownership by the Wrigley family. The total price was $21.5 million, including the ballpark and the land.

"Go get him!" Cook said.

There was a problem. Green was in his third season of managing the Phillies. The year before, in 1981, he had guided them to their first World Series title in 97 years. Talk about the Cub drought. The Phillies had suffered through a century of failure. Their last world championship was in 1883, baseball's "stone age."

The Phillies were now trying to repeat. Because of a lengthy mid-season strike, 1981 was a split-season. The Phillies were still alive and competing for the playoffs. Also, Green had deep roots, three generations in the Philadelphia area. Except for two seasons in exile, near the end of his undistinguished pitching career, the Phillies had been his only club. It didn't seem likely he would leave a contender for the perennial second-division Cubs.

Green balked.

"Invite him and his wife to dinner," Cook suggested to McKenna.

On the next to last weekend of the regular season, the Phillies were at Wrigley Field. Green accepted the invitation. The McKennas arranged a lavish production at their suburban

Winnetka estate. The Cooks were also present along with Tribune Co. executive vice president John Madigan and his wife Holly.

"I'll serve veal marsalla," Joan McKenna announced. It was her best dish. "Maybe that will get him."

Green was impressed. A big man, 6 feet 6 inches and 250 pounds, he had a second serving, complimented Mrs. McKenna on her culinary skills, and then dove in for a third helping. Stomach filled, he departed and rejoined his club.

The Phillies were eliminated by the Dodgers. When the cheering stopped, Green packed his bags for Chicago. There could be no turning back. He intended to dig in for life. He was rewarded with a generous salary, a million dollars for five years, with gilded options. According to an unconfirmed report, his four children would be provided with dancing lessons.

There was an additional test. Green flew to Tucson, Arizona, to meet the widow of Colonel Bertrand McCormick, the long-time Tribune powerhouse.

"She liked him," McKenna reported to the Tribune Tower. "She said he was tall and handsome."

It was the clincher, the ultimate endorsement. Tall and handsome was a Tribune preference.

When Jerry Reinsdorf, then the rookie owner of the cross-town White Sox, heard that Green had agreed to the conditions, he said he wasn't surprised. "Even God rested on the last day."

It wasn't long before Green made his first mistake. A stranger to Chicago, he opened with the slogan "Building a New Tradition." What he didn't know was that the Cubs had a wonderful tradition. Though they hadn't finished first in 36 years, 16 pennants had flown from their flagpole.

Though unaware of Chicago history, Green knew how to stitch a winning team together. The entire eight-man starting lineup and the four leading pitchers on the Cubs' 1984 N.L. East Division championship team were acquired in trades, except for third baseman Ron Cey who was signed as a free agent.

Green began by plucking talent from the Philadelphia organization. This is not unusual. A new man, especially a farm director, knows the players he left behind. Within 18 months, 22 former

Phillies had crossed the Rubicon: nine players, a manager, Lee Elia, three coaches, a half dozen scouts, two public relations men, an attractive and pleasant secretary, etc. In Chicago they soon became known as the Cub-Phils, in Philadelphia as the Phil-Cubs.

Dozens of deals were consummated. The best was among the first: Ryne Sandberg, a minor league infielder and veteran shortstop Larry Bowa of the Phillies for Ivan DeJesus, a middling shortstop. Sandberg was a supposed throw-in but Green refused to make the deal without him, confident he had the discipline and physical capabilities of a potential all-star.

There was little progress in 1982. With Sandberg at third base, a weary Bowa at shortstop and Keith Moreland, another Philadelphia import, in left field, the Cubs finished fifth (73-89) and next to last in the N.L. East. Sandberg started slowly—one hit in his first 31 at-bats—but got into the swing and finished with a respectable .271 average. Fleet afoot, he led the club in runs with 103 and set a Cub rookie record of 32 stolen bases.

The next season (1983) the Cubs won two fewer games. Another fifth-place finish. Manager Elia, who had been Green's third base coach in Philadelphia, was fired on August 22. Elia compounded his misery when he committed the cardinal sin. He had blasted the fans earlier in the season, on April 29 after the 19th game during what was expected to be a routine press conference.

Elia's diatribe, five minutes of uninterrupted profanity, was captured on tape by Les Grobstein, a free lance radio reporter, and replayed in dugouts and press boxes at every big league outpost. It was triggered after some fans had abused Moreland and Bowa following a losing performance. The next day Green made a public apology.

"We were walking down the left field line to the clubhouse," Elia later explained. "One guy poured beer on Moreland. Moreland went after him. Then someone hit Bowa in the neck with something. We were lucky nobody was hurt."

Within minutes, Elia was in his clubhouse office. He was unable to contain his rage and erupted with the blasphemy, an obscene and hilarious soliloquy of such heroic proportions that it was put on public sale and became known as the infamous "Elia Tape."

What bothered him, Elia later said, was the interpretation that his comments were directed at all Cub fans. The tape includes the following, which offers a general view of Elia's frustration—the Cubs had sunk into the cellar with a 5-14 record:

"There are about 3,000 fans who have been watching us each day and they have been very negative, expecting too much. Why don't they rip me instead of the ballplayers? Eighty-five percent of the world is working but the 15 percent who come out here to Wrigley Field have nothing better to do than heap abuse and criticism on the team. Why don't they go out and look for jobs?"

Charlie Fox, a baseball lifer then among Green's front office confidantes, replaced Elia as an interim manager. Fox had been raised on the streets of New York City. He had a beautiful baritone, knew all the sentimental Irish ballads and had sung at bar mitzvahs and weddings, and occasionally in pubs. He had managed the San Francisco Giants and Montreal Expos and is remembered for adding to baseball's lexicon when he told a departing player, "Be sure the door doesn't hit you in the ass on the way out."

Jim Frey succeeded Fox at the start of the memorable 1984 season. "There are two things I like about the new manager," a Chicago columnist observed. "(1) He isn't from Philadelphia and (2) according to the record books he has been in Philly only once, for the 1980 World Series."

A line-drive hitting outfielder, Frey had a 14-year playing career, all in the minors. He had a career .302 batting average and won two batting titles at the Triple A level. In 1957 he led the Texas League in seven offensive categories. After he retired as a player, he spent 15 years in the Baltimore organization, the last 12 as the Orioles' batting coach.

His expertise was especially beneficial to Sandberg, now playing second base after his rookie year. Frey told him to stop spraying singles, that he wasn't aggressive at the plate and was big and strong enough to reach the fences. He should concentrate on pulling the ball, i.e., hitting for distance. Sandberg listened.

He responded in 1984 with 19 home runs, four more than in his previous two seasons combined, batted .314 and led the league with 550 assists. As Green had envisioned, Sandberg began to hit with power and developed, even sooner than expected, into a premier player. One more home run and another triple in 1984 would have made him the first major league player with 200 hits, 20 doubles, 20 triples, 20 home runs and 20 stolen bases in the same season.

Sandberg's biggest day was on June 23 against the St. Louis Cardinals at Wrigley Field. With the Cubs trailing 9-8 in the bottom of the ninth, Sandberg connected for a game-tying home run off Bruce Sutter, the former Cub who was among the best closers of the time. Sandberg stepped in against Sutter again in the 10th and responded with another game-tying home run. The Cubs won 12-11 in 11 innings. Sandberg drove in seven runs.

After the game Cardinal manager Whitey Herzog told reporters Sandberg was the best player since Babe Ruth. More than likely, as author Norman Mailer would say, Herzog was "feeding the goat." Herzog was known for tweaking the press. But the Chicago newspapers, like author Mailer's goat, gobbled it up and ran with it for another Sandberg touchdown.

Green had supported Frey with a blockbuster trade—with the Phillies, of course—on March 26, at the conclusion of spring training. It may have been his best deal because he acquired Gary Matthews and Bob Dernier, two-thirds of his starting outfield, at virtually no cost. The only possible explanation is that the Phillies were dumping salaries.

The Cubs yielded two fringe players, Bill Campbell, an aging relief pitcher who was approaching retirement, his best seasons behind him, and Mike Diaz, an obscure outfielder who disappeared four years later without leaving a footprint.

Dernier was an outstanding center fielder who strengthened the defense and, equally important, provided Frey with an established leadoff hitter. Combined, Dernier and Sandberg, who batted second, stole 77 bases and scored 208 runs. Matthews played left, was a strong hitter and the ultimate team man. His teammates called him "The Sarge."

"When we got those two players, I knew we had a chance," Frey said.

Green wasn't finished. On June 13, two days before the trading deadline, pitcher Rick Sutcliffe came aboard in a seven-player deal with Cleveland. Outfielder Joe Carter, then a prize rookie who developed into a big star, was sacrificed. The deal was a risk. Sutcliffe had undergone surgery and had lost 15 pounds. Worse, he had won only four of nine decisions with the Indians.

It was a masterstroke. Sutcliffe won his first two Cub starts, lost to the Dodgers, and finished with 14 successive victories for 16-1 over-all, a .941 winning percentage, still the Cubs' one-season record. Appropriately, he won the clincher on September 24 in Pittsburgh with a route-going nine-strikeout, two-hitter. Said Frey, "Sutcliffe was a godsend."

After the Cubs had defeated the pursuing New York Mets for the seventh time in a row, Frey admitted, "If anybody has the advantage, it's us. I don't anticipate the jockey falling off."

But Frey was cautious. Wise in the ways of the world, he knew there were no guarantees and spoke of the day in 1961 when he was in the minors and had gone to the Fort Erie racetrack with Pittsburgh Pirates coach Joe Lonnett: "Our horse, Puss 'n' Boots, had an eight-length lead. The horse jumped a hedge and landed in a pond. That's when I stopped playing horses."

The Cubs were slow out of the gate, in second place a half game out at the All-Star break. They went into the lead to stay on August 1. Seven days later, Ed Lynch, then with the Mets and in the next decade the Cubs' general manager, hit Moreland with a pitch that triggered a baseball war. The Cubs had their biggest lead, 9½ games, on September 15 when they were 32 games over .500.

They won breezing, with a 96-65 record, 31 games over .500, 6½ games ahead of the Mets, 12½ ahead of the third-place Cardinals. They had wonderful balance, six hitters with 80 or more runs batted in—third baseman Cey (97), catcher Jody Davis (94), first baseman Leon Durham (86), Sandberg (84), Matthews (82) and Moreland (80). Cey led in home runs with 25.

For Cub fans and the Tribune Co. it was a time of immense joy, the first championship of any kind in 39 years. The "Billy Goat Curse" had been lifted. The Bleacher Bums ordered another case of beer. And while the fans were lining up for playoff and World Series tickets, the parent Tribune Co. was placing full-page local and national advertisements: "ONE OF OUR SUBSIDIARIES HAD A GREAT YEAR."

"Dallas Green deserves the credit," said McKenna, his original sponsor. "He turned the club around in just three years."

Total victory was denied. The Padres, upstarts from the West Division, eliminated the Cubs in the playoffs. The Cubs won the first two games of the N.L. Championship Series and needed only one more victory for their first pennant since 1945. Incredibly, the Padres recovered and won the last three games.

The Cubs took the opener in a 13-0 rout. Sutcliffe went seven innings and was supported with six home runs, two by Matthews. They won the second game 4-2 behind Steve Trout who worked 8⅓ innings and held the Padres to five hits. Big Lee Smith, who had 33 saves during the regular season, finished for him.

The Padres responded with a 7-1 win. Dennis Eckersley was the loser. They also won the fourth game, 7-5, to square the series at two apiece. Steve Garvey, the Padres' veteran first baseman, was the batting star with four hits and five RBI, including a ninth-inning, game-winning home run off Lee Smith.

The fifth and final game was anticlimactic and would have been forgotten if not for a crucial error by first baseman Durham. With one out in the seventh and the Cubs leading 3-2, Tim Flannery's grounder rolled through Durham's legs, Carmelo Martinez scoring to lift the Padres into a 3-3 tie. A two-run double by Tony Gwynn and Garvey's single gave the Padres three more runs and a decisive 6-3 victory.

All six San Diego runs were charged to Sutcliffe. It was his first loss since June 20. As Sutcliffe trudged into the clubhouse, he said, "This will stay with me for a long time." Durham, who had connected for a two-run, first-inning home run, told newsmen, "I've got to let it go, man. Somebody has to win and somebody has to lose. All you can do now is look forward to next year."

Green remained in seclusion for the next three days. The Tribune executives, fearful of published reports that he would be rejoining the Phillies, rewarded him with a three-year contract extension with a sweetener, the club presidency. The rumors about his imminent departure were hokum and flew from the typewriters of his sportswriter friends in Philadelphia.

The Cubs swept the board in the post-season awards. Sandberg, with 22 of a possible 24 first-place votes, was named the N.L. Most Valuable Player, the Cubs' first since Ernie Banks in 1959. Sutcliffe won the Cy Young. Frey was Manager of the Year, Green the Executive of the Year. The Cubs had a record home attendance of 2,108,055, 81 percent of capacity.

One championship often begets another but the Cubs were unable to maintain the pace. The 1985 club was troubled with what may have been an unprecedented flood of injuries. The entire five-man pitching rotation was simultaneously immobilized in mid-August.

Sutcliffe, Trout, Eckersley, Scott Sanderson and Dick Ruthven missed 60 starts, combined, and finished with a cumulative 35-35 record. Sutcliffe, the hero of 1984, was 8-8 and on the disabled list three times. Eckersley (11-7) was the biggest winner. The most significant statistic: 20 pitchers appeared, 18 winning at least one game.

A half dozen position players were similarly affected. Matthews, Dernier and Davis also broke down. Confronted with an aging and ailing club, Frey used 101 different lineups. The result was a fourth-place finish, a major tumble, seven games under .500 at 77-84, and 23½ games out. Right fielder Moreland played in 161 games and had his best year with .307, 14 home runs and 106 RBI.

The next year, 1986, was more of the same. Frey got the ax early, on June 12. The club was struggling at 23-23 in fifth place. Coach John Vukovich managed the next two games before Gene Michael arrived. Michael, a former shortstop, was accustomed to the tumult. He had had three brief shots managing George Steinbrenner's New York Yankees.

Michael completed the season without incident. But for the first time in the 20th Century during a full season the Cubs didn't have a 10-game winner. Sutcliffe lost six of his first seven decisions, went on the disabled list, and was replaced by Ed Lynch, acquired in a deal with the Mets. Lee Smith had 31 saves. Greg Maddux, a future star, was called up from the minors and won two of four decisions.

The Cubs dropped to fifth place, 37 games out, with a 70-90 record. A frustrated Green told reporters, "I don't want this kind of season to happen again."

The next season was worse, a disaster. Last place with a 76-85 record. Andre Dawson, a superstar outfielder, was the only saving grace. The baseball owners were then in the midst of a collusion. In an attempt to curb the soaring salaries, they ignored the top free agents. Green broke the boycott and signed Dawson for $500,000, twice below his value.

Instead of shirking in discontent, Dawson, 33, an 11-year veteran, with shattered knees, batted .287 and led the league with 49 home runs and 137 RBI. The fans in the right field bleachers salaamed in unison every time he took his position. He was a landslide MVP, the first from a last-place club, and a daily inspiration to his teammates. He had had 12 surgeries. The players watched in awe as the trainers taped his knees.

On September 17, 1987, prior to the last home game, with the club in last place, Green summoned the press: "I want to apologize to the fans of the Chicago Cubs. The reason I have to apologize is because we quit, with a capital Q." He spelled it out, Q-U-I-T. "There is no other explanation for it.

"I'm a fighter and I'm a screamer and yeller. I hurt so bad I don't know where to start. I have done everything I could possibly do for the players and their families. I didn't expect them to give up with some 30 games to play. I was slapped in the face, and so were the Cub fans.

"Talk about collusion! There's collusion in our clubhouse. It's collusion to keep your mouth shut. There's collusion to take my money. For the last month, all the players have been talking about is their hunting and fishing trips and the damn cruises. They forgot we had a month to play. No, they didn't forget. They didn't care."

A month later, on October 29, Green also quit, following a severe skirmish with John Madigan, the Tribune executive vice president who was overseeing the Cub operation.

Green wanted coach John Vukovich to manage the club. Madigan withheld approval. Green then indicated he would be willing to get back into uniform to manage. Madigan had no objection providing Green abdicated his upper-management position. Madigan insisted that Green could no longer continue as the club's general manager. Green was given a "golden parachute" and departed without comment.

He took a well-earned sabbatical, then returned for the 1989 season to manage the Yankees. "I might bring something to the table that might carry us over the hump," he announced. "And if it doesn't work, I'll go the way of all Yankee managers."

He lasted one season. From 1993 to 1996 he managed the Mets. He was dismissed in late August, replaced by Bobby Valentine. He then went home to rejoin the Phillies as senior advisor to the general manager.

LOOKING GOOD, WINNING UGLY

Doug Rader, a former big league third baseman, coach, manager and bon vivant, out of Northbrook, Illinois, wanted to put the record straight.

"I was falsely accused," Rader insisted.

In 1983 when the White Sox were enroute to the title in the American League West, Rader was quoted as saying they were "winning ugly."

Rader revealed the credit should go to Darrell Johnson, the advance scout for the Texas Rangers. It was Johnson's invention. In filing a report on the Sox, he wrote that they were "winning ugly." An example of the ugliness, according to Johnson: "They are scoring six runs on six hits."

Rader, the Texas manager, repeated Johnson's observation a week or two later. The Chicago players converted it into a battle cry. Soon thereafter, the Sox were almost invincible and won the West by 20 games, a league record. It was their first championship of any kind since the 1959 A.L. pennant-winning club.

"Winning Ugly" signs were plastered throughout the Chicago area on billboards, caps, sweaters, T-shirts, automobiles, store windows and repeatedly popped up on the Comiskey Park center field message board.

"I thanked Mr. Rader many times," White Sox manager Tony La Russa recalled. "We were dead in the water when he said that."

A closet intellectual, Rader is also street smart and a revisionist historian. Later he offered an amendment. "There's no such thing as winning ugly, only losing ugly."

Four months after the comment first appeared, on August 29, the Rangers made their second and final trip to Comiskey Park. The White Sox were in first place, 7½ games ahead and 15 over .500. It was a festive occasion. The fans welcomed them with "Winning Ugly" bedsheet banners and dozens of home-made signs carrying the same message.

Each time Rader appeared on the field, or when he poked his head out of the dugout, there were gleeful shouts of "Ugly! Ugly!"

The Sox swept the two-game series, 2-1 and 5-0, behind Rich Dotson and Britt Burns to hike their lead to 9½ games. As the defeated Rangers were departing, Rader was surrounded by Chicago reporters eager for his comments.

"I'm no oil painting myself," Rader acknowledged. "Do you remember 'Dumbo,' the little elephant in the Walt Disney movie? A crow gives Dumbo a feather and as long as he had it in his trunk he believed he could fly. He believed and they (White Sox) believe, and when you believe something hard enough it'll happen."

It happened but it wasn't a sure thing until the September stretch. The Sox were slow out of the gate but won at a glorious pace during the last two months of the season. The joy came to an end when the Baltimore Orioles eliminated them in the play-offs. Still, a chapter of memorable events was added to the sum of White Sox history.

In past successes, because of the vast old Comiskey Park acreage, the Sox relied almost completely on pitching, defense and speed. They usually had a pitch-and-putt offense. But the '83 club had excellent balance, led the league in runs with 800, had four sluggers with 20 or more home runs, and had a golden-armed pitching rotation, the only team with a pair of 20-game winners. Lamar Hoyt was 24-10, Rich Dotson 22-7.

The Sox lost their first three games, all to the Rangers and, except for one day, were in fourth place or lower until June 28. Two of the big hitters, cleanup-man Greg Luzinski and Carlton Fisk, who batted behind him, slumped so badly that La Russa benched them.

Fisk's frustration was such that in early May, after he had grounded into a double play, he slammed his helmet on the dugout floor. It bounced back and struck his chest. He picked it up, threw it a second time, and it hit La Russa in the leg. Fisk was hitting .136.

Luzinski, alias "The Bull," went three weeks without an extra-base hit. He didn't get his average over .200 until early June. Superstitious, La Russa was making up the lineups without vowels in the players' names.

Luzinski began to find his stroke on May 21. He homered in five consecutive games. On June 26, he connected for a 445-foot home run off Minnesota's Bryan Oeckers that bounced on the left field Comiskey Park roof, an accomplishment previously only achieved by a dozen gargantuans. Later in the season Luzinski did it again.

The Sox, who had been 14 games under .500, began climbing. They were in third place, two games over, at the All-Star break. Hoyt, with the help of relievers Dick Tidrow, Juan Agosto and Salome Barojas, picked up his 11th win on July 18, in a 3-2 decision over Cleveland that lifted the Sox into first place to stay.

The Sox were unbeatable thereafter. The pursuing Kansas City and Texas clubs were trampled in the stampede. Floyd Bannister, after a discouraging 3-9 start, was 13-1 in the stretch, while Hoyt was 15-2 and Dotson 14-2, a collective performance over a long period that may be without equal. They finished with a combined 62-27 record, 35 games over .500.

Rookie outfielder Ron Kittle, like Luzinski, connected in five consecutive games, and led the club in home runs with 35 and in RBI with 100. The others with 20 or more home runs were Luzinski (32), Fisk (26) and Harold Baines, the DH (20).

There was also an unlikely hero, Jerry Dybzinski, a little-known, 155-pound utility shortstop who in two previous seasons never had more than 248 at-bats. He was picked up in a trade with Cleveland three days before the regular season began.

Scott Fletcher, the starting shortstop, was slumping, both at the plate and in the field. La Russa decided a day or two of rest would be beneficial and summoned Dybzinski from the bench. It wasn't quite a reenactment of the Lou Gehrig–Wally Pipp extravaganza but "The Dybber" remained much longer than expected.

From May 1 through June 5, a stretch of 34 games, he was absolutely sensational. He steadied what had been a leaky infield and batted .321 with 14 RBI, most of them with two outs. On the season, he batted a deceiving .230 in 127 games. Essentially a singles hitter, almost half his hits were for extra bases. He also led the club in sacrifice bunts with 11, only four fewer than league-leader Alan Trammell of Detroit.

"We couldn't have done it without him," said reliever Tidrow. "He's the guy who got us over the hump."

La Russa agreed: "He gave us a lift when we were struggling."

Six years later, when Vance Law was with the Cubs, manager Don Zimmer asked him about the '83 Sox, particularly Dybzinski. Law had been the Sox regular third baseman.

"Sure, he was a good player," Law replied. "He was the difference. He set the whole club on fire. He taught me a club is only as strong as its bench."

Also riding the Sox bench was Harvey Misel, a heavyweight hypnotist out of St. Paul. Pleasant and genial, Misel had worked with dozens of A.L. players when they were in Minnesota for a series with the Twins. Some of them gave him a high endorsement, including Eric Soderholm, a former White Sox slugger who had played with the Twins.

Not all of the White Sox submitted to Misel. According to the clubhouse chatter, Greg Walker, a left-handed hitting rookie first baseman who had come up with Kittle from the Pacific Coast League, was Misel's most successful patient. Walker was in a slump. Misel put him under and told him he was a great hitter, etc. Walker jumped off the couch and drove in 21 runs in the next 14 games.

When the Sox arrived in Seattle, Frank Funk, the Mariners' pitching coach, was asked how he would pitch to Walker, what was the best way to get him out.

"The same way I'd pitch to Ted Williams," Funk advised. "Low and behind his back."

Hoyt, a husky right-hander, was the ace of the White Sox pitching staff and led the league in victories with 24. The previous year Hoyt also led with 19 but didn't receive a single vote in the Cy Young award balloting. This time he was an overwhelming choice. Kittle was named Rookie of the Year, La Russa, Manager of the Year, and general manager Roland Hemond, Executive of the Year.

It was Hemond's "genius" season.

He made a half dozen trades for front-liners before and during the season that worked to perfection. He acquired center fielder Rudy Law from the Dodgers, third baseman Vance Law from the Pittsburgh Pirates, second baseman Julio Cruz from the Mariners, Tidrow and Fletcher from the New York Yankees, pitcher Dennis Lamp from the Cubs, and gambled on Bannister who was signed as a free agent.

Owner Jerry Reinsdorf also contributed. Engaged in an on-going feud with Yankee owner George Steinbrenner, Reinsdorf said, "I know how to tell when George is lying—his lips move."

Commissioner Bowie Kuhn fined Reinsdorf $5,000.

Hemond's gray suit, soaked with champagne and beer during the victory celebration, is on display and hangs in a glass case at the new Comiskey Park, the last remnant of the White Sox division championship.

When the Orioles won the A.L. championship playoff guess who was the goat?

In the fourth and final game, with one out in the ninth inning and the tying run at the plate, Dybzinski overran second base on Cruz's single to left and was tagged out in a rundown between second and third on the front end of a game-ending double play.

PLEASURES, PAIN, BIG HURT

Lulled to complacency by the ease with which they won a division title by 20 games over second-place Kansas City in 1983, the White Sox felt assured of climbing to greater heights. Owner Jerry Reinsdorf was among many who thought all the team had to do was show up to claim another title in 1984 on the way to a World Series date.

"We were making plans in the spring of '84 for how we were going to handle the playoffs in the fall," Reinsdorf confessed after the Sox plunged to fifth place with a 74-88 record.

Neither Reinsdorf, manager Tony La Russa nor anyone else could suspect 10 years would pass before the White Sox won again. Nor that their next post-season adventure, in 1993, would come in a new ballpark with a far different cast of players.

Not even the acquisition of great veteran pitcher Tom Seaver nor the arrival of promising rookies such as outfielder Daryl Boston and catcher Joel Skinner could keep the Sox from disaster in '84. Such an outcome didn't seem possible when a seven-game winning streak vaulted them into first place just before the All-Star break, but they lost 13 of the next 17 enroute to fading into oblivion.

The collapse was a team effort with both pitchers and hitters contributing. LaMarr Hoyt, the 1983 Cy Young award winner, went from 24-10 to 13-18, Richard Dotson from 22-7 to 12-15, and Britt Burns dipped to 4-12. Seaver, 39, was the stalwart of the rotation at 15-11 and Floyd Bannister contributed 14-11.

Sluggers Greg Luzinski and Kittle also fell off. Luzinski's home run output dropped from 32 to 13, and he decided to retire. While Kittle hit 32 home runs, his batting average dipped to .215 and his runs batted in sank from 100 to 74. The only offensive standout was right fielder Harold Baines, who batted .304 with 29 home runs and 94 RBI. Boston and Skinner both disappointed, as did other newcomers.

If there was a high point to a low season it came on May 8 and 9. The White Sox defeated the Milwaukee Brewers 7-6 in a game that lasted 25 innings and spanned two nights, ending on a home run by Baines. It was the longest A.L. game ever, just an inning shy of the major league record.

One consolation in 1984 was that Sox attendance climbed to a record 2,136.988, a remarkable feat in the face of the "Cub Fever" sweeping Chicago. The Cubs won a division title, their first championship of any sort in 39 years, and also set an attendance mark with 2,107,655.

General manager Roland Hemond's main effort to recharge the Sox for 1985 was to trade the fading Hoyt to San Diego for rookie infielder Ozzie Guillen and pitchers Bob Long and Tim Lollar. The latter pair didn't help, but Guillen emerged as the latest in a long line of outstanding Sox shortstops, a fine fielder and acceptable hitter. He won the Rookie of the Year award.

Not that 1985 was a memorable season. The Sox made a modest recovery, finishing third with an 85-77 record. Burns snapped back to lead the pitching with 18-11, but was overshadowed by Seaver, who on August 4 won the 300th victory of his career, beating the Yankees in New York. He finished 16-11. Baines (.309, 22 home runs, 111 RBI) and Fisk (.238, 37 home run, 107 RBI) led a modest offense.

The lackluster showing, traceable in part to the failure of the farm system to develop adequate young talent, cost Hemond his job after the season. In a surprise move, Reinsdorf chose broadcaster Ken "Hawk" Harrelson, a former major league outfielder, to replace Hemond.

The result was confusion, dissension and further backsliding in 1986. Harrelson didn't last out the season. The White Sox started 7-18 to heighten tension between the flamboyant, outspoken Harrelson and La Russa. Of the many players acquired by Harrelson, only backup catcher Ron Hassey, who came from the New York Yankees in exchange for Kittle, was of much help. With the Sox 26-38 on June 20, Harrelson fired La Russa, replacing him with Jim Fregosi, a veteran manager and former star shortstop of the California Angels.

Fregosi couldn't right the sinking craft which sank to fifth place with a 72-90 record. Harrelson bailed out on September 25. Even as he confessed that front office duties weren't his strong suit, Harrelson defended his record.

"We're only a couple of hitters away from being a good team," he said. "I wouldn't trade pitching staffs with anybody in the league. By 1988 we'll have a club that can compete with anybody."

The '86 team hadn't been able to compete. Only Baines (.296, 21 home runs and 88 RBI) stood out on offense, though outfielder John Cangelosi set a major league rookie record by stealing 50 bases. The only pitcher to win more than 10 games was Joe Cowley (11-11), who threw a no-hitter against the Angels on September 11. Harrelson traded Seaver (2-6) at midseason.

The two most important developments of 1986 were a decision by the ownership to investigate the possibility of building a new ballpark to replace Comiskey Park, now 76 years old, and Reinsdorf's hiring of Larry Himes, director of scouting and player personnel for the California Angels, as Harrelson's successor.

"The Angels have a very impressive record of guys who made it to the major leagues," Reinsdorf explained, "and he (Himes) is the guy who did it."

He was also to do it for the Sox. Principal among Himes' new recruits during the next few seasons were first baseman Frank

Thomas, third baseman Robin Ventura and pitchers Jack McDowell and Alex Fernandez.

They were acquired one by one in successive first rounds of the annual summer draft of amateur players by Himes, whose expertise was in scouting. An All-American catcher in college, Himes played in the minor leagues for 10 years without rising above Triple A. He spent 14 years as a scout and in the front office of the Angels.

Himes understood the subtleties and in his first four years with the Sox selected college players in the first round of the summer draft. He considered the 17- and 18-year-old high school prospects the bigger risk. The collegians were three or four years older and much more mature physically and emotionally. There was also less agony. The waiting period was shorter.

So Himes went to college. The first White Sox draft choices, one year at a time, in order: McDowell, Stanford; Ventura, Oklahoma State; Thomas, Auburn; Fernandez, Miami (Florida). By 1990 they were at Comiskey Park and three years later were among the principals in a successful playoff bid.

McDowell made the initial impact, winning all three of his decisions in a late-season call-up in September 1987. It made little difference in the outcome of the campaign, the White Sox finishing fifth again with a 77-85 record.

Among the few position players to distinguish themselves were Baines (.293, 20 home runs, 93 RBI), first baseman Greg Walker, back from a spate of injuries to lead the team in home runs with 27 and RBI with 94, and a recruit from Seattle, outfielder Ivan Calderon (.293, 28 home runs and 83 RBI). Bannister turned around a 3-7 start by winning 13 of his final 17 decisions for a 16-11 mark to lead the pitchers. Reliever Bobby Thigpen began to come into his own with a 7-5 record and 16 saves.

Just as the Sox continued to flounder on the field, they struggled until after the '87 season to secure a deal to build a new ballpark with public help. It was not until Reinsdorf's group flirted with St. Petersburg, Florida interests that an Illinois Sports Facilities Authority to erect Comiskey Park II won joint final approval from both the state of Illinois and the city of Chicago. Even then it took many more months of bickering until ground was broken on May 7, 1989.

By that time, the 1988 campaign had passed without much to recommend it. Another fifth place finish at 71-90. Injuries to Fisk, who hit 19 home runs in just 76 games, Walker and Calderon hampered manager Fregosi and even Baines, reduced to being a designated hitter because of a knee injury, slipped to .277, 13 home runs and 81 RBI. Guillen, however, continued to sparkle in the field, and stole 25 bases for the second successive season.

Himes' efforts to rejuvenate the starting pitching by trading away veterans Bannister, the long-fading Dotson and temporary pickup Jose DeLeon were unfruitful. Yet the DeLeon deal with St. Louis gained center fielder Lance Johnson, a future standout. The over-all pitching suffered, veteran pickup Jerry Reuss leading a motley rotation at 13-9 and McDowell (5-10) experiencing rookie growing pains. Closer Thigpen's 34 saves and five wins were factors in more than half the team's victories.

To no one's shock, certainly not Fregosi's as he had ridiculed Himes' "rebuilding with youth" claim as "going cheap," the manager was fired after the season.

"We haven't seen eye-to-eye a lot," Fregosi said, referring to a long-running feud with Himes. "This is probably best for everyone concerned. It's up to somebody else to judge whether I was given a fair chance or not."

Himes turned the team over to Jeff Torborg, a former pitching coach and catcher, on whom he counted to develop the young staff. Torborg, a gentlemanly well-spoken leader, may have made headway in 1989 but it didn't show on the record. The Sox swooned to last with 69-92, their worst mark in 13 seasons. Poor defensive play and pitching inadequacies greased the skids, keeping the Sox last from April 21 to the end.

"It was the worst defense I've ever seen," Torborg lamented. "It was a struggle for us. I kind of overrated us, but it was based on what other people told me. I was new, and we made a big turnover in personnel."

The most shocking turnover came July 29 when Himes sent Baines, Reinsdorf's pet and a fan favorite, to Texas in a deal that brought second baseman Scott Fletcher, left-handed pitcher Wilson Alvarez and a raw young outfielder named Sammy Sosa. Reindorf showed his regard by retiring Baines' uniform number 3 though his hero was to play another dozen years, including two more stints with the White Sox.

Calderon was the leader of a thin offense, batting .286 with 13 home runs and 87 RBI. Guillen, who stole 36 bases, and Fletcher teamed up well to improve the middle of the infield. "I'll match up our double play combination with any in the league," Torborg said.

As for the pitching, Reuss was alone over .500 with 8-5, though Melido Perez (11-14) and Thigpen (2-6, 34 saves) were respectable.

Expectations weren't high for 1990, the last season at old Comiskey Park whose faded charms were featured in a marketing campaign based on nostalgia, but the White Sox astonished the world. They improved to 94-68, a record often good enough for a division title. Not this time. They finished second, nine games behind the Oakland A's.

"It wasn't a dream season because we didn't finish first, but it was certainly a satisfying season," Torborg said. He earned a Manager of the Year award.

What made the season more satisfying was the promise and performance of youth. Three rookies, Ventura, Thomas and Fernandez, and other youngsters such as pitchers McDowell and Greg Hibbard and outfielders Lance Johnson and Sosa sparkled.

After spending all of 1989 in the minors, McDowell emerged as the staff ace with a 14-9 record, with Hibbard matching his totals. Unheralded Eric King was 12-4 and Perez, 13-14. Bullpen ace Thigpen set a major league record with 57 saves.

The most significant event of the season came on August 2 when Himes recalled first baseman Thomas and starter Fernandez from the minors. Thomas immediately demonstrated his superior hitting skills by batting .330 in 60 games. Fernandez, a future ace, went 5-5 in 13 starts. Harrelson, back in the White Sox broadcast booth after a two-season exile to New York, soon nicknamed the 6-feet-5 Thomas "The Big Hurt."

Calderon (.273, 14 home runs, 74 RBI and 32 stolen bases), Fisk (.285, 18 home runs, 65 RBI) and Johnson (.285 with 36 steals) led the batters. Ventura and Sosa flashed great promise. Ventura took over third base and, despite an 0-for-41 slump, finished at .249. Sosa batted only .233 but hit 15 home runs, drove in 70 runs and with 32 steals was the third player on the team with more than 30. Even the ailing and fading Kittle, retrieved as a free agent in 1988, contributed with 16 home runs.

One who did not benefit from the Sox revival was its architect, Himes, whom Reinsdorf fired before the season ended. Reinsdorf's partial explanation was that Himes "couldn't get along with anybody." Reinsdorf recruited Ron Schueler, a former pitcher, from Oakland's front office to replace Himes, who resurfaced in a major way on November 14, 1991 as general manager of the Cubs.

Schueler was to stay in command 10 years, during which he engineered the team to two division titles (1993, 2000). Not all of his moves panned out, but he enjoyed Reinsdorf's total confidence throughout. His first moves, in preparation for the inauguration of new Comiskey Park in 1991, brought veteran outfielders Tim Raines and Cory Snyder and knuckleballer Charlie Hough to the White Sox, with Calderon among those departing. Also added was another veteran, outfielder Bo Jackson, a storied athlete with a hip injury that required surgery so he couldn't play until late in the season.

The first game played at Comiskey Park II on April 18, 1991 was a debacle, the Detroit Tigers trouncing the White Sox 16-0. While the season wasn't exactly similarly disastrous it wasn't any great shakes either, the Sox finishing second with an 87-75 record. Attendance at the new park soared to a Chicago record of 2,934,145.

The veterans acquired by Schueler didn't add much to the mix but most of the youngsters continued to develop. In his first full season, Thomas batted .318 with 32 home runs and 109 RBI.

Ventura, who won a Gold Glove, hit .284 with 23 home runs and 100 RBI, the most ever for a Sox third baseman. Guillen and Johnson also had fine seasons, but Sosa backslid, dipping to .203 with just 10 home runs in 116 games.

The young pitchers also made strides. McDowell (17-9) and Fernandez (9-13) turned into standouts and rookie Alvarez (3-2) made a splash by pitching a no-hitter against Baltimore in his second major league start.

Schueler, increasingly impatient with Torborg's methods, encouraged the manager to accept an offer from the New York Mets after the 1991 season. Schueler replaced him with Gene Lamont, a longtime coach for the Pittsburgh Pirates. He provided Lamont with veteran firepower in slugger George Bell, as well as experience at second base with Steve Sax. At the time, the price paid for Bell to the Cubs didn't seem exorbitant—the struggling young Sosa. It's noteworthy that the Cubs general manager who made the deal was Himes, who got him from Texas for the White Sox two years before.

Certainly, Bell didn't disappoint in 1992, with 25 home runs and 112 RBI to team up with Thomas (.323, 24 home runs, 115 RBI) and Ventura (.282, 18 home runs and 93 RBI) for a potent heart of the Sox lineup. Speed came from Raines (45 steals) and Johnson (41 steals). Amidst acrimony, solid-fielding Ron Karkovice took over from the fading and oft-injured Fisk.

The campaign was marred almost at the beginning, however, when Guillen suffered a severe knee injury in a collision on April 22. He was out for the season, part of the reason the Sox finished third with a record of 86-76.

While McDowell emerged as a full-fledged star with 20-10, including a league-leading 13 complete games, he also gave management headaches. He was particularly peeved at being ignored while Thomas and Ventura were offered long-term contracts.

"I'm all for Frank and Robin," he growled. "They're great players. I hope they get what they deserve. What do I get? More grief!"

The other young starting pitchers, Fernandez (8-11) and Alvarez (5-3) were still learning, but a new bullpen ace, Roberto

Hernandez (7-3, 12 saves) emerged to replace the receding Thigpen.

A decade after the "Winning Ugly" success of 1983, Lamont finally led the White Sox once more into the promised land of a division title in 1993. It was the culmination of Himes' process of building with youth, augmented by Schueler's "fine tuning."

Guillen summed it up: "It shows you baseball is like putting up a building. You build and build and build until you've made a building."

The White Sox, with a 94-68 record, won the A.L. West by eight games over Texas. They took over first place to stay on July 7 and clinched on September 27 by beating Seattle 4-2 on a three-run home run by Bo Jackson, the surgically-repaired former football star who contributed 18 home runs and 45 RBI in 85 games.

Pacing the Sox was Thomas and the youngest starting pitching rotation—average age 24—ever to win a division title. Thomas hit .317, drove in 128 runs and set a Sox record with 41 home runs. He won the Most Valuable Player award. Ventura contributed 22 home runs and 93 RBI and a judicious free agent pickup by Schueler, outfielder Ellis Burks (.275, 17 home runs, 74 RBI) helped offset a steep decline by Bell.

The pitching, though, was the chief factor in the title run. McDowell won the Cy Young award with 22-10, Fernandez blossomed at 18-9, Alvarez contributed 15-8 and Jason Bere, a rookie called up from the minors on May 25, added the completing touch with 12-5. Alvarez and Bere each finished the season with seven consecutive victories. Hernandez was the big man in the bullpen with 38 saves.

Lamont, like Torborg three years earlier, won the Manager of the Year award, an honor whose glow was to fade just about as quickly as it did for his predecessor.

A rare sour note to the regular season was the forced retirement of Fisk six days after he caught his 2,226th game on June 22, 1993 to set a major league durability record behind the plate.

Even the pleasure of finally gaining a division title wasn't complete because the White Sox, just as they had in 1983, stumbled in the post-season. They fell to the Toronto Blue Jays in the A.L. Championship Series in six games. The young Sox pitching staff, so solid earlier, yielded a record 65 hits for a six-game series.

The highlight for the Sox came in Game 4 after losing the first two games at Comiskey Park then winning the first in Toronto. They tied the series on a triple and a home run by Johnson and a home run by Thomas. Johnson's home run was his first of 1993 after 540 regular season at-bats without one.

"I try to hit triples," Johnson said. "If I was going to go out and try to hit home runs, I'd hit seven or eight a year and be out of the game in two years."

Game 4 was the final spark of life in '93 for the Sox. Toronto won the next two and the series on its way to a World Series title. What was most distressing for the disappointed Sox was that they lost all three games in Chicago.

"When you have a team of 25 guys and nothing works at home," said Raines, who led the Sox in hitting with 12-for-27 for a .444 average, "it's just frustrating for guys to take. If it was just one or two or three guys, you could understand. But it was the whole ball club."

All the same, the ball club appeared to have an excellent chance of winning another division title in 1994 and redeeming itself in a second successive post-season venture.

It certainly seemed so well into the '94 season as the White Sox, reinforced with free agent outfielders Julio Franco and Darrin Jackson as replacements for Bell and Burks, battled for first place in the newly-constituted A.L. Central Division. Their chief rivals were the Cleveland Indians, from whom they wrested first place on July 18.

They were in first place as well on August 12 when the race ended abruptly. A long-festering labor dispute between owners and players resulted in a stand-off that wiped out the rest of the regular season and post-season competition.

The "lost season" did however contribute to baseball lore and statistics despite not confirming championship teams. The celebrated "Bat-gate" incident in which Cleveland slugger Albert

Belle was accused of using a "corked" bat, one confiscated by the umpires and then stolen from their dressing room, spiced the campaign.

More positively, Thomas reaffirmed his status as a great hitter by batting .353 with 38 home runs and 101 RBI in just 113 games of the curtailed season. He gained his second consecutive Most Valuable Player award. Franco batted .319 with 20 home runs and 98 RBI and Jackson hit .312.

The pitching continued to be outstanding. By winning his first eight decisions after having won his last seven of 1993, Alvarez achieved a 15-game winning streak before settling for a final season record of 12-8. Bere was 12-2, Fernandez 11-7 and McDowell 10-9.

It was doubly galling that with such a superb collection of talent, the White Sox couldn't claim another division title in an effort to advance to their first World Series in 35 years.

Schueler lamented: "I might not have an opportunity to have this club again. We have a lot of free agents. You don't know what's in store."

What the future held was a half dozen years of turmoil and controversy before the White Sox would emerge again as a potent force.

Ryno, Grace, Sammy Make 'em Run

23

I t is curious and inexplicable how the course of the Cubs' fortunes in the second half of the 20th Century always ran rigorously true to form. Brief bursts of hope were inevitably succeeded by long stretches of ineptitude. This was certainly so in the final baker's dozen seasons from 1988 through 2000, none of which produced total satisfaction and most of which turned out frightfully appalling.

No matter who the general manager, manager, or players, the result was the same—endless frustration for Cub fans, who in defiance of the accepted baseball wisdom that attendance follows success in the standings turned out massively to watch mostly inept teams. In 11 of the 13 seasons attendance topped two million and often approached three million in a ballpark that could hold just over 40,000.

The introduction of night baseball to Wrigley Field on August 9, 1988 undoubtedly contributed to attendance, but only partly since the vast majority of home games (63 of 81) continued to be played in the daytime. "Beautiful Wrigley Field" became the major attraction rather than the oft-struggling Cubs.

They continued their wayward course under Jim Frey, who replaced Dallas Green as general manager after the 1987 season. As if in loyalty to Cub tradition, Frey began with a trade that challenged the notorious Lou Brock–for–Ernie Broglio deal of 1964 as a disaster. He sent outstanding closer Lee Smith to the Boston Red Sox for pitchers Calvin Schiraldi and Al Nipper, both failures in 1988.

Fortunately, Frey's choice to manage the team, Don Zimmer, a boyhood friend and major league infielder for 12 seasons, turned out better. The Cubs were the outgoing, aggressive and hunch-playing Zimmer's fourth major league managerial stop and he had polished a rough-hewn knack of winning player confidence and inspiring enthusiasm.

Zimmer's immediate task was to make the most of a crop of talented youngsters produced in the mid and late 1980s by a farm system revived by the Green regime. Shortstop Shawn Dunston, outfielder Rafael Palmeiro, first baseman Mark Grace and right-hander Greg Maddux were the cream of the crop, all entering the early phases of long and successful careers. Another novice, catcher Damon Berryhill, replaced Jody Davis, a hero of '84, who was sent packing late in the 1988 season.

Under Zimmer's hand, the youngsters blended in well with veterans such as second baseman Ryne "Ryno" Sandberg, right fielder Andre Dawson and third baseman Vance Law, a free agent pickup who hit .293 with 78 RBI. Dawson (.303, 24 home runs, 78 RBI) and Sandberg (.264, 19 home runs, 77 RBI and 25 stolen bases) provided power and a steadying influence.

Left fielder Palmeiro, playing his first full major league season, was the runner-up in the N.L. batting race with .307, though he hit only eight home runs, failing to show the consistent power that was his after he left the Cubs. Rookie Grace, a superb fielder, replaced fading veteran Leon Durham and batted .296.

Brightest of all was Maddux, 22, who boasted a 15-3 record at the All-Star break and finished 18-8 to lead a starting rotation that included Rick Sutcliffe (13-14), Jamie Moyer (9-15) and Schiraldi (9-13). The bullpen was lacking, Smith who had 36 saves in 1987 being sorely missed, with veteran pickup Goose Gossage no answer as he picked up only 13 saves.

Yet the Cubs appeared to be progressing, finishing fourth with a 77-85 record in 1988. Zimmer was hugely pleased, musing, "The question is, how much better are these young guys going to get?"

He found out the next season when the Cubs came up with their second and last title of any sort in the 20th Century, another East Division championship. It came at a price, however, a nine-player trade with the Texas Rangers on December 5, 1988 in which the major figures yielded were Palmeiro and Moyer, whose careers were to thrive. The Cubs' only meaningful acquisition was erratic left-handed closer Mitch "Wild Thing" Williams, who enjoyed a brief but crucial burst of success.

Luckily, Williams' career season came for the Cubs, and right away in 1989 as he contributed 36 saves. He was one of many heroes. Sandberg extended an errorless streak to 90 games and batted .290 with 30 home runs. Grace hit .314. Dawson, despite mangled knees, led the team with 77 RBI and hit 21 home runs. Center fielder Jerome Walton batted .293 and had a 30-game hitting streak, the longest by a Cub since 1900, and won the Rookie of the Year award. Another rookie outfielder, Dwight Smith, batted .324.

Maddux led the pitchers with 19-12, a revived Sutcliffe was 16-11, but the bonus was provided by journeyman Mike Bielecki with an unexpected 18-7. Another major contributor was setup pitcher Les Lancaster, 4-2, who was almost unhittable with a 1.36 earned run average for 42 appearances.

The Cubs clinched first place on September 26 and finished with a record of 93-69, six games ahead of the second-place New York Mets. They set an attendance record with 2,491,492 to round out Frey's joy and that of the Tribune Co.

"I couldn't be prouder of a ball club that this one, in all my 41 years in baseball," Zimmer said. "This has been my most satisfying season."

It would have been even more satisfying if the Cubs could have negotiated the next obstacle, the N.L. Championship Series. They failed, falling to the West Division champion San Francisco Giants in five games.

The Cubs' pitching short-circuited, Maddux suffering severe batterings in Games 1 and 4. Only Bielecki stood out with a strong effort in Game 5 before finally succumbing 3-2 as the Giants wrapped up the N.L. pennant.

The confrontation was notable chiefly for the batting duel between rival first basemen Will Clark and Grace. Clark produced 12 hits in 20 at-bats for a .650 average, hit two home runs and drove in eight runs. Grace virtually matched him with 11 hits in 17 at-bats for .647, a home run and also drove in eight runs.

Despite the numbing finish, Sandberg paid tribute to Zimmer: "He gambled all year and we won every time. He went against the book for an entire season and we won the division. You can't change your style just because it's the playoffs."

Nine years were to pass before the Cubs gained the playoffs again and then not with a division title but rather the consolation prize of a "wild card" berth. By that time Zimmer was a coach with the Yankees and Sandberg had retired as a player.

The long years of travail and tribulation began in 1990 and continued for eight seasons with only occasional individual achievements softening the hard times. A pitching collapse in Zimmer's third season at the helm dragged the Cubs into a fourth-place tie with 77-85. Williams was often wildly ineffective, Sutcliffe injured most of the campaign and Bielecki sank to 8-11. Even Maddux (15-15), the ace of the staff, struggled, failing to win in 13 consecutive starts. Rookie Mike Harkey (12-6) defied the trend in a false dawn.

The offense held up far better. Sandberg batted .306, drove in 100 runs and with 40 home runs was the first second baseman to lead the league in that category since Rogers Hornsby in 1925. Dawson hit .310 with 27 home runs and 100 RBI, and Grace batted .309. Their performances offset steep declines by Walton and Dwight Smith, who had been so outstanding as rookies the previous season.

Sandberg, in addition to his hitting prowess, continued to be a defensive gem. He won an eighth consecutive Gold Glove and broke two major league records at his position—most successive games (123) and most chances (582) without an error.

Zimmer later was moved to marvel, "He made so few errors that when he made one you thought the world was coming to an end. Then he hits 30 or 40 homers and scores 100 runs. I saw them all...I saw the best second basemen who ever played, and in my opinion Ryne Sandberg is the best second baseman who ever played baseball."

Frey sought reinforcements for Zimmer after the 1990 season by diving into the free agent market for three veterans, slugging outfielder George Bell, starter Danny Jackson and reliever Dave Smith. Only Bell proved worth his share of the aggregate one-year outlay of $8 million for new talent. Jackson and Smith combined for a record of 1-11 and 17 saves in 1991. An April deal sent 1989 hero Mitch Williams to Philadelphia for reliever Chuck McElroy who was only marginally better.

Bell did round out a sort of "Murderer's Row" heart of the lineup. He contributed 25 home runs, batted .285 and had 85 RBI. Sandberg (.291, 26 home runs, 100 RBI) and Dawson (.272, 31 home runs, 104 RBI) were solid, but Grace fell off to .273 with merely eight home runs and 58 RBI. The Cubs led the league in home runs with 159.

Notwithstanding, all that firepower didn't add up to success in 1991, partly because the pitching staff lacked depth. Maddux (15-11) and Bielecki (13-11) were the only dependable starters. Onetime ace Sutcliffe (6-5) was released before the season ended and the promising Harkcy (0-2) was injured. At season's end, the Cubs, at 77-83, were fourth.

Zimmer wasn't around by that time and Frey was gone a few months after his buddy left. In an efffort to save the season when the Cubs started out 18-19, Frey replaced Zimmer as manager with Jim Essian, a former big league catcher managing in the Cubs' farm system. Under Essian the Cubs were 59-63 the rest of the way but he was discarded, as was Frey when former White Sox general manager Larry Himes took command of the team on November 14, 1991. None other than Himes has been general manager of both Chicago teams.

Vigorous, opinionated and often abrasive, Himes plunged into his new challenge with zest, hiring as manager Jim Lefebvre, who had been fired by the Seattle Mariners after the 1991 season. Lefebvre was overflowing with enthusiasm, quick to laugh and prone to angry outbursts at underachieving players. The Cubs gave him plenty of scope to exercise the latter weakness.

Himes' major moves for 1992 were to sign free agent starter Mike Morgan and, far more important in the long run, trade Bell to the White Sox for struggling young outfielder Sammy Sosa. Himes' strength was an ability to recognize incipient talent and in dealing for Sosa a second time—he acquired him for the White Sox in 1989—he achieved one of the greatest coups in Cub history.

A mid-season deal also brought veteran third baseman Steve Buechele but 1992 was pretty much a re-run of the previous two seasons, the Cubs again finishing fourth, winning one more game (77-84) than in 1990 and '91. Sandberg (.304, 26 home runs, 100 RBI), Dawson (.277, 22 home runs, 90 RBI) and Grace (.307) stood firm, but an ailing back sidelined shortstop Dunston and the rest of the cast was undistinguished.

That is except for three starting pitchers, most notably Maddux, who won the Cy Young award with a record of 20-11 and earned run average of 3.28. Morgan (16-8, 2.55 ERA) and young Frank Castillo (10-11, 3.46 ERA) also stood out.

What didn't stand out, and forever besmirched Himes' reputation among Cub fans, was his failure to sign Maddux to a long-term contract. (Actually, Himes' Tribune Co. bosses made the decision to let Maddux go.) After an acrimonious dispute, free agent Maddux joined the Atlanta Braves and extended his string of Cy Young awards to four while establishing himself as the outstanding pitcher of his generation.

Paradoxically, while holding back on Maddux, the Tribune Co. permitted Himes to make Sandberg baseball's highest paid player for 1993. He was awarded a four-year contract extension for $30.5 million in the spring of '92.

Himes put a brave face on Maddux's departure. Upon signing free agent Jose Guzman before the 1993 season he remarked, "I've now got the starter to replace him."

Not quite, though Guzman was 12-10 in '93 before melting away with arm trouble. Greg Hibbard (15-11) a free agent from the White Sox, led the starters. Morgan was 10-15 and Harkey

10-10. The ace of the staff was reliever Randy Myers, an expensive free agent signee, who set a N.L. record with 53 saves.

As part of the reshaping for '93, Dawson also was let go, opening right field for Sosa, who responded by emerging as a star at the age of 24. He led the team with 33 home runs, drove in 93 runs and stole 36 bases to join Grace (.325, 14 home runs, 98 RBI) and surprising young catcher Rick Wilkins (.303, 30 home runs, 73 RBI) as the leaders on offense. Injuries hampered Sandberg, who batted .309 with only nine home runs and 45 RBI, to 117 games. Back surgery sidelined Dunston almost all year.

Even though a feud raged between Himes and Lefebvre, adding to player discontent with the general manager, the 1993 Cubs finished above .500 (84-78) for the first time in four years by winning 20 of their last 28 games. Not that the improvement saved Lefebvre's job. Himes fired him for not doing even better.

Lefebvre angrily told reporters "This is what I get for busting my butt for two years." He said that when he asked Himes why he was fired, Himes told him, "'I don't want to get into it.' He said he was doing it because it was best for him. He doesn't care what's in the best interest of the team."

Himes replaced Lefebvre with Tom Trebelhorn, an upbeat, enthusiastic type who had managed the Milwaukee Brewers for five seasons. Among other changes for 1994 was the realignment of the N.L. into three parts, assuring the Cubs they could finish no lower than fifth place in the Central Division. They accomplished that with a record of 49-63 when a players' strike curtailed the season abruptly on August 12.

Trebelhorn's brief tenure (less than a full season) was remarkable only for his attempt at reconciliation with unhappy fans after the team lost its first 12 home games. He conducted chats with the disgruntled fans in front of the firehouse next to Wrigley Field. "A lot of heart and emotion comes with the Cubs," he said. "The fans are terrific. They root hard, but they root fair."

Fair or foul, the fans had little to cheer about in '94. Rookies Steve Trachsel (9-7) and Kevin Foster (3-4) showed promise, but the overall pitching was dismal, other than that of Myers who accumulated 34 saves. Grace (.298) and Sosa (.300, 25 home runs, 92 RBI) led a sporadic attack. Wilkins declined to a one-year "wonder," sinking to .227 and seven home runs.

The most sensational development came on June 13 when Sandberg, dismayed by family problems as well as alleged dissatisfaction with management's failure to build a winning team, announced his retirement at the early age of 34 after 13 seasons. At the time he was batting just .238 in 57 games and was only in the second year of his $30.5 million contract.

Chicago Tribune columnist Mike Royko, an ardent, if realistic and hard-bitten, Cub fan, remarked whimsically: "Maybe that's what they should put on his plaque when he goes into the Hall of Fame: 'Ryne Sandberg, who walked away from one of the biggest paychecks in baseball, because he didn't think he was earning it.'"

The Tribune Co. concluded that neither Himes nor Trebelhorn was earning his pay either after the '94 failure. They turned to Andy MacPhail, whose Minnesota Twins had won two World Series under his guidance as general manager, as the new Cub president. He hired Ed Lynch, a former Cub pitcher who had been working in the San Diego Padres front office, to be his general manager. Lynch in turn named Jim Riggleman, who had managed the Padres for two years, to guide the Cubs.

Riggleman's approach to managing was to emphasize strong fundamental play, enforce strict discipline without being a martinet, demand all-out effort and communicate freely with his players.

"Jimmy epitomizes the manager of the 1990s because the bottom line with him is he's reasonable," Lynch said. "He's an outstanding communicator, not confrontational."

Nevertheless, confrontations did occur during Riggleman's five-year run, the longest by a Cub manager since Durocher's tenure (1966–72). Lynch signed two major free agents to ease Riggleman's task going into the '95 season, pitcher Jaime Navarro, who was to cause the manager trouble, and outspoken center fielder Brian McRae. Other deals brought in catcher Scott Servais and outfielder Luis Gonzalez.

In a 1995 season limited to 144 games because of the late set-tlement of the players' strike that had begun in 1994, Riggleman led the Cubs to a 73-71 record and third place. Navarro paced the starters with 14-6. Youngsters Foster and Jim Bullinger each won 12 and Castillo 11. The consistent Myers had a league-high 38 saves.

Grace emerged as the veteran team leader, led in batting with .326 and hit 51 doubles, six short of the club record. Sosa continued to grow with 36 home runs, 119 RBI and 34 stolen bases. McRae was a revelation as the Cubs' best leadoff man in two decades. He batted .288 with 92 runs, 12 home runs and 27 stolen bases.

The plus-.500 finish heightened expectations for 1996 and they soared when Sandberg decided to return at the age of 36. He made a solid contribution with 25 home runs and 85 RBI to a title bid that disintegrated with a devastating skid of 14 losses in the season's final 16 games.

Grace and Sosa again stood out. Grace won his fourth Gold Glove and batted .331, highest for a Cub since Bill Madlock's .339 in 1976. Sosa was leading the league in home runs with 40 and had 100 RBI when on August 20 he suffered a hand fracture that ended his season. McRae had another fine season, scoring 111 runs, hitting 17 home runs and stealing 37 bases in his lead-off role.

Inadequate pitching undermined the team. Myers was gone, having left as a free agent after the '95 season, and no replacement was entirely satisfactory, though Turk Wendell earned 18 saves in 21 chances. Navarro led the rotation with 15-12 and Trachsel developed to 13-9 but none of the other starters was consistent. To compound the problems, Navarro rebelled against Riggleman's regimen, ensuring his departure as a free agent after the season.

Lynch's efforts to shore up the pitching for 1997 included signing free agent closer Mel Rojas and veteran starters Kevin Tapani and Terry Mullholland. Dunston was retrieved from San Francisco, where he had spent 1996, to plug the hole at short-stop.

It was all in vain as the Cubs tumbled to their worst showing (68-94) since 1980, starting out fittingly with a N.L. record season-opening losing streak of 14 games. Rojas was a bust and was traded to the Mets in August along with McRae and Wendell for pitcher Mark Clark and outfielder Lance Johnson. Tapani was sidelined with finger surgery the first four months, but finished strong with 9-3.

Rojas was 0-4 with six blown saves in 19 opportunities before he departed. He understood the Cub fans' unhappiness with his poor performance. "I don't blame the fans for booing me," he said. "I can handle that. I owed them something. I came over here (to Chicago) with a good attitude to have a good year. It didn't work out that way."

As bad as it was overall, 1997 did offer a few positive aspects. Grace batted .319, Sosa hit 36 home runs and drove in 119 runs, and Sandberg ended his career by hitting a respectable .264 with 12 home runs and 64 RBI as well as establishing a career record for second basemen with 277 home runs. Rookie outfielder Doug Glanville broke in with .300 and Clark finished 6-1 for the Cubs. Rookie starter Jeremi Gonzalez was 11-9.

Despite the horror of 1997, Riggleman got a vote of confidence from MacPhail and Lynch for his fourth season as manager and also a revamped roster. In addition to Clark and Lance Johnson, Lynch added veterans in slugging outfielder Henry Rodriguez, second baseman Mickey Morandini (obtained from Philadelphia for Glanville), shortstop Jeff Blauser and closer Rod Beck.

"We're better right now than we were last year," Lynch proclaimed. "With Henry (Rodriguez) hitting behind Sammy (Sosa) in our lineup, that should help run production."

Neither Lynch nor anyone else could have expected the sort of "run production" the Cubs got in 1998. It was the year of the national attention-riveting home run battle between Sosa and Mark McGwire of the St. Louis Cardinals in which both broke Roger Maris' record of 61 home runs in a 162-game season. Longtime superstar McGwire won out, finishing with 70, but

Sosa's total of 66 finally vaulted him into the top echelon of baseball's hierarchy of great players.

It took an extra effort, a 5-3 victory in a wild-card tiebreaker game with the Giants, as well as a superlative achievement by Sosa, for the Cubs to gain their first post-season berth in nine years. But they accomplished it, finishing second in the Central Division in the regular season with a record of 89-63 before beating the Giants. A two-run home run by late-season pickup, third baseman Gary Gaetti, provided the impetus.

The N.L. Division Series was almost anti-climactic as well as disheartening, the Cubs falling in three straight to the Atlanta Braves. The only Cub solace was Tapani's pitching in Game 3 in which the Cubs led 1-0 before losing 2-1 in 10 innings. Braves pitchers limited the Cubs to 17 hits in series.

Nonetheless, 1998 was a remarkable season for Sosa and the Cubs, though they again failed to capture first place. Among its highlights, in addition to Sosa's 66 home runs, 158 RBI, .308 average and 134 runs scored, which earned him the Most Valuable Player award, the most spectacular was a major league record-tying 20 strikeout performance by 20-year-old rookie right-hander Kerry Wood. It came on May 8 in a 2-0 victory over Houston in his fifth big league start.

Wood went on to win the Rookie of the Year award with a 13-6 record, a 3.40 earned run average and 233 strikeouts in $166\frac{2}{3}$ innings. Ominously, however, arm problems plagued him late in the season. It eventually called for surgery that kept him out of the 1999 campaign and limited him in 2000.

Among those contributing to the partial success of 1998 on offense were Grace (.309, 17 home runs, 89 RBI), Morandini (.296, 93 runs), Rodriguez (.251, 31 home runs, 85 RBI) and utility outfielders Brant Brown (.291, 14 home runs) and Glenallen Hill (.351 in 131 at-bats). Veteran shortstop Blauser was a flop, hitting just .219.

In addition to Wood, Tapani (19-9) and Trachsel (15-8) stood out as starters. Mulholland (6-5, three saves) excelled in a dual role. Beck was outstanding with 51 saves and three wins.

Yet above all it was Sosa's season, vaulting him to international fame. The poor kid, a former shoeshine boy from the Dominican Republic, may not have outduelled McGwire but he also surpassed two legendary players, Roger Maris and Babe Ruth, whose record of hitting 60 home runs in 1927 the former broke in 1961. Sosa also set a record for most home runs in a calendar month by hitting 20 in June.

Baseball Commissioner Bud Selig was on target when he said, "This is what will be remembered about the summer of '98, two players hitting more home runs than Babe Ruth and two players breaking Roger Maris' record."

Leonard Coleman, president of the N.L., focused on what Sosa and McGwire had done for baseball, which suffered from being suspended during the labor dispute from the late 1994 season into the early 1995 campaign. He also noted the friendly nature of their heated competition as well as their contributions to charitable causes.

"They not only provided exciting entertainment but they also have been great models for the dignity of the human spirit, caring for each other, caring for the game of baseball, caring for all of society," Coleman said.

"They transcended their unparalleled actions on the playing field by their personal actions. They are two super human beings."

While the McGwire-Sosa friendly rivalry continued at a steaming pace for another season, the brief burst of sunshine for the Cubs clouded over instantly. Their next two seasons, 1999 and 2000, ranked among the worst in the franchise's 125-year history. Changing players, managers and general managers made no difference.

Under Riggleman, the Cubs were 67-95 in 1999, finishing last. An unbelievable record home attendance of 2,813,854 witnessed the journey into oblivion.

Under Don Baylor, Riggleman's successor for 2000, the Cubs were two games worse at 65-97 and took a firm grip on last place. The Wrigley Field turnout was only a few thousand fewer.

MacPhail and Lynch, bemused by the unexpected modest success of 1998, handed Riggleman a recipe for disaster in 1999, a team of "graybeards." The Cubs started the season with an infield of Grace (34), Morandini (32), Blauser (33) and Gaetti (40), an outfield of Sosa (30), Johnson (30) and Rodriguez (31), and catcher Benito Santiago (34).

Lynch termed the ages irrelevant, "not a factor for '99."

The Cubs certainly weren't, whether advanced age played a role or not, collapsing after a decent 32-23 start. They won only 35 of their remaining 107 games.

One of the major pitching additions held up well, starter John Lieber (10-11) doing a fair job of replacing the sidelined Wood. The other, veteran closer Rick Aguilera (6-3, 8 saves) who replaced the faltering Beck, was no bargain. Trachsel (8-18) and Tapani (6-12) went into reverse gear, as did almost the entire staff except for young reliever Terry Adams (6-3, 13 saves).

Sosa's second duel with McGwire was almost as heated as the first, the Cardinal winning out with 65 home runs to the Cub's 63. Sosa finished at .288 with 141 RBI to lead a strong offense. Grace batted .309, Rodriguez had a good year with .304, 26 home runs and 87 RBI and part-timer Hill contributed 20 home runs and .300 in 99 games. But the middle and left side of the infield collapsed, Morandini and Blauser fading, and third base a nagging problem. Santiago's once-bright catching skills were in free-fall.

Riggleman paid the price, walking the plank after five seasons, as Lynch admitted, "It is clear a lot of changes need to be made in our roster. Our pitching has not performed as well as we thought."

Neither did most of the old-timers, many of them gone by the 2000 season as Lynch cleaned house. To replace Riggleman, he brought in Baylor, who had managed the Colorado Rockies for six years through 1998.

Baylor's opening statement was in sharp contrast to Dallas Green's "new tradition" blunder of almost 20 years earlier. "There aren't too many times that you have a chance to manage a franchise with a great tradition like the Chicago Cubs," Baylor rejoiced, later adding, "You're talking about a team that's recognized all over the world."

Sadly, recognized only as "lovable losers" by many who are unaware of their real tradition and the Cubs continued in that vein in 2000 despite Lynch's and Baylor's fervent efforts. Lynch continued to recruit veterans, bringing in catcher Joe Girardi, shortstop Ricky Gutierrez, second baseman Eric Young, third basemen Willie Greene and Shane Andrews, center fielder Damon Buford and starting pitcher Ismael Valdes.

As the season progressed it became evident neither Baylor nor the new personnel were transforming the team into a winner though some "retreads" such as Girardi, Young, Gutierrez and Buford were playing well. With the Cubs a disappointing 39-53 on July 19, Lynch resigned as general manager after more than five years in the role.

MacPhail, who decided to act as general manager as well as president, recounted Lynch's offer to step aside.

"He said, 'I feel responsible (for the team's woes)'," MacPhail recalled. He added later that Lynch had not done all that badly. "If you evaluate all the trades individually, with maybe one exception, they were all either favorable or at least neutral. The frustrating part was that he never seemed to get rewarded for plugging individual holes."

The turmoil continued through the rest of the 2000 season and even into the following spring after MacPhail took over Lynch's duties. Much of the turbulence was caused by several bumbling and—to many injudicious—attempts to trade away Sosa because of his bid for an expensive contract extension. Despite all the furor, Sosa began the 2001 season as a Cub, remaining their chief fan attraction.

Sosa finished 2000 with a major league–leading 50 home runs, a mid-season injury to McGwire ruling out a third home run derby between the two, and hit a career-high .320 with 138 RBI. Young (.297 and 54 stolen bases), Gutierrez, Buford and Girardi met expectations. Grace fell off a bit to .280 and Rodriguez, along with Hill, was traded away at mid-season when it became apparent it was another lost campaign. A mid-season pick-up, outfielder Rondell White, was hurt soon after joining the Cubs.

Lieber (12-11) again stood out among the starters and Wood (8-7) made a promising recovery from surgery. Tapani (8-12) struggled, as did a horde of youngsters tested for the rotation, while Valdes (2-4) flopped abysmally. Closer Aguilera picked up 29 saves but was clearly on the downgrade.

It was no surprise that Valdes and Aguilera were among the deported after the failures of 2000, but fans were shocked when MacPhail let Grace, a mainstay of the Cubs for 13 seasons, leave as a free agent to join the Arizona Diamondbacks rather than extend his contract at the age of 36.

Grace's feelings were hurt though he realized it was a "business decision." Accordingly, he couldn't resist a parthian shot: "It's good to be on a team at last that's committed to winning," intimating that the Cubs weren't.

MacPhail retooled for 2001 with a flood of veterans of variable caliber and state of health, among them catcher Todd Hundley, the son of "iron catcher" Randy, third baseman Bill Mueller, first baseman Ron Coomer, outfielder/first baseman Matt Stairs, closer Tom Gordon and starting pitchers Julian Tavarez and Jason Bere. Youngsters such as outfielders Corey Patterson, Gary Mathews Jr., and Roosevelt Brown and first baseman Julio Zuleta also figured in the new mix.

The future, of course, guarded the secret of how the Cubs would fare with their new cast in the 2001 season and afterwards. But if the past were any guide their fortunes would probably repeat the usual form. Either a brief burst of hope followed by a period of despair, or a period of despair followed by a brief burst of hope.

It's been that way since 1946, and the Cubs have always run strictly true to that inconsistent pattern since their last pennant in 1945. The 13 seasons from 1988 through 2000 offered further proof of that with no N.L. pennant, a lone first place finish, one hard-won "wild card" berth and just four campaigns over .500.

THE KIDS REALLY CAN PLAY

If Ron Schueler knew how to steer a straight course it wasn't evident during his 10-year term as general manager of the White Sox in the final decade of the 20th Century. Yet when he stepped down after the conclusion of a successful 2000 campaign it was clear his flexibility was a major asset.

Schueler's adaptability to varying circumstances was demonstrated after the disappointment of the 1994 season, terminated prematurely on August 12 by a players' strike with his team in first place and likely to win a second consecutive division title. For the next three years Schueler attempted to re-energize the White Sox with mostly veteran, sometimes high-priced free agents. When that didn't succeed, he began to build with young talent from the minor leagues, which did work by 2000.

Schueler was put to the test even before the 1995 season got underway after being delayed three weeks until the labor dispute was settled. It was a bob-tailed campaign held to 144 games but far too long for the White Sox. Schueler's replacements for Julio Franco and Darrin Jackson, solid offensive contributors in 1994, didn't measure up. Veterans John Kruk and Chris Sabo were no help, even if outfielder Dave Martinez (.307 in 119 games) was steady. Rookie second baseman Ray Durham also struggled to take the place of departed sparkplug Joey Cora.

It was the steep decline in pitching that hurt most. Jack Mc-Dowell, the contentious former ace of the staff, was gone as a free agent. Of the other three earlier standouts only Alex Fernandez (12-8) fared reasonably well though not until he won his final seven decisions. Wilson Alvarez (8-11) and Jason Bere (8-15) became unreliable. Closer Roberto Hernandez (3-7, 32 saves) held up under an added load.

So did the offensive spearheads, first baseman Frank Thomas, third baseman Robin Ventura and center fielder Lance Johnson. Thomas led the team in batting for the fifth consecutive year with .308, hit 40 home runs and batted in 111 runs. Ventura contributed 26 home runs and 93 RBI and Johnson batted .306, led the league in triples with 12, hit a surprising 10 home runs and stole 40 bases.

If there were high points to the season they were individual feats provided by Ventura and Johnson. Ventura tied a major league record by hitting two grand slam home runs in a game at Texas on September 4. Johnson set a team record with three triples among six hits in a nine-inning game on September 23 at Minnesota.

By that time, manager Lamont, the toast of fandom with first place teams the previous two years, was long gone. After the White Sox were swept in a four-game series by the surging Cleveland Indians, dropping their record to 11-20 on June 2, Schueler pulled the plug on Lamont, whom he considered too "laid back" to inspire his players.

"If they can't get up for a series like the Cleveland series, I can't let it go further," Schueler asserted. "I'm not going to ask our owner to put out good money for a team nine or 10 games under .500."

Schueler handed the baton to fiery coach Terry Bevington, at first on an interim basis, eventually also for the 1996 campaign. Bevington was certainly not "laid back" but prone to contend with everyone in sight, including his own players, foes and the media. He not only fought with the umpires on the field, but in one case even off it.

When the season ended, the Sox were 55-54 under Bevington, 68-76 overall and in third place.

Schueler gave the free agent market another whirl for 1996. His chief prize was designated hitter Harold Baines, now 37, a former White Sox hero and owner Jerry Reinsdorf's favorite player whose uniform No. 3 had to be "unretired." Other major veteran newcomers were pitcher Kevin Tapani, outfielder/infielder Tony Phillips and outfielders Danny Tartabull and Darren Lewis.

Under the combative Bevington's aggressive management, the White Sox got off to a fine start. They won 19 of 22 games between May 15 and June 10 to gain first place but then lost 10 of the next 11 to surrender the top spot to the Indians for the rest of the season. They finished second with a record of 85-77.

Bevington, however, finished last with some of his players, who resented his abrasiveness and dictatorial handling, particularly that of pitchers. Yet he held on to his job in part because Schueler was unable to persuade Jim Leyland, a former Sox coach under La Russa, to return to Chicago. Leyland chose to lead the Florida Marlins to a World Series title in 1997.

"I don't believe in letting players dictate who the manager will be," Schueler said, defending his retention of Bevington. "That's my decision. I don't hire any of them to manage. They all think they can manage. They all think they can play too."

Many did play well in 1996, especially Thomas. Despite a foot stress fracture that kept him out of 18 games, Thomas carried the offense again, hitting .349 with 40 home runs and 134 RBI. Ventura (.284, 34 home runs, 105 RBI), Baines (.311, 22 home runs, 95 RBI) and Tartabull (.254, 27 home runs, 101 RBI) also contributed to a record team total of 195 home runs.

Alvarez (15-10) and Fernandez (16-10) recovered to lead the starting pitchers, Tapani, 13-10, helped and rookie James Baldwin (11-6) developed quickly. Hernandez (6-5, 38 saves) turned in another strong season and setup man Matt Karchner, 7-4, distinguished himself.

Hoping to put the White Sox over the top in 1997 and boost sagging attendance, Reinsdorf opened the vault for Schueler, who lured free agent slugger Albert Belle away from the Indians with a five-year, $52.5 million contract that made him the highest-paid player in the game. Pitcher Jaime Navarro came from the Cubs for a four-year, $20 million deal. Neither lived up to expectations in 1997. Navarro, who along with veterans Doug Drabek and Danny Darwin, was supposed to help offset the departures of Fernandez and Tapani, was a failure for three seasons with the White Sox.

Reinforced by Belle, who was coming off a strong '96 season with the Indians in which he hit .311 with 48 home runs and 148 RBI, the White Sox seemingly had a powerhouse attack with Thomas, Ventura and Baines the other offensive leaders.

But the '97 season unravelled early, Ventura suffering a broken leg in spring training and missing the first 99 games. Belle struggled, as did the pitching, yet the White Sox hung in the race until late July. They were 3½ games behind Cleveland on July 31 when they shocked their fans and the baseball world by trading three of their top pitchers, Alvarez, Hernandez and Darwin, to San Francisco for six minor leaguers.

The deal was denounced as the "White Flag Trade." Reinsdorf and Schueler were accused of dastardly and premature surrender with two months left in the season. Reinsdorf defended the action, saying, "Anyone who thinks this White Sox team will catch Cleveland is crazy." Of course, they didn't, plodding to second place with a record of 80-81.

Belle totaled 30 home runs and 116 RBI, but batted only .274. Thomas, however, had another fine year, with 35 home runs, 125 RBI and a .347 average to become the first White Sox to lead the league in batting since Luke Appling in 1943. Baines contributed .305 in 93 games before he was sent to Baltimore to finish the season. Durham (.271 and 33 stolen bases) teamed up well with veteran shortstop Ozzie Guillen.

The pitching failure was the most marked, Drabek (12-11), Baldwin (12-15) and Alvarez (9-8), carrying the starting load until July 31 with Navarro (9-14) extremely erratic. After Hernandez (5-1, 27 saves) left, Karchner (3-1, 15 saves) surprised as the closer.

The sorry experience of 1997 triggered a radical change in approach by Schueler and Reinsdorf. The emphasis shifted from costly free agents to cheaper young talent. It was made easier by a bumper crop of prospects in the White Sox farm system.

"We've been trying to win every year for a long time with veterans and we haven't given our kids a chance," Schueler explained. "I think this year we have to give our kids an opportunity to show what they can do."

He also gave Jerry Manuel, a former journeyman infielder and minor league manager, an opportunity to see what he could do. The gentlemanly, soft-spoken, yet candid Manuel was a sharp contrast as a manager and person to Bevington, who was fired at the end of the '97 season.

Among the youngsters Manuel worked with in '98 were three obtained in the maligned deal with San Francisco, shortstop Mike Caruso and pitchers Keith Foulke and Bobby Howry. Altogether 18 rookies played for the Sox in what was clearly a rebuilding season. Caruso seemed among the most promising as he replaced veteran shortstop Guillen, who was let go after 14 seasons as a fixture. Caruso batted .306 but was erratic on defense.

A more solid rookie performance was that of outfielder Magglio Ordonez (.282, 14 home runs, 65 RBI). He joined a resurgent Belle who batted .328 and set team records with 49 home runs and 152 RBI and a recovered Ventura (.263, 21 home runs, 91 RBI) in having outstanding seasons. So did Durham (.285, 19 home runs, 36 stolen bases). Thomas, however, fell off to .265, skidding under .300 for the first time in his career though he hit 29 home runs and drove in 109 runs.

The best among the young starting pitchers Manuel nursed along were Mike Sirotka (14-15), John Snyder (7-2) and Jim Parque (7-5), while Baldwin (13-6) also progressed, if erratically. Navarro (8-18) disappointed again. Bill Simas (4-3, 18 saves) and Howry (0-3, 9 saves) shared the closer's role.

It all added up to an 80-82 second place finish, not bad considering the inexperience of the team, the youngest in the league. The Sox finished strong with a 45-31 record after the All-Star break and, surprisingly, hit 198 home runs, the most in team history.

"We've made some progress, no question about it," said Schueler cautiously. "We'll have to build on that."

Belle and Ventura didn't continue as part of the building process. Rather than attract fans with his batting prowess, Belle repelled them with a surly, belligerent attitude. The Sox were glad to let him move on as a free agent to the Orioles. They were less happy to see Ventura leave the same way to the New York Mets but felt unable to meet his terms to stay.

Schueler's chief imports for 1999 were catcher Bruce Fordyce and young first baseman Paul Konerko who had been touted as a Rookie of the Year candidate the previous season at Los Angeles before the Dodgers gave up on him as did the Cincinnati Reds.

An advertising campaign, built around the slogan "The Kids Can Play," emphasized the White Sox youth movement for 1999, but once the season began it became obvious some of them weren't yet ready for mature company.

A conflict between Thomas, suffering from personal problems and an ankle injury that required surgery, and Manuel over his star's reluctance to play first base rather than serve as designated hitter, didn't basically affect the rebuilding though the Sox staggered to a 75-86 record. They finished second but an astounding 21½ games behind the runaway Indians.

Thomas batted a weak .305 in 135 games with just 15 home runs and 77 RBI and Caruso's faults in the field were magnified when he slid to .250. But Ordonez (.301, 30 home runs, 117 RBI) and Durham (.296, 13 home runs, 34 stolen bases) came on strong. So did two rookie outfielders, Chris Singleton (.300, 17 home runs, 72 RBI, 20 stolen bases) and Carlos Lee (.280, 16 home runs, 84 RBI). Fordyce's .297 was the best offense from a catcher since Carlton Fisk's days. Konerko proved a rare bargain, batting .294 with 24 home runs and 81 RBI.

The pitching remained deficient, Navarro wasting regular starts for the third consecutive season with an 8-13 record. Sirotka (11-13), Baldwin (12-13), Parque (9-15) and Snyder (9-12) rounded out an inconsistent rotation. Yet Howry, 5-3, 28 saves, was a beacon of the bullpen with Foulke, 3-3, 9 saves, a solid collaborator.

Despite the progress, the White Sox didn't look like contenders in 2000, not even after Schueler finally unloaded Navarro, sending him along with the disappointing Snyder to Milwaukee for shortstop Jose Valentin and surgically-repaired veteran starter Cal Eldred. Valentin's fielding also was suspect, but he could hit far better than Caruso.

The trade with Milwaukee was the first of three moves that helped turn the Sox into a winner, the others being the pickup on waivers of obscure veteran utility infielder Herbert Perry and a six-player swap with Baltimore on July 29 in which the Sox got catcher Charles Johnson and Baines (again), yielding Fordyce and three others.

Eldred's major contribution before arm trouble struck again was a 10-2 record by mid-season, three of those wins coming over the White Sox's chief rivals, the Indians. Valentin was an offensive catalyst, if defensively uncertain, batting .273 with 25 home runs and 92 RBI. Perry plugged the troublesome hole at third base and batted .301 with 12 home runs and 61 RBI in 109 games. Johnson steadied the pitching staff while hitting .326 with 10 home runs and 36 RBI in 44 games for the White Sox.

Above all, the key to success was the hitting of Thomas, who came alive after two subpar seasons with .328 and career-highs in home runs, 43, and RBI, 143. He was given a wake-up call during an angry confrontation in spring training with Manuel who denied his request for special treatment and demanded compliance with team rules and managerial decisions. Thomas burst out angrily, Manuel responded forcefully. The heated session benefited both.

"I didn't have anything to get out," Manuel explained. "It was good that Frank got it out. I hope I was honest and expressed how I felt. I always wanted to talk to him and communicate on different things."

With Thomas back on track, Ordonez (.315, 32 home runs, 126 RBI), Konerko (.298, 21 home runs, 97 RBI), Lee (.301,

24 home runs, 92 RBI) and Durham (.280, 17 home runs, 75 RBI) joined in a fearsome Sox offense.

Sirotka (15-10) stood out among the starters, with Baldwin (14-7) and Parque (13-6) also major contributors along with Eldred. Foulke (3-1, 39 saves) and Howry (2-4, 12 saves) were bullpen stalwarts.

Manuel, who won the Manager of the Year award, pointed to an 11-game winning streak on the road in early and mid-June, including three victories at Cleveland and four in Yankee Stadium, as triggering the eventual Sox first-place finish with a record of 95-65, five games ahead of the Indians.

"We won this thing on that road trip to Cleveland and New York,"Manuel said. "That's when the Central Division was won. We never let up, we never let up. I feel a great deal of pride for these men."

Owner Reinsdorf denied he felt vindicated by capturing the division title, but was quick to point out that people had made a snap judgment in condemning the so-called "White Flag Trade" of 1997.

"The one thing people have to understand is the people who criticized us in '97 were White Sox fans," he said. "They weren't fans of any other team. The only reason they were criticizing us is because they thought we were doing the wrong thing. Those people, I'm sure today are as happy as I am. And they're happy that they were wrong."

During the 1999 season "The Kids Can Play" slogan rang almost comically hollow, but after the surprising success of 2000 it was clear the kids had grown up and really could play.

Up to a point, that is. The White Sox fell swiftly to the Seattle Mariners in the A.L. Division Series, losing all three games—7-4 in 10 innings, 5-2 and 2-1. Seattle pitching held the highest scoring team in the major leagues to seven runs and 17 hits and limited the "Big Four"—Thomas, Ordonez, Lee and Konerko—to a 3-for-40 performance.

"We played good baseball, they played magnificent baseball," Manuel insisted. "It took that kind of effort to beat us. They pitched extremely well, they played great defense. They did everything you have to do to win."

It was a disappointing finish, nevertheless it couldn't entirely dim the luster of what had been an outstanding, exciting 2000 season. The promise was apparent.

"The veterans beat us this time," Thomas said of the Mariners, "but before long the veterans will be in this clubhouse."

Durham also was upbeat in defeat, looking toward an even brighter future.

"A lot of people didn't know about the White Sox this year," he said. "Now a lot of people know who we are. They know who Magglio Ordonez is. They know who Carlos Lee is. They know who Jim Parque is. People can finally put faces with names. This is definitely a stepping stone for great things to come."

Stepping stone or false step, the 2000 season with its unexpected joys and painful final rebuff, joined a long parade of memorable White Sox campaigns, some bitter, some sweet, yet all integral to a lengthy, fascinating and ever-growing tradition.

CHARACTER
DEVELOPMENT

General "Wild Bill" Donovan was in command of the European theater of the Office of Strategic Services (OSS), later known as the Central Intelligence Agency (CIA). World War II was raging. Donovan received a telegram from headquarters in Washington:

"Moe Berg is on his way. Do you know him?"

"Sure, I know him," Donovan responded. "He's the slowest runner in the American League."

Morris Berg, the son of a New Jersey pharmacist, is a footnote to Chicago baseball history. He was with the White Sox from 1926 through 1930, five full years. In three of those seasons he failed to steal a base. He was also a weak hitter. Only once in this stretch was his batting average over .246.

Yet he has emerged as baseball's leading cult figure. He earned degrees from Princeton University and the University of Columbia Law School and studied at the Sorbonne in Paris. He was learned in seven languages and was a founding member of America's most prestigious linguistic society.

While at Princeton, where Berg was a fleet-footed shortstop and team captain, he had tea with Albert Einstein, the great mathematician and scientist. According to a published account, the professor suggested they teach each other their specialties. Moe thought it was a good idea. Einstein had second thoughts.

"It wouldn't work," Einstein said. "You would learn mathematics faster than I would learn baseball."

Because of his verbal skills and the rare gift of silence, Moe was perfect for espionage. Tall and handsome, 6-feet-3 and 190 pounds, he was the original James Bond, the conqueror of a chorus line of eager contessas.

Moe was pushed into service as a secret agent for the OSS and was dispatched to Italy to gather information on Germany's effort to launch nuclear bombs. His mission, according to published reports, was to assassinate Werner Heisenberg, one of the world's leading physicists. But only if Heisenberg was close to producing an atomic bomb. Moe attended a Heisenberg lecture in Zurich and kept his loaded gun in its shoulder holster. Heisenberg was still at first base.

Before that, when Berg was a player, he went to Japan on an exhibition tour with many of baseball's celebrity figures, Babe Ruth included.

Japanese hostility toward the United States was increasing. The U.S. ambassador's daughter was having a baby. Disguised in Japanese garb, Moe went to visit her. He reached the roof of St. Luke's Hospital undetected and filmed Tokyo's skyline with a camera he had concealed in his kimono.

The photographs were helpful to Jimmy Doolittle's air raid on Tokyo. In 1946, Berg declined the Medal of Freedom given for outstanding service during the war. By this time he was engaged in a prolonged dispute with the government. The feds dunned him. They insisted he had been overly reimbursed for several of his OSS adventures. Some of his expense accounts had not been completed according to the standards.

Whatever, Moe's experiences in baseball and in war are ideal for a John leCarre mystery novel, with a major film to follow, starring agent 007. Moe's intellectual "groupies" could be included. They were unaware the mysterious Mr. Berg seldom was comfortable in the company of triple-domed scholars.

To Berg, most were boring stuffed shirts, buried in academic minutiae. What he enjoyed most was associating with the ballplayers of his time. Except for one occasion, he never flaunted his erudition. Two years after he had played his last game he wrote a 5,000-word ramble on the nature and purpose of the game for the *Atlantic Monthly*, a middlebrow magazine tending toward the high.

He described the catcher as "Cerberus" and threw in a few Latin and French phrases but otherwise kept it clean. He explained in detail the battle between the pitcher and the hitter and emphasized the importance of team balance, pointing out as an example that in 1908 when Ed Walsh won 40 games the White Sox finished third. He also said the players are not interested in the score but only in how many runs are necessary to tie and to win.

Once they hang it up, professional ballplayers have little, if any, desire to return to the ballpark. Not Moe. He attended as many as 50 games a year. The ballpark, he said, was his theater. He watched every pitch and every move of the catchers. Having been a catcher, he often criticized them, not so much for what they did but more for what they didn't do.

There was a night in 1969 when Baltimore beat Vida Blue of the Oakland A's in the first A.L. playoff game. The critical moment was in the seventh inning when Blue was pitching to Paul Blair of the Orioles. Blue got two strikes on Blair and then fired four or five fastballs in succession. With each succeeding pitch, Blair improved his timing, getting a little piece of the ball at first, then a bigger piece. His timing down perfect, Blair pulled a game-winning double to left field.

Hours later Moe was still upset. "Why didn't he give him the hook?" Moe asked in unaccustomed anger. "Why didn't he give him the hook?"

Moe knew if Blue had changed speeds and had thrown a breaking ball Blair probably would have struck out, lunging. Typically, Moe didn't blame Blue. The Oakland catcher was at fault. It was the catcher's responsibility to call for the curve.

Several times in a hotel lobby when ballplayers were nearby Moe was asked if he wanted to be introduced. He always declined. He didn't want a player asking who he was, when he played or who he played with. He considered the need for such identification demeaning.

"They think it all started with them," Moe would say. "Don't they know there were many of us here before they got here?" Their lack of baseball history and indifference to the past annoyed him. So he avoided them.

Moe had a 15-year big league career. A reserve catcher, he only once had as many as 351 at-bats, with the White Sox in 1929 when he hit .288, a career-high. That same season he stole five of his 11 bases. He had a .243 lifetime average and scored 150 runs, an average of only 10 a season.

Statistics never tell the full story. He was of unique value during his last few years as a player-coach with the Boston Red Sox. He caught the second games of doubleheaders and tutored the younger players, Ted Williams among them. A half- century later, Williams was still talking about "Wonderful Moe." More than once, Williams said, "Most fascinating ballplayer I ever met."

Moe died at 70 on May 29, 1972, in Belleville, New Jersey, of an abdominal aortic aneurysm. Harold Kaese of the *Boston Globe* wrote a tender farewell titled: "Goodbye, Moe Berg, in any language."

The Chicago teams have had their share of unusual characters in baseball's passing parade. Rabbit Maranville, a Hall of Fame shortstop who had a 23-year major league career, was the annual league leader in eccentric behavior.

Maranville had a brief and memorable stay in Chicago. In mid-season of 1925 he was appointed the Cubs' player-manager. He celebrated his promotion by walking through the club's Pullman railroad car, pouring ice water on all of the players who were sleeping. "No sleeping, especially at night, while I'm the manager," he announced.

The Rabbit didn't sleep much, day or night. He was fired for failing to discipline one of his players, i.e., Rabbit Maranville. A week or two before he was dismissed, a small, loud character was observed hawking newspapers outside of Ebbets Field in Brooklyn.

"Extra! Extra! Maranville Fired!" yelled the newsboy who turned out to be Maranville. He had a scoop. He was fired when the Cubs returned to Wrigley Field.

Maranville went into vaudeville and was playing in a theater in Lewiston, Maine.

"Here's how I stole second off Joe Bush," the Rabbit said, and in a state of high excitement he slid clear across the footlights, landing so hard on a drum in the orchestra pit that he fractured his leg.

In Philadelphia he demonstrated the sure control he exercised under difficult conditions. Returning to his 25th floor room at the Majestic Hotel, he found that a party of card players had locked him out so they could enjoy their game in peace. Rabbit did not waste time at the door. A few minutes later the card players heard a tapping at an unopened window. It was the Rabbit. He had walked a narrow ledge high above the street to get there and bless them with his company.

To win a bet, he dove into a pool of water in St. Louis with his clothes on. "There's a tough fish in there," the Rabbit said. "He bit me."

"What'd you do?" a teammate asked.

"I bit him back," Maranville replied. And he pulled half a fish from between his teeth to prove it.

Only 5-feet-5 and 150 pounds, Maranville had an outstanding career. He wasn't much of an offensive threat, with only 28 home runs in 10,078 at-bats, and never hit .300 in 17 seasons as an every-day player. But he was outstanding in the field, and according to some latter day super-statisticians saved his team as many as 50 runs every season. He also invented the basket catch, later made famous by Willie Mays.

And then there was the White Sox outfielder who could hit a ton but couldn't field. Smead Jolley joined the White Sox in 1930 and remained for only two and a half seasons. Considering his brief stay, he was among the most popular players in White Sox history and had his own fan club, unusual at that time.

Defensively, Jolley was totally inept. The enemy was a routine fly ball, sometimes a harmless grounder. Once a ball went through his legs twice, the first time when it scooted to the wall, the second time on the way back.

When he was in the minors with the San Francisco Seals of the Pacific Coast League, Jolley had five seasons when he batted .447, .346, .397, .404 and .387. He drove in 105 runs or more in 11 years, with a high of 188, both PCL records. A power hitter, he once hit a ball with such force it broke a window of a lady's apartment almost a full block beyond the left field fence.

"They told me to ask her for a date so the club wouldn't have to repair the window," Jolley recalled. "She was attractive. Nice and sweet as could be. But I was bashful. Besides, I was engaged."

Jolley was impressive physically, 6-feet-4 and 220 pounds. In 1932, his last season with the White Sox, manager Lew Fonseca converted him into a catcher. In his first appearance behind the plate he handled Ted Lyons in a winning game. Wonderful! No longer would he be a defensive liability. But the conversion lasted only five games before he was returned to the outfield.

Jolley was far ahead of his time. He was born 50 years too soon. He would have been a strong designated hitter.

Art Shires was another frustrated White Sox hand. Shires fancied himself as a boxer, not a ballplayer. He was a first baseman and a good hitter with a .291 lifetime average, and referred to himself as Art "The Great" Shires.

He adopted the appellation, he explained, because it was rooted in Shakespeare.

"Remember in the play *Twelfth Night*," he wrote, "it says, 'Some are born great, some achieve greatness, and some have greatness thrust upon them.' Well, I was born great."

After two informal fights with White Sox manager Lena Blackburne, he decided to have a second career as a professional boxer. He knocked out "Mysterious Dan" Dailey in his debut but was smitten by "Tornado" George Trafton, a center with the Chicago Bears. Nonetheless, he continued fighting and had matches in Boston and St. Paul.

After he was banned from the ring in 29 states, baseball Commissioner Judge Kenesaw M. Landis stepped in and requested Art the Great confine his hitting to baseballs. Landis went so far as to issue the following manifesto:

"Hereafter any person connected with any club in this organization who engages in professional boxing will be regarded by this office as having permanently retired from baseball. The two activities do not mix."

Round No. 2 with Blackburne came when the manager, hearing a commotion in Shires' hotel room, looked in. Shires was using empty whisky bottles as Indian clubs and shouting for more liquor. Catching sight of Blackburne, he threw a bottle at him.

"Are you drunk again?" Blackburne asked.

Shires threw another bottle and hit Blackburne in the head. Blackburne fell to the floor. Lou Barbour, the White Sox traveling secretary, appeared.

"Stay out of this," Shires warned. "I can lick a dozen guys like you and Lena."

Shires soon found employment elsewhere.

RULING DYNASTIES

"Baseball is too much of a business to be a sport and too much of a sport to be a business."

So observed Philip K. Wrigley, the long-time Cub caretaker when testifying before a Congressional committee 50 years ago. Big league clubs, for a variety of sensible reasons, are an alluring attraction for wealthy investors. Like ballplayers, the owners are transients. They come and go.

Except in Chicago.

The Cubs and White Sox have been a family "heirloom" and are the only major league clubs that have had three generations of uninterrupted family ownership. The Wrigleys and Comiskeys controlled the Cubs and Sox for almost three-quarters of a century.

The Comiskeys were first. Charles A. Comiskey, known as the "Old Roman," was a baseball pioneer, the co-founder of the American League, and operated the White Sox from its birth in 1901. William Wrigley, Jr., bought majority ownership of the Cubs in 1918 after the "outlaw" Federal League folded.

The story of Comiskey's so-called "defining moment" has been told many times and is included in most of the White Sox histories. Young Charles, then 17, was driving a brick wagon in

1876, hitched his horses to a post, and stopped to watch a semi-pro game at Jackson and Laflin streets.

One of the pitchers was woefully ineffective. Comiskey was not a stranger. He was a pitcher with a growing reputation. He approached the manager and told him, "I can do better than that." The manager sent him in in relief. Young Comiskey squelched the rally and remained in the game.

His father, "Honest John" Comiskey, for 13 years an alderman in Chicago's 10th Ward, had been waiting for the bricks to arrive. They were to be used in the construction of a new city hall. Exasperated, he took off in search of his missing son. He found him on the mound in the midst of striking out the side. Rather than order him to complete his assignment, Honest John delivered the bricks himself. The son never again drove a brick wagon.

Another version, more believable, is that the Libertys, a well-known semi-pro club, were without a pitcher. He had failed to appear. Comiskey volunteered and did so well that later, in the same year, he was offered $60 a month to play for a Milwaukee semi-pro team.

Comiskey began to climb the baseball ladder and in 1879 joined the Dubuque, Iowa, club in the Northwestern League. Two years later, in the winter of 1881, he received a letter from Al Spink of St. Louis, founder of the *Sporting News*. Acting as an agent, Spink advised Comiskey that owner Chris von der Ahe would double his salary and pay him $125 a month to play first base for the St. Louis Browns in the newly-organized American Association in 1882.

Comiskey was with the Browns for the next eight years. He was appointed player-manager in his second season and directed the Browns to four consecutive pennants, 1885–1888. He was a right-handed batter and a reliable hitter but was cheered mostly for his speed and defensive brilliance. He stole 122 bases in 1887.

It was during this time Comiskey introduced a new way to play first base. It was a significant and lasting contribution. Instead of staying moored to the bag, as was the custom, he moved about 15 to 18 feet to his right, narrowing the gap between first base and second.

He now was able to field groundballs and catch line drives that would have gone through the infield for base hits He also ordered his pitchers to cover first when he had ranged too far from his position to return and accept a throw for the putout. Soon, the other first basemen did the same.

In 1890, with the guarantee of an $8,000 salary, he was the player-manager of the Chicago franchise in the idealistic, employee-controlled Brotherhood (or Players) League. The players had a voice in all policy decisions and in addition to their wages were to share in the profits. The Brotherhood collapsed in chaos after one season.

Comiskey returned to St. Louis for one more season as a playing manager. He was transferred to Cincinnati of the National League the next year. In early April of 1892, Cap Anson brought his Chicago White Stockings to Cincinnati. It was the first regular season matchup between baseball's two most prominent managers.

Ban Johnson, sports editor of the *Cincinnati Commercial-Gazette*, jumped on the story:

"For many nights has the boastful Anson dreamed on conquests over his hated rival, Comiskey. The fond hopes of the old warrior were not realized. Yesterday, the two great baseball leaders met, and it was indeed a royal sight to see them contest for the honors of the diamond. The colors of Anson's Chicago club went down to defeat, 5-2. More than 5,000 enthusiastic Cincinnati supporters howled themselves hoarse with delight. As old Anson trailed off the field with his ball tossers, a motley crowd of Cincinnati rooters followed him to the clubhouse, chiding him in his misery."

It was during his Cincinnati stay that Comiskey strengthened his acquaintance with Ban Johnson, a fireball and an ambitious sportswriter. Together, they began laying the foundations of what was to become the American League. It would be a second major league, equal in status to the established N.L.

After a brief period as a minor league, the "upstart" American League planted a franchise in Chicago and claimed major league status in 1901. James A. Hart, president of the Chicago entry (Cubs) in the N.L., vigorously opposed the intrusion. War was declared.

The new league was too strong to be denied. Hart managed to win the concession that Comiskey would not use the word "Chicago" in front of White Stockings (quickly changed to White Sox). When the first World Series was played in 1903, it was the ultimate acknowledgment that the Johnson-Comiskey creation was a major league. Johnson was elected president. Comiskey was the owner of the Chicago franchise, the anchor of the new league.

Now a full-fledged entrepreneur, Comiskey became aware of the benefits of advertising, and in 1913 the White Sox embarked on a post-season world tour with the New York Giants. Twenty-one games were played in this country before they put to sea and played exhibitions in Japan, China, the Philippines, Australia, Egypt, Italy, France and England.

The 30,000-mile, 142-day trip, made under the auspices of the United States government, was a big success and drew huge, cheering crowds that marveled at the strange game. U.S. ambassadors greeted the teams at every stop. They were honored at 136 dinners, lunches and banquets. Forty-four games were played overseas; Chicago won 24 and lost 20. Eleven years later the Sox and Giants made a second and shorter tour, limited to games in Great Britain, Paris and Rome.

There were also many days of agony for Comiskey, particularly in 1920 with the discovery that White Sox players had dumped the 1919 World Series. Comiskey's reputation was sullied. He knew the Series was fixed after the first game. Rather than expose his crooked players, he tried to cover it up as if it was all a bad dream and never happened.

The Old Roman, a multi-millionaire, died in his sleep on October 16, 1931, at the age of 72. The club passed on to his only child, J. (John) Louis. Louis grew up in the shadow of his father and like the sons of many famous and wealthy men cultivated an opposite persona. He was quiet in manner, shy and reclusive and, above all, abhorred flash and flamboyance.

Lou Comiskey was athletic in his youth and played on the baseball and football teams at DeLaSalle Institute, a Catholic high school within easy distance of the ballpark bearing his name. In his mid-20s, he took ill and began gaining an enormous amount of weight. He was constantly dieting and had three sets of clothes to accommodate his weight changes.

Again unlike his father, he was generous, possibly to a fault. He never had a serious holdout. Almost anonymous, he built the club's farm system and for the first time sent scouts on the road. Typically, he funded Andy Frain and his brother Pat, helping them launch an usher service that blossomed into a national success. Lou died young, in 1939 at the age of 54. He weighed in excess of 300 pounds.

The former Grace Reidy, Lou's widow, the Old Roman's daughter-in-law, took control—but not quite. Lou's will stipulated that the First National Bank of Chicago oversee the operation. In effect, Grace Comiskey was in a minority position. She spent two years in court fighting the bank and won control in February 1941. She "abdicated" in 1948 and seemingly passed the torch to her 22-year-old son, Charles A. "Chuck" Comiskey II.

Chuck Comiskey began functioning as the club's owner, confident he would reign forevermore. Both his grandfather and father had said so. More than that, they promised an orderly male succession. But his heritage had not been carved in stone. When his mother died in 1956, she left him 46 percent of the team's stock. The remaining 54 percent was inherited by his sister, Dorothy, 11 years older, who had had her choice of two White Sox suitors, pitcher John Rigney and first baseman Zeke Bonura. Rigney got the call.

Chuck's mother obviously was fearful her son, as Los Angeles Dodger executive Al Campanis would have said, "lacked the necessities." What mom surely didn't anticipate was a brother-sister feud that carried into the courtroom. The enterprising Bill Veeck, who had operated clubs in St. Louis and Cleveland, swooped in for the kill.

Supported by a seven-man investment group, Veeck & Co. purchased Mrs. Rigney's holdings for $2.7 million on June 10, 1959. Veeck and former slugger Hank Greenberg, his principal partner, then tried to buy out Comiskey for tax reasons. If 80 percent of a company's stock changed hands within 360 days of the initial purchase a new federal tax depreciation schedule was allowed. Like oil wells and manufacturing equipment, ballplayers were depreciable. The savings would have approached Veeck's purchase price.

Young Comiskey defiantly held out for a year and a half until Chicago's first 1961 snow. He sold his 46 percent for $3.5 million on December 14 to a local 11-man combine that included Bill Bartholomay, later a baseball fixture. And for the first time in 62 years the Comiskey ownership brigade had joined the exodus out of baseball.

The Wrigley family had an identical run of 62 years, from 1919 until 1981 when the Tribune Co. bought the Cubs from Bill Wrigley, the third generation owner. Before Bill there was his father, Philip Knight Wrigley, and before P.K. there was William, Jr., who was the genius.

Unlike his son and grandson, William, Jr. was robust, an extrovert, loud and garrulous. If he had something to say, and he always did, he said it so everyone could hear him. Above all, he was a super salesman. He made the family fortune, starting from scratch, in the chewing gum business. In the year 2000, the Wm. Wrigley Co. had worldwide sales in excess of $2.1 billion. Wrigley was also a fan who cheered.

A typical story that illustrates his behavior:

He was watching the Los Angeles Angels, then the Cubs' top farm team, play Salt Lake in a Pacific Coast League game. Bill Lane, the Salt Lake owner, was beside him. When Lefty O'Doul came to bat Wrigley asked, "Who is that fellow?"

"That's the guy one of your scouts wanted to buy some time back. He's the best hitter in the league, a swell fielder, a valuable man."

"What did you say his name was?"

Lane spelled it out for him. "O'Doul—O-D-O-U-L."

"Wrap him up. I'll take him."

The son of a soap manufacturer, Wrigley was born in Germantown, Pennsylvania, a Philadelphia suburb. Seeking fame and fortune, he ran away to New York at the age of 11 and started his first enterprise, selling newspapers in front of the *New York Tribune* building. He returned home two months later. When he was 13, his father sent him on the road selling soap.

Restless, he journeyed West and began manufacturing baking soda. Chewing gum was used as a premium. His customers devoured the gum. The shipping cost for 100 pounds of baking soda was five dollars. For that same five dollars, he reasoned, he could ship 10 times as much gum. He dove into the gum business.

It was a Horatio Alger story. After he moved the family to Chicago, a friend asked why it was that the Cubs were owned by Cincinnati businessmen. Wrigley didn't have the answer. He began buying Cub stock. He enjoyed going to the ball games. He bought more stock.

These purchases helped keep Charles Weeghman afloat. A cafeteria king, Weeghman had been the owner-president of the Chicago Whales in the Federal League. It folded in 1916 after two seasons. During the peace process, the National League awarded Weeghman the right to buy its Chicago franchise.

Three years later Wrigley had majority control. He ran the Cubs for the next 13 years. Eager for a winning team, he spent freely and approved a half dozen trades for high-priced players, most of whom were in the twilight. The Cubs won only one pennant, in 1929, during his term but he had laid the foundation for three more pennants in the 1930s.

Wrigley died in his Phoenix, Arizona mansion in January 1932, at 70. P.K. came in from the bullpen in 1934 and had the longest reign of all, 43 years, until his death at the age of 82 in 1977. P.K.'s son, Bill, mopped up and sold the family jewels to the Tribune Co. four years later.

Philip was reclusive. He never appeared on radio or television. He preferred anonymity, another instance where the son adopted a completely different personality from the father. *Sports Illustrated* magazine referred to him as "The best unknown man in the realm of sports." His biography, written by Paul Angle, a distinguished scholar, is subtitled, *A Memoir of a Modest Man*.

Whereas his uninhibited sire, William, Jr., could spot and

smile at a photographer at 100 yards, P.K. refused to pose for a color photograph for the cover of *Fortune* magazine, and expressed delight that he was the first competing owner to negotiate a World Series without being photographed.

Phil Erbes, an executive with the Wrigley Co., insisted P.K. made only two public speeches, both when he was honored at the Chicago baseball writers' annual dinner. The first time he said, "Thank you," and sat down. Several years later he was more effusive and said, "Thank you very much."

He also tried for the common touch. He didn't allow his secretary to answer the phone. He took the calls, and delighted in telling of his many conversations with a carpenter whom he had never met and often talked to for an hour. Wrigley said he listened and "he's very interested in baseball and sometimes offered useful advice." He was also the most truthful owner of his time, perhaps of any time.

Wrigley's fellow owners cringed when he appeared before the Congressional anti-trust committee for a "Study of Monopoly Power." The committee, chaired by Congressman Emanuel Celler of New York, conducted two witch hunts against baseball.

Wrigley testified that the reserve clause should be abandoned because it bound players to one club until they were traded, sold or released. He also said he was in favor of salary arbitration and limited free agency. This was on October 17, 1951, a quarter of a century before impartial arbitrators forced these adjustments.

Gabe Paul, who operated four big league clubs and was among Wrigley's contemporaries, insisted Wrigley "Is probably the most visionary owner we have ever had. And he's the only owner who would vote against his best interests if he thought it would help the league."

Wrigley was a contrarian. Always eager to play the pioneer and plow new ground, he wasn't one to follow the leader. The best example was the advent of night baseball. The first major league night game was played in 1935 at Cincinnati. More than half a century, 53 years, passed before lights were installed at Wrigley Field.

"He didn't think of it first so he never liked the idea," said

John C. Hoffman, a long-time Chicago baseball writer.

James T. Gallagher, the Cubs' general manager, conceded that "Mr. Wrigley had his quirks. But he authorized me to go ahead. This was in 1941, right after the season. We were going over the books, suffering, losing a lot of money, wondering what the hell we were going to do and so he said, 'All right, we'll put in lights.'

"By late November we had everything we needed. All the material was stockpiled under the stands. We kept it a secret. I went to the winter meetings and got back home on December 7, the day the Japanese bombed Pearl Harbor. I called Mr. Wrigley and he said, 'Call the War Department the first thing tomorrow morning and ask them if they want the material.'

"So Monday, promptly at eight o'clock in the morning, I called the War Department—today they call it the Defense Department. I told them we had a few tons of steel and I don't know how many miles of cable. It wasn't against the law but the government didn't want everybody buying steel. And they said, 'Good, we'll take it.'

"Mr. Wrigley was delighted to have an excuse to call the whole thing off. We put a little story in the papers that the Cubs had given the steel, all the material, to a defense plant. Later, I remember asking where the steel went. I never did find out."

In 1962, when the Cubs hosted the All-Star game, Wrigley told Jack Kuenster, now the eminent editor of *Baseball Digest*, then a beat writer for the *Chicago Daily News*, he would not be in attendance. He didn't want two tickets for himself, and preferred they be made available to a fan. He explained further he would watch on television because it gave him a better view.

Young Bill Veeck, who had been operating the cross-town White Sox, slapped his good knee in amusement and said, "He's telling the fans to stay home and watch the game on television."

Wrigley was amused by the massive (newspaper) interest in professional baseball. "You can put up a new hotel or something and it wouldn't make a difference. But just hiccup something about baseball and everybody turns out."

Early on he was a fan. He attended a nominal amount of

games and as the vice president of the National League participated in management affairs. Eventually, he dropped out. During the last 20 years of his ownership he was almost never at the ballpark and when he was it was in mid-morning before the games began.

Once, Peanuts Lowrey, the Philadelphia Phillies' third base coach who had played five full seasons with the Cubs, told reporters that Mr. Wrigley had watched the game in a box seat five or six rows behind the Cub dugout. A reporter hurried to the clubhouse for confirmation.

"I saw him," said Ernie Banks. "I waved to him." Ron Santo and Billy Williams, who claimed they, too, were well acquainted with the boss, acknowledged this rare sighting. The next day brought the discovery it wasn't Mr. Wrigley. It was his cousin.

He overpaid his players and, unlike his fellow moguls, awarded mid-season raises. In 1957 when pitcher Dick Drott was performing for the rookie minimum of $6,500, Wrigley boosted him to $15,000 with the explanation, "Why should he have to wait until next season? He's doing the job right now."

Not all of his employees were enthralled. He dismissed manager Bob Scheffing after the 1959 season. Scheffing had done a good job. Insiders insisted Wrigley fired him to take the headlines away from the White Sox who the next day were to make their first World Series appearance in 40 years.

"He just doesn't think people are very smart, especially if they don't have any money," Scheffing said in an interview three years later. "And at the same time he's suspicious of people who have a million or two."

Wrigley's principal concern was maintaining "Beautiful Wrigley Field," more than the team itself. "We can't guarantee a winning team," he said, "but we can guarantee the physical properties. We can take care of that."

Almost every season Wrigley used the meager profits to reinforce and repair the aging "temple." The press howled in anger: the money should be used to buy better ballplayers, etc. Wrigley knew better. The players were transient. The ballpark is the permanent attraction.

P.K. died in 1977 and the Cubs passed to his son, Bill, who before and after inheriting the club showed little interest in baseball. He had a brief, uneventful term and on June 16, 1981 sold his 81 percent Cub holdings to the Tribune Co. for $18.5 million. He died in 1999 at 66. At the time of his death, *Forbes* magazine estimated his wealth at $3 billion.

Aside from the Comiskeys and Wrigleys, Jerry Reinsdorf of the White Sox leads in longevity. Reinsdorf will be in his 22nd season of ownership in 2002. The Allyn brothers, Arthur, Jr., and John, held the White Sox for 15 years. Bill Veeck of the White Sox was the only two-term owner, from 1959–61 and 1975–80.

FRONT OFFICE MUSICAL CHAIRS

Managers are hired to be fired. And most of them are. Throughout the years both Chicago teams have been active in this perpetual game of musical chairs but the Cubs had a unique experience, the dismissal of baseball's only "Athletic Director."

He was Colonel Robert V. Whitlow of the Air Force Academy. Whitlow had no previous baseball experience but was tall and handsome and with a pleasant personality. Owner Philip Wrigley, in another pioneering move, anointed the colonel during the tumult of the early 1960s.

Whitlow drew the assignment because he was an expert in nutrition and conditioning. During his term he was constantly supplying players with chocolate milk balls, at the time believed to be spiked with a secret and mysterious ingredient. When sent to the lab it was exposed as a Vitamin C pellet.

"I was ahead of my time," Whitlow said after he was relieved of command. "The players were eating too many hot dogs. I was trying to come up with an energy food. The players liked them, but after a while they lost interest."

While at the Air Force Academy, Whitlow was attached to the space program and aware of the latest advances, not only in nutrition but in the general area of physical fitness. He crammed the clubhouse with exercise and weight training machines. This was long before they became standard equipment.

Wrigley was also impressed with Whitlow's bulk, 6-foot-5-inches and 230 pounds. "He's got the size that commands respect," Wrigley said.

The 43-year-old Whitlow, who played football at West Point, had been in town for a morning conference with the late Mayor Richard J. Daley about the first Chicago appearance of the academy's football team. He called on Bud Offield, Wrigley's nephew, an executive with the chewing gum company. Offield was among Whitlow's golfing buddies in Michigan.

"Bud said, 'Come on over (to the Wrigley Building Restaurant) and have lunch with us,'" Whitlow explained. "Mr. Wrigley came down—joined us. And that's how it all started."

Three months later, on January 10, 1963, Whitlow was hired. It would have been a minor appointment and of no significance if his role had been limited to whipping players into shape. What was astonishing was that he was put in charge of the entire baseball operation. The three reigning vice presidents, including John Holland who had been functioning as the general manager, and Clarence Rowland and Charlie Grimm were to report to him.

When Whitlow joined the club in spring training, equipment manager Yosh Kawano gave him uniform No. 1. He had a locker in the clubhouse and during the workouts stationed himself in left field shagging fly balls, an effort that would bring him closer to the players.

In the beginning, Whitlow said he might even take a turn as the head coach. He never did. Two weeks before the '63 season began, with Wrigley's approval, the colonel killed the College of Coaches. Bob Kennedy, a former White Sox third baseman who had been a Navy pilot, was appointed manager and had a two-and-a-half year run.

Holland continued making the trades. Whitlow was also peripherally involved but Holland had the final word. The Lou Brock–Ernie Broglio deal, one of the most embarrassing trades in Cub history, was consummated during Whitlow's watch. Years later, Whitlow revealed he was against the trade. So was Kennedy.

Threatened, the vice presidents, who were often feuding, teamed together and soon pushed Whitlow into the background. He became an inconsequential player. Defeated, Whitlow resigned on January 31, 1965, without the courtesy of a routine press release.

Two weeks later, Dick Dozer of the *Chicago Tribune* asked Holland, "Where is the colonel?"

Holland replied, "Since you asked, he has tendered his resignation."

This bizarre chapter of baseball roulette is not uncommon, certainly not in the last several decades. With each passing season the stakes increase and with it the pressure to win. Today general managers are fired almost as often as field managers. Still, the Cubs in the last 84 years have had only seven general managers, the White Sox 11. Holland, who lived in constant fear of Wrigley, held on the longest and holds the Cub record, 18 seasons including the Whitlow intrusion.

In the beginning, team presidents functioned as general managers. They set the policy and ran the entire organization from top to bottom, including player signings and acquisitions, as well as such mundane tasks as scheduling, transport, and hotel accommodations. It was, in the main, a one-man show.

Eventually a baseball bureaucracy surfaced. The first-born were the general managers. They were rarely invited to league meetings (limited to owners and club presidents) and usually were former players, sophisticates who could judge player talent and their financial value, specialists in the movement of the uniformed personnel, including those assigned to minor league affiliates.

Harry Grabiner of the White Sox had the longest Chicago run. Grabiner joined the Sox in 1905 at the age of 14. He started at the bottom, swept the grandstands, sold scorecards and peanuts, and in 1915, for his good work, was elevated to secretary/treasurer and functioned as general manager.

He negotiated contracts, initiated trades, player acquisitions and sales, and, like a modern-day public relations chief, also shielded owner Charles A. Comiskey, the so-called Old Roman, from the press before and during the 1919 Black Sox scandal.

Always optimistic, Grabiner often told reporters, "Boys, this is the year we win the pennant." The Sox won in 1917 and 1919.

Grabiner was dismissed in 1945 by Mrs. Grace Comiskey the Old Roman's daughter-in-law who took command when her husband, Lou, died in 1939. When Grabiner departed the team was unraveling and in deep financial trouble. Grabiner was hired by young Bill Veeck, who then was running the show in Cleveland. Grabiner died three years later at the age of 57.

John Davis Holland of the Cubs was the second in longevity in Chicago. He was a second generation baseball lifer. His father, John. A., owned minor league clubs in Oklahoma City and St. Joseph, Missouri, and in later life was president of the old Western League.

Holland had a lengthy apprenticeship. He was a minor league general manager and field manager, and joined the Cubs in 1943. Thirteen years later he was in charge of the Cubs' Los Angeles operation in the Pacific Coast League. Almost immediately, he brought the Angels from last place to first. He became the Cubs' front office chief prior to the 1957 season.

Holland lacked flamboyance and had a quiet and shy nature. He preferred anonymity and endured Wrigley's follies with silence. Privately, he opposed the rotating head coaching scheme. The biggest blunder was the Brock trade. But he shouldn't be faulted. It was made at Wrigley's request.

Prior to Holland's arrival, the Cubs had been buried in the second division. Eleven more lean years followed. The Cubs didn't come up for air until 1967, their first successful season in 20 years. From 1967 to 1972 they were in constant contention. No pennants but never lower than third place. They were second three times.

The '69 season was among the most exciting in Cub history. With Leo Durocher firmly in command, they held the lead most of the way but faded in the September stretch. It was Durocher's best and worst year during his six-and-a-half year term as the Cubs' field manager.

Despite contrasting personalities, Holland and Durocher were never in conflict. Durocher was hired at Wrigley's suggestion.

Garrulous, Durocher didn't mingle with the troops and was constantly telling reporters how he had been at the theater or had attended a dinner party hosted by Wrigley and his wife, Helen. Again, Holland endured. He didn't have access to this inner circle and obviously was not regarded as a social equal. He retired after the 1975 season.

William Louis Veeck, Bill Veeck's father, was another long-term general manager. He also held the title of club president and reigned for 14 seasons, from 1919 through 1933. He had been a baseball writer for the *Chicago American* under the house byline of Bill Bailey and was the inspiration for the then popular song, "Won't You Come Home, Bill Bailey?"

Self-educated, Veeck never used coarse language. He arrived in Chicago at the age of 25 and went to work on the *Chicago Inter-Ocean* newspaper which folded a year later. He then joined the *American* as a reporter and rewrite man and was transferred to sports at the recommendation of Ring Lardner, the great sportswriter, who was a close friend.

According to the romantics, Veeck had been critical of the Cubs and was hired by William Wrigley, Jr., Philip's father, who had become the majority owner in 1918. Wrigley supposedly said, "All right, if you're so smart, let's see what you can do!"

Closer to the truth was that Veeck, while covering the Cubs in spring training, was invited to a dinner at Wrigley's winter home in Pasadena, California. Wrigley was impressed and a year later hired Veeck and another sportswriter, John O. Seys, as the club secretary. For all practical purposes, Veeck was the Cubs' first general manager and easily the most successful in Chicago history.

Dignified and respected, the senior Veeck lacked the promotional flair of his son but was not hidebound to tradition. He was the first baseball executive to propose inter-league play and did so at a 1922 joint owners' meeting but it was brushed aside. He was a thousand miles ahead of the times. Inter-league play was adopted 75 years later.

Veeck was also the first to allow local radio stations to broadcast big league games, without charge, in defiance of the other N.L. owners. Later, he introduced Ladies' Day, another successful innovation. In addition, he supervised the installation of facilities on Catalina Island, California, the Cubs' spring training site for most of the next four decades, and convinced Wrigley to purchase the minor league Los Angeles Angels as a nursery for potential prospects.

Veeck brought the Cubs two pennants, in 1929 and 1932, and unaccustomed prosperity. Anticipating a rise in attendance, he double-decked the Wrigley Field grandstand. From 1925 to 1931, Cub attendance more than doubled. The 1929 home gate of 1,485,166 was a Wrigley Field record and a Chicago record that held until 1960.

He was equally astute in building a winning team. He acquired first baseman Charlie Grimm, shortstop Rabbit Maranville and outfielder Kiki Cuyler from the Pittsburgh Pirates, and picked up Hack Wilson, a barrel-chested outfielder, in the minor league draft for $7,500. Five years later, in 1930, Wilson hit a N.L. record 56 home runs and drove in 191 runs, still the one-season major league record.

By 1928, the Cubs were ready. Veeck had rescued manager Joe McCarthy from the minor leagues. It was a bold move. McCarthy had never played or managed in the big leagues. Veeck also assembled one of baseball's strongest hitting outfields—Riggs Stephenson in left field, Wilson in center and Cuyler. In the pennant-winning '29 season they had a combined .355 batting average—Stephenson (.362), Cuyler (.360), Wilson (.345). Though the Cubs finished 10½ games in front, it wasn't a completely enjoyable season. Veeck was enraged when Wrigley purchased Rogers Hornsby from the Boston Braves for $125,000 and five players. Veeck thought the price was too high, even for Hornsby, still considered the best right-handed hitter in baseball history.

Only a promise by Wrigley never to interfere again persuaded Veeck to rescind his resignation. Hornsby turned out to be what the Cubs needed, at least for that season. He batted .380 with 39 home runs and 149 runs batted in and helped lead the club to its first flag since 1918.

Wrigley had cajoled Veeck into firing McCarthy who was replaced by Hornsby with four games remaining in the 1930 season. Hornsby, in his first year as player/manager, had guided the St. Louis Cardinals to the 1926 pennant. He had no such success with the Cubs and had an abrasive and arrogant manner.

Soon, Wrigley and Veeck became disenchanted with Hornsby's martinet methods which triggered several player revolts. Hornsby was also a racetrack regular, and it was alleged that he was consorting with gamblers and bookmakers. When Wrigley died in January 1932, Veeck was still stuck with Hornsby.

Veeck had reinforced the club with a sparkling new double-play combination of shortstop Billy Jurges and second baseman Billy Herman but the Cubs were struggling and in third place on August 1, 1932, when Veeck fired the Rajah. The easy-going Charlie Grimm succeeded Hornsby.

Relaxed, the Cubs embarked on a 14-game winning streak and went on to win the pennant. Veeck died of leukemia the following year and left the nucleus of a good team, good enough to win two more pennants in the 1930s. His *Sporting News* obituary described him as "the most popular and progressive of all baseball executives."

Harold Walker, a minority stockholder, and Charles "Boots" Weber, who had been in charge of the Los Angeles club, were on the throne for the next decade. Measured by pennants, Weber's tenure was a resounding success. His trades were mostly engineered by vice president Clarence "Pants" Rowland.

Rowland landed pitchers Larry French and Tex Carlton and third baseman/outfielder Fred Lindstrom, all of whom helped in the winning of the 1935 pennant. Three years later the Cubs won again, their fourth flag in 10 years, with the addition of first baseman Rip Collins and Dizzy Dean, previously a star pitcher with the Cardinals.

Dean had suffered an arm injury the year before and was acquired in a highly-publicized trade at a cost of $185,000 and four players. The deal was consummated at Philip Wrigley's insistence despite Weber's objections. Used sparingly, Dean won seven of his eight decisions.

Hard times followed—five consecutive second-division finishes. Wrigley, who had inherited the club in 1932, reached into the press box for a general manager, as his father had done a quarter of a century earlier. James Timothy Gallagher, a baseball writer for the *Chicago Herald-American*, was brought aboard.

Gallagher came in with a "five-year plan," which was mocked by the press. But precisely five years later, in 1945, the Cubs won their last pennant. Gallagher swung the deal that put the Cubs across, the mid-season waiver purchase of veteran pitcher Hank Borowy from the Yankees for $97,000. It was a deal without precedent.

When Borowy reported, the Cubs had the top winners in both the American and National leagues. Borowy was 10-5 with the Yankees, Hank Wyse was 11-5 with the Cubs. Borowy was 11-2 for the Cubs, completed 11 of his 15 starts, and finished with eight consecutive victories.

"I was just doing my job," Gallagher said many years later, at the age of 94, in a telephone interview from his home in Port Republic, Virginia. "I was a baseball man and I feel I was good at what I did." Then the modest Mr. Gallagher added, "I have a lot of good memories but I keep them to myself. I'm not anxious to tell my life story."

Another deal which was a resounding success was Gallagher's acquisition of Hank Sauer, a power-hitting outfielder from the Cincinnati Reds in 1949. A fan favorite, Sauer soon became known as the "Mayor of Wrigley Field." He fueled the offense and three years later, in 1952, hit 37 home runs and drove in 124 runs to win the N.L.'s Most Valuable Player award.

Gallagher had a 10-year reign and was then rotated to vice president/business affairs. He was the chairman of the Official Scoring Rules Committee and a member of the Rules Committee for many years, helping to clarify the rules. A Philadelphia lawyer was no longer needed for an interpretation. Gallagher left the Cubs in 1956 and finished his baseball career in the commissioner's office.

While all this was going on, the White Sox were floundering. From 1938 through 1948 they finished in the first division only once. The '48 club struck bottom with 101 losses, one shy of equaling the team record. Attendance dropped accordingly. The club was approaching bankruptcy.

Grace Comiskey turned to her son, Charles A "Chuck" Comiskey II, and entrusted him with active supervision of the club's affairs in 1948. His mother retained the office of president and had final veto power. Young Comiskey made an outstanding move. He installed Frank Lane as the club's general manager. And three years later excitement returned to Comiskey Park.

Lane was a dynamo. Born in 1896 in Cincinnati, he had been going nonstop ever since. His father, a druggist, died when the boy was four years old. His mother had to support herself and her son by taking to sewing. The energetic young Frank Lane was earning his keep at the age of 12.

Weary of playground fights and determined to convert his blubber into muscle, Lane began intensive calisthenics. "That changed my whole life," Lane told an interviewer. "Up to then I'd been a big, fat sissy." When he was 16 he was playing for pay on Cincinnati's Northside semi-pro football team. By his senior year he was paid $100 a game.

He took two years of law at the University of Cincinnati but gradually sports officiating became his principal occupation. Then in 1934, at the age of 38, he landed his first baseball job as traveling secretary of the Cincinnati Reds. For 10 of the next 14 years, except during World War II, he bounced around the minor and major league level in secondary executive positions.

Patriotic, he enlisted in the Navy a month after Pearl Harbor, in January 1942, as a lieutenant at the age of 46. The general cut-off age was 40 but Lane convinced the recruiting officers he had the stamina and energy of men half his age. His principal assignment was to whip Navy personnel into shape. He served as a physical training instructor at a half dozen naval bases. He was in the service for four years. When he was discharged he held the rank of commander.

Returning to civilian life, Lane rejoined Larry MacPhail who had been his boss in Cincinnati. MacPhail, now with the Yankees, appointed him the general manager of the Kansas City club, the

Yankees' top farm affiliate. Two years later, in 1946, the dynamo was the president of the Triple A American Association.

His first move with the White Sox may have been without precedent. To determine the value of his players, he put the entire 40-man 1949 roster on waivers. The waiver price was only $10,000. Still, only two players were claimed, second baseman Cass Michaels and pitcher Howard Judson.

And so Lane began dealing. He acquired pitchers Billy Pierce and Saul Rogovin from Detroit and Joe Dobson from the Boston Red Sox. Pierce was a steal. Lane got him, plus $10,000, for Aaron Robinson, an obscure catcher who three years later vanished from the big league scene. Pierce, 21, had pitched only 65 innings for Detroit. Lane projected him as a big winner. Lane was right. Pierce won 211 games.

In another sleeper, Lane sent catcher Joe Tipton to the Philadelphia A's for second baseman Nellie Fox who had a Hall of Fame career. Outfielder Minnie Minoso came from Cleveland in an elaborate three-club swap. Eddie Robinson, a power-hitting first baseman who broke the club's single-season home run record, was acquired from Washington. In another major coup shortstop Chico Carrasquel was plucked out of the Brooklyn farm system for $35,000 and two players.

In Lane's first season, the Sox moved up two notches, to sixth place. Two years later, in 1951, under the command of Paul Richards, an innovative dugout wizard whom Lane had rescued from Buffalo of the International League, the Go-Go Sox amazed the baseball world. They had a long stretch in first place and finished fourth, the highest since 1943, and had an attendance of 1,328,234, an all-time record broken by the 1959 pennant-winning club.

It was the club's first million gate, double the season attendance in 1948, the year before Lane arrived. The excitement continued. For the next four years the Sox finished third and drew more than a million fans. Lane had achieved the impossible. He had taken a demoralized last-place club and had turned it into a strong contender.

According to Edgar Munzel of the *Chicago Sun-Times*, from

October 1948 to February of 1953 Lane made 155 deals involving 220 different players but some of those transactions were internal, such as recalling players from the club's farm system. Later, when he was no longer with the Sox, Lane traded managers, believed to be without precedent, swapping Joe Gordon for Jimmie Dykes.

Lane resigned on September 21, 1955. After he left the White Sox he became a baseball nomad and may have set a major league record for "most clubs, general manager, career, four." His next stop was St. Louis, then to Cleveland and Kansas City. He never again duplicated his Chicago success and died in 1981 at the age of 85.

Chuck Comiskey and his brother-in-law, John Rigney, a former White Sox pitcher, ran the club for the next three years. Though they were not always in agreement, the Sox didn't retreat. They were third again in 1956 and then had a two-year stay in second place, the first time since 1920 they finished in such a lofty position.

"Barnum" Bill Veeck arrived in March 1959, a month before the season opener. He assembled a huge group, more than 50 individual investors that included Hall of Fame slugger Hank Greenberg. Veeck took advantage of a brother-sister squabble which had reached litigation and purchased Dorothy Rigney's 54 percent holdings for $2.7 million. Chuck Comiskey refused to sell his 46 percent and hung on as a minority stockholder.

It was the first time since the birth of the A.L. in 1901 the Comiskey family had yielded control. Greenberg, the biggest single stockholder in the Veeck syndicate with 36 percent, was named the club's general manager but was comparatively inactive. Veeck was in command and had the good fortune to inherit a pennant-winning team that had been put together by Chuck Comiskey and Rigney.

Veeck patched the club but the only major transaction was an August waiver deal for first baseman Ted Kluszewski, an aging power hitter then in his 15th big league season. Klu's first 14 hits were singles. Collectively, the Sox hit 97 home runs, the only club in the league with fewer than 100. The pennant was won with pitching, speed, defense and a pitch-and-putt attack.

The Sox had a team batting average of .250, which ranked sixth in the league, were 35-15 in one-run victories and outscored their opponents by more than 100 runs, 699 to 588. In one game they scored 11 runs in one inning on one hit, a single by Johnny Callison. They led the league in stolen bases. Shortstop Luis Aparicio, a defensive marvel, tied the club record with 56. Center fielder Jim Landis, also brilliant defensively, had 20 steals and was even faster than Aparicio going from first to third.

Manager Al Lopez and Ray Berres, a premier pitching coach, had a solid staff. Early Wynn, Bob Shaw, Pierce and Dick Donovan were the rotation starters. Wynn led with 22 wins, which included a one-hitter. Pierce also had a one-hitter, a near-perfect game in Washington, broken up by Ed Fitzgerald who doubled with two outs in the ninth. Gerry Staley and Turk Lown were the closers.

This edition of the Go-Go Sox captivated the populace as never before. The clinching was in Cleveland on September 22. Mayor Richard J. Daley, a lifelong Sox fan, was among the thousands who met the players at Midway Airport. In a midnight welcome-home salute, Daley had allowed fire commissioner Robert Quinn to set off the city's air raid sirens. Many of the citizens were frantic and looked skyward. They thought the Russians were attacking.

It was the last Chicago pennant of the 20th Century. Forsaking the future, Veeck traded away four of his young players: Outfielder Callison to the Philadelphia Phillies, outfielder/first baseman Norm Cash to Cleveland and catcher Earl Battey and first baseman Don Mincher to Washington, all of whom prospered. The Sox finished third in 1960, 21 games out.

In ill health, suffering from a neurological disorder, Veeck sold his holdings to Chicagoan Arthur Allyn, Jr., the following year, in June 1961. Six months later Chuck Comiskey unloaded his 46 percent to a consortium of local businessmen which included Bill Bartholomay who subsequently became the chairman of the board of the Atlanta Braves.

Allyn elevated Ed Short into the general manager's chair. Short, who had been the club's traveling secretary, was a Horatio

Alger story. Self-educated, he began as a statistician for Hall of Fame broadcaster Bob Elson, then worked as the sports director for a local radio station.

Lane and Chuck Comiskey hired Short as the director of press relations. Hard-working, Short assumed the general manager's chair in 1961, and had a nine-year run, with three second-place finishes. Two of his clubs, in 1964 and 1967, went into the final day of the season with a chance to tie for the pennant.

Three years later, Arthur Allyn sold to his younger brother, John, who to almost everyone's surprise had been an equal partner. Short departed late in the 1970 season and was replaced by Roland Hemond who was a pup out of Frank Lane. During the 1970 winter meetings in Los Angeles, Hemond traded or sold 16 players in less than 18 hours.

Hemond had a 14-year stay, second in longevity to Grabiner. Hired away from the California Angels, he had an encyclopedic knowledge of all active players, including those in the minors. He inherited a club that had lost 106 games. In his first season, 1971, the Sox lost 26 fewer games. The next year, after Hemond acquired slugger Richie Allen, the Sox were in second place, 25 games above .500.

The Sox were unable to maintain the pace and for the next 10 seasons floated between third and sixth place. Hemond stayed at his post when Veeck regained control of the team in late 1975 and held on through the 1980 season after which ownership passed to a group headed by Jerry Reinsdorf.

Hemond's greatest triumph was in 1983 when the Sox won the West Division title, their first championship since 1959, but were eliminated by Baltimore in the first round of the playoffs. Hemond was dismissed two years later and was succeeded by the colorful Ken "Hawk" Harrelson, a former big league outfielder who had been on the club's broadcasting crew.

Harrelson was out of his element. A scratch golfer, he was accustomed to the outdoor life and couldn't be chained to a desk. He soon gave way to Larry Himes, who, not many years later, would become unique in Chicago baseball history: the only general manager of both Chicago clubs.

Like Hemond, Himes had been with the California Angels, for 14 years. His expertise was in scouting. Al Goldis, another good scout, came aboard as Himes' assistant. For four years in succession the White Sox struck it rich in the draft of amateur free agents: pitcher Jack McDowell, third baseman Robin Ventura, first baseman Frank Thomas and pitcher Alex Fernandez, all of whom developed into premier performers.

Never before had the White Sox tapped into the draft with such astonishing success. Himes also reorganized the farm system and merged the player development and scouting departments. Initially chairman Reinsdorf was delighted but later became disenchanted. When Himes was dismissed, Reinsdorf's principal explanation was: "He thinks he owns the club."

Himes was in charge for four years, from 1987 through 1990. The Sox climbed out of the second division once, in 1990. Three years later, after Himes was gone, they won the American League West. Himes had laid the foundation but most of the credit went to his successor, Ron Schueler, a tall and sometimes stoic out of Hayes, Kansas.

Schueler had the ideal credentials. He had pitched in the big leagues for six full seasons and parts of two others and had an undistinguished 40-48 career record, only once winning as many as 11 games. He had been a pitching coach with the White Sox and Pittsburgh and a special assignment scout and assistant general manager with the Oakland A's.

"Scouting is a lonesome job," Schueler observed. "But you learn a lot."

Most of all, he learned patience and silence. He seldom rambled. In his 10 years as Reinsdorf's right hand the club never finished lower than third and then only twice. And if not for the 50-day 1994 mid-season player strike the Sox might have won three division titles—in 1993, 1994 and 2000—in his time, a remarkable record considering that the club's player payroll was usually in the middle and sometimes in the bottom third.

The 1993 season was a dream. The Sox went in front to stay on June 21 and won the A.L. West cruising. Himes' four first-round draft choices led the club. McDowell, 22-10, won the Cy

Wrigley Field originally was built in 1914 for the "outlaw" Federal League and became the home of the Cubs in 1916. Many subsequent alterations have turned it into one of baseball's most revered "shrines," considered by many the perfect setting in which to attend a baseball game.

Wrigley Field

Photos courtesy of the Chicago Cubs and the authors.

Ron Santo and Lou Boudreau

Lou Boudreau (right) was third baseman Ron Santo's first manager as a Cub rookie in 1960. Boudreau retreated to the radio broadcast booth after the season while Santo went on to an outstanding career that someday may enshrine him in the Hall of Fame alongside Boudreau, a great shortstop and successful manager for the Cleveland Indians.

Leo Durocher

Leo Durocher revived the Cubs to pennant contention in the late 1960s and early 1970s as their controversial and contentious manager.

Jim Frey

Jim Frey managed the Cubs to their first division championship in 1984 and as general manager assembled the talent that won again in 1989.

Don Baylor

Don Baylor suffered greatly in his first season as Cub manager in 2000 but steered the team to division title contention in 2001.

Joe Tinker

Joe Tinker for 11 seasons (1902–12) was an outstanding shortstop for the Cubs, with his name immortalized in verse by Franklin P. Adams.

Johnny Evers

Johnny Evers was the middleman at second base on the storied "Tinker to Evers to Chance" Cub double-play combination.

Frank Chance

Frank Chance was the "Peerless Leader" as the star first baseman and manager of four Cub pennant-winning teams (1906–08, 1910). His Cubs won the World Series in 1907 and 1908, the last Chicago teams to do so.

Three-Finger Brown

Three-Finger Brown was the ace of the great Cub pitching staffs of the early 20th Century, winning 20 or more games in six consecutive seasons (1906–11).

Fred Merkle

Fred Merkle gained dubious "immortality" as a New York Giant by making a base-running "boner" that led to a Cubs' pennant in 1908. Merkle played for the Cubs 1918–20.

Rabbit Maranville

Rabbit Maranville was a fine-fielding, light-hitting shortstop and a memorable character who briefly managed the Cubs in 1925.

Charlie Grimm

Charlie Grimm is best remembered as the three-time manager of the Cubs (1932-38, 1944-49, 1960) and the last to lead them to a N.L pennant in 1945.

Riggs Stephenson

Riggs Stephenson was a great hitter with a career average of .336 for 14 seasons, nine of then (1926–34) as a Cub outfielder.

Gabby Hartnett

Gabby Hartnett gained lasting fame for his "homer in the gloamin'" that propelled the Cubs to a pennant when he was their manager in 1938. He was a great defensive catcher and a formidable slugger.

Charlie Root

Charlie Root won 201 games in 16 seasons (1926–41) as a Cub. He always denied that Babe Ruth's home run off him in the 1932 World Series was a "called shot."

Hack Wilson

Hack Wilson drove in 191 runs for the Cubs in 1930 to set a still existing major league record. The stumpy center fielder led the N.L. in home runs four times, his 56 in 1930 remaining the league record until 1998.

Stan Hack

Stan Hack as an outstanding all-around third baseman from 1932 to 1947. He twice reached career batting high of .317. Hack managed the Cubs for three seasons (1954–56).

Phil Cavarretta

Phil Cavarretta was a teen-aged sensation when he joined the Cubs at 18 in 1934 and helped them to three pennants (1935, 1938 and 1945). He won the N.L. MVP award in 1945 when his .355 led league batters. He managed the Cubs for three seasons (1951–53).

Claude Passeau

Claude Passeau won 20 games for the Cubs in 1940 and pitched a one-hitter in Game 3 on the 1945 world Series to beat the Detroit Tigers 3-0.

Bill Nicholson

Bill Nicholson was the Cubs' prime slugger of the 1940s. He led the N.L. in home runs and runs batted in, in 1943 and 1944 and won the MVP the latter year.

Andy Pafko

Andy Pafko was among the Cubs' finest center fielders for nine seasons (1943–51) and drove in 110 runs in the pennant year of 1945.

Ernie Banks

Ernie Banks earned the title of Mr. Cub s the team's most popular player during 19 seasons (1953–71) in which he hit 512 home runs and twice won the MVP.

Billy Williams

Billy Williams was among the best left-handed hitters of his term of 16 seasons (1959–74) with the Cubs and led N.L. batters with .333 in 1972 when he also hit 37 home runs and drove in 122 runs. He finished his career with 426 home runs.

Lou Brock

Lou Brock became a Hall of Famer outfielder with the St Louis Cardinals after the Cubs gave up on him in a notorious trade in 1964.

Dallas Green

Dallas Green became general manager of the Cubs in 1981 and later also vice president until he was forced out in 1987. He put together the 1984 division champions.

Randy Hundley

Randy Hundley revolutionized catching with his one-handed style and became the "iron man" behind the plate with a record 160 games in 1968.

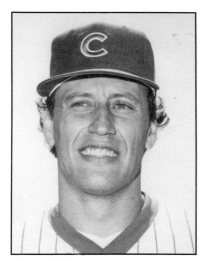

Ken Holtzman

Ken Holtzman was an outstanding left-hander who won 17 games for the Cubs in both 1969 and 1970. He pitched no-hitters in 1969 and 1971.

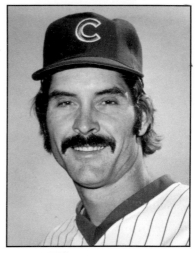

Dave Kingman

Dave Kingman produced a career season for the Cubs in 1979 when he hit 48 home runs and drove in 115 runs but he was an indifferent outfielder.

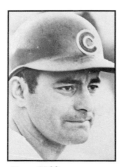

Lee Elia

Lee Elia managed the Cubs in 1982 and part of 1983 until his fate was sealed with an ill-judged and widely reported outburst against rambunctious Wrigley Field fans.

Ferguson Jenkins

Ferguson Jenkins was a 20-game winner six seasons in succession (1967–72) to match Three-Finger Brown's feat early in the century. Jenkins won the Cy Young award in 1971 when he went 24-13.

Steve Stone

Steve Stone pitched well for both the Cubs and White Sox and won the Cy Young award in 1980 when he went 25-7 for the Baltimore Orioles. He later became a highly-respected analyst of Cub games for WGN-TV in Chicago.

Rick Sutcliffe

Rick Sutcliffe was obtained in a trade from Cleveland by the Cubs in June 1984 and went 16-1 the rest of the season to pitch them to a division title.

Bill Madlock

Bill Madlock replaced Ron Santo as the Cub third baseman in 1974 and led the N.L. in batting with .354 in 1975 and .336 in 1976 before being traded away.

Bruce Sutter

Bruce Sutter became the Cubs' closer in 1976 and in 1979 carried the Cy Young award with 37 saves, 6-0 record and a 2.23 earned run average.

Lee Smith

Lee Smith took over as the Cubs' premier closer in 1982, saved 29 games to lead N.L. relievers in 1983 and saved 33 in 1984 to help the Cubs to the division title.

Ryne Sandberg

Ryne Sandberg was "stolen" by Dallas Green as a "throw-in" in a trade with Philadelphia in 1982 and became one of the game's greatest fielding and slugging second basemen. He won the MVP in 1984 for his part in the Cubs' division title run by batting .314 with 19 home runs, 84 RBI and 32 stolen bases.

Sammy Sosa

Sammy Sosa became an international celebrity in 1998 as the Cub right fielder battled Mark McGwire for the honor of breaking Roger Maris' record of 61 home runs in a season. McGwire prevailed with 70 as Sosa hit 66. The duel continued in 1999, McGwire again topping Sosa 65 to 63. But Sosa led the major leagues with 50 in 2000.

Kerry Wood

Kerry Wood struck out 20 Houston Astros in only his fifth start for the Cubs on May 6, 1998, to tie the major league record for most strikeouts in a nine-inning game. Wood was voted National League Rookie of the Year for 1998.

Young award. Fernandez was 18-8. Thomas hit .317 with 41 home runs and 128 runs batted in and Ventura, a Gold Glove third baseman, hit 22 home runs and drove in 94 runs.

Schueler had gambled and signed center fielder Ellis Burks, a free agent who had been suffering with injuries. Burks came through big-time: 17 home runs, 74 RBI. Late in the season, when McDowell and Fernandez were struggling, rookies Jason Bere and Wilson Alvarez picked up the slack and were a combined 14-0 the last six weeks of the season (both were 7-0). It was the best two-man performance in the stretch since Tom Seaver and Jerry Koosman went 19-2 for the 1969 New York Mets.

More than likely, the Sox would have won again in 1994. But there were no winners. Weary of unproductive talks with the players' union, the owners canceled the rest of the season on August 10 when the Sox were 21 games over .500 and a game ahead of Cleveland in the Central Division. At the time of the shutdown, Thomas was second in the league in home runs with 35 and third both in RBI, 101, and batting, .353.

After the season, Schueler indicated he might resign. Reinsdorf persuaded him to stay. Six years later, in the first year of the new millennium, Schueler did resign after another glorious season when the Sox, under the field direction of Jerry Manuel, won another division title. Schueler was succeeded by Kenny Williams, who had been Reinsdorf's special assistant since 1994.

The Cubs also won two division championships in the last two decades of the 20th Century. They came five years apart in 1984 and 1989. The general managers were Dallas Green and Jim Frey, opposites in temperament. Green was 6-feet, 6-inches and full of bluster. Frey was almost a foot shorter and seldom raised his voice.

Green was hired on October 9, 1981, a year after he had managed the Phillies to a World Series victory, their first world championship in 97 years. It was Green's first full season as a big league manager. The Phillies qualified for the playoffs the next season but were eliminated.

A right-handed pitcher, Green had a modest playing career, 20 wins, 22 losses. He had two notable moments: Giving up Pete

Rose's only career grand slam home run, and Jimmy Piersall's 100th home run. To celebrate, Piersall circled the bases backwards.

When Green ended his playing career, he found work in the Phillies' farm system. He did it all during 24 seasons with the Phillies: pitched, coached, managed in the minors, ran the farm system, and then moved into the front office as the assistant to general manager Paul Owens. His managerial career with the Phillies was brief, less than two and a half seasons.

The Tribune Co. had purchased the Cubs in May 1981, ending three generations of Wrigley family ownership. Andrew McKenna was named president and immediately began searching for a general manager. McKenna listed four requirements: (1) a former player or field manager; (2) farm system experience; (3) someone between the ages of 40 and 50; and (4) somebody who never had been the front office chief of a big league club. McKenna didn't want a recycled general manager.

Green filled the bill. He took over a last-place club and had a stormy reign which peaked three years later with a division championship, the Cubs' first title in 39 years. Green built the team with a series of outstanding deals, many with the Phillies. In all, during his first three years with the Cubs, 22 former Phillies, including field manager Lee Elia, were imported to Wrigley Field.

Green's biggest long-term strike was the acquisition of infielder Ryne Sandberg who had been buried in the Phillies' farm system. Also arriving from the Phillies were Gary Matthews, Bob Dernier and Keith Moreland, the entire 1984 Cub outfield, shortstop Larry Bowa, the principal in the Sandberg deal, and three pitchers, none of whom blossomed.

To strengthen the pitching, Green landed Dennis Eckersley, then a starter, from Boston. More important, he got Rick Sutcliffe in a seven-player June 13, 1984 swap with Cleveland. Sutcliffe came at a stiff price: Green had to relinquish rookie outfielder Joe Carter who went on to have an outstanding major league career. But the Cubs couldn't have won without Sutcliffe.

Sutcliffe was 16-1, for .941, the best winning percentage in Cub history. A 6-foot-7 right-hander, Sutcliffe (4-5 with

Cleveland) was a Wrigley Field sensation. He finished the regular season with 14 consecutive decisions, including the clincher, a two-hit, route-going performance at Pittsburgh on September 24. He won the Cy Young award.

Second baseman Sandberg won the Most Valuable Player award. He hit .314, had a 62-game errorless streak, and came within one triple and one home run of being the first player with 200 hits, 20 doubles, 20 triples, 20 home runs and 20 stolen bases in the same season. It was just the beginning for Sandberg who had a sensational 14-year Cub career.

For his good work, *The Sporting News* named Green the Executive of the Year. His Tribune bosses, fearing he would return to the Phillies, rewarded him with a big salary boost and the club presidency. But it was soon apparent the magic was gone. The Cubs dropped to fourth place in 1985, then to fifth and sixth.

Frey, who had managed the club to the '84 division title, was fired two years later but agreed to remain with the Cubs as a broadcaster. Frey was replaced by Gene Michael whom Green had lured away from the Yankees. Michael, an independent, resented Green's interference and was dismissed after the 1987 season.

Instead of remaining silent, Green told reporters hiring Michael was his "worst mistake." Michael responded with a blistering salvo. "Dallas has a big mouth and is a big buffoon," Michael told reporters. "I can't believe how he keeps making excuses for himself. He's trying to make himself look good for the bad job he did. How long is he going to live off '84?"

Frustrated, Green announced third base coach John Vukovich would be the next Cub manager. The executives in the Tribune Tower vetoed Vukovich's appointment. Green responded by saying that he would manage the club. The Tribune approved. Green could descend into the dugout proving he yield his general manager's job. Green refused to compromise and resigned on October 29.

Irony of ironies! Frey, whom Green had fired, replaced him as the club's general manager prior to the 1988 season. It was a surprise, but a logical appointment. More than anyone, Frey had an insider's knowledge of the uniformed personnel and understood the club's problems. A year later the Cubs won another division title under manager Don Zimmer.

It was the first time Frey had been elevated to a front office position but he was a savvy warrior who had been in professional baseball since 1950. A left-handed hitting outfielder, he never played in the major leagues but had a cumulative 14-year .302 average and won two minor league batting championships.

He surfaced to the majors with Baltimore and was the Orioles' batting coach for 10 years. Before joining the Cubs he had managed the Kansas City Royals to the 1980 A.L. pennant. The only area in which he was lacking was making player trades but he picked it up quickly. He made two crucial deals that helped lift the Cubs to the top of the East Division in 1989: the acquisition of closer Mitch Williams, who had 36 saves, one short of Bruce Sutter's club record, and Mike Bielecki, an obscure starting pitcher who won 18 games.

Frey also promoted outfielder Jerome Walton, who had been in Double A, to the parent club. Walton, leading off, had a major league high 30-game hitting streak and was named the N.L.'s Rookie of the Year. Greg Maddux replaced Sutcliffe as the team's pitching ace and won 19 games. Sandberg hit 30 home runs and set a major league record with 90 consecutive errorless games and won his seventh consecutive Gold Glove.

Two fourth-place finishes followed and on November 19, 1991, without a specific explanation, Frey was rotated to the rear as a "consultant" and never heard from again. Larry Himes stepped in, knighted by Stanton Cook, formerly the head of Tribune Co., then in charge of the Cubs.

The hope was that Himes would repeat his success and stock the farm system with outstanding talent as he had done with the White Sox. Himes was ousted three seasons later, after a front office shakeup, and was replaced by Ed Lynch.

Andy MacPhail, who had great success at Minnesota, was now the Cub president. When Lynch came aboard, MacPhail expressed confidence that the club was certain to improve. A former big-league pitcher who had a one-year stint with the Cubs,

Lynch was on the job five and a half years and had only one season, 1998, when the Cubs finished above .500.

The '98 club (90-73) won the wild card berth, the first time the Cubs gained the playoffs since 1989. Sammy Sosa, with 66 home runs, and pitcher Kerry Wood, a rookie sensation who set a one-season club strikeout record for a first-year man with 233 in 167 innings, led the team to the title.

The Cubs dropped into the cellar the following season and when Lynch resigned on July 19, 2000, MacPhail assumed the dual responsibilities as president and general manager.

The Firing Line

"The owners are not baseball people. They think they're running a department store. They change managers like they change underwear."
—Al Lopez, White Sox manager, 1957–65, 1968–69

"I hate to say it but I don't think the owners really respect what the manager does. They feel like it's something almost anybody can do."
—Whitey Lockman, Cub manager, 1972–74

The Chicago teams have had 88 different managers, the Cubs 51, the White Sox 37. Charlie Grimm holds the Chicago record with three managerial terms with the Cubs. James Callahan, Paul Richards and Al Lopez managed the White Sox twice as Joe Tinker did the Cubs.

Jimmy Dykes of the White Sox had the longest Chicago run (since 1901), 13 seasons, from 1934 through 1946. Frank Chance of the Cubs, "The Peerless Leader," is next with seven full seasons and part of an eighth, one more than Leo Durocher who commanded the Cubs for six and a half seasons. Chance reigned from 1905 to 1912, Durocher from 1966 to 1972.

It's a game of musical chairs. All of the clubs play it. A manager is hired, then fired, and hired by another club, fired again, and so on. The only guarantee for longevity is to own the club. Connie Mack, who owned the Philadelphia A's, survived for 50 years, the entire first half of the 20th Century.

The modern record, since 1900, for most clubs managed is six, shared by Dykes, who succeeded Mack, Rogers Hornsby, Dick Williams and John McNamara. Billy Martin is believed to be the all-time yo-yo. He managed five clubs and was hired and fired nine times.

There have been 583 managers since the birth of the National League in 1876, from Bill Adair, who directed the White Sox for 10 games in 1970, to Don Zimmer, a dugout wizard for 13 seasons, the last four (1988–91) with the Cubs. Alvin Dark, who played for the Cubs, holds the record for most years collecting his manager's salary after he had been aborted, five, three at San Diego, two at Cleveland.

Chris Von der Ahe, owner of the St. Louis Browns, played roulette. He had seven managers in 1896 without gain. The Browns finished 11th in the then 12-team National League, 50½ games out of the lead. The 1882 Louisville club employed a manager for home games, another for the road. The 1977 Texas Rangers had four managers. Eddie Stanky, who was first, quit after the season opener.

Philip K. Wrigley, long-time Cub caretaker, weary of firing managers, used rotating head coaches for two years. Everyone laughed. But George Steinbrenner, who made 26 managerial changes in his first 18 years of ownership of the New York Yankees, has been a closet disciple. In search of the quick fix, Steinbrenner routinely rotated his coaches and managers. Manager Billy Martin was up and down five times.

Charlie Finley, equally impatient, had 18 different managers in 20 seasons, seven at Kansas City (A's), 11 at Oakland. Finley had a red phone plugged into the dugout. From his office in Chicago, he made suggestions in critical moments. His managers usually obeyed. After he sold the Oakland club, Finley couldn't contain his contempt. "Managers are overrated," he said. "They're a dime a dozen."

Two owners, neither of whom had been a professional player, descended into the pit. To trim his payroll, owner Emil Fuchs dismissed Rogers Hornsby and directed the Boston Braves for the entire 1929 season. Atlanta's Ted Turner, frustrated after 16 consecutive 1977 losses, managed one game. The Braves lost again, 2-1 to Pittsburgh. Turner said: "That wasn't so bad. We lost by only one run."

Worse, a sportswriter, Oliver P. Caylor of the *Cincinnati Enquirer*, managed the 1890 Reds. Not only did the Reds finish last but they were expelled from the National League for the next season for "Violations of the rules, particularly of the regulations forbidding the sale of liquor on the grounds or in buildings owned or controlled by the club."

The 1891 *Spalding Guide* offered "Five Hints to Managers."

No. 4: "It takes all summer for a nine to get used to each other's peculiar style of play, and just when they have got to the right point the season closes, and the next season the nine is divided up among a half dozen other clubs. Here is where the mistake is made. Get rid of your weak men, but retain every man who has worked well for the club, even if he is not quite up to the high mark of playing strength you aim at."

Casey Stengel, after guiding the Yankees to nine pennants in a 10-year sequence, said, "I couldn't a done it without the players." It wasn't a burst of modesty. The nine years before that, when Stengel was managing at Brooklyn and Boston, he never escaped from the second division.

Anxious to continue working, managers almost always accept the transfers without complaint. They know how the game is played, take the rap, keep your mouth shut, and move on. Sparky Anderson, since retired, the only manager whose teams won the World Series in both leagues, expounded on the manager's life.

"I'm not saying this in disrespect, but what does the Manager of the Year mean? I've got four of them. They're the most useless awards I've ever seen. All it means is that I had four pretty good teams in those years.

"Motivation is the word they use when they want to get rid

of somebody. 'He doesn't motivate.' I laugh about it all the time. It's the most over-used word in the world. It doesn't mean anything. I can't call a player in and say, 'Now, you've been a good boy, so I want you to get out there and drive in the winning run.'

"And sometimes they double up and plant the word 'dissension.' If you have a losing club and half the players are at each other's necks, that's dissension. But when you're in first place there's never dissension. It's 'good chemistry.'"

This lengthy preamble is offered in explanation of the perils of managing. Neither the managers of the Cubs nor the White Sox, so far as is known, were confronted with these dangers. But like their colleagues they must contend with meddling, know-nothing owners, the radio talk show babble, and depressed player payrolls.

Frank Chance was the most successful Chicago manager. He was named "The Peerless Leader" by Charles Dryden, a famous Chicago baseball writer. He drove the Cubs to four pennants (1906–08, 1910) and two World Series championships (1907–08). Chance was in command for seven full seasons. None of his teams finished lower than third in an eight-team N.L.

"Husk" Chance was 6-feet, 200 pounds, strong as an ox. "What qualification, Mr. Chance, above all others, is responsible for your success as a manager?" a reporter asked.

"My ability to lick any man on the club," he replied.

His players were intimidated but admired him because of his honesty and competitive spirit. He was a disciplinarian and furious if his players talked to opponents. When Owen "Chief" Wilson of the Pittsburgh Pirates spiked him in a play at third base, Wilson said, "I hope you're not hurt."

Returning to the dugout, Chance told his teammates, "What should he have said, 'The next time I hope you lose your leg.'"

Big Ed Reulbach, who was among the most effective pitchers in Cub history, was occasionally faint-hearted and sometimes wilted in late-inning pressure. From his position at first base, Chance would shout at him, telling him what would happen in the clubhouse if he didn't get down to business. With new courage, born of terror, Reulbach was suddenly invincible.

Chance's wife, the former Edith Pancake, insisted that off the field he had a quiet, diffident personality. Once at the ballpark, he had a fighting spirit and was an inspiration to his men. When his predecessor, Frank Selee, became ill late in the 1905 season, instead of selecting a replacement, owner Charles W. Murphy called a clubhouse meeting and asked the players for their preference. Chance was their choice.

The son of a bank president, Chance was born in Fresno, California. He attended Washington College in Irvington, California, and majored in baseball, football and dentistry. He was recommended to the Cubs by Bill Lange, a Cub outfielder of the previous generation. Chance never played in the minors. He joined the Cubs in 1898.

Originally Chance was a catcher, but Selee moved him to first base. A right-handed hitter with only occasional power (20 home runs in 17 seasons), he hit .300 or better five times, had a .297 lifetime average, and twice led the league in stolen bases, with a career high of 67 in 1903. To protect himself on the outside pitch, he hung over the plate and was repeatedly knocked down. In a 1904 doubleheader, he was hit by a pitch five times. Frequently beaned, later in life he suffered from chronic migraine headaches.

In 1906, his first full season as a manager, the Cubs won 116 games, still the record for most victories in one season. They won the pennant in each of the next two seasons, finished second in 1909 (6½ games out), and won again in 1910. Miracle of miracles: four Cub pennants in five years. His teams won 768 games, twice as many as they lost.

Chance quarreled with Murphy in 1912 over the amount of money the club was willing to spend for quality players. Chance resigned in protest after the season and that winter underwent surgery for his headaches. He managed for three more seasons without success, two with the Yankees and one with the Boston Red Sox. He died in 1924, six days after his 63rd birthday.

Jimmy Dykes, who managed the White Sox for 13 seasons, a club record, was a polar opposite. Called the "Little Round Man" for his ample girth and lack of height, Dykes was the Will

Rogers of baseball. He rarely met anyone he didn't like. Considering his assignment and that he was constantly burdened with inferior talent, he was genial beyond belief. A popular after dinner speaker, he entertained his players and the sportswriters with a seemingly endless bag of good humor.

One night when umpire John Flaherty bent over to dust the plate a seventh time, Dykes, then managing Detroit, turned to pitcher Jim Bunning in the dugout and asked, "Do you know why Flaherty's using the brush all the time?"

"No."

"He's trying to find the plate. He hasn't been around it all night."

Connie Mack, his manager with the A's, once asked Dykes why he didn't slide into third base.

"My cigars were in my back pocket," Dykes replied. "I was afraid I'd break them."

He often told about his first at-bat against the great Walter Johnson.

"Walter rears back and whizzes two strikes past me. Talk about a batter being slow to get the bat off his shoulders. I didn't have time to even think about swinging. He winds up again, wham, another one zips past me. I didn't know what it was or where it was, high or low, inside or outside. I figure he'd struck me out, so I head for the bench."

"'Take your base, he hit you,' the umpire says.

"I didn't know what he was talking about. 'Hit me?'

"'Well, tell me this: Do you always wear your cap the way you're wearing it now?'

"I reach up and feel for my cap. The bill is turned clear around on the side where Johnson's last pitch had clipped it."

When he discovered his coaches and players were openly betting on the ponies, Dykes pinned a notice on the bulletin board:

"No tips on horses are allowed in this dressing room. If you think a horse is good, bring him in here where we can all appraise him."

He dropped pearls of wisdom: "Don't ever trade for a guy

who hits .400 against you and .200 against everybody else. When you get that guy he'll hit .200 for you."

Dykes began his career as Connie Mack's boy, a tough little infielder who helped the A's win three consecutive pennants from 1929 through 1931. He played 22 years, the last seven for the White Sox, and was the starting third baseman in the first All-Star game in 1933. He had a .280 lifetime average and was the first modern player to play more than 100 games at each of the four infield positions.

Approaching bankruptcy, Mack broke up his team. He sold Dykes and outfielder Al Simmons and Mule Haas to the White Sox at the end of the 1932 season for $100,000, in those days a princely sum. Two years later, Dykes was the Sox manager, succeeding Lew Fonseca. Typically, they were in last place.

They never finished last again, not with Dykes in the dugout. Seven of his teams finished in the second division, only three soared as high as third, but his reputation grew. Said the astute Birdie Tebbetts, who managed three clubs: "He was the best manager of worn-out talent. Everybody knew he brought his clubs higher than they should have been."

Alfonso Ramon Lopez, the seventh son of a seventh son, led the White Sox out of the wilderness. He was the perfect manager. He had been an iron-man catcher and had broken the record for most games caught. And he was a natural leader. At 25, when most major league players are beginning to climb out of the crib, he was the captain of the Brooklyn Dodgers.

In 1925, after the World Series, a barnstorming squad of big league players was traveling through Florida on an exhibition tour. Tampa was one of the stops. Walter Johnson, who threw with lightning speed, had agreed to pitch five innings for the home team. For a week there was concern in the Tampa baseball community; was there a local catcher who could handle him?

"What about Alfonso?" asked a sportswriter named Montono of the *La Traduccion*, an Ybor City Spanish language newspaper.

"He's only 16. He could get hurt."

"I know," Montono replied. "But he can catch."

Before the game, Johnson took Lopez aside and told him not to call for too many curveballs.

"Mr. Johnson, you throw whatever you want," Alfonso replied. "I'll put down the sign and if you don't want it then shake it off."

Johnson then informed Lopez he would "let it all out" only against Jacques Fournier of the Dodgers and Ike Boone of the Red Sox.

Lopez was the Dodgers' regular catcher five years later. But there were moments of depression. One year as the Dodgers were breaking their spring training camp and heading north, he was sent back to the minors.

Gary Schumacher of the *New York Journal* told him, "Don't worry, kid. You've got too many tools to stay down. You'll be back."

Tom Meany, then with the *Brooklyn Times*, was nearby. After Lopez was gone, he asked Schumacher, "Do you really think he'll make it?"

"Naw," Schumacher said, "but he's a nice kid. The least I could do is cheer him up."

Lopez bloomed. He was in the starting lineup in 1930. Casey Stengel was the manager. Two years later, Lopez was traded to the Boston Bees (as the Braves were briefly renamed).

"The club's in trouble," Stengel told him. "You were the only one the other clubs wanted."

Five years passed. Stengel, now the Boston manager, traded Lopez a second time, to Pittsburgh for catcher Ray Berres and $40,000. Again Stengel was apologetic. The explanation was familiar.

"Al, I don't like to see you go but the club needs the money."

Many years later Stengel elaborated. "As a catcher, Lopez was the best, one of the very best. It wasn't long before I knew I could take a snooze with him behind the plate. He put effort into his work. He had baseball on his mind all the time. He wasn't one of those question-answer players, not that they're bad. But he didn't ask because he knew the answers. Now, that's a pretty bright man, you gotta agree."

Lopez repeatedly said that Gabby Hartnett of the Cubs, at that time, was the best defensive catcher in the National League. If so, Lopez was second. One year, Lopez doesn't remember which, he went through the entire season with one passed ball.

Danny McFayden, who was the pitcher, told the sportswriters they should change it and charge him with a wild pitch. "I crossed him up," McFayden insisted.

Lopez' first managerial assignment was with the Cleveland Indians. He guided them for six years, from 1951 through 1956. His Cleveland clubs never finished lower than second and won the pennant with 111 victories in 1954, a league record that broke Stengel's string of five consecutive Yankee pennants.

Lopez left Cleveland prior to the 1957 season and moved to Chicago's South Side, to Comiskey Park. He reconstructed the team around pitching, speed and defense. Three more second-place finishes were absorbed. Marshall Smith of *Life Magazine* captured the scene in the spring of 1959:

"A Yankee desperado named Casey Stengel has been shooting up the American League and getting away with the swag. Catching him seems almost impossible. Not only does he know all the tricks and short cuts but his equipment is superb. He has guns capable of firing accurate, murderous shots that make an enemy helpless.

"He also has the horses—the finest, swiftest horses that money can buy. If any of his guns fails to shoot straight, he has others cached away in carefully protected arsenals. If any of his magnificent horses gives out, he has others hidden in the cane-brakes, waiting for his whistle. With all his limitless resources and daring, the Yanqui should feel completely safe from pursuit.

"But he does not. Every time he looks over his shoulder he sees the same relentless, inescapable figure. The pursuer is not a glamorous hero but a threadbare man wearing a big sombrero. He is riding a burro so forlorn that every step looks as though it might be his last. His guns are peashooters. He has no arsenal, no spare mounts, no resources. But he is always there, always following."

As Marshall Smith had foreseen, Stengel and the Yankees were overtaken by Señor Lopez' "peashooters." Last in the league in home runs, the White Sox won the 1959 pennant, their first flag in 40 years. That broke another Yankee reign. If not for Lopez, Stengel's Yankees more than likely would have won 10 pennants in a row.

Ty Cobb, second only to Babe Ruth as baseball's greatest player, wrote a fan letter. Cobb was 72. The letter, dated September 30, 1959, said:

"This is a brother ballplayer's greeting. Your being in the other league (Lopez played virtually his entire career in the N.L., Cobb all of his in the A.L). Frank Lane admired your ability and I more than you know. I want to add my congratulations to the very many you will receive. You have done a wonderful job, you and your team. I admire much how you did it. You play a type of game I know well.

"Baseball is an attractive game as it was planned out to be and played for 60 or more years before these muscle guys came in with the lively ball. Some of them are lunks and do not know 'beans.' You have done a great job over several years. My salutations!"

In 1995, seventy years after a 16-year-old schoolboy had caught Walter Johnson's overwhelming fastball, the citizens of Tampa erected a life-size bronze statue honoring Alfonso Ramon Lopez. Senor Lopez is wearing an old-style chest protector and throwing his mask in pursuit of a foul popup.

There is no statue of Charlie Grimm but his ashes were strewn over Wrigley Field. A three-time Cub manager, Grimm is difficult to categorize. He had the heart of a vaudevillian and often entertained with his mimicry when he was in the coaching box. He was among baseball's leading troubadours and the ultimate contradiction to Leo Durocher's dictum that "Nice guys finish last." In his first seven seasons as manager his teams never finished lower than third.

Grimm was prominent in four Cub pennants (1929, '32, '35 and '45). He was the first baseman on the 1929 club, the second-half season manager in 1932, the season-long manager in 1935, and managed the first 126 games in 1938 before he was relieved by Hartnett. After a three year hiatus in Milwaukee, then a minor league bastion, Grimm returned to Chicago at the urging of front office chief James T. Gallagher and managed the Cubs in 1945 when they won their last pennant.

He also had two separate stretches in the radio booth and three terms in the front office. Almost every time he returned to the field he would announce, "These hands weren't made to carry a briefcase." A slick-fielding first baseman, Grimm had hands the size of hams. He led the league's first basemen in fielding nine times. When he retired he held the career record for most putouts and chances.

Trainer Ed Froelich said that in all the years he was with the Cubs only one groundball eluded Grimm. Hack Wilson, the Cubs' stumpy slugger, came running in from right field and, in mock surprise, shouted, "Charlie, what's wrong? Did the gamblers get to you?"

Grimm was a solid hitter—a .290 career average—but was overshadowed by his slugging teammates. He hit a creditable .289 in 1930 when the Cubs had a .309 team average. Grimm was among the club's weakest hitters and batted eighth. Five of his teammates batted .325 or higher.

To Grimm, baseball was fun, not war. He scoffed at the managerial "master minds," particularly the spindly martinets who were not satisfied until they had complete and unchallenged control. In the end, Grimm's relaxed approach diminished his achievements. He made everything look too easy.

"I like to be close to my players," Grimm explained. "I'm supposed to be an easygoing guy but you've got 25 different dispositions and you've got to treat them differently. If I think a guy isn't putting his best foot forward, I take him aside and talk to him. There's no sense embarrassing someone in front of everybody. Ballplayers have feelings like everyone else. I've handled some pretty tough ones in my time and gotten good performance out of them.

"They call me 'Jolly Cholly.' That's the way I always was and that's the way I'll always be."

A native of St. Louis, Grimm dropped out of school in the

sixth grade. He was raised in a musical family. His father played the bull fiddle, his mother the harmonica, a sister at the piano, one brother on the guitar and another on the bass tuba. Charlie was a left-handed banjo player, skilled enough to perform professionally with Eddie Peabody.

In 1916, Grimm broke in with Connie Mack's Athletics, sat on the bench, and three years later was traded to the Pittsburgh Pirates where he remained the next six seasons. His appealing, nonchalant manner was appalling to owner Barney Dreyfuss. After the 1924 season, Dreyfuss decided, "It's about time we get rid of our banjo players," and traded Grimm and his comrades, Rabbit Maranville and Wilbur Cooper, to the Cubs.

Even before he unloaded his gear, Grimm, his banjo in tow, joined the Cubs' string band. He played 12 seasons with the Cubs, the last four as player/manager. He was owner Philip Wrigley's favorite player. He was kept on the payroll beyond his time and lived happily ever after.

Adrian Constantine Anson, named for two Roman emperors, ruled the baseball world in the 19th Century. The first white child born in Marshalltown, Iowa, founded by his father, Anson was a baseball lifer, generally acknowledged the best player of his time and as well known as Babe Ruth, who surfaced almost 50 years later.

The lead of Anson's *Sporting News* obituary, written by Chicago baseball writer John Sheridan, follows:

"The mighty manager-captain of the almighty Chicago White Stockings, the greatest hitter of his day, if not, indeed, all days, the giant of giants, most beautiful man on a club of beautiful men—man of highest personal character and finest self-respect, a man who never did aught to bring that profession into disrepute or disfavor, a man who indeed did more than any other to elevate baseball from its humble beginnings to the great sport of a great nation, was truly a man to whom a nation might rally, of whom a nation might well be proud. Now the mighty athlete of 37 years of play on the diamond is laid in the dust to the sorrow of all lovers of sport."

Now for some of the facts:

Anson was with the White Stockings, later renamed the Cubs, for 22 years, then a record for longevity. He was a player-manager for the last 19 seasons. In the first eight years of this dual role his teams won five pennants. Innovative, he has been credited with inventing the hit-and-run, encouraged base stealing and may have been the first to rotate his pitchers.

More than that, Cap Anson was the original centerpiece of the National League, founded in 1876 by William Hulbert, a weathy Chicagoan who made his fortune in wholesale groceries and coal. It was Hulbert, a civic booster, who made the endearing comment: "I'd rather be a lamppost in Chicago than a millionaire in any other city."

Albert Goodwill Spalding, out of Byron, Illinois, who later presided over a profitable worldwide sporting goods empire, assisted Hulbert on the sly. Then a star pitcher with Boston of the National Association, Spalding recruited three of his outstanding teammates for Hulbert's Chicago franchise in the new league.

Hulbert then went after Anson, the star of the National Association's Philadelphia Pearls. Anson was the ultimate prize. He agreed to come aboard and was guaranteed a $2,000 salary. Anson's wife didn't want to leave Philadelphia. Anson tried to negate his contract. He offered Hulbert a $1,000 buyout. Hulbert refused. Anson suited up and finished his career in Chicago.

Within months, the Association folded. It had been riddled with corruption, fixed games and uncertain scheduling. Five of its 13 teams didn't finish the 1875 season. As planned by Hulbert and Spalding, the Association's four major eastern teams—the New York Mutuals, Philadelphia Pearls, Boston Red Stockings and Hartford Blues—were absorbed by the National League.

In a peace-making effort, Hulbert threw the Association survivors a bone. He installed Morgan G. Bulkeley, owner of the Hartford club and later a United States senator from Connecticut, with the league presidency. A figurehead, Bulkeley resigned

10 months later. Hulbert succeeded him and remained in office until his death in 1882.

The Bulkeley appointment became a source of embarrassment a half century later, in 1937, when he was voted into the Hall of Fame in the first election of executives. It was clearly a case of mistaken identity. Hulbert, not Bulkeley, had saved the game. Still, 61 years passed before Hulbert was enshrined.

Anson was the first N.L. player to accumulate 3,000 hits. He hit .399 in 1991 and .421 in 1887, when walks were counted as hits. He won three batting titles and hit .300 or better in 20 of his 22 seasons. He had a .331 career average, led the league in runs batted in four times, in doubles twice, and in errors three times.

He was well over 6 feet tall, weighed 210 pounds and sometimes was described as a "blond giant." Gruff, he was a disciplinarian, didn't allow his players to drink or smoke, and constantly skirmished with the umpires. He is also believed to be the first player to write his biography, *A Ball Player's Career*, published in 1900 by the Era Publishing Co. of Chicago.

Anson was a racist and twice didn't allow his team to take the field against African-American opponents. His prejudice against black players, never fully explained, was a source of comment throughout every professional league, and, without doubt, delayed their acceptance into the major leagues.

Anson was dismissed after the 1897 season. He remained in Chicago, owned a bowling and billiard hall and also organized a semi-pro baseball league. Both foundered financially. He went into politics and from 1905 to 1907 served as Chicago's city clerk.

N.L. president John Heydler, aware Anson was short on funds, offered him a pension. Anson rejected all efforts of financial assistance, saying, "Nobody owes me anything." He died in 1922 and is buried in Chicago's Oakwoods Cemetery. A huge monument, "In belated appreciation of Captain Anson," was paid for by the N.L.

WHEELERS,
DEALERS

The three saddest words in the Cub lexicon:
"Broglio for Brock."

It was June 15, 1964, two hours before the trading deadline
and it seemed to be nothing more than another routine deal between the Cubs and Cardinals. A promising but obscure young
left-handed hitting outfielder in exchange for Ernie Broglio, an
established pitcher, once a 21-game winner, expected to help in
the pennant drive. In essence, that was the genesis of Broglio-for-
Brock. Such mid-season trades are common: youth for experience.

Leaping ahead, it is 31 years later, January 22, 1995. The
Cubs are opening their annual winter fan convention at the
downtown Hilton Hotel. The honored guests are gathering in a
private mezzanine chamber. In comes Ernie Broglio. He sits
down at a table with Lou Brock.

"If it wasn't for you, I wouldn't be here," Broglio announces.

"I know," Brock replies. "We're joined at the hip. History put
us together."

It was among the worst deals in Cub history. Brock, then 23,
went on to a Hall of Fame career. Broglio? Cub fans wish you

wouldn't ask. He reported with a sore arm. Over the next three seasons, all with the Cubs, he won a *total* of seven games.

Bob Smith of the *Chicago Daily News* was ecstatic when the trade was made: "Thank you, thank you, oh, you lovely St. Louis Cardinals. Nice doing business with you. Please call again any time."

Most of the players from both sides agreed with Smith's assessment. Bill White, then the Cardinals' first baseman and later president of the National League, was emphatic.

"We thought we had given up too much," White said. "Brock was not a good fielder, he struck out a lot and he didn't know how to run the bases."

Brock made his Cardinal debut in Houston at old Colt Stadium. Inserted as a pinch hitter, he struck out on three pitches.

Bing Devine, the Cardinals' general manager, was sitting behind the plate. "A group of fans were just behind me, riding Brock and the Cardinals," Devine recalled. "And one of them said, 'Broglio for Brock? Who could make such a deal?'

"And I remember saying to one of my associates, 'I guess I've got to agree. Who in the world would make such a deal?' "

John Holland, the Cubs' general manager, was the aggressor. Holland and Devine had been discussing a deal since the previous winter. Brock was available. Two days before the trading deadline, on June 13, Holland telephoned Devine and left a message to call him. Devine returned the call as the Cardinals were boarding a plane for Houston.

Devine: "John said, 'You're going badly and we're going badly. We need a pitcher. You mentioned Brock.'

"I said, 'All right, John, but I'm traveling. I'll call you tomorrow from Houston.'

Devine was sitting next to manager Johnny Keane on the flight to Houston. "Keane always liked Brock," Devine said. "I told him, 'If we're ever going to get Brock, it looks like now.'"

Devine remembers Keane's response. "He said, 'What are we waiting for?' "

In Chicago, the reaction was mixed. Bob Kennedy, the Cubs' head coach—the Cubs were then experimenting with rotating head coaches—was against the deal. Three of the other coaches, Lou Klein, Verlon "Rube" Walker and Fred Martin, sided with Kennedy.

"We just liked Lou Brock a lot more than that," Kennedy recalled years later. "And we didn't like Broglio. Lew Burdette (acquired from the Cardinals two weeks earlier) was on our club and told us Broglio had been having arm problems. He'd been getting shots."

The deal was consummated on a Monday when the Cubs had an open date. "I told the coaches to go someplace and not tell anyone where they would be," Kennedy later revealed.

"We didn't want Mr. Holland calling us and asking for our approval. I went out and played golf. I remember I was golfing in the rain. I told Claire (his wife) not to tell anybody where I was. But they found me and I had to go into the office.

"I told Mr. Holland, 'John, this guy's got a bad arm.' But he assured me his arm was in good shape."

The indications are that Cub owner P.K. Wrigley, not Holland, had pushed for the deal. Holland apparently was following orders. Rarely quoted on personnel matters, Wrigley told reporters, "If you want to hit the bull's-eye, you have to take a shot at it."

In two and a half season and 1,207 at-bats with the Cubs, Brock had a cumulative .257 batting average, with a one-season high of .263. His principal achievement was a blockbuster home run into the right-center field bleachers in the old Polo Grounds, then the home of the New York Mets. The distance was estimated at 458 feet. That Brock was able to hit a ball that far was surprising. At 5 feet, 11 inches and 170 pounds, he had not been regarded as a power hitter.

Outfielder Bob Will, who was among Brock's Cub teammates, had a vivid memory of the home run.

"It seemed like it didn't want to come down," Will recalled. "It just kept going and going and disappeared. Richie Ashburn (the Mets' center fielder) started after it and stopped. I've never forgotten how he stood watching the ball. Then he turned and looked toward the plate, like he couldn't believe it. We talked about it for weeks. We knew he had some power, but that was a long way."

And, of course, Brock, hasn't forgotten:

"The pitch was almost over my head. I chopped down on it and began running as fast as I could. Bill Jackowski, the second base umpire, gave me a home run sign. I thought he meant if I kept on running I'd have an inside-the-park home run. I came around home plate as fast as I could. All the Cubs were looking out to the outfield. Nobody shook my hand. Ron Santo then began pounding me and said, 'Did you see where that ball went? Did you see the ball? I needed binoculars.'"

Babe Ruth had hit two home runs into that same sector 40 years earlier but the bleachers were then closer to the plate. Joe Adcock in 1953 and Hank Aaron (who connected the night after Brock did) were the only sluggers to reach the Polo Grounds bleachers. Brock's home run came on June 17, 1962, in his 56th big league game. It was two years before the trade and was off Al Jackson, who hung a curveball. It was Brock's first home run against a left-handed pitcher.

When he was traded, Brock was hitting .258 with two home runs, certainly no indication of what was to come later. In 103 games with the Cardinals he hit .348 and led the Redbirds to the pennant. Before Brock, they were 28-30. Thereafter they were 65-39, 26 games over .500.

Contrary to Wrigley's expectations, the Cubs didn't hit the bull's-eye. The sore-armed Broglio, a 21-game winner in 1960, was 4-7 with the Cubs, who wound up in last place, 17 games out. When the deal was consummated they were 27-27 and tied for fifth, 5½ games out of the lead.

Brock helped the Cardinals win two more pennants, in 1967–68, batted over .300 six times and is a member of the exclusive 3,000 Hit Club (3,023). He led the league in stolen bases eight times and in 1974 set a single-season record with 118 steals. He had a career total of 938 stolen bases, a major league record since surpassed. His record of 14 World Series steals still stands. He batted .297 lifetime, .391 in World Series play, and was elected to the Hall of Fame in 1985, his first year on the ballot.

The Broglio-Brock trade still hasn't been forgotten almost 50 years later and more than likely probably will continue to have a lengthy shelf life. The deals that turn out poorly are remembered. There have been dozens of other "bloopers" by the Cubs and White Sox, but some of these deals occurred so long ago that it's difficult to put them in the proper perspective.

Certainly, Cub fans were provoked in 1917 when Cy Williams, a slugging outfielder, was sent to the Philadelphia Phillies for Dode Paskert, also an outfielder. Paskert had a brief Cub career—four home runs in four years. Williams played 13 seasons with the Phillies, had a lifetime total of 251 home runs and in 1923 tied Babe Ruth for the major league lead with 41.

The White Sox were equally guilty of misjudgment and 43 years later, after they won the 1959 American League pennant, traded prize rookie Johnny Callison, also to the Phillies, for third baseman Gene Freese. Owner Bill Veeck made the deal in a hasty effort for a second successive flag but it was a big flop. Callison matured with the Phillies and had a career total of 226 home runs. Freese was traded to Cincinnati a year later.

White Sox farm director Glen Miller, who nursed Callison through the minors and was aware of his potential, was heartsick. Miller's condition worsened three months later when Veeck, in an identical deal, sent first baseman Norm Cash to Cleveland, which quickly traded him to Detroit. Cash, who appeared in only 71 games in his two years with the Sox, also blossomed. He led the A.L. in batting in 1961 with a .361 average and had a career total of 377 home runs.

Veeck blundered again a month later when he dealt two more of his young players, catcher Earl Battey and first baseman Don Mincher, to the Washington Senators for outfielder-first baseman Roy Sievers, who four seasons earlier had led the A.L. in home runs with 42 and in RBI with 114. Sievers was installed in the cleanup spot but was unable to pull the wagon. He was traded two years later.

The Cubs made their share of similar mistakes. Impatient with his progress and high strikeout totals, they traded first baseman Dolf Camilli to the Phillies in June 1934 for Don Hurst, who was in the twilight of his career. Camilli had played in only 32 games with the Cubs. Overnight, he developed into one of the N.L.'s premier power hitters and had eight consecutive seasons with 23 or more home runs. He was the 1941 MVP when he drove the Brooklyn Dodgers to the pennant and led the league with 32 home runs and 120 RBI. Of his 239 career home runs, only six were for the Cubs.

Other ex-Cubs who flourished elsewhere: outfielder Andy Pafko, relief pitcher Lee Smith, first basemen Rafael Palmeiro and Andre Thornton, and outfielder Joe Carter, who was sacrificed in the Rick Sutcliffe deal. The Carter trade wasn't a "bummer." It was a good deal for both sides. If not for pitcher Sutcliffe's 16-1 record, the Cubs would not have won the 1984 division title.

The Chicago clubs have made dozens of good deals. Frank "Trader" Lane of the White Sox, within a two-year period, traded for Hall of Fame second baseman Nellie Fox, pitcher Billy Pierce—who should be similarly honored but has been ignored by the Cooperstown brigade—and Chico Carrasquel, who was among the best shortstops of the time (1950s).

Pierce arrived in a 1948 deal with the Detroit Tigers for Aaron Robinson. Fox checked in the next season from Connie Mack's Philadelphia A's for Joe Tipton, another obscure catcher. To get Carrasquel, Lane bamboozled Branch Rickey, a legendary and shrewd operator then with the Brooklyn Dodgers. Carrasquel was their most prized prospect.

Rickey had a dozen good players stockpiled in the minors in 1949 and advised Lane he was willing to deal outfielder Sam Jethroe, then with the Dodgers' Montreal farm club. Lane repeatedly expressed interest in Carrasquel. Rickey was noncommittal.

Two weeks later Lane called Rickey:

"When can I announce the Carrasquel deal to the press?"

"What deal?"

"Don't you remember?"

"Well, all right, if I made the deal, I'll keep my word."

And the White Sox had baseball's next Mr. Shortstop for $45,000.

Trader Lane picked up Pierce when he was 22 and 3-0 in two seasons combined with Detroit. Pierce went on to win 208 additional big league games. Fox was also a 22-year-old novice when Lane brought him to Chicago. He had had three mediocre seasons with the A's—262 at-bats, eight extra base hits, no home runs—and, miraculously, soon became a White Sox fixture, the MVP in the 1959 pennant season.

Another shrewd Lane deal was the acquisition of veteran right-hander Virgil "Fire" Trucks during the 1953 season from the St. Louis Browns. Trucks went 15-6 the rest of the season for the Sox to finish with a 20-12 record. He was 19-12 the next year and 13-8 in 1955 before leaving Chicago.

On occasion, the Cubs also prospered. Shortstop Ernie Banks, alias Mr. Cub, was acquired in 1953 from the Kansas City Monarchs of the Negro American League for $15,000, legitimate larceny. Mordecai "Three-Finger" Brown was another steal, from the Cardinals for pitcher Jack "The Brakeman" Taylor in 1903. Brown helped the Cubs win four pennants. He had six consecutive (1906–11) 20-win seasons as did Ferguson Jenkins, his brother Hall of Famer who was captured at an early age from the Phillies in 1966.

Sammy Sosa is entitled to dual mention and listing in both the "best" and "worst" columns. Both Chicago teams traded for him. The "hero" in the Sosa saga is Larry Himes, who had four seasons as White Sox general manager then three in the same role with the Cubs. Convinced Sosa had all the "necessities," Himes traded for him twice.

The first time was the bigger risk. Sosa, then 22, was an obscure outfielder with the Texas Rangers. Himes acquired him from the Rangers in a mid-season deal in 1989 at the cost of Harold Baines, a popular White Sox outfielder—so popular that the next season, with Baines still in mid-career, owner Jerry Reinsdorf retired his uniform number, an act of admiration without precedent.

Three years later, Ron Schueler, who had succeeded Himes as White Sox front office boss, traded the late-blooming Sosa to the Cubs for aging slugger George Bell. And who, of all people, was then the Cub general manager waiting to welcome Sosa at the Wrigley Field players' gate? None other than Larry Himes. Once with the Cubs, Sosa began pounding home runs and became an international hero.

Himes also had a huge blot on his ledger. He allowed Greg Maddux to escape, a blunder equivalent to the Brock-Broglio trade. A farm product, Maddux had been with the Cubs for seven years. He had a combined 95-75 record, a considerable achievement with mostly sub-.500 clubs.

In 1992, his last season in Chicago, Maddux was 20-11, tied for the league in victories with Tom Glavine of the Atlanta Braves, and won the Cy Young award. Maddux led in innings pitched (268), was third in fewest hits allowed (6.7 for each nine innings) and had a 2.18 earned run average, lowest in the league among starting pitchers. And he was only 26.

He opted for free agency following the 1992 season. Remarkably, Himes let him get away. A year or so later, Maddux revealed he had been waiting for Himes to call. He was eager to re-sign with the Cubs. Himes was unable to bend and spoke only to Maddux' agent. Disenchanted, Maddux departed. He jumped to the Braves, won three more Cy Young awards in a row, and became one of the most effective pitchers of all time, easily the best of his generation.

The White Sox lost Denny McLain, a two-time Cy Young winner and the last pitcher to win 30 games. McLain had a distinguished but troubled big league career. Losing McLain was not of wrenching consequence and barely a bleep on the White Sox screen. A native Chicagoan, he grew up five miles from Comiskey Park and was signed out of Mount Carmel High School in 1962 for a $17,000 bonus.

Farmed out, McLain pitched in two games in 1962 with the Harlan, Kentucky club of the Appalachian League. He broke in with a no-hitter and lost his next and last start for Harlan. What was especially impressive to the brass in Chicago was his strikeout total, 32 in 18 innings, almost two an inning. The next season he was 4-7 with Clinton, Iowa, in the Class D Midwest League.

For a closer look, the Sox invited him to their 1963 spring training camp. But there was a problem. McLain was one of three young bonus pitchers in the organization; only two could be carried into the regular season. At that time bonus players, if not placed on the active roster after their first full season, were left unprotected, subject to an $8,000 waiver claim.

Dave DeBusschere and Bruce Howard survived. Neither had much success. DeBusschere, later a basketball star with the New York Knicks, won three games with the Sox. Howard hung on for five seasons and won 25 games. Detroit acquired McLain on waivers. Farm director Glen Miller and manager Al Lopez had no regrets. While in the minors, McLain was often out of control and twice had gone AWOL.

McLain was suspended three times in 1970, a one-season record, by baseball Commissioner Bowie Kuhn. The charges were for allegedly consorting with gamblers and participating in a bookmaking operation in Flint, Michigan, dousing two Detroit beat baseball writers with a bucket of ice water, and carrying a gun.

After his playing career ended, McLain was twice convicted of racketeering and extortion and fraudulent business practices. He did time in stronghold federal prisons. Still, he had some great seasons. He was the last 30-game winner with 31-6 in 1968, led the Tigers to a pennant that year and captured both the Cy Young and Most Valuable Player awards.

One of his three biographies is titled *Nobody's Perfect.*

Hear It Now, See It Live

On April 23, 1924, a young newspaperman named Hal Totten completed his pioneering play-by-play radio report of a Chicago Cub game, a 12-1 victory over the St. Louis Cardinals. It might have been the first time he closed a broadcast with what was to become his signature sign-off, "G'bye now."

"G'bye now" lacks the fervor of later signature phrases such as "Hey-Hey!" and "Holy Cow!" but it's just as significant. Totten blazed a trail through the airwaves for Jack "Hey-Hey!" Brickhouse and Harry "Holy Cow!" Caray, and dozens of other Chicago radio and TV baseball broadcasters.

Totten, 23, a lively-voiced reporter for the *Chicago Daily News*, was embarking on an untried venture for radio station WMAQ (frequency 670), owned by the newspaper. He broadcast every 1924 Cubs and White Sox home game. Previously no station in any major league city had gone beyond broadcasting an occasional game.

The experiment was successful. The audience for Cubs and White Sox games grew steadily during the season. By its end, Totten was securely launched on a long and distinguished career that extended to World Series and "Game of the Day" assignments for several national networks.

Brickhouse, whom Chicagoans heard for the first time in 1940, acknowledged the debt to Totten, as well as other pioneer broadcasters, when interviewed by Curt Smith, the author of *Voices of the Game,* a history of baseball broadcasting.

"...if these guys, announcers like Totten, had bombed, if they hadn't turned baseball on, then broadcasting wouldn't have clung to baseball," Brickhouse told Smith.

It's also possible that baseball wouldn't have clung to broadcasting.

Unbelievable as it may seem at a time when a great portion of major league baseball's revenue is derived from TV and radio, the broadcast media wasn't always welcome, but once was feared and shunned by many in the game. The three New York–area teams, Yankees, Giants and Brooklyn Dodgers, signed an agreement in 1934 barring radio broadcasts through 1938.

Chicago, however, heartily embraced baseball broadcasting almost from the advent of radio receivers after World War I. Totten took to the air less than three years after radio's first baseball game. Announcer Harold Arlin had described a Pirates game at Forbes Field on the country's first radio station, KDKA in Pittsburgh, on August 5, 1921.

The idea caught on quickly, and the 1921 World Series entertained listeners just two months later with celebrated *New York Herald-Tribune* sports columnist Grantland Rice describing the action in the all-New York duel between the Yankees and Giants. An annual October ritual had been established to continue ever since.

The popularity of the World Series broadcasts encouraged WMAQ's decision to put Totten on the air for all Chicago home games in 1924. Rival station WGN started more modestly by having Sen Kasey report the 1924 City Series in October.

Before long, with no fear of exaggeration, Chicago could have been called the baseball broadcast capital of the country. Other stations followed the lead of WMAQ and WGN and by 1929 Cubs' games were heard on five and those of the White Sox on two.

The disparity might be explained partly by the fact that the Cubs won the National League pennant in 1929, while the White Sox were also-rans. Additionally, Cub owner William Wrigley, Jr. and team president William Veeck, Sr. were enthusiastic about broadcasting from the start, prizing the free publicity for their team.

"The more outlets, the better," Wrigley bubbled. "That way we'll tie up the whole city."

Anyone who had a license and the equipment to broadcast games was free to do so. Free in more ways than one because in the early days teams did not charge fees—or grant "exclusivity"—to stations for the privilege of airing games.

As a result, Totten soon became just one of a crowd of broadcasters by the late 1920s and into the early 1930s. His colleagues included Pat Flanagan, Joe E. Brown (future movie star), Quin Ryan, Truman Bradley, Johnny O'Hara, Jack Drees, Russ Hodges and Bob Elson. There was even Charlie Grimm, who occasionally turned to radio between his three terms as the Cub manager.

It was Elson who made the greatest and most enduring impact in Chicago sports broadcasting. If a triumvirate of the city's most notable baseball announcers were chosen, he would rank with latecomers Brickhouse and Caray.

A native Chicagoan, Elson in 1928 joined WGN's Quin Ryan on Cub and White Sox games. After Ryan left play-by-play a couple of years later, Elson became the virtual Voice of Chicago baseball for 40 years, and a broadcaster of national reputation with a dozen World Series and nine All-Star Games to his credit. After naval service in World War II, he gloried almost as much in his nickname, The Old Commander.

Elson's casual, matter-of-fact, almost impartial method of describing games contrasted sharply with the frenetic, boisterous and boosterish styles of most later announcers, among them his enthusiastic protégé Brickhouse and the ebullient Harry Caray. Elson's level, cultivated voice seldom betrayed excitement. He merely reported what happened on the field, though with frequent digressions to interject a commercial or "recommend" a favorite restaurant, bar or entertainment.

Elson insisted he made it "a point never to criticize a player on the air, never second-guess a manager, never rap an owner. I hope people can say that as long as Bob Elson was on the air he never hurt anybody."

Elson's understated manner served him well, keeping him on the air for 40 years and more than 7,000 games, mostly those of the White Sox after the 1940s. But critics began to emerge in the late 1950s. They preferred "cheerleading" announcers such as Bert Wilson, who first went on radio with Cub games in 1944. Quibblers savaged Elson's style as "dull" in comparison.

In Curt Smith's book, Brickhouse and Vince Lloyd, a later Cubs announcer, condemned the criticism of Elson as ignorant and unwarranted.

"I know there were idiots—know-nothings who said in the sixties that he was boring," Brickhouse said, "but to me he was a pioneer, the most marvelous broadcaster who ever lived."

Lloyd enthused, "The first time I heard him, I thought he was the greatest I'd ever heard."

Merit aside, Elson's great influence is undeniable. He was the radio voice of both the Cubs and White Sox throughout the 1930s on various stations (broadcasts had a tendency to drift year-by-year until the system of exclusivity and payment to teams for rights was fully developed in the mid-1940s). In the post–World War II years, the White Sox claimed his major attention, and he stayed with them until he was dismissed after the 1970 season.

During that long run, Elson had many on-the-air partners, among them Brickhouse, Dick Bingham, Don Wells, Ralph Kiner, Milo Hamilton, Bob Finnegan and Red Rush. Several went on to fine careers of their own.

Naturally, the relationship between teams and the electronic media changed a great deal during the four decades in which Elson's voice entertained and informed fans throughout the Midwest (affiliated smaller city stations often picked up broadcasts emanating in Chicago). The most dramatic change, of course, came with the rise of TV in the late 1940s.

By that time radio stations were paying teams for the exclusive rights to broadcast their games, and the early practice in two-team cities such as Chicago of not airing games at competing times was dropped. For awhile, Chicago became the only two-team city in which almost all games were broadcast on both radio and TV.

This was still in the future, but was to become of extraordinary importance to Brickhouse, the second member of Chicago's baseball broadcasting "triumvirate," who came on the scene in 1940. Elson, then with WGN, had met Brickhouse, a young announcer working in Peoria, Illinois. Needing an assistant, Elson invited Brickhouse to audition for the job.

Brickhouse became Elson's partner on Cubs and White Sox games over WGN in 1940, then went it alone during Elson's military service from 1942 to 1944. WGN dropped baseball briefly in 1944, leaving the loud, boisterous Bert Wilson as the Cubs' primary voice on another station.

On Elson's return, he and Brickhouse resumed as a team to broadcast the White Sox games in 1945 before they finally split. Elson continued with the White Sox, but Brickhouse wandered to New York for a brief stint before returning to Chicago in 1947 to confront his true destiny. TV had arrived on the scene!

Actually, it had debuted in Chicago while Brickhouse was absent. Joe Wilson was at the mike on April 20, 1946, when WBKB-TV televised the Cub home opener. Brickhouse joined Wilson the next year for a handful of games, but his breakthrough year was 1948 when WGN-TV became the visual outlet for both Chicago teams. Brickhouse's 34-year reign as monarch of Chicago baseball TV had begun. He covered many activities other than baseball, including Chicago Bear games for decades. He also aired several World Series.

What made the early days of TV especially exciting and "wonderful" Brickhouse told Curt Smith, was that "we knew we were on the groundfloor of something tremendously important. I'm very proud that I wasn't just the first voice of the Cubs—I was the first voice ever heard on WGN (TV), airing a boxing tournament from Chicago Stadium. So we were making history. We could sense it even then."

Brickhouse's broadcasting style, while not as frenetic and emotional as Bert Wilson's or Caray's, was much more "gee whiz" and partisan than Elson's. He often interjected pleas of "Boy, do we need a hit" or "Come on, let's get a run," into his commentary. His "Back...Back...Back...Hey-Hey!" shriek on a Chicago home run drive became his "calling card."

"I never thought you couldn't have excitement and integrity at the same time," he explained. "Or that if you were accurate it meant you had to be boring."

Over 34 years, Brickhouse shunned being boring as he broadcast with Harry Creighton, Marty Hogan, Lou Boudreau, Charlie Grimm, Vince Lloyd, Lloyd Pettit, Jim West, Milo Hamilton, among others, before retiring in 1981.

He even worked an inning or two with a former baseball announcer, one Ronald Reagan, who had "re-created" Cub games off the telegraph tape as a young man in Des Moines, Iowa, in the early 1930s before becoming a movie star and eventually president of the United States. Re-creation of play-by-play started concurrently with the first World Series aired in 1921, and was a staple for Brickhouse, Elson and all early broadcasters for "away" games.

In retrospect, it's hardly surprising that Brickhouse's name became associated far more with the Cubs than with the White Sox. While the Cubs remained with WGN, the Sox shifted to WFLD (Channel 32) after the 1967 season and for five years (1968–72), the personable Jack Drees, with a revolving cast of partners including former pitching star Billy Pierce, was No. 1 on White Sox telecasts.

But in 1973, Caray, who had replaced Elson on radio for the 1971 season, started to do double duty as the chief attraction on telecasts. At the same time, the team left WFLD for WSNS (Channel 44) to begin a trek to various "free" and pay-TV outlets over the next three decades. It even returned to WGN for part of the schedule after 1989.

Caray's uninhibited, "fan as announcer" style of broadcasting had made him wildly popular during his 25 years in St. Louis until he was fired in 1969 because of a personal conflict with the team owners. He spent 1970 broadcasting Oakland A's games, then leaped at the chance to replace Elson, who had been let go by the

White Sox after the season. (Ironically, Elson took Caray's job in Oakland for a final year of broadcasting baseball in 1971.)

A greater contrast in men or broadcasting styles between Caray and Elson, or for that matter the relatively restrained Brickhouse, is unimaginable. Caray was loud, boisterous, opinionated, often outrageous, very much the "blue collar fan as broadcaster" who leered at attractive women in the crowd, swilled beer with admirers, and loudly and openly criticized his team's players, managers, general managers and owners.

From the upper deck TV booth at old Comiskey Park, Caray snared foul balls with an oversized fish net, led his "Hey, Harry"–yelling admirers in bellowing "Take Me Out to the Ball Game," blurted "Holy Cow!" at startling or sensational events in games, emerged into the crowd to shake hands with men or to kiss girls, and in general stole the show with his act.

"My whole philosophy has always been to broadcast the way a fan would broadcast," Caray explained to Curt Smith. "I'm so tough on my guys because I want them to win so much. I've often thought that if you gave the microphone to a fan, he'd sound a lot like me. The disappointment, the hurt, the anger, the bitterness, the love, the ecstasy—they'd all be there."

Caray's lack of restraint infuriated many baseball people, especially the players and front office personnel he criticized, often aggravating even the team owners, first John Allyn, who hired him, and later Bill Veeck, who kept him on because of his proven value in attracting fans to the ballpark as well as to his radio and TV broadcasts.

During Veeck's second term as chief owner of the White Sox, from 1975 through 1980, he considered Caray his greatest asset.

"There were years when Harry was the only performer we had," Veeck said. "They say guys in his business don't put people in the ball park. Well, he draws more people than any player on our club or the opposition. And I've had front office people tell me that Harry even draws people to their parks."

Among those working with Caray on TV and radio during his 10 years with the White Sox, the most enduring were former outfielder Jimmy Piersall of "Fear Strikes Out" fame, Lorn Brown and Joe McConnell.

The latter two took over on radio for several years after Caray departed from the White Sox in 1982, but it was Piersall who made the greatest impact during his tenure from 1977 until he was fired in late 1981 for outrageous on-the-air remarks about players' wives and women in general. He even angered Veeck by calling the owner's wife "a colossal bore," but he and Caray were a "hot act" until Piersall self-destructed.

Chicago's teams both changed hands in 1981. The Tribune Co. bought the Cubs from the Wrigley family, and a syndicate headed by Jerry Reinsdorf purchased the White Sox from Veeck's group. When Brickhouse retired that year, it was widely expected, and especially by Milo Hamilton himself, he would take over the chief role in Cub telecasts. He had been assisting Brickhouse for several years.

Unfortunately for Hamilton, Caray thought the grass greener on the Cub side than on the White Sox side, and decided to jump the fence. The Cubs were delighted, being well aware of the impact Caray had made with White Sox fans. Hamilton had to settle for a secondary role to Caray both on television and radio until their incompatibility led to his departure in 1984.

Although Caray, whether because of greater discretion or encroaching age, was far less outspoken during his 15 years as a Cub broadcaster than he had been earlier, he was widely popular as ever until his death in early 1998. His most enduring legacy may be the singing of "Take Me Out to the Ball Game" during the seventh inning stretch, which has since become a Wrigley Field tradition.

He kept up much of his act on the North Side of Chicago, including attempting to catch foul balls with the fish net, spelling names backwards, reading notes from fans over the air, and "shilling" for restaurants.

Caray eventually teamed up on television with Steve Stone, a thoughtful analyst and Cy Young Award winning pitcher who had joined WGN in 1983. Among his radio partners were former Cub manager and general manager Jim Frey and finally onetime star third baseman Ron Santo, who came on board in 1990.

While Caray, Brickhouse and Elson were undeniably the dominant figures of Chicago's baseball broadcast media during the 1900s, there were many other talented men among their contemporaries, as there are among their current successors. Some have already been mentioned, others should be to avoid neglect.

One of the most highly-regarded was Jack Quinlan, who succeeded Bert Wilson in 1956 as the chief radio voice of the Cubs. Quinlan established a strong, literate, glib and genial presence until his death in an auto accident in 1965.

"He was quick, polished, had a great Irish sense of humor, and we would never have been able to keep him," Brickhouse said. "Jack would have been a network star for sure."

Vince Lloyd replaced Quinlan, and he and Boudreau, who in 1960 had switched places with manager Grimm to handle the team for the rest of the season, formed an effective partnership for two decades until Caray's arrival in 1982. Among Caray's later partners were Thom Brennaman and Josh Levin.

Skip Caray took over the main role on television after his grandfather's death in 1998, and was paired with Stone until the color commentator quit after being dogged by health problems in 2000. On radio, velvet-voiced Pat Hughes took hold in 1996 in a jovial, teasing partnership with analyst Santo.

Among Harry Caray's successors on White Sox radio and TV were onetime Dodgers pitching star Don Drysdale, Hall of Fame pitcher Early Wynn, and most notably former slugging outfielder Ken Harrelson, who exhibited the most staying power.

Harrelson began as Drysdale's partner in 1982, and for one season (1986) became general manager of the White Sox. His tenure was no success, and he left Chicago until he returned to the air for the White Sox in 1990. He was paired with Tom Paciorek through 1999, then with another ex-Sox player, Darrin Jackson.

The White Sox radio side has been remarkably stable for the last decade, with John Rooney and Ed Farmer teamed as play-by-play announcer and color commentator since 1992.

Like everything else, much has changed about baseball broadcasting since the voices of Elson, Brickhouse and Caray rang out loud and clear on Chicago's radio and television stations. That's not surprising when one considers that Elson's career started in 1928 and Caray called his last game seven decades later in 1997, a period equal to the Biblical lifespan of man.

Today's broadcasters are required to be more analytical than either Elson or Brickhouse, though both were highly knowledgeable about baseball, and are not permitted to be as critical and outspoken as was Caray at his outrageous peak.

Whether that's of major benefit to listeners and viewers is open to debate.

What's not is that Elson, Brickhouse and Caray, all three enshrined in baseball's Hall of Fame as recipients of the Ford C. Frick Award honoring broadcasters, were Chicago's most distinguished baseball announcers of the 20th Century.

Statues of Caray and Brickhouse have been erected in Chicago to declare their extraordinary talents. Perhaps one day they will be joined, as they should be, by one of Elson to round out a sculptural triumvirate of virtuosity on the air.

MEDIA RARE

It has been an oft-troubled relationship, but baseball and journalism—as well as the latter's upscale cousin, literature—have been closely linked ever since Henry Chadwick in the 1850s convinced the *New York Times* that its readers were interested in the game and those who played it.

Chadwick, inventor of the box score, began to inform and entertain followers of the Knickerbockers and other New York–area teams with reports of games and players in the mid-19th Century. He became the country's first sports editor with the *New York Clipper*, then held the same post with the *Brooklyn Eagle* for almost half a century.

What Chadwick wrought, others copied, and newspapers around the nation were quick to seize on baseball as a circulation builder. In Chicago, which at one time housed about two dozen daily newspapers, baseball fever was intense by the 1860s. The *Chicago Tribune, Chicago Times*, and rival journals made the most of the rising mass entertainment, often with unabashed local partisanship and boosterism.

By 1876 stories about games and players were routine. When the National League and the current Cub franchise (then–White Stockings) were born, the *Chicago Tribune* carried an account of the team's first game, a 4-0, three-hit victory pitched by manager

Al Spalding over Louisville in Kentucky on April 25, 1876. Part of the story:

"The credit for the victory belongs to Spalding more than to anyone else, and it is safe to say that better pitching was hardly ever seen.

"Third baseman (Cap) Anson and shortstop (Johnny) Peters faced some stiff hits and fielded them in beautiful style, the throwing of both men being as accurate as rifle shooting. Taken as a whole, the first game of the Chicagos of 1876 was a creditable one and promises well for the score at the end of the season."

Chadwick became intrigued with the Spalding-led White Stockings, who won the first N.L. pennant in 1876, and six of the first 11. By 1878 he was collaborating with Spalding in the publishing arm of the latter's booming sporting goods firm to write and edit a stream of rule books, guides and other publications.

Other publishers, editors and writers also seized the opportunities provided by the rise of baseball through the rest of the 19th Century. Daily newspapers devoted increased space to the game, as did a host of new periodicals such as *The Sporting News*, founded in 1886. Chadwick may have been the first "baseball writer" but quickly became the pioneer veteran of a swelling crowd.

The most literary-talented among Chicago's early baseball writers was Finley Peter Dunne, who at the age of 19 in 1886 covered the White Stockings for the *Chicago Daily News*. Dunne was to gain enduring international fame as a *Chicago Evening Post* columnist with his character, Mr. Martin Dooley, the aging barkeep/philosopher of Archer Ave. in the South Side Irish neighborhood of Bridgeport who delivered shrewd commentary in Irish brogue on the foibles, ills and injustices of society.

Not surprisingly, given Dunne's past as a baseball writer, Mr. Dooley sometimes teased the game, as in the following observation:

"In me younger days 't was not considhered rayspictable f'r to be an athlete. An athlete was always a man that was not sthrong enough f'r wurruk. Fractions dhruv him f'rm school an' th' vagrancy laws dhruv him to baseball."

Dooley set the pattern for a literary tradition among Chicago baseball writers—as well as for a later Chicago newspaper columnist, Mike Royko, a similarly caustic observer of the city's turbulent political scene. Among many writers with baseball interest who were to follow in Dunne's footsteps were such notables as humorist author Ring Lardner, drama critic and historian Lloyd Lewis, and novelist James T. Farrell.

Lardner began covering baseball in Chicago in 1907 for various newspapers. He left to edit *The Sporting News* in St. Louis from 1910 to 1911, then returned to write an often satirical sports column for the *Chicago Tribune* (1913–19) until a syndicate offered him national exposure in a move to New York.

Lardner's masterpiece is *You Know Me, Al*, the correspondence of Jack Keefe, a fictional semi-literate pitcher with the White Sox, published in 1916. Less memorably, in 1910 he contributed the lyrics to a tune written by White Sox pitcher Doc White. The song was called "Little Puff of Smoke, Good Night."

Lewis came on the Chicago newspaper scene a decade or so after Lardner, and firmly established himself as a man of many talents. During more than three decades with the *Chicago Daily News*, into the 1950s, he served as sports writer, editor, drama critic, historian, managing editor, playwright and war correspondent.

Lewis gained widespread recognition as a historian of the Civil War with the book *Lee's Lieutenants*, while also turning out exceptional sports stories such as an account of the grief he suffered when his childhood idol, New York Giants pitcher Christy Mathewson, lost a World Series game in 1911. It became part of the collection of similar stories, assembled and often written by *Daily News* sports columnist John P. Carmichael under the heading, *My Greatest Day in Baseball*.

Born in Chicago in 1904, Farrell became best known for a series of novels about the city's Irish community which featured the character Studs Lonigan. He was a lifetime White Sox fan and in 1957 published an account of his devotion to the game called *My Baseball Diary*.

In one of Farrell's novels, protagonist Danny O'Neill's most vivid childhood memories involved having attended a no-hit, no-run game pitched by Ed Walsh of the White Sox in 1911. Farrell comments that to Danny "this thing of athletic beauty is his first exposure to art" and causes him to resolve to become a professional baseball player.

Numerous Chicago writers of fiction and history other than Dooley, Lewis and Farrell have used baseball as a theme, or made mention of it in a novel. Among them is Nelson Algren, whose best known work, *The Man With the Golden Arm*, however, had nothing to do with the game despite its deceptive title.

Chicago Sun-Times television critic Paul Molloy wrote *A Pennant for the Kremlin* (1964), a fantasy about the possible relationship among the sport of baseball, big business and international relations in the 1960s. Angered by the United States' inability to get along well with the Kremlin (Soviet Union), a wealthy Chicagoan wills his fortune and the Chicago White Sox (which he owns) to the Soviets.

Another tale of baseball is Marvin Karlins' 1969 *Last Man in Is Out*. This is a futuristic novel, relating what occurs when a college professor inherits a baseball team in 2002. The title seems to echo Eliot Asinof's *Eight Men Out*, the semi-fictional account of the Black Sox scandal published in 1963.

Baseball music hall acts and theater melodramas graced the stage even before "Casey at the Bat" appeared in 1888, so it was hardly an innovation when in 1978 the Organic Theater of Chicago performed a new musical play, *Bleacher Bums*. The difference was that this time the Chicago association was central. The setting was Wrigley Field, the Cubs were playing the St. Louis Cardinals, and the audience saw the action through the "eyes," words and antics of eight frenetic fans. *Bleacher Bums* was also televised.

While the vast majority of writing about baseball, whether fact or fiction, is done by those who watch the game rather than play it, there are exceptions. Players, managers and front office people have turned out books, generally with professional assistance, yet sometimes on their own.

Jim Brosnan, who pitched for the Cubs, White Sox and other teams in the 1950s and 1960s, wrote a much-praised book, *The Long Season*, about his experiences in 1959 with the St. Louis Cardinals and Cincinnati Reds. When Brosnan joined the White Sox in 1963 general manager Ed Short demanded that he give up writing. Brosnan refused to do so and the Sox released him. Brosnan continued his writing career after leaving baseball.

Short's intransigence was in stark contrast to the attitude of White Sox founder and owner Charles Comiskey, who not only encouraged Frank Chance, manager of the rival Cubs, to publish a novel but obligingly provided a preface.

Chance wrote his romance, *The Bride and the Pennant: The Greatest Story in the History of America's National Game, True to Life, Intensely Interesting*, in 1910, the year he also led the Cubs to their fourth pennant in five years. This forgotten literary curiosity was published by Laird and Lee, a Chicago firm. The reason Comiskey wrote or had someone write the preface in his name remains a mystery.

The novel tells of a star pitcher at the University of Chicago who flunks out of school in his senior year and is hired by a New Orleans professional team. However, much of the action takes place in Chicago where the deciding games for the league pennant are played. Baseball fans, familiar with today's game, would consider the 1910 version fascinating if they could obtain a copy of Chance's hard-to-find creation.

While Chance was churning out his melodrama, the first Cub manager and onetime team owner Spalding was laboring on a tome of his own. Spalding long had urged Henry Chadwick to compose a history of baseball, but Chadwick died at the age of 83 in 1908 before he could comply. Spalding decided to write the history himself.

Though Spalding dedicated his book to Chadwick (and also to William Hulbert, founder of the Cubs and of the National League, and to the league itself), he sought to refute the pioneer writer's contention that baseball developed from games played during his childhood in England. Spalding strongly supported the Abner Doubleday myth and argued that baseball was wholly an American development.

All this was laid out in *America's National Game*, published in 1911 by Spalding's own firm. In the foreword, Spalding wrote that the hoped the book was "the simple story of America's National Game as I have come to know it." It is far from that, the uncompromising text reflecting Spalding's views and prejudices. Its greatest value is as Spalding's autobiography, the personal reminiscences of a founding father.

Biographies and autobiographies, like Spalding's, were commonplace by the 1910s, though few baseball people wrote their own as he did. Most such books were produced by professionals, often sportswriters, with or without their subjects' permission or cooperation.

Gustav Axelson, a baseball writer for the Hearst chain of newspapers, wrote *Commy, the Life Story of Charles Comiskey*, published by Reilly and Lee in 1919, just before the notorious World Series between the owner's White Sox and the Cincinnati Reds. The book was highly laudatory, keeping author and subject the best of friends.

Comiskey's affinity with and affection for sports writers was pronounced. Among his boon companions were such well-known newspapermen of his day as Axelson, Irving Vaughn, William Veeck, Sr., the father of future White Sox owner Bill, and Jim Crusinberry.

At a time early in the 20th Century when Chicago still was home to a dozen daily newspapers there was a large corp of baseball writers. The best known were Lardner, Hugh Fullerton, Charlie Dryden, Forrest B. Myers and I.E. "Cy" Sanborn.

During this period, and well into the 1950s, becoming a baseball writer was the burning ambition of many young journalists. The job's relative freedom of expression, the game's dramatic unpredictability, and its many vivid personalities and "heroes" attracted talented writers. Until the 1920s, before the rise of college football, then the professional variety, as well as other sports, baseball had no major competition for mass outdoor entertainment.

A stanza of doggerel in the *Sporting News* in 1912 made the point:

"There is only one sport that appeals to them all.
When you size up the dope on the case,
There is only one sports and its name is base ball,
Others follow; it sets the pace."

Marshall Hunt, longtime managing editor of the *Daily Olympian* (Olympia, Washington), spent his early years as a sportswriter in New York (he was reputedly closer to Babe Ruth than any other writer) during what has been called The Golden Age of Sports. His opinion of the relative merits of newspapermen and especially of baseball writers of the 1920s: "The sportswriters were absolutely the best writers on the papers in those days, and baseball writing was the best of all jobs on a newspaper."

So it remained, by and large, until at least the 1960s when other sports "beats" began to match or overshadow it in appeal to talented writers.

Many Chicago baseball writers remained at their coveted posts for virtually their entire careers, sometimes 25, 30 or even 40 years. A few, like Lardner and Veeck, and later Carmichael, Warren Brown and Gene Kessler, became sports columnists but kept their primary focus on baseball despite writing about other sports.

Fullerton, who gained national fame for his investigative reporting of the Black Sox scandal of 1919–20, spent 25 years as a Chicago baseball writer. He started with the *Chicago Record* in 1896, then was hired by the *Chicago Tribune*. He moved to New York in the 1920s, and was one of the founding fathers of the Baseball Writers Association of America (BBWAA).

Among those who became familiar household names in Chicago because their bylines appeared almost daily for several decades in the city's newspapers were Vaughn, Dryden, Carmichael, Crusinberry, Warren Brown, Harry "Señor" Neily, Jimmy "The Cork" Corcoran, Harold "Speed" Johnson, Wayne "T-bone" Otto, Larry Woltz, Ed Burns, Ed Prell, Edgar Munzel,

Howie Roberts, Jim Gallagher, Francis J. Powers, Herbert F. Simons (founder in 1942 of *Baseball Digest*, baseball's oldest magazine), John Kuenster, Jim Enright, Wendell Smith, Dick Dozer, Joe Goddard and Dave Van Dyck.

Wendell Smith's career was exceptional because of his ethnic background. After he joined the *Chicago American* in 1947 he became the first African-American member of the BBWAA. He played a vital role in helping Jackie Robinson break the color barrier of major league baseball and later on was instrumental in integrating spring training facilities in Florida.

Smith was honored posthumously by being chosen as a writer member of the Baseball Hall of Fame at Cooperstown, N.Y. Among other Chicago baseball writers who became recipients of the J.G. Taylor Spink Award, named in honor of a publisher of *The Sporting News*, were Lardner, Fullerton, Dryden, Brown, Carmichael and Munzel.

Some writers have taken jobs with the Cubs and White Sox. The most notable instance was that of William Veeck, Sr., a *Chicago American* writer whose thoughtful criticism of the Cubs induced owner William Wrigley Jr. to name him team vice-president in 1918. A year later, Veeck became president of the Cubs and ran the team until his death in 1933.

William Wrigley's son, Philip K., used similar rationale in 1940 to choose a new general manager. He challenged Gallagher, a *Chicago American* sportswriter, to demonstrate what he could do to improve the team he had been criticizing. Gallagher eventually moved on to the baseball commissioner's office.

Before his long baseball writing stint with the *Chicago Sun-Times*, Munzel was a publicist for the White Sox. Roberts left the *Chicago Daily News* in 1961 to become the team's traveling secretary, and eventually moved into the Cubs' ticket office. After Carmichael left the *Daily News* in 1972, he employed his talents as a toastmaster and raconteur to serve as a community relations representative for the White Sox.

For nearly 40 years, beginning in the early 1930s, Carmichael and Warren Brown were the most durable and celebrated sports columnists in Chicago. Baseball was a passion for both of them, though they didn't neglect other sports.

Brown arrived in Chicago in the early 1920s, preceding Carmichael on the staff of the *Chicago Herald and Examiner.* Carmichael switched to the *Daily News* in 1932. His witty "Barber Shop" column appeared in that newspaper from 1934 until the mid-1970s, continuing for a couple of years after his official retirement.

Brown's "So They Tell Me" column appeared in the *Herald and Examiner* and its successor Hearst papers in Chicago for more than four decades. He had a breezy style, a distinctive satirical bent, and a gift for the telling anecdote and reminiscence. At times, Brown could be harsh and biting and was seldom reluctant to voice his true opinions

When asked which World War II talent-riddled team, the Cubs or Detroit Tigers, would win the 1945 World Series, Brown quipped, "I don't think either of them can." After the Tigers did win in seven games, Brown called it the "worst World Series ever played."

Brown wrote of Cubs slugger Hack Wilson: "He was a highball hitter on the field, and off it."

Carmichael seldom had a harsh word for anyone. His unfailingly positive attitude made him extremely popular with the major sports figures of his time, including such giants as Connie Mack and George Halas.

An interviewer once asked Carmichael why he was a "nice-guy" writer.

His reply, in part: "I never believed in castigating a lot of people. I don't know why. Maybe it was because I always had a feeling that if you turn out to be wrong, you've done irreparable damage."

This gentle approach served Carmichael well, as did an exceptional ear and tenacious memory. He interviewed without taking notes, other than to mark a date, yet captured even subtle turns of phrase and eccentricities of speaking perfectly. His columns and stories were informative, entertaining and often humorous. His ability to depict character—and characters—in anecdotal form was outstanding.

Nowhere is this better displayed than in the pages of the book, *My Greatest Day in Baseball*, the collection of 57 "as-told-to" stories of which he wrote 15. They were originally published one by one in the *Daily News* in the early 1940s and have been reprinted as a collection several times.

Regrettably, Carmichael never published another book, though a collection of his outstanding columns—he once estimated that he wrote 11,000—or a venture into baseball history or biography, something not infrequent among baseball writers or sportswriters in general—might have been welcome to his faithful readers.

Brown, however, did produce a lengthy work apart from his newspaper writings. He wrote the first extended history of the White Sox. Published in 1952, his book, *The Chicago White Sox*, drew heavily on the Axelson biography of Comiskey mentioned earlier, but added a few breezy and witty touches.

Since Brown's book came out half a century ago, there has been an ever-enlarging flood of White Sox and Cub histories, biographies, autobiographies, commentaries, exposés, encyclopedias and pictorial books. Some have sold well, others have sunk without a trace

During that long stretch of time much has changed, including the style of writing about baseball, as well as the conditions of the game itself, influenced as it has been by television and the riches it has brought to those who play it or own the teams.

And just as baseball, harassed by competition from rival sports and other sources of entertainment, has lost the dominant position it once held as the acknowledged "national pastime," the baseball writer is no longer the undisputed "golden boy" of the sports department. Ironically, his job is probably more difficult than it was in the past.

He can bolster his spirits with the knowledge that in Chicago he is the heir of a great tradition, one handed down by a phalanx of outstanding predecessors. Carmichael, Brown, Lardner, Fullerton, Dryden, Smith and many others have left a rich legacy of fine, sometimes even inspired, writing and reporting about the game and its players.

Here is Carmichael capturing the larger-than-life essence of Dizzy Dean as the Cardinals pitcher recalls a clubhouse conversation with his manager, Frankie Frisch, before defeating the Detroit Tigers 11-0 in the seventh game of the 1934 World Series:

"Frisch came by and do you know what he said? 'Anybody with your stuff should have won 40 games instead of a measly 30. You loaf. That's the trouble. Thirty games! You ought to be ashamed of yourself.'

"Imagine that, and me just winning the series for him. Ol' Diz pitchin' outta turn too, don't forget that. He wanted me to pitch although he'd said Bill Hallahan was gonna work the last game. But he came to me the night before and he asked, 'Diz, you wanna be the greatest man in baseball?' I told him I already was, but he didn't even hear me because he went on, 'You pitch that game tomorrow and you'll be tops.' I just told him, 'Gimme that ball tomorrow and your troubles are over.' He wanted me to pitch. I knew that. Hell, I was afraid he would let Hallahan start."

That's baseball-writing *Chicago Style*, a form of literature in itself.

DAWN OF TRADITION

32

The White Sox and Cubs, that's what it has come down in our day, the venerable pair of rivals for the hearts and fervent support of Chicago fans being the city's surviving and sometimes thriving major league baseball teams.

Yet it would be remiss to entirely forget the many pioneer major league, semi-pro, amateur and African-American teams that strutted briefly on the diamond before they vanished into the dust bins of history.

A few of their names: Excelsiors, Eckfords, Blues, Firemen, Mutuals, Jacksons, Aetnas, Laflins, Libertys, Dreadnaughts, Pastimes, West Ends, the original White Stockings, Unions, Pirates, American Giants, Union Giants and Whales.

These teams may have been transitory but they contributed mightily during the parallel emergence of both baseball and the city of Chicago from modest beginnings onto the center stage of the American experience during much of the 19th Century and the early 20th.

While Chicago was born in the 1800s, being incorporated in 1837, baseball can reach much farther into the past for its roots. Perhaps even into the Middle Ages. A medieval manuscript depicts a game played with stick and ball. It's more certain, however, that baseball began to evolve by the time of the Revolutionary War.

A belligerent 1920s mayor of Chicago, Big Bill Thompson, once threatened to punch England's King George V on the nose if he visited the city.

Thompson might have felt more kindly toward the monarch had he known that his majesty's great-great-grandfather, George III, had played base ball—or "baste-ball"—as a child, thus anticipating what was to be hailed as the "national pastime" of his former colonies after they became the United States of America.

Despite the myth that Abner Doubleday, a Civil War general, invented baseball in Cooperstown, New York, in 1839, its origins can be traced to the English games of rounders and cricket. Development was well under way in the 18th Century. Novelist Jane Austen even casually referred to "baseball" in *Northanger Abbey*, the first version of which was written in 1798.

Austen employed the word a decade after Princeton College in 1787 forbade the students to "play with balls and sticks in the back common of the college," ostensibly because their pastime was too rough!

By the 1820s, various rudimentary forms of the game, named "base ball," "rounders" and "townball," among other labels, were thriving in New England and much of the eastern United States.

Baseball found a more solid footing in 1845 when Alexander Joy Cartwright, a young shipping clerk, and fellow members of the New York Knickerbocker Base Ball Club crafted the basic rules that channeled the evolution of baseball toward the game that it is now.

Another enthusiast, Henry Chadwick, a later recruit to the Knickerbockers, was equally instrumental in popularizing the game as a newspaperman, publicist and record-keeper. His devising of the box score made possible a valid comparison of current and past player and team performances, enabling baseball to accumulate its rich tradition.

Cartwright's rules spread across the nation in the late 1840s, quickly reaching then-frontier Chicago. Baseball soon overshadowed its cousin cricket, which had preceded it as an organized team sport with the formation of the Chicago Wicket Club in 1849.

While the cricketeers—mostly English immigrants—played matches on the lakefront, the baseball pioneers held their games on the outskirts of town. Clubs from Chicago were soon called "prairie teams" because they generally played on the large empty lots bordering the city.

By 1860 when Abraham Lincoln won the presidency after being nominated by the Republican Party at its convention in Chicago, baseball was already the "national pastime."

A Currier & Ives cartoon (labeled "The National Game, Three Outs and One Run") depicts Lincoln holding a ball and bat (in the form of a rail because of his youthful prowess as a rail-splitter) while telling his three disgruntled rivals in the election how he had been able to make a "home run."

The Civil War (1861–65) was a great catalyst for baseball because it provided a pleasurable outlet of energy for the huge assemblies of young men in both the Union and Confederate armies. It could be played on almost any fairly level patch of ground with minimal equipment and little preparation.

When the war ended the discharged soldiers took the game home with them. Amateur teams flourished. By 1867 the National Association of Base Ball Players, an amateur body founded in 1858, numbered 300 member clubs, the most notable in Chicago being the Excelsiors.

Soon after the Union Stock Yard opened southwest of Chicago's main business district in 1865, investors built nearby Dexter Park Pavilion, which accommodated baseball games as well as horse races.

Dexter Park's claim to historical significance—in addition to it being the forerunner of such ballparks as Wrigley Field and Comiskey Park II—rests primarily on a game played in July 1867 during a three-day national tournament sponsored by the Chicago Excelsiors. Such tournaments were extremely popular. The sponsors charged up to 25 cents admission and offered cash and other prizes to winning teams.

Albert Goodwill Spalding, the most important figure in Chicago's early baseball history, attracted widespread public attention for the first time when he pitched for the unheralded

Forest City's of Rockford, Illinois, against the Washington Nationals, reputedly the best team in the nation.

The Nationals had crushed all other opposition with routs such as 90-10 over Columbus (Ohio) and 106-21 over Indianapolis. The Chicago Excelsiors, the pride of the burgeoning metropolis, also had crumbled, losing 49-4 to the Nationals.

But to general amazement, the Forest City's from small-town Rockford upset the powerhouse from the national capital 29-23 behind Spalding. He may not have pitched a masterpiece by today's standards, but conditions and the game were vastly different in those days, and Spalding, only 16 years old, was hailed as a hero.

Henry Chadwick, by this time the leading baseball writer in the country, testified to Spalding's decisive role in Forest City's victory, saying that it was because of his "very effective pitching...the Nationals suffered their first and only defeat of their tour."

Spalding so impressed the Excelsiors that they made him an offer he couldn't refuse to move to Chicago and pitch for them. One of their sponsors, a wholesale grocer, hired him as a clerk at $40 a week (about ten times the normal pay for such a job) with the stipulation that his duties would not conflict with pitching for the Excelsiors.

Spalding appeared in an Excelsiors uniform only once because the grocer's business quickly failed, but the hypocrisy revealed by hiring him as a clerk made it clear that amateur baseball was becoming "shamateur." Spalding returned to Rockford and during the next three years helped the Forest City's win 45 of 58 games, supporting the team's claim to be "champions of the West."

The undisputed top team in the nation, however, was the first openly all-professional club, the Cincinnati Red Stockings, who in 1869 won all of their 65 games to give their backers more than their money's worth. The Red Stockings cast aside all pretense of amateurism and paid their players handsomely. Manager Harry Wright getting $1,200 a season and his star player, brother George, $1,400.

Professional baseball had arrived! Neither Chicago nor Spalding was slow to take advantage of the shift from "shama-teurism" to above board pay-for-play, whose benefits had been demonstrated by Wright's Red Stockings, who ran their winning streak to 92 before losing 8-7 on June 14, 1870 to the Brooklyn Atlantics.

Less than three months later, on September 7, 1870, the Red Stockings fell 10-6 in Cincinnati to a visiting Chicago team, the original White Stockings, who played their home games at Dexter Park. Civic pride had induced Chicago promoters to spend lavishly to recruit a team capable of challenging the Red Stockings.

"The Chicago club is a $20,000 article, and for that money a dozen of the best players in the country may be had," a critic explained.

Encouraged by the turnouts at Dexter Park, several Chicago businessmen enrolled the White Stockings in the first profession-al league, the National Association of Professional Base Ball Players (N.A.), founded on March 17, 1871. Spalding left Rockford (though the Forest City's also entered the N.A.) for a $1,500 per-season offer from Harry Wright, now managing the new Boston Red Stockings. It was a turning point for Spalding— and eventually baseball in Chicago.

In his memoirs, Spalding wrote: "I had determined to enter Baseball as a profession. I was neither ashamed of the game nor of my attachment to it. Mr. Wright was offering us...cash...to play on the Boston team.... Why, then, go before the public under the false pretense of being amateurs?"

Spalding and baseball had "come out of the closet."

While Spalding and the Red Stockings flourished during the five-year existence of the N.A. (the young man from Rockford becoming the game's dominant pitcher), the Chicago White Stockings struggled as if under a black cloud.

The White Stockings built Lake Park, the first enclosed Chicago baseball field, capacity 7,000, on a city dump between Lake Michigan and Michigan Avenue, barely in time to watch it turn to ashes in the Great Chicago Fire of 1871.

Their second home, called 23rd Street Grounds, was more enduring even if the White Stockings were not. They declined into semi-pro status in 1872, though they reentered the N.A. in 1874. Poor attendance and financial problems kept them teetering on the verge of collapse until William Hulbert, an energetic Chicago merchant, took charge as chief owner and president in 1875.

A pragmatist, Hulbert realized that the N.A. was doomed by its lack of a coherent structure. Among its problems were charges of "thrown" games, alcoholic and gambling players, the frequent collapse of underfinanced teams, the jumping of franchises from city to city, no set schedules, and lack of a central authority.

Hulbert attacked vigorously on two fronts. He first set out to transform the White Stockings into a contender. He raided the top two N.A. teams, Boston and Philadelphia, for their best players. In mid-1875, he signed pitchers Spalding and Jim "Deacon" White, infielder Ross Barnes and catcher/outfielder Cal McVey of Boston, and first baseman Adrian "Cap" Anson and third baseman Ezra Sutton of Philadelphia.

When the uproar over the raids threatened to result in the expulsion of the White Stockings from the N.A., Hulbert decided on a pre-emptive strike. He proposed a new, more solidly-based, tightly-knit, firmly-ruled league.

Assisted by Spalding, who had been named manager and captain of the White Stockings and was to receive 25 percent of gate receipts in addition to his salary, Hulbert accomplished his goal at a meeting of prospective owners on February 2, 1876 in New York City. The National League of Professional Base Ball Clubs (N.L.) was born with eight charter members, including Hulbert's franchise to which he transferred the name White Stockings. The old White Stockings franchise and the National Association disappeared.

The new league was determined to enforce both financial solvency and fixed schedules on its franchises and to require its players to abide by a rigid code of conduct or face expulsion.

It's largely owing to Hulbert and Spalding, who had pitched the Boston Red Stockings to four consecutive N.A. pennants

(1872–75), that the new White Stockings—eventually Cubs—survived and prospered. (The Cubs are the sole charter member of the N.L. to remain in one city and not miss a season from their birth in 1876.)

Hulbert's White Stockings took over their predecessors' ballpark, the 23rd Street Grounds, but with a difference. Spalding managed and pitched them to a pennant in the N.L.'s first season of 1876. The team won 52 of 66 games, with Spalding's record 47-13. Cap Anson established himself as a major star by hitting .356 as the third baseman, and second baseman Ross Barnes led the league in batting with .429.

The White Stockings' first game was played April 25, 1876, in Louisville, Kentucky, and *The Chicago Daily News*, also a "rookie" that year, printed the following account the next day:

"THE CHICAGOS VS. LOUISVILLE—The baseball match yesterday between the Chicago and Louisville clubs, at Louisville, was won by the former with the score of 4-0. Considerable money changed hands on the results of the game, the Chicagos being favorites at odds of three and four to one. The professors (fans) may feel thoroughly satisfied, therefore, with the opening record this year. Mr. Warren of St. Louis served as umpire."

Despite their success in 1876, arm problems ended Spalding's playing career in 1877 and the White Stockings sank to fifth place in the N.L., which had shrunk to six teams by season's end.

When Hulbert assumed the presidency of the N.L. as well as of the team in 1877, he named Spalding the club's secretary (in effect, general manager). Spalding concentrated increasingly on team business as well as personal interests. He was also building what was to become a major sporting goods firm, A.G. Spalding & Brothers.

By the time Hulbert died in 1882 he had put the N.L. on a solid footing. Perhaps the owners' most significant—if ominous—step under his leadership was the insertion of a reserve clause into players' contracts in 1879.

This restriction on freedom of contract became a source of endemic conflict between players and owners for a century until the "free agent" development of the 1970s. Yet it might also have provided an economic shield for baseball to become financially secure during its developmental stage.

With Hulbert gone, Spalding became president and chief owner of the White Stockings and the major power broker of the N.L. Bolstering his influence was the enormous success of the White Stockings on the field and financially during the 1880s.

Earlier, even while the White Stockings continued to flounder in competition in 1878 and 1879, they were profitable enough to pay for a new home called Lakefront Park. It occupied virtually the same site on Michigan Avenue as the N.A. team's Lake Park, which had burned down in 1871.

Spalding took another significant step in 1879 when he named Anson manager. Anson kept the job for 19 seasons, during most of which he was the league's outstanding first baseman.

The earlier part of Anson's reign was one of the most glorious eras in the team's history. During a seven-year span from 1880 through 1886 his White Stockings won five pennants, played in what might be called an early World Series, went South for spring training, and "barnstormed" around the world.

Anson and Spalding built the White Stockings into a powerhouse, acquiring Ed Williamson, George Gore, Abner Dalrymple and Frank Flint in 1879. The next year, two great pitchers, Larry Corcoran and Fred Goldsmith, came aboard, as well as outfielder Mike "King" Kelly and shortstop Tommy Burns.

The legendary Kelly, who also backed up catcher Flint, has been called the Babe Ruth of the 19th Century, and was a natural showman. With Gore and Williamson, Kelly formed the finest outfield of the day. Corcoran never won less than 27 games in each of the next five seasons, reaching a peak of 43 in 1880. Goldsmith was a 20-game winner for four consecutive years.

Kelly was a flamboyant, larger-than-life personality as well as a great hitter, fielder and baserunner who inspired a popular song, "Slide, Kelly, Slide." His talents were not confined to the diamond. He displayed considerable skill in off-season stage appearances, often reciting "Casey at the Bat," to audiences that thought of him as the protagonist of the poem.

With Kelly aboard, the White Stockings captured three consecutive pennants, 1880–1882. In '80, they won 21 consecutive games, a feat unsurpassed for 36 years until the 1916 New York Giants had a string of 26. The White Stockings' winning percentage of .798 for the 1880 season, on a record of 67-17, has never been matched.

The White Stockings' enormous success in the early '80s made baseball ever more popular in Chicago and encouraged wider participation in semi-pro and amateur play. Diamonds such as the Leavitt Street grounds at Leavitt and Van Buren were laid out on empty lots, and later also in the city's new parks, such as Jackson and Lincoln.

An indoor variety of the game, eventually to become softball, also took hold by the late 1880s, with the diamonds often placed over roller skating rinks.

The semi-pro and amateur teams of the day frequently traveled to other cities for Sunday games. In 1881 the Chicago Eckfords visited St. Louis to play the then-independent Browns run by sports journalist Al Spink, who was to become one of the co-founders of *The Sporting News.*

(In the same year Spink lured Charles Comiskey, the son of a Chicago alderman, to St. Louis from minor league Dubuque, Iowa, to play first base for the Browns, who joined the new professional American Association [A.A.] in 1882. Almost two decades later, Comiskey was to found the present White Sox.)

Even as baseball fever spread, Anson's team faded in '83 and '84. But fresh talent, including another superlative pitcher, John Clarkson, and swift outfielder Billy Sunday, who later became a charismatic evangelist, enabled the White Stockings to again win pennants in '85 and '86. Clarkson was 53-16 in '85 and 35-17 in '86.

Anson sparkled both as hitter and manager while the White Stockings were riding high. He led the league in batting three times. Gore was the leader with .360 in '80 and Kelly topped all hitters with .354 in '84 and .388 in '86. Williamson's 27 home runs in '84, though tainted by the short distance of 180 feet down the left field foul line to a six-foot high fence, stood as a record until Babe Ruth hit 29 in 1919.

The Sporting News, in its first issue, dated March 17, 1886, acknowledged the supremacy of Anson's White Stockings in a report detailing the team's prospects for the coming season and preparations for spring training in Hot Springs, Arkansas.

After a visit to Spalding's sporting goods store in Chicago, the unnamed reporter wrote: "There is no city in America that is prouder of its ball team than is Chicago and the general impression seems to be that the White Stockings will successfully defend the pennant during the season of '86."

The White Stockings did do that, but the '86 season marked the zenith of Anson's managerial career. The White Stockings failed to win a pennant during his remaining 11 years at the helm. Kelly and Gore were gone after the '86 campaign, and Clarkson departed after the '87 season.

Gore was sold to New York and Kelly was shipped to Boston for $10,000, the most paid in a player transaction to that time. Kelly had no complaints because the Red Stockings raised his salary to $5,000, almost double his White Stockings pay.

Among other important developments of the 1880s was another new ballpark for the White Stockings, this time West Side Park at Congress and Throop streets, which originally was called Congress Street Grounds. The 10,000-seat facility opened in 1885.

West Side Park was the site of the first "World Series" games played in Chicago. After the '85 season, the White Stockings were challenged to a postseason series by the champion St. Louis Browns of the American Association, which by 1883 had achieved recognition as a major league. By 1885, Comiskey was managing the Browns as well as playing first base.

A 12-game championship series was agreed on, with the first game to be played at West Side Park, the next three in St. Louis, and the rest at other A.A. sites. The opener in Chicago was a 3-3 tie called because of darkness. The series ended abruptly after six games, either in a three-games-to-two victory for the Browns, according to their fans, or in a tie at three wins apiece, according to the Chicago rooters. The Browns considered one of the games a Chicago forfeit and the White Stockings claimed it a victory.

The teams met again after the '86 season, this time in a best-of-seven games home-and-home series. The Browns won in the 10th inning of the seventh game, at St. Louis. The series was no contest as to fan interest, the White Stockings drawing merely 13,106 to four games at West Side Park while the Browns drew a near-capacity turnout of 29,460 to the three games at Sportsman's Park.

The "World Series" defeat signaled the end of the glory years on the field for the White Stockings of Spalding and Anson with storm clouds gathering in the form of increasing hostility between players and owners. The White Stockings would not win another pennant until 1906, by which time they were known as the Cubs.

Though the White Stockings went nowhere in the N.L. standings after Clarkson, Gore and Kelly left, they did go around the world between October 1888 and April 1889.

Spalding, ever the impresario, took his White Stockings and a competing squad of "All-Americas" drawn from other clubs to Australia, Ceylon, Egypt (where they played in the shade of the Pyramids) Italy, France, England, Ireland and Scotland.

In London they met the Prince of Wales, George III's great-grandson and the future King Edward VII, who was polite enough not to suggest that his ancestor had invented the game, which he considered "excellent" though not superior to cricket.

Spalding said the tour was intended to introduce baseball to "crowned heads, nobles and peasantry in the Old World," and perhaps also to extend his "sporting goods business to that quarter of the globe and to create a market for goods there...."

Chadwick called the trip, "The greatest event in the history of athletic sports."

Spalding might well have felt on top of the world during the tour. His White Stockings did rule Chicago, even if not the N.L. in the standings. And so far, through 1889, he had not had to contend with any serious major league rival in his domain.

The only challenge to the White Stockings from the A.A. had come in the form of post-season clashes with Comiskey's Browns because the younger major league in its 10-season lifespan (1882–1891) never put a franchise into Chicago.

And while another "upstart" had invaded the city, it had quickly failed. That was a franchise from the 13-team Union Association (U.A.), a league led by Henry Lucas, a St. Louis railroad millionaire who sought to lure N.L. and A.A. players by eliminating the reserve clause. Spalding bullied his star pitcher, Corcoran, from deserting to the Chicago Unions, and rallied the N.L. and A.A. into a joint effort that succeeded in crushing the U.A. after just one season (1884).

Six years later, in 1890 the Chicago franchise of the newly-formed Brotherhood or Players' League, posed a far greater threat to the White Stockings than any previous invader. Led by John Montgomery Ward, a lawyer as well as a star player in the N.L., the Players' National League of Baseball Clubs recruited many disaffected N.L. and A.A. players with promises of profit-sharing, no reserve clause and long-term contracts.

The Players' League (P.L.) was represented in Chicago by a team bankrolled by John Addison, a wealthy contractor. It was managed by Comiskey, who had bolted from the Browns. Fugitives from Anson's White Stockings were also on the roster.

Called the Pirates by foes, and White Stockings by friends, the P.L. team started out well, but attendance quickly fell off. The Pirates sputtered out their sole season—and that of the league—in South Side Park, at 35th and Wentworth streets, almost directly across the street from the site that would later be occupied by the original Comiskey Park.

Spalding hastened the process of disintegration of the P.L. by buying out Addison's team for something less than $25,000. His victory statement: "The Players League is deader than the proverbial door nail! It is now undergoing the embalming process."

Despite the triumph of Spalding and his N.L. colleagues in crushing the P.L., a cry of defiance by Comiskey was to prove a harbinger of the future. Comiskey lamented that the P.L. had the N.L. at its mercy and let it off the hook. "The N.L. was in such a bad way that a child could have pushed the organization over but nothing would do the Players League people but a compromise," he said.

A few years later, Comiskey played a major role in what was to become the successful challenge of the N.L. by the American League, and of Spalding's club by his own team, the White Sox.

Despite the eventual outcome of the battle in 1890, the P.L. defections hit the White Stockings hard. Surprisingly, however, they finished second that year with a cast of largely over-the-hill, minor league and sandlot players. A wit tagged them "Anson's orphans," quickly transmuted to the new nickname, Orphans, which displaced that of White Stockings.

Though many of White Stocking defectors and those from other teams, including Comiskey, returned to their former employers after the P.L. folded, Anson's problems were soon compounded further. Spalding stepped down as team president after the '91 season, though he remained a stockholder until 1902. James Hart, a Chicago businessman and minority owner, took his place as president.

Hart and Anson quickly fell out. Anson soon made his grievances public, charging that his new boss was tight-fisted, unwilling to approve good trades, and undermining his authority with the players.

If Hart was parsimonious it might have been because of the cost of another new home for the team going up in 1892 at the corner of Polk and Lincoln (now Wolcott) streets. The West Side Grounds, with the first double-decked wooden grandstand built in Chicago, was larger (16,000 seats compared to 10,000) than West Side Park, and more luxurious. It was to serve until the move in 1916 to what now is Wrigley Field.

West Side Grounds, however, did not become a full-time home until 1894. Many games in 1892 and 1893 were played at South Side Park, the field at 35th Street abandoned by the P.L. team. This was done in an attempt to lure fans from a new section of the city and also as a convenience to those attending the 1893 Columbian Exposition, a world's fair on the South Side.

While the team was flitting from one venue to another, Anson was also struggling with a revolving cast of players. Among them were such rising stars as Clark Griffith, Bill Dahlen and Bill Lange. Anson's Orphans soon earned the new nickname of Anson's Colts—or just Colts—because of the team's overall youth.

Despite the ancient adage, youth was not served. Nor was maturity when Anson was dismissed by Hart on February 1, 1898, at the age of 45. He had led the team to five pennants in 19 seasons as manager, had played on six White Stockings pennant-winners, had won three batting titles, and was the first major league player to amass more than 3,000 hits.

As the 19th Century wound down, not even pitcher Griffith's six consecutive 20-game winning seasons (1894–99), the superlative play of outfielder Lange, a .330 lifetime hitter, and the fine fielding of shortstop Dahlen throughout the 1890s, could bring home a winner for Anson or his successors as manager in its final decade.

But the closing year of the century, 1900, presaged the major development of the era which was about to dawn. A vigorous new rival to the Colts for fan favor and support arrived in Chicago.

Weakened by the battle with the P.L., the American Association had collapsed after the 1891 season. The N.L. embraced four of its teams, the rest disbanded. As the sole major league, the N.L. kept an unwieldy membership of 12 teams until after the 1899 season when it cut back to eight.

With the A.A. defunct, an ambitious and canny young sportswriter, Byron "Ban" Johnson, detected an opening for a new major league built around the cities abandoned by the N.L. .He began slowly, laying the groundwork by organizing the minor Western League in late 1893. One of his colleagues was Comiskey, who purchased the Sioux City, Iowa, franchise, which in 1895 he moved to St. Paul, Minnesota.

When the N.L. slimmed to eight teams after the 1899 season, Johnson decided the time was ripe for the second step. He renamed his organization the American League, persuaded Comiskey to move from St. Paul to Chicago, and transferred several other teams into cities abandoned by the N.L.

Hart had no choice, under baseball's prevailing National Agreement, other than to stand by as Comiskey entered the Chicago "market" though the Colts president realized the potential threat. He met with Comiskey, obtained a few minor concessions, and tried to comfort himself with the thought that, after all, the A.L. was still a minor league.

As if bound by tradition, Comiskey named his team the White Stockings, but that nickname was almost immediately abridged to White Sox in the spirit of the 20th Century, which was about to dawn.

Before it did, Comiskey's White Sox finished out the 19th by winning the American League's first pennant while playing in a hastily-built tiny ballpark called 39th Street Grounds, located near the corner of 39th and Princeton streets. The pennant was a decided triumph even if on a minor league note.

It was not "minor" much longer. After the A.L.'s opening season of 1900, Johnson, Comiskey and their allies claimed major league status for their creation. It was a declaration of war against the N.L.

The A.L. immediately joined battle by ruthlessly raiding the N.L. for players and managers. In his most important acquisition, Comiskey added injury to insult by luring ace pitcher Clark Griffith from Hart's Colts and naming him manager of the White Sox.

With the advent of the 20th Century, baseball's long period of gestation in Chicago was over. The city now had two major league teams, and both would endure for the next 100 years and beyond.

Fields of 33 Dreams 'n' Screams

Age cannot seem to wither Wrigley Field nor stale the infinite variety of its attractions. Season after season, whether the home team plays well or ill, its "friendly confines" are often crammed to capacity by crowds composed not only of Cubs fans but of "pilgrims" from all over the nation enticed by its mystique as the greenest of baseball's green cathedrals.

Possibly more than any other ballpark ever built, Wrigley Field has become an attraction on its own, a baseball monument considered worthy of landmark designation. It's the genuine, nonfictional "field of dreams," an entertainment center blending history, tradition, myth, heroics, hopes and heartbreaks in what many consider the perfect setting for a baseball game.

Yet despite its present stature as the exemplar of what most fans imagine such a edifice should be, the present Wrigley Field with its seating capacity of 39,056 is a far cry from the single-decked, relatively modest structure erected at a cost of $250,000 in 1914 as the home of the short-lived Chicago Whales of the "outlaw" Federal League.

Wrigley Field has undergone numerous alterations, some major, such as moving a section of the stands 60 feet—home plate once was located where the pitcher's mound is now—and double decking the original grandstand from the right field corner to the left.

The configuration and location of the stands, the outfield dimensions, the material of the fences and walls, the location of the scoreboard, and even the level of the playing field have changed radically in the numerous projects that have kept the park viable into the 21st Century. The latest major innovation was the installation of lights in 1988, making Wrigley Field the last major league ballpark to offer night games.

It's good to keep the evolution of Wrigley Field to its current revered status in mind when considering Chicago's newest baseball park, Comiskey Park II, which has been criticized for various alleged shortcomings since it opened in 1991. The most fire has been directed at the elevation—or 35-degree pitch—of the upper deck and the "mall-like" concourse for concessions and washroom facilities.

The upper deck concern was addressed in a major renovation for the 2001 season that included relocating several thousand seats from the upper deck to the bleachers and along the foul lines beyond each dugout. The expansion of the bleachers required reduction of the outfield dimensions, an adjustment perhaps only coincidentally in keeping with the current trend to encourage more home runs.

Comiskey Park II may never arouse the veneration accorded Wrigley Field, or serve as long. Still it's noteworthy that it has been the flexibility to adjust to the changing expectations, needs, and demands of generations of fans that has kept Wrigley Field vigorous far beyond the useful life of virtually every other ballpark. Some replaced in recent years were as much as 60 years younger than Wrigley Field.

Most of Chicago's earlier ballparks, with the exception of the first Comiskey Park, which housed the White Sox for 81 seasons from 1910 through 1990, had brief useful lives, often shorter than a decade.

The Cubs have played in Wrigley Field for so long, since 1916, that it's almost a shock to realize that it's actually the sixth home of the team since its birth in 1876 as a charter member of the National League. As for the White Sox, they've had three homes since the American League claimed major status in 1901, if one dismisses nine- and 11-game diversions to Milwaukee's County Stadium in 1968 and 1969 when then-owner Arthur Allyn considered moving the team to the city recently abandoned by the Braves.

Like baseball itself, the ballpark evolved in stages from a relatively crude and simple form to the current complex structure with its emphasis on fan creature comforts.

In baseball's earliest days, in Chicago as elsewhere, games were played on open fields without seating arrangements for spectators, who were free to position themselves at convenient viewing points around the edges of the playing area. The well-off even looked on while seated in carriages or on horseback. When the game turned professional it became necessary to limit spectators to those who had paid their way into an enclosed area. That led to the fenced-in park.

Horse racing preceded baseball as a mass spectator sport, and so its wooden grandstands furnished the pattern for similar structures in the first enclosed ballparks in the 1860s. Some facilities, such as Dexter Park Pavilion, built soon after the Union Stock Yard opened southwest of Chicago's main business district in 1865, accommodated baseball games as well as horse races.

The success of baseball's first professional team, the Cincinnati Red Stockings of 1869, inspired the founding in 1871 of the National Association of Professional Baseball Players (N.A.). Chicago's member team, the White Stockings, hurriedly put up an enclosed wooden ballpark on a city dump between Lake Michigan and Michigan Ave., within walking distance of the downtown business district.

This first purpose-built Chicago baseball stadium had a capacity of 7,000 and separated the seating for men and women (for protection from hooligans and improper language). Season tickets (for an undependable schedule) cost $15. A six-foot board fence surrounded the park, the wall being some 375 feet from the plate at the foul lines.

The stadium apparently was officially called Union Base-Ball Grounds, but became variously known as Lake Street Dumping Ground, White Stocking Park and Lake Park, the last sticking as the favored label.

Lake Park was not only the first enclosed park built specifically for baseball in Chicago, but its site eventually housed the team that was to become the Cubs. Not however, before a disaster that required the future Cubs to debut elsewhere in 1876.

The N.A. White Stockings started out well, battling for the championship into late season, when misfortune struck. On October 9, 1871, the Great Chicago Fire began, not only devastating the city for three days, leaving 100,000 homeless and causing an estimated $196 million in damage, but burning down Lake Park.

The White Stockings built a new home for the 1872 season. It was located at 23rd St. and State St. Unimaginatively called the 23rd Street Grounds, it was to become the first home of the team eventually named the Cubs.

The White Stockings struggled on for five seasons, even sinking to semi-pro status for a time, while the Boston Red Stockings, led by pitcher Albert G. Spalding, dominated the N.A. by winning four consecutive pennants.

William Hulbert, the energetic Chicago businessman who became White Stockings president in 1875, played the principal role in founding the National League a year later. He raided the N.A. before it broke up. Two of his recruits, Spalding and first baseman Adrian "Cap" Anson, became the major 19th Century figures in Cub history.

The N.L. teams took over the existing ballparks of the defunct N.A. Hulbert's White Stockings moved into their predecessor's 23rd Street Grounds, where they played for two seasons. It was the first of five stops en route to Wrigley Field.

Just two years later the White Stockings, who won the N.L.'s first pennant in 1876 with Spalding as manager and pitching ace, were able to afford a new venue, Lakefront Park, built on the Michigan Ave. site of the N.A. team's original ballpark of 1871. The new park cost $10,000 and its original capacity was 3,000 spectators, which soon was expanded to 10,000, including standees. It featured 18 "luxury boxes" for the well-to-do, among them Spalding, who became chief owner after Hulbert's death in 1882. Spalding had named Anson manager in 1879.

The next shift came in 1885, after the team had won three more pennants in succession from 1880–82. Spalding spent $30,000 for a larger and fancier stadium. West Side Park stood at Congress and Throop streets. It had seating for 10,000, including private roof boxes, as well as facilities for track, cycling and lawn tennis. The stadium served the White Stockings well. They won pennants the first two years (1885–86) they played there after having been also-rans the previous two seasons.

The next change came in 1891 when the White Stockings used two home fields, West Side Park as well as another at 35th and Wentworth streets, near the future location of Comiskey Park. It was the second facility of three on the site, all known as South Side Park, and had been the home of the short-lived Chicago Pirates of the upstart Players League during the 1890 season. The White Stockings of 1891 played there on Tuesdays, Thursdays and Saturdays and at West Side Park on Mondays, Wednesdays and Fridays. No Sunday games were permitted by the National League until 1893.

In 1892 the team, now also nicknamed the Colts (as well as Orphans, among many other ephemeral labels), played its entire home schedule in South Side Park, but the next year again used two fields, playing Sunday games exclusively at the new West Side Grounds, Spalding's largest, most expensive and fan-friendly effort yet.

West Side Grounds had a capacity of 16,000 though overflow crowds of 20,000 and more were not unusual. It was the first double-decked stadium in Chicago even if being constructed of wood it was backward-looking because steel and concrete parks were already coming in. Located at Polk and Lincoln (now Wolcott St.), West Side Grounds was the team's exclusive home from 1894 until the move in 1916 to the former Federal League park which was to become known as Wrigley Field.

West Side Grounds flourished in the first decade of the 20th Century, with the Cubs winning a record 116 games in 1906 (while losing only 36) as they rolled to a pennant, their first of four in five years (1906–08 and 1910).

The Cubs' success was not unalloyed, however, as it was marred by being upset in the 1906 World Series by the cross-town White Sox, who had stolen their former name in capsule form after invading Chicago in 1900. The Cubs, however, did win the 1907 and 1908 World Series, both over the Detroit Tigers. West Side Grounds thus was the site of the Cubs' first four World Series appearances, two successful. They since have played five at Wrigley Field, winning none, and losing another played oddly enough at Comiskey Park as their home field.

The move to what is now Wrigley Field came after the team was purchased in 1916 by "Lucky Charlie" Weeghman, who had built a chain of lunchrooms in Chicago into an $8 million fortune. Weeghman entered baseball by buying a franchise in the minor Federal League for $25,000 in 1912.

Weeghman's Federal League team, originally called the Chifeds, played home games at DePaul University on the North Side, the first time a professional team had ventured into that area of Chicago. In the beginning Chicago had grown chiefly to the south, then to the west, which was why the earlier major league parks were located in those areas. Expansion to the north came last.

Weeghman sought to capitalize on the boom on the North Side when the Federal League challenged the established N.L. and A.L. by declaring itself a major league for 1914. The site at Clark and Addison streets he chose for his new park had been occupied by the Chicago Lutheran Theological Seminary, so even then it was "hallowed ground." One reason for the choice of the location was that fans could easily reach the park on the Milwaukee Road train and the elevated from the Loop.

Architect Zachary Taylor Davis, who had designed Comiskey Park a few years earlier for the White Sox, was commissioned to plan what at first was called North Side Ball Park. It was to seat 14,000. Ground was broken on March 4, 1914. Weeghman's team, renamed the Whales, played their first home game just seven weeks later, on April 23, defeating Kansas City 9-1.

The Whales, and Federal League, lasted two seasons. North Side Park became Whales Park then Weeghman Park. Early attendance success encouraged Weeghman to expand capacity to 18,000, but when the Federal League's efforts to gain recognition of major league status failed so did the league. As part of a settlement, Weeghman was permitted to buy a franchise in an existing major league.

Weeghman formed a 10-man syndicate that bought the Cubs for $500,000 on January 20, 1916 from principal owner Charles Taft. A member of the group was William Wrigley Jr., a Chicagoan who had made a fortune in chewing gum.

Named president, Weeghman moved the Cubs out of West Side Grounds to the newer park, where they played their first game, defeating Cincinnati 7-6 in 11 innings on April 20, 1916. It soon became known as Cubs Park until 1926, when it was renamed Wrigley Field after the man who took control when Weeghman sold his interest in 1918.

Wrigley Field has become a virtual baseball "shrine." The availability for a time of almost all Cubs games on television cable networks and satellite systems in much of the country has spread the ballpark's fame far beyond the Chicago area and made it a major tourist attraction to dedicated fans from all over the nation.

The field has accumulated a treasure trove of legendary events, such as Gabby Hartnett's "homer in the gloamin'," Ernie Banks' 500th career home run, the notorious "two balls in play" game between the Cubs and St. Louis Cardinals, Babe Ruth's alleged "called shot" home run in the 1932 World Series, Lou Gehrig's home run as a high school boy, and many others similarly memorable.

The ivy-covered brick outfield walls, the huge manually-operated scoreboard built by a young Bill Veeck beyond center field, the "Bleacher Bums" and the fame of great Cubs hitters such as Banks, Hack Wilson, Rogers Hornsby, Phil Cavarretta, Ron Santo, Billy Williams and Sammy Sosa, as well as pitchers, among them Grover Cleveland Alexander, Charlie Root, Ferguson Jenkins and Greg Maddux, have contributed to the aura of a facility often called the ideal setting for a baseball game.

Additionally, the history of the Chicago Bears football team is inextricably linked to Wrigley Field, where it played for almost

50 years before moving to Soldier Field in 1971. Many legendary Bears, including Red Grange, Bronko Nagurski, Bulldog Turner, George McAfee, Sid Luckman, Johnny Morris, Mike Ditka, Dick Butkus and Gale Sayers, performed their greatest exploits in home games on a football field crammed into what now is exclusively a baseball park.

Beyond its crowded history, Wrigley Field's natural advantages, meticulous maintenance and frequent improvements have kept it up to date without betraying tradition. Among its assets are easy access from public transportation, good sightlines, nearness of the fans to the field, almost perfectly proportioned dimensions and a picture-book setting for games, especially on a warm, sunny summer day.

The Cubs' current ownership, The Tribune Co., has declared that Wrigley Field is sure to serve its needs and those of fans well into the 21st Century.

So is the home of the White Sox, Comiskey Park II, but its history is far briefer. The White Sox played their first game there on April 16, 1991, losing 16-0 to the Detroit Tigers. It is just the third ballpark occupied by the team since it arrived in Chicago in 1900, a year before the American League claimed major league status.

When owner Charles Comiskey moved his then-minor league team from St. Paul, Minnesota, to Chicago, he took over a decrepit former cricket grounds at the corner of 39th St. and Princeton Ave., in the Irish Bridgeport section of the South Side. The field was just a few blocks from the current location of Comiskey Park II.

Comiskey put up a wooden, whitewashed grandstand on the site where his team played its first game on April 21, 1900, losing 5-4 to Milwaukee. When the White Sox won pennants in 1900 and 1901 (the latter their first as a major league team) the ballpark, called 39th Street Grounds or South Side Park, seated fewer than 5,000. Its capacity was enlarged to 6,600 for 1903, but proved inadequate as the team's popularity grew. A crowd of 30,084—including standees in the roped-off outfield—reportedly witnessed Doc White extend his consecutive shutout streak to 45 innings on October 2, 1904.

South Side Park reached the zenith of its brief glory in 1906 when the "Hitless Wonder" White Sox upset the Cubs, winners of 116 regular season games, in the third World Series ever played, and the only one between the two Chicago teams.

With the White Sox becoming solidly established in Chicago, and attendance booming in the pre-World War I era, it became clear to Comiskey that South Side Park was inadequate. His team needed a far larger, more sumptuous home.

Comiskey purchased a large plot of land fronting Wentworth Ave., and on a section at 35th St. and Shields Ave. in 1910 built what was hailed as the "Baseball Palace of the World." Designed by architect Zachary Taylor Davis, who planned Wrigley Field four years later, Comiskey's new ballpark cost between $500,000 and $750,000, and was the fifth baseball facility in the nation to be constructed of concrete and steel.

When it housed its first game on July 1, 1910, a 2-0 St. Louis Browns victory over the White Sox, Comiskey Park scarcely resembled its appearance after a major expansion in the 1920s. It started out as a single-deck concrete grandstand running from the left-field corner into the right-field corner with bleachers in the outfield except for center. The grandstand was not totally covered. The park held about 30,000.

It was in this form that Comiskey Park housed three consecutive World Series from 1917 through 1919. In the first, the White Sox defeated the New York Giants to become Chicago's last lords of all baseball. The next year, because Comiskey Park had a larger capacity than their field, the Cubs of 1918 called it home while losing to the Boston Red Sox. And 1919 was the year of infamy, the White-Black Sox throwing the World Series to the Cincinnati Reds.

Forty years were to pass until Comiskey Park hosted another World Series, its last, that of 1959 in which the Los Angeles Dodgers defeated the White Sox of Nellie Fox, Luis Aparicio, Ted Kluszewski and Jim Landis. Between 1919 and 1959, the White

Sox endured many bleak years on the field, though not necessarily in fan support.

Despite the Black Sox scandal of 1919, the White Sox prospered at the gate in the early 1920s, and Comiskey spent almost $1 million in 1926 to renovate and expand the park. The stands were double-decked all around except for a small bleacher section in center field, increasing the capacity to 52,000. Comiskey Park assumed the bulky appearance that remained nearly unchanged until it was torn down.

Like those of Wrigley Field, Comiskey Park's dimensions waxed and waned during its 81-season lifespan. When it opened, the field measured 362 feet down each foul line and 440 to straightaway center. For a while it settled down to 352 feet down the foul lines and 415 feet to center after frequent mutations. A chicken-wire fence briefly reduced the dimensions in 1949 and 1969, and home plate was shoved back and forth from the wall now and then. Yet the principle of symmetry was generally maintained.

The three most significant changes to the park after 1926 were the installation of lights in 1939 (the White Sox defeated the Browns 5-2 in the first night game on August 14), the exploding scoreboard devised by showman-owner Bill Veeck in 1960, and the "skyboxes" for the well-heeled in the early 1980s.

By the late 1980s, the owners group headed by Jerry Reinsdorf that had purchased the team from Veeck's syndicate in 1981 decided that the old park "was nearing the end of its useful life," as a structural survey stated. After massive political machinations, the Illinois General Assembly on July 1, 1988 approved an appropriations bill to build a new Comiskey Park across the street from the old one. The Illinois Sports Facility Authority was to provide the new park for lease to the White Sox.

The final game in the onetime "Baseball Palace of the World" was played on Sept. 30, 1990, with a crowd of 42,849 watching the White Sox defeat the Seattle Mariners 2-1. A few months later old Comiskey Park yielded to the wrecker's ball.

While Comiskey Park I never won the hearts of fans nationally as did Wrigley Field, it was undeniably just as dear to several generations of ardent White Sox followers. It certainly accumulated a comparable wealth of treasured memories of great players, remarkable achievements and historical events.

It was the site not only of four World Series, but of baseball's first All-Star Game on July 6, 1933. Other all-star games followed, among them an annual East-West Negro League event, which made it all the more meaningful when Larry Doby of the Cleveland Indians batted for the first time as a major league player on July 5, 1947, breaking the A.L. color barrier just as Jackie Robinson had done in the N.L. earlier that season. Doby later was to play for and manage the White Sox.

The Chicago (later St. Louis and Arizona) Cardinals of the National Football League called Comiskey Park home for a while, and college football teams, including Notre Dame, played games there. Several notable boxing title bouts, including Joe Louis vs. Jimmy Braddock and Floyd Patterson vs. Sonny Liston, took place in the infield.

But most of all, the old park will be remembered for baseball, and such outstanding players as Shoeless Joe Jackson, Eddie Collins, Ray Schalk, Urban Faber, Luke Appling, Ted Lyons, Zeke Bonura, Minnie Minoso, Chico Carrasquel, Billy Pierce, Nellie Fox, Luis Aparicio, Wilbur Wood, Dick Allen, Bill Melton, Harold Baines, Ozzie Guillen and Frank Thomas.

It also will be remembered for the teams those men played on, if grimly for the Black Sox more fondly for manager Jimmy Dykes' overachievers of the Great Depression days, the Go Go White Sox of general manager Frank Lane, manager Al Lopez's pennant-winners of 1959, the South Side Hit Men of 1977, and the "Winning Ugly" modestly successful winners of a division title in 1983.

The old park's replacement, also named Comiskey Park, began to take shape with ground-breaking on May 7, 1989, and was completed at a cost of $119 million in 22 months, in time for the opening of the 1991 season. Designed by architect Rick deFlon, the structure lacked the nostalgic feel of some later-built stadia, such as Baltimore's Camden Yards and Cleveland's Jacobs Field. Its design was thoroughly modern and functional, if somewhat austere.

Comiskey Park II was a new departure in Chicago ballparks with its emphasis on fan convenience with unobstructed sight lines, 118 luxury suites, a stadium club, state-of- the-art electronic scoreboard, numerous concession stands, souvenir shops and even a museum. When opened, it had a seating capacity of 44,321 and symmetrical outfield dimensions of 347 feet down each foul line and 400 to center field. Both crowd capacity and fence distances shrank with the alterations made for the 2001 season.

But as the long histories of Wrigley Field and Comiskey Park I suggest, a ballpark is almost a living entity, developing and re-shaping over decades until it scarcely resembles the original Comiskey Park II, no doubt, will follow a similar pattern.

Whether it will ever accumulate a tradition comparable to that of its predecessors remains to be seen. A start has been made with the White Sox division titles of 1993 and 2000, the introduction of interleague play with the Cubs and most of all the feats of outstanding players such as Frank "Big Hurt" Thomas.

Tradition, like Rome, Wrigley Field and old Comiskey Park, can't be built in a day but accumulates decade after decade.

ALL-TIME CHICAGO TEAM

Among the more dubious blessings of the advent of the new millennium, whether on New Year's Day 2000 as incorrectly celebrated by the impatient or greeted accurately a year later, was a deluge of All-20th Century teams.

One of these squads, The Top 100 Players of the Century, chosen by the Society for American Baseball Research (SABR), included eight players whose names are welded to the Cubs or White Sox. Cubs Ernie Banks, Mordecai "Three-Finger" Brown, Ferguson Jenkins and Ryne Sandberg were rated as No. 27, 75, 96 and 98, respectively, and White Sox Joe "Shoeless Joe" Jackson, Ed Walsh, Luke Appling and Luis Aparicio ranked 52nd, 85th, 86th and 88th. Eddie Collins, No. 49, and Carlton Fisk, 92, spent about half their careers with the Sox and Grover Cleveland Alexander, 25, and Greg Maddux, 40, somewhat less with the Cubs.

All such aggregations, whether chosen by the admirable SABR or by magazines, newspapers, book authors, television networks and baseball card and breakfast cereal vendors, were skewed by a bias toward the current and more recent. Old-time players, unless of towering magnitude and reputation, were given short shrift or even totally ignored despite high standing among their contemporaries.

That was regrettable if understandable. It's impossible to objectively compare players never seen in action to those observed in person, often day-to-day as by baseball writers and radio and television sportscasters. Only statistics and the testimony of peers and the media of their time survive to testify to the comparative skills of those whose playing days have receded far into the past.

Statistics lie, memory fibs. What's more, conditions change vastly from decade to decade with new ballparks, altered dimensions, rules tinkering and a host of other modifications. Despite the incantations of poets and the delusions induced by nostalgia, baseball is not impervious to change. The game is different from what it was a century ago even if most modifications have come in small increments, often almost imperceptible, or huge ones such as introduction of the designated hitter.

Consider Ed Walsh's memory of his experience with the White Sox when they were The Hitless Wonders in light of the way baseball is played today: "There was one season, 1908, the year I won 40 games, when our whole club hit exactly three homers in the entire year. (Fielder) Jones, the manager, hit one, (Frank) Isbell hit another, and I got the third."

As another example of changes in the game, Walsh pitched 464 innings the season he was 40-15, double the workload expected of a first class starting pitcher these days. Yet only devoted baseball fans recall Walsh and most of his compeers.

Of course, the names of a few giants of the distant past are known even to those ignorant of the latest inductee into the Hall of Fame, such as Kirby Puckett in 2001, whose career ended just five years earlier.

Babe Ruth transcends baseball, and so do Lou Gehrig, Shoeless Joe Jackson, Ty Cobb and a handful of others. A statistical table in *Baseball Digest* magazine illustrated forcefully why Ruth, aside from his home run feats, is invulnerable as the all-time monarch of the game. In a tabulation of "players with most runs scored, season" (since 1900), Ruth's name occupied six of the 18 lines, starting with a record 177 in 1921. In fact, Ruth was listed four times among the top six, Gehrig taking second and fourth places, further demonstrating why he, too, is assured of enduring status among the titans.

The foregoing exposition is intended not as an alibi but to emphasize the difficulty of selecting any credible and valid all-star aggregation from among several generations of players spread over a century. Some, like Ruth, Gehrig and Shoeless Joe Jackson, defy time which ravages memory and levels reputation. The vast majority, however, no matter how highly-regarded in their day, sink beneath the weight of decades, ignorance of history and limited modern attention spans.

Nonetheless, duty demands selection of a Chicago All-Time Team of the finest of the White Sox and Cub players whose exploits have been detailed in the preceding chapters. Unlike Jim Crusinberry, who began his sportswriting career in 1903, the authors cannot claim a headline such as the one trumpeting his "White Sox All-Time Best" in the October 1949 issue of *Baseball Digest*. It boasted, "Picked by one who has seen them all." A half century later, no one can make such a claim.

Because the pre-1900 era of baseball was vastly different from even the first years of the 20th Century, certainly until the pitching distance was extended to 60 feet, 6 inches in 1897, no early players were considered for the Chicago All-Time team. Not even such luminaries as Albert Spalding, Cap Anson and King Kelly of the Cubs, in whose day the definition of what constituted a foul, walk or base hit changed frequently as the game developed from the time when a pitcher was required to comply with the batter's request as to where to throw the ball. The problem did not arise with the White Sox because they were born in 1901, our arbitrary choice as the starting point.

Because a 25-man roster has been the general practice in the major leagues for much of the last 100 years, that number of players has been chosen to **Baseball,** *Chicago Style*'s all-time team. It comprises two lineups of nine men each and seven extra pitchers, two of them relievers. Two managers were selected.

THE ALL-TIME CHICAGO TEAM

1B: Ernie Banks, Cubs; Frank Thomas, White Sox.

2B: Eddie Collins, White Sox; Ryne Sandberg, Cubs.

SS: Luke Appling, White Sox; Luis Aparicio, White Sox.

3B: Ron Santo, Cubs; Heinie Zimmerman, Cubs.

C: Gabby Hartnett, Cubs; Carlton Fisk, White Sox.

OF: Billy Williams, Cubs; Joe Jackson, White Sox.

OF: Hack Wilson, Cubs; Riggs Stephenson, Cubs.

OF: Sammy Sosa, Cubs; Minnie Minoso, White Sox.

SP: Ted Lyons, White Sox; Three-Finger Brown, Cubs.

SP: Red Faber, White Sox; Ferguson Jenkins, Cubs.

SP: Ed Walsh, White Sox; Billy Pierce, White Sox.

SP: Eddie Cicotte, White Sox.

RP: Bruce Sutter, Cubs; Lee Smith, Cubs.

M: Frank Chance, Cubs; Al Lopez, White Sox.

Any such all-star team inevitably invites disagreement over the relative merits of the players chosen and those left off. That's understandable, particularly when some of the players omitted won various awards, led the league in some category of hitting, pitching or fielding or—to take it to the extreme—are enshrined in the Hall of Fame.

Since the achievements and merits of most of the exceptional Cub and White Sox players have been discussed in the preceding pages of this book it seems superfluous to go into further detail about those left off the **Baseball,** *Chicago Style* All-Star Team. Yet since two or three of the selections are probably controversial, brief explanations might be appropriate, though in the cases of Joe Tinker and Johnny Evers it's sufficient to reiterate that their skills were exaggerated by Franklin P. Adams' poem.

White Sox fans might be annoyed at the selection of Collins at second base rather than Nellie Fox, the hero of the 1959 pennant-winning season and the A.L. MVP that year. Fox had a fine career, no doubt, but hardly one comparable to that of Collins, who finished with a career average of .333 for 25 seasons, 12 of them with the Sox. In seven of his Sox years he hit over .330 with a high of .369 in 1920. He also led the A.L. in fielding percentage nine times and in stolen bases four times, with a high of 81.

Old-timer Crusinberry, who "has seen them all," wrote of Collins in 1949—pre-Fox, of course—that "he is just about the universal choice among the experts as the best second baseman the A.L. ever had." During Collins' playing days an umpire—surely an unbiased observer—called him the best baseball player ever, a rather large compliment in the era of Babe Ruth, Ty Cobb and Rogers Hornsby.

Another controversial choice might be Fisk rather than Ray Schalk, whose defensive skills were undisputed. Yet Schalk was never a dangerous hitter, with an average of .253 for 19 seasons and just 12 home runs. Fisk was a major offensive threat as well as a standout receiver—like Hartnett—and ended his 24-year career with 376 home runs.

When it comes to starting pitchers, the debate could be furious with such standouts as Ed Reulbach, Charlie Root and Lon Warneke of the Cubs and Doc White, Gary Peters and Wilbur Wood finding strong support.

No one could seriously dispute the inclusion of Chance as one of the two top managers nor perhaps that of Lopez. Chance's record of four N.L. pennants and two World Series titles in seven full seasons as Cub manager is unmatched. Charlie Grimm led the Cubs to three pennants but it took him far longer and he never won a Series.

"Frank Chance was a great baseball manager," said John McGraw, his bitter rival as manager of the New York Giants. "He could fight on the field and forget his enemies afterward. He was a great leader. He asked no man to take any chance he would not take himself. He had the power to instill enthusiasm even in a losing cause."

No major league manager ever lost less often than Chance over an extended period. The Cubs won almost twice as many games as they lost (768-389) during his reign from 1905 through 1912 for a winning percentage of .664.

Lopez won merely one pennant (1959) during his major run as White Sox manager from 1957 through 1965 but his often undermanned teams were always competitive and well over .500. His guiding principle, he said, was that "a manager must adapt his style to what material he's got. There's no other way to do it."

And there's no other way to choose an All-Time Chicago Team than to just do it and let the debate begin to rage.

Top
of the
Charts

O ne might call them the M&M Boys, but it would seem
presumptuous to use a tag invented in 1961 for New York
Yankees Mickey Mantle and Roger Maris during their assault on Babe Ruth's single-season record of 60 home runs set in
1927. Maris, of course, prevailed with 61 to Mantle's 54 for a
new mark that held for 37 years, until Mark McGwire hit 70 in
1998, outgunning Cub Sammy Sosa's 66 that same season.

Yet Bill Madlock and Bill Melton also share a few similarities
other than the first letter of their surnames. Both were outstanding third basemen. Both played in Chicago, though not on the
same team. Madlock was with the Cubs from 1974 to 1976 and
Melton with the White Sox from 1968 to 1975. Both led their
leagues in a major batting category. Melton paced the A.L. in
home runs in 1971 and Madlock topped the N.L. in batting an
impressive four times, twice as a Cub in 1975 and 1976.

What links them most dramatically is that both waited until
the last possible moment to nail down an individual league leadership. That also sets them apart from the many other Cub and
Sox players who have reached the top of the charts in N.L. and
A.L. batting and pitching categories. Both went to the limit, winning championships in final games of a season.

Each man told his story in a first person narration a few years after the last-gasp effort snatched jubilant success from the jaws of incipient disheartening failure.

First, here's Madlock's account:

"I had a few good years in Chicago with the Cubs and would have been happy to stay there the rest of my career. People said, 'Madlock is going to be the Cub third baseman the next 10 years,' but it didn't work out that way.

"But, like I say, I enjoyed playing in Chicago and when I think of the game that gave me the most individual satisfaction it naturally has to be the last game I played there as a Cub in 1976. The reason, of course, is that I won my second N.L. batting title in that game. It gave me even more satisfaction than the 1975 All-Star game in which I got the big hit.

"I'd won the batting title for the first time in 1975 (with .354), but as the 1976 season went on I really had little hope of winning it again. I was down around .310 going into the latter part of the season and there were several people ahead of me. People were asking, 'Where's he been?' But I thought that wasn't bad hitting. It's just that when you do well one year you raise everyone's expectations after that.

"The other thing about it is that some years you get a lot of breaks on close plays from the official scorer and they give you hits. The nest year things might be different and they don't give you the close ones. There were some plays in '76 that I thought were hits that the official scorer called errors.

"Another reason I wasn't hitting for as high an average in '76 was that while talking contract with the Cub management the previous winter it had been mentioned that I hadn't hit too many homers and that they thought I should have more ribbies (runs batted in). So I tried to hit a few more homers in '76—and succeeded.

"In spite of that in early September I got on a hot streak and lifted my average into the .330s. I can't remember how many hitters were ahead of me at that point, but I know Ken Griffey (of the Cincinnati Reds) was ahead of me. He was having a great year. I didn't know if I could catch him, but I thought I had a chance if the hits kept dropping in.

"But all that was forgotten after we went to New York to play the Mets with about two weeks to go in the season and I got mugged in a hallway of the Waldorf Astoria Hotel. The muggers banged my head against the wall and I suffered a concussion. I spent 10 days in the hospital and I wasn't even thinking about the batting championship anymore. I just wanted to get out of the hospital. When I did get out, I wasn't sure if I could play.

"Our last series of the season was at home, three games against the Montreal Expos at Wrigley Field. Manager Jim Marshall asked me if I felt like I could play and I said I'd give it a try. I was still weak, but I felt all right otherwise and the doctors had given me the green light so there was no reason to sit it out.

"I went 0-for-4 the first game on Friday. The next day I got a hit in three times at bat. The next game was on Sunday, the last day of the season (October 3, 1976), and the reporters were asking me before the game whether I could catch Griffey and if I was feeling the pressure. Griffey was hitting .338 and I was at .333, five points behind.

"I told people, 'No, I'm not feeling any pressure because I'm not even thinking of catching Griffey. I'm just going to do the best I can to close out the season with a good feeling. That's all I'm looking for.'

"But everybody was wondering what would happen. When I passed the bullpen before the game, Darold Knowles, one of our relief pitchers, said, 'You've got a chance, Bill, but you're going to need at least three hits to do it.'

"There'd been talk about Griffey sitting out the last game for the Reds to protect his average. I don't think it was Ken's idea but manager Sparky Anderson's. And he did keep Griffey out of the starting lineup in the final game at Cincinnati.

"Woody Fryman was the starting pitcher for Montreal against us which was an advantage for me, him being a left-hander and me being a right-handed hitter.

"My first time up in the first inning I laid down a bunt, nice and soft. The third baseman came charging in to pick up the ball barehanded but I beat the throw to first for a single. So I had one hit.

"My next turn came in the third inning—which was the big inning for us because we scored five runs and knocked Fryman out of the game. Joe Wallis led off with a single and I came up with a man on and nobody out. I hit a chopper toward the hole to the left side. Larry Parrish, the third baseman, got a glove on it but the ball got past him for my second hit.

"The third time up was the toughest. It was in the fourth inning and Dale Murray was pitching—a right-hander who was probably the best relief pitcher in the league at that time and off whom I hadn't got a hit in two years. We had a man on first, so Montreal had the infield playing in.

"I figured my job was to hit behind the runner so I tried to hit to right. Murray got two strikes on me, then I fouled off about three balls. I can't say I ever got a pitch I was looking for but I blooped a ball over the first baseman's head. He was playing in so the ball fell in short right field. If he'd been playing back, he would've been able to make a routine play on it. Instead, I had my third straight single.

"In the seventh inning I got my fourth straight hit, a single like the rest. This one was solid, a line drive to left field. That pushed my average up to .339.

"We'd scored eight runs in the game so I got a chance to bat for the fifth time in the eighth inning. Just before I went to the bat rack, Marshall grabbed me and said, 'I'm sending in Rob Sperring to bat for you. I know what I'm doing.' He'd been told that in Cincinnati Anderson, hearing what kind of day I was having, had sent Griffey in to pinch hit and that he'd struck out. That meant I was ahead of him.

"The funny thing is that Sperring got a hit, which meant that between us we went 5-for-5.

"By the time the game ended, we learned that Griffey went out again in his second time at bat to finish the season at .336.

I'd won the batting title for the second straight season with my 4-for-4 game.

"I was still weak from my stay in the hospital and I didn't dream I could catch Griffey, but I guess I just was supposed to win that batting title. I know I was very fortunate.

"What pleased me most was how the fans at Wrigley Field reacted that day. They were just great, a good crowd for the final day of the season, very excited about what they were seeing. Of course, nobody—including myself—had any idea it was my last game in a Cub uniform.

"But that's a game I'll never forget, my last home game in Chicago when I won a batting title."

The game Melton had good reason to remember was far from his last with the home team in Chicago, but one (rather, two games, as he made evident) that also concluded a season in fine fashion. Here's Melton's account:

"It was a combination of two games rather than just one that figures as my top thrill in baseball, but it all took place in less than 20 hours so you could call it the day I'll never forget. It happened in 1971, Chuck Tanner's first year as White Sox manager, and sort of put a cap on our revival after finishing a terrible last in 1970.

"Few people paid much attention to the fact I'd hit 33 home runs and had 96 runs batted in in 1970. It was one of the best-kept secrets in baseball, but I guess with a last-place team you can't expect much attention. Still, it was the most home runs any White Sox had ever hit, although it didn't lead the league. I thought it was worthy of some notice, especially since I had missed 20 games with an injury.

"When 1971 came everything was different. Tanner took over the club and all of a sudden we were playing good baseball and for a time even made a run at the Oakland Athletics, who won the division title.

"I started out hitting home runs at a good pace, leading the league most of the way. I had a real hot streak in June and July when I hit 19. But I fell off in August, hitting only two that month, and found myself in a battle for the home run lead with Reggie Jackson of Oakland, Norm Cash of Detroit and Reggie Smith of Boston. I was trying too hard to hit home runs, that's all. But the other guys didn't get far ahead of me. They must have been trying too hard, too.

"Going into the last two games of the season I had 30 home runs, two less than Jackson and Cash and the same number as Smith. My chances of winning the home run title at that point didn't look too good, going against three guys. But I had one advantage; we had two games to play and their clubs had only one.

"I guess Chuck (Tanner) knew how much I wanted the home run title and he wanted it for me, too. In order to give me some extra at-bats he moved me up to leadoff from my usual cleanup spot for the last two games against the Milwaukee Brewers at White Sox Park.

"The first game was Wednesday night, September 29, 1971. The Brewers started Jim Slaton, a right-hander with a pretty good fastball. I don't remember the count now but I was up there looking for a fastball when I led off the game. I got it, too, and drove it into the left field bleachers for home run No. 31.

"The next time at bat Slaton tried to finesse me with a couple of changeups and I couldn't do anything with them. But then he came in with the fastball again and I hit it to almost the same spot and the ball again landed in the left field bleachers. That was No. 32.

"I knew what to expect the next time I went up. Slaton didn't disappoint me. He knocked me down with a high, hard pitch. I can't say I was surprised. When you hit two straight you've got to expect to be brushed back.

"I grounded out my last time at bat that night, but I didn't feel too bad about it. I figured I had one game left to win the home run title clear if neither Cash nor Jackson hit one that night. They finished their seasons that night with 32. Smith stayed at 30, and he was out of the running.

"The next day, Thursday, we closed the season with an afternoon game and it's tough sometimes hitting in a day game after a night game. You've got to make an adjustment. I had only one thought in that game, to hit a home run. We'd already clinched third place so the game didn't mean anything in the standings.

"But hitting a home run when you set out to do it is almost impossible. If you play long ball you never hit 'em. You choke up or turn your head or something goes wrong. It just doesn't work. Yet that's what I had to do in this last game and the Brewers had a tough pitcher going, Bill Parsons, who could really throw hard. He got me out when I led off the game so there was one chance gone. I was relieved about one thing—he *was* pitching to me.

"I went into the game a little leery because I didn't think they were going to give me a chance to hit. They could have pitched me outside and not given me anything good. But they challenged me. And I knew Parsons would be throwing fastballs. That's what I hit.

"The second time up, to lead off the third inning, the count went up to 2-2 before Parsons came in with a fastball. When I hit it I was worried it wouldn't reach the wall. It was a line drive to left field. But it carried into the seats. I hit the ball good. It was the hardest hit of the three. When I saw it going over the wall I couldn't believe it. I didn't even know how I touched the bags when I went around the bases. But I put both feet on home plate.

"I was so excited I threw my helmet into the stands. When we made the third out of the inning the fans were still cheering when I went out into the field. Tanner took me out of the game and I sailed my baseball cap into the seats after the helmet.

"We won the game 2-1, but all the excitement in the clubhouse was about my 33rd home run. I'd won the home run title outright, the first White Sox player ever to do it. Tanner was just as excited as I was. He pulled out a bottle of champagne which had been lying around since 1967—when the White Sox almost won the pennant—and poured it over my head. It smelled funny but it felt good."

It may seem strange that the White Sox had to wait until the 71st season of their major league existence to claim their first A.L. home run champion in Melton but they weren't known as the "Hitless Wonders" much of that time without cause. And Melton didn't open any floodgates though Dick Allen also led with 37 in

1972 and 32 in 1974. Melton and Allen remain the only White Sox to lead in home runs even if Albert Belle's 49 in 1998 set a new team high and Frank Thomas has surpassed 40 several times.

As if a White Sox home run champion wasn't rare enough, a league leader in runs batted in is even scarcer. In fact, unique. Allen with 113 RBI in 1972 is the only Sox player to lead the A.L. during its entire first century of play.

Batting champions? Madlock with his pair in successive seasons for the Cubs equaled two-thirds of the entire White Sox total over 100 years. Luke Appling led with .388 in 1936 and .328 in 1943. Thomas became only the second Sox player to top the A.L. when he hit .347 in 1997.

When it comes to pitchers leading or sharing the league crown for wins, the White Sox have fared far better. Ten Sox have topped the A.L. in 14 seasons, four doing it twice. The roll call: Doc White, 27-13 in 1907; Ed Walsh, 40-15 in 1908; Eddie Cicotte, 28-13 in 1917 and 29-7 in 1919; Ted Lyons, 21-11 in 1925 and 22-14 in 1927; Billy Pierce, 20-12 in 1957; Early Wynn, 22-11 in 1959; Gary Peters, 20-8 in 1964; Wilbur Wood, 20-17 in 1972 and 24-20 in 1973; LaMarr Hoyt, 19-15 in 1982 and 24-10 in 1983; and Jack McDowell, 22-10 in 1993.

Comparisons may be odious, but baseball fans love them which is reason enough to also survey the list of Cub players who led the league in batting average, home runs and pitching victories to compare it to that of the White Sox. (Of course, the starting point is 1901, when the Sox became a major league team.)

Only five Cubs have won batting titles, Madlock being alone in doing it twice. The others: Heinie Zimmerman, .372 in 1912 (also led league in home runs and RBI for rare batting Triple Crown); Phil Cavarretta, .355 in 1945; Billy Williams, .333 in 1972; and Bill Buckner, .324 in 1980.

Home run leaders have been plentiful, Cubs winning or sharing the N.L. title 17 times between 1901 and 2000. Hack Wilson did it four times, while Frank "Wildfire" Schulte, Bill Nicholson and Ernie Banks led twice each. The roster: Schulte, 10 in 1910 and 21 in 1911; Zimmerman, 14 in 1912; Cy

Williams, 12 in 1916; Wilson, 21 in 1926, 30 in 1927, 31 in 1928 and 56 in 1930; Nicholson, 29 in 1943 and 33 in 1944; Hank Sauer, 37 in 1952; Ernie Banks, 47 in 1958 and 41 in 1960; Dave Kingman, 48 in 1979; Andre Dawson, 49 in 1987; Ryne Sandberg, 40 in 1990; and Sammy Sosa, 50 in 2000.

A dozen Cubs have won or shared the N.L. title for most victories in a season, only Pat Malone doing it twice. The rundown: Three-Finger Brown, 27-9 in 1907; Larry Cheney, 26-10 in 1912; Hippo Vaughn, 22-10 in 1918; Grover Cleveland Alexander, 27-14 in 1920; Charlie Root, 26-15 in 1927; Pat Malone, 22-19 in 1929 and 20-9 in 1930; Lon Warneke, 22-6 in 1932; Bill Lee, 22-9 in 1938; Larry Jackson, 24-11 in 1964; Ferguson Jenkins, 24-13 in 1971; Rick Sutcliffe, 18-10 in 1987; and Greg Maddux, 20-11 in 1992.

Of course, like many baseball facts and figures, the above lists of Cub league leaders glide smoothly and silently past a remarkable anomaly. The players who hold the Cub records in each category—batting average, home run total and most pitching wins—all failed to lead the league the season of peak accomplishment. Rogers Hornsby hit .380 in 1929 for the highest batting average by a Cub since 1900. Brown had the most wins when he went 29-9 in 1908. Sosa hit 66 home runs in 1998 when he finished second to McGwire's 70.

The White Sox record-setters have fared better. Only Albert Belle's team-high in home runs, 49 in 1998, failed to lead the league. Appling's batting average of .388 in 1936 and Walsh's 40 wins in 1908 led the league as well as set franchise records.

A league championship in batting average, home runs or pitching victories achieves a form of immortality, inclusion in that most hallowed of baseball tomes, the record book, which preserves for all time the names of players who otherwise might be quickly forgotten.

Chicago's M&M Boys, Melton and Madlock, deserve a gilded column of their own in that "good book." Each proved in the closing game of an otherwise lackluster season the indisputable validity of the adage, "Better late than never."

It beats all hollow that old and familiar Chicago cry of sorrow and despair, "Wait 'til next year!" The M&M Boys didn't have to.

No one could hope to predict accurately whether White Sox and Cub fans would need to repeat that lament in 2001 or in the years beyond. While White Sox hopes faded as the 2001 season approached its climax, the Cubs inflamed their followers' expectations to a fevered pitch with a stirring division title bid reinforced by the late July acquisition of slugger Fred McGriff. Whether the final result would be the Cubs' first pennant since 1945 or a calamitous reprise of the 1969 debacle was in the laps of the baseball gods, as unfathomable as ever, their intent never to be devined by experience or knowledge of former events. Despite what historians sometimes suggest, the past is no guide to the future, rather just a parade that has marched out of sight.

Nonetheless, a virtual journey into bygone days, a sort of tour through the colorful panorama of Chicago's baseball past, lends depth and appreciation to the pleasures of the game, especially if fleshed out with an understanding of its traditions and an awareness and recognition of those who shaped it into its present form.

It's all part of **Baseball,** *Chicago Style*.

INDEX

A

Accumulated memory, *x*
Adair, Bill, 157, 280
Adams, Bobby, 126
Adams, Franklin P., 49, 357
Adams, Terry, 225
Adcock, Joe, 296
Addison, John, 336
Advertising campaign, 234
Agee, Tommy, 144, 154–55, 167
Agosto, Juan, 197
Aguilera, Rick, 225, 227
Ahe, Chris von der, 248, 280
Air Force Academy, 259
Alexander, Grover Cleveland, 346
   acquisition of, 35
   honors, 353
   playing career, 14, 37, 60, 62
   records, 367
Algren, Nelson, 316
All-American Football
   Conference, 99
Allen, Richie "Dick," 158–59,
   271, 351, 365–66
Allison, Bob, 170
All-Star Game, 97–101, 351
All-Time Chicago Team, 355–58
Allyn, Arthur, Jr., 121, 153–56,
   270–71, 257, 343

Allyn, John, 156–60, 257, 271,
   309
Altman, George, 118
Altrock, Nick, *xi*, 26–28, 40–41
Alvarez, Wilson, 206–11,
   231–32
Amalfitano, Joey, 180–82
American Association, *xii*, 248,
   332, 338
American League, *ix*, 249–50,
   336, 338–39
Anderson, Bob, 117
Anderson, Sparky, 281–82
Andrews, Shane, 226
Angle, Paul, 253
Anson, Adrian Constantine
   "Cap," *xi*, 249, 330, 355
   background, 290
   career stats, 338
   death of, 292
   dismissal of, 292, 338
   managerial tenure, 290–92,
     334, 345
   playing career, 292, 314, 331,
     333, 344
Anti-trust issue, 254
Aparicio, Luis, *xi*, 351
   All-Time Chicago Team, 356
   Hall of Fame, *xiii*
   honors, 353

playing career, 111, 115–16,
121–22, 132–34, 155–57,
270
World Series, 349
Appalachian League, 300
Appling, Luke, 96, 351
All-Star Game, 100
All-Time Chicago Team, 356
Depression Era squad, *xiii*,
90, 93–95, 104–5, 232
Hall of Fame, *xiii*, 87, 92
honors, 353
records, *xiv*, 87, 157, 366,
367
Arizona Diamondbacks, 227
Arlin, Harold, 304
Ashburn, Richie, 126, 128, 295
Asinof, Eliot, 2, 316
Athletic Director, 259–61
Atlanta Braves
1969 season, 143, 144
1970 season, 145
1977 season, 281
1998 season, 223
Atlantic Monthly, 241
Attell, Abe, 3, 7–9, 18–19
Auditorium, 40
Auker, Eldon, 67
Austen, Jane, 326
Austrian, Alfred, 2–3
Austrian confessions, 2
Axelson, Gustav, 318

B

Baer, Bugs, 91
Bagley, Gym, 44
Bahnsen, Stan, 158, 159
Baines, Harold, 163–64, 197,
202–6, 231–32, 235, 299,
351
Baker, Gene, 109–10, 113
Baldwin, James, 231–36

Ballpark
dual purpose, 343
enclosed, 343–44
evolution of, 343–44
Ball tampering, 167–69
Baltimore Orioles
1954 season, 108
1959 season, 132, 271
1969 season, 241
1971 season, 86
1983 season, 196, 199
1991 season, 208
1997 season, 232
1999 season, 234
trades with, 155, 235
World Series, 144
Banks, Ernie, *xi*, 146, 174
acquisition of, 109–10, 299
All-Time Chicago Team, 356
College of Coaches Era,
118–20, 129
Cubs Great Collapse, 141,
142
Hall of Fame, *xiv*
honors, 353
MVP, 114, 117, 191
playing career, 109–17,
139–42, 145–46
records, 346, 366, 367
retirement of, 146
Ruth (Babe) comparison,
114
Bannister, Alan, 160, 162
Bannister, Floyd, 197, 199, 202,
204–5
Barbour, Lou, 245
Barnes, Ross, 330, 331
Barojas, Salome, 197
Barr, George, 81
Barrios, Francisco, 161
Bartell, Dick, 69
Bartholomay, Bill, 252, 270
Base-ball, 326

Baseball
  amateur clubs, 327–28
  bureaucracy, 261
  early parks, 327, 329, 330
  first commissioner, 4
  first professional team, 328
  indoor variety, 333
  league beginnings, 330
  origins of, 325–27
  popularity, 333
  prairie teams, 327
  recovery policy, 24
  rules, 326
Baseball Digest, 74, 255, 320, 355
Baseball Magazine, 27, 98
Baseball Writers Association of
    America, 16, 319
Basket catch, 243
Bat-gate incident, 170–72,
    210–11
Battey, Earl, 121, 135, 270, 297
Baumgarten, Ross, 163
Baumholtz, Frank, 105, 107,
    109
Baylor, Don, 224–26
Beck, Rod, 222, 223, 225
Beckert, Glenn, 120, 139–42,
    146, 174–75
Bell, George, 208–10, 217–18,
    299
Belle, Albert, 170–72, 210–11,
    232–34, 366–67
Bench, Johnny, 148, 150–51
Bender, Chief, 31
Bennett Field, 29
Benton, Al, 71
Bere, Jason, 209, 211, 227, 230
Berg, Morris "Moe," 90–91,
    239–42
Bernazard, Tony, 163
Berra, Yogi, 169
Berres, Ray, 270, 286
Berry, Ken, 122, 154, 157, 169

Berryhill, Damon, 214
Bevington, Terry, 230–31, 233
Bielecki, Mike, 215–17, 276
Bingham, Dick, 306
Black Sox Scandal, *xii–xiii, xvi,*
    1–20, 22, 38, 250, 261
Blackburne, Lena, 89, 244, 245
Blair, Paul, 241
Blauser, Jeff, 222, 223, 225
Bleacher bums, 346
Blomberg, Ron, 162
Blue, Vida, 241
Bonds, Bobby, 162
Bonham, Bill, 173–76, 178–79
Bonura, Zeke, 93, 251, 351
Boone, Ike, 286
Borowy, Hank, 71, 266
Bossard, Gene, 168–69
Bossard, Roger, 168–70
Bossard's Swamp, 169–70
Boston Bees, 286
Boston Braves, 72, 99, 281
Boston, Daryl, 201, 202
Boston Globe, 242
Boston Red Sox, 55
  All-Star game, 101
  1959 season, 133
  1967 season, 154
  trades with, 91, 214, 268, 271
  World Series, 36, 349
Boston Red Stockings, 291, 329,
    330, 334
Boudreau, Lou, 117, 308, 311
Bowa, Larry, 186, 274
Boxing bouts, 351
Box score, 313
Braddock, Jimmy, 351
Bradley, Tom, 157, 158
Bradley, Truman, 305
Brennaman, Thom, 311
Brickhouse, Jack, *xii,* 303, 304
  on criticism of Elson (Bob),
    306

broadcasting style, 307–8
Hall of Fame, 312
honors, 312
partners, 307, 308
retirement of, 310
WGN-TV, 307
Bridges, Tommy, 67
Bridwell, Al, 43
Broadcasters, 303–12
Brock, Lou, 119–20, 214, 260, 293–96
Broglio, Ernie, 119–20, 214, 260, 293–96
Brooklyn Atlantics, 329
Brooklyn Dodgers, 101, 107, 134, 147
Brooklyn Eagle, 313
Brooklyn Times, 286
Brosnan, Jim, 317
Brotherhood. *See* Players' League
Brown, Bobby, 171
Brown, Brant, 223
Brown, Clint, 93
Brown, Joe E., 305
Brown, Lorn, 310
Brown, Mace, 82
Brown, Mordecai "Three-Finger"
  acquisition of, 299
  All-Time Chicago Team, 356
  Golden Era, 21, 26, 27, 29–32, 39, 40, 47–48
  Hall of Fame, 320
  honors, 353
  records, 367
  World Series, 27, 29–31, 40, 41
Brown, Roosevelt, 227
Brown, Warren, 50, 71, 109, 319–22
Bryant, Clay, 68
Buckner, Bill, 177–82, 366
Buechele, Steve, 218

Buford, Damon, 226
Buford, Don, 154, 169
Buhl, Bob, 119
Bulkeley, Morgan G., 291–92
Bullinger, Jim, 221
Bunning, Jim, 284
Burdette, Lew, 295
Burk, Robert, 12
Burks, Ellis, 209, 210
Burns, Bill, 7–9, 18–19
Burns, Britt, 163, 164, 196, 202
Burns, Ed, 319
Burns, Ken, *x*
Burris, Ray, 176, 178
Busby, Jim, 106, 107
Bush, Donie, 89–90, 132
Bush, Guy, 61, 65, 76
Bush, Joe, 243
Butkus, Dick, 348
Buzhardt, John, 122, 169–70

C

Calderon, Ivan, 204–7
California Angels, 101, 167, 203, 272
Callaghan, Marty, 61
Callahan, James, 279
Callahan, Nixey, 24–25
Called-shot incident, *xv*, 65, 73–79, 346
Callison, Johnny, 121, 132, 135, 145, 270, 297
Camden Yards, 351
Camilli, Dolf, 297–98
Campbell, Bill, 188
Camp Ojibwa flap, *xv*
Cangelosi, John, 203
Cannon, Raymond, 15
Capone, Al, 69, 172
Caray, Harry, *xii*, 303
  broadcasting style, 307–9
  Cub career, 164

death of, 310
departure of, 164
firing of, 160
Hall of Fame, 312
partners, 310, 311
popularity of, 310
re-hiring of, 160
Caray, Skip, 311
Cardenal, Jose, 147, 174–79
Cardwell, Don, 117, 118
Carleton, Tex, 66
Carlos Hotel, 53
Carlson, David, 19
Carlton, Tex, 265
Carmichael, John P., 82, 315,
319–23
Carrasquel, Chico, 351
acquisition of, 104, 268,
298
Go-Go Sox Era, *xiii*, 105–8
trade, 111
Carriage parades, 22–23
Carroll, Clay, 160
Carter, Joe, 189, 274, 298
Carter, Nick, 15
Cartwright, Alexander Joy, 326
Caruso, Mike, 233, 234
Cash, Norm, 121, 136, 168,
270, 297, 364
Castillo, Frank, 218
Cavarretta, Phil, *xi*
Depression Era, 66, 67, 82
managerial tenure, 107–9
playing career, 109–10, 173,
346
records, 366
World Series, 71
Caylor, Oliver P., 281
Celler, Emanuel, 254
Central Intelligence Agency
(CIA), 239
Cermak, Anton, 76
Cey, Ron, 185, 189

Chadwick, Henry, 313, 317,
326, 328, 335
Chance, Frank, *xi*
All-Time Chicago Team, 356,
357–58
as author, 317
background, 283
career stats, 282
death of, 283
double play skills, 22, 49–51
firing of, 32
Golden Era, 21, 26, 29–32,
39–40, 45, 47, 283
Hall of Fame, 49–50
longevity of, 279
managerial tenure, 32, 88
Merkle's Boner, 44
player intimidation, 282
resignation of, 283
World Series, 27–32, 41, 42
Chandler, Happy, 101
Chapman, Ben, 79
Chappas, Harry, 162
Chase, Hal, 3, 4
Cheney, Larry, 367
Chicago American, 155, 263,
320
Chicago Bears, 347–48
Chicago Cardinals, 351
Chicago Daily News, 82, 255,
294, 303, 314, 315,
320–22, 331
Chicago Daily Post, 314
Chicago Eckfords, 332
Chicago Excelsiors, 327–28
Chicago Herald-American, 266
Chicago Herald Examiner, 5,
321
Chicago Inter-Ocean, 263
Chicago Lutheran Theology
Seminary, 346
Chicago Pirates, 336, 345
Chicago Record, 319

Chicago Sun-Times, 127, 139,
    172, 268, 316, 320
Chicago Times, 313
Chicago Tribune, 12, 20, 25, 44,
    59, 78, 97–101, 127, 220,
    261, 313–15, 319
Chicago Unions, 336
Chicago Whales, *xii*, 22, 33, 253,
    341, 346
Chicago White Stockings. *See*
    White Stockings
Chicago Wicket Club, 326
Chicago World's Fair, 97
Chifeds, 346
Childers, Jack, 142
Cicotte, Ed
    All-Time Chicago Team, 356
    arrival of, 32
    Black Sox Scandal, 6
    confession, 2, 4
    game fix role of, 19–20
    Golden Era, 12, 22, 33, 34,
        37, 86
    indictment of, 4
    records, 366
    salary, 12
    suspension of, 85
Cincinnati Commercial-Gazette,
    249
Cincinnati Enquirer, 281
Cincinnati Red Stockings, *vii*,
    328, 329, 343
Cincinnati Reds, 234
    1890 season, 281
    1917 season, 35
    1935 season, 66
    1949 season, 105
    1967 season, 150
    1969 season, 142
    1971 season, 146, 147
    1972 season, 148
    trades with, 266

World Series, *xii*, 19–20,
    37–38, 69, 349
City Series, 22, 42
Clark, Mark, 222
Clark, Will, 216
Clarkson, John, 333–35
Clean Sox, 4, 85, 86–87
Cleveland Indians
    bat-gate incident, 170–72,
        210–11
    1920 season, 85
    1947 season, 351
    1949 season, 104
    1954 season, 108, 111
    1955 season, 110
    1959 season, 115, 133, 270
    1983 season, 197
    1994 season, 210
    1995 season, 230
    1996 season, 231
    1997 season, 232
    1999 season, 234
    success of, 107
    trades with, 111, 136, 189,
        198, 268–70, 274, 297
    2000 season, 235, 236
Cobb, Ty, 13, 29–30, 64, 132,
    288
Cochrane, Mickey, 67
Colavito, Rocky, 101
Cole, Dave, 112
Cole, Dick, 126
Cole, King, 31
Coleman, Leonard, 224
College All-Star football game,
    99
College of Coaches Era, 119,
    125–29, 260, 280
Collins, Eddie, 351
    acquisition of, 13, 33
    All-Time Chicago Team, 356,
        357

Black Sox Scandal, 87
career stats, 89
Clean Sox, 4
Golden Era, 22, 33, 36–37, 86, 89
Hall of Fame, *xiii*, 87
honors, 353
managerial tenure, 88–89
World Series, 34
Collins, James "Rip," 68, 126, 265
Collins, Shano, 4, 86
Colorado Rockies, 225
Columbian Exposition, 337
Comiskey, Charles A., 4, 317
acquisitions/trades, 33, 339
American League role, 249–50, 337
biography, 318
Black Sox Scandal, 2–3, 9, 10, 250
building ballpark, 349
contributions of, 22, 24–25, 247
death of, 90, 250
defining moment, 247–48
franchise owner, 250, 339
investigation of, 18
managerial tenure, 336
payments to Clean Sox, 86–87
payroll, 11–12
player parades, 22
playing career, 248–49, 333–34
rebuilding of Sox, 88
reward offer, 17
Comiskey, Chuck
acquisitions/trades, 111
active management of, 267, 269
front office changes, 96, 104, 267

inheritance, 114
ownership feud, 251
sale of Sox, 252, 270
Comiskey, Dorothy, 94, 114, 251
Comiskey, Grace Reidy, 90, 94–96, 104, 114, 251, 262, 267
Comiskey, "Honest John," 248
Comiskey, John Louis "Lou," 90, 91
acquisitions/trades, 92
background, 250–51
contributions, 251
death of, 94, 251
Comiskey Park
All-Star Game, 100–101, 351
architect, 346, 349
attendance, 87, 103–7, 156, 158, 202, 268
construction of, 349
dimensions, 350
expansion of, 349
final game at, 350
lifespan, 342
lights, 350
media defamation, *xii*
memories, 351
night games, 94
opening of, 28
rebuilding of, 204–5
re-dedication of, 89
renovation, 88, 350
scoreboard, 120, 350
skyboxes, 350
sport venues, 351
Comiskey Park II, 348
attendance, 207
design, 351
fan convenience, 352
groundbreaking, 351
inauguration of, 207
upper deck concerns, 342

Concession stand, 23–24
Condon, Dave, 99
Congress Street Grounds, 334
Consuegra, Sandy, 108
Cook, Stanton, 184, 185, 276
Coombs, Jack, 31
Coomer, Ron, 227
Cooper, Wilbur, 290
Cora, Joey, 229
Corcoran, Jimmy, 319, 336
Corked bat incident, 170–72,
    210–11
Corriden, Red, 106
Corum, Bill, 74, 75, 78
Cowley, Joe, 203
Craft, Harry, 118, 126–28
Craig, Roger, 135
Crawford, Sam "Wahoo," 30
Creighton, Harry, 308
Cricket, 326–27
Cronin, Joe, 126
Crosetti, Frank, 68
Crowder, Alvin, 67
Crusinberry, Jim, 318, 319, 355
Cruz, Julio, 199, 200
Cub, Mr. *See* Banks (Ernie)
Cub Fever, 202
Cubs
    All-Star Game, 100, 101, 255
    Athletic Director, 259–61
    Broglio/Brock trade, 293–96
    City Series, 42
    College of Coaches Era,
        118–20, 125–29, 137, 260,
        280
    1876 season, 313–14
    exhibition games, 42
    farm system, 214
    front office, 259–61, 262–66,
        273–77
    Golden Era, *xiii*, 14–15, 23,
        26–32, 35–40, 47, 61, 347
    graybeards, 225

Great Collapse, *xiii*, 141–45
Grimm Era, 59–72, 105, 264
Hall of Fame, *xiv*
Homer in the Gloamin',
    81–84
individual achievements, *xiv*
inter-league play, 42
iron man, 149–51
major league status, *ix*
media defamation, *xii*
Merkle's Boner, 43–48
minor league affiliates, 127
1950s, 105, 107–17
1960s, 117–18, 138–45
1970s. 145–48, 173–80
1980s, *xiii*, 181–82, 186–93,
    213–16, 274–76
1990s, *xiii*, 216–23, 224,
    225, 277
origins. *See* White Stockings
park, 60, 347. *See also* Wrigley
    Field
Silver Age, *viii, xii*, 21
Tribune Co. ownership, 257
2000 season, 224, 226–27
World Series, *xi–xiii*, 21, 23,
    27–32, 36, 40–42, 63,
    65–68, 71–79, 346, 349
Wrigley family ownership,
    247, 252–57
Cuccinello, Tony, 95, 170
Cullenbine, Roy, 71
Cunningham, Joe, 122
Cuyler, Kiki, 54, 62, 119, 264

D

Dahlen, Bill, 338
Dailey, "Mysterious Dan," 244
Daily Olympian, 319
Daley, Richard J., 115, 260, 270
Dark, Alvin, 280
Darwin, Danny, 232

Davis, George, 28, 40, 41
Davis, Jody, 189, 191, 214
Davis, John, 54
Davis, Zachary Taylor, 346, 349
Dawson, Andre, 192, 214–19,
　　367
Deadball era, 26
Deadened ball incident, 167–69
Dean, Dizzy, *xv*, 67–68, 82, 323
DeBartolo, Edward, 163
DeBusschere, Dave, 301
DeJesus, Ivan, 177, 181, 186
DeLaSalle Institute, 250
DeLeon, Jose, 205
Demaree, Frank, 66, 69
Demeter, Don, 168
Dent, Bucky, 159, 161
Dernier, Bob, 188, 191, 274
Detroit Tigers
　　All-Star Game, 101
　　1948 season, 104
　　1959 season, 115
　　1965 season, 167–68
　　1966 season, 154
　　1974 season, 170
　　1979 season, 162
　　1983 season, 198
　　1991 season, 207, 348
　　trades with, 164, 268, 298
　　World Series, 29, 30, 67, 69,
　　　71, 323, 346
Devine, Bing, 294
Devlin, Art, 47
Dexter Park, 329
Dexter Park Pavilion, 327, 343
Diaz, Mike, 188
Dickey, Bill, 68, 79, 92
Dickshot, Johnny, 95
DiMaggio, Joe, 68, 92
DiMuro, Lou, 170
Disco Demolition Night, *xv*, 162
Ditka, Mike, 348
Dobson, Joe, 108, 268

Doby, Larry, 111–12, 162, 351
Donahue, Jiggs, 41, 42
Donovan, Dick, 110–12,
　　115–16, 133, 135, 270
Donovan, General "Wild Bill,"
　　239
Doolittle, Jimmy, 240
Dotson, Richard, 163–64,
　　196–97, 202, 202, 205
Doubleday, Abner, 318, 326
Double-play combination,
　　49–51, 64, 107, 110
Douglas, Phil, 4
Dozer, Dick, 261, 320
Drabek, Doug, 232
Drabowsky, Moe, 113
Drebinger, John, 76–77
Drees, Jack, 305, 308
Dressen, Charlie, 154
Dreyfuss, Barney, 290
Dropo, Walt, 110
Drott, Dick, 113
Drovers National Bank, 12
Dryden, Charles, 44, 282,
　　318–22
Drysdale, Don, 311
Dungeon Derby, 103
Dunne, Finley Peter, xv, 314–15
Dunston, Shawn, 214, 218–21
Durham, Leon, 182, 189–91,
　　214
Durham, Ray, 229, 232–37
Durocher, Leo, *xi*, 129, 153,
　　177, 262–63
　　acquisitions/trades, 138, 143,
　　　147
　　attitude towards Banks
　　　(Ernie), 140
　　career stats, 147
　　contract extension, 146
　　criticism , by, 146
　　dictum, 288
　　hiring of, 137–38

leadership, 139–40
longevity of, 279
secret mission of, 143
on Stanky (Eddie), 153
successor, 173
tenure of, 220, 241–43
Dybzinski, Jerry, 198, 200
Dykes, Jimmy, *xi, xiii*, 269, 280
acquisition of, 92
All-Star Game, 100
career stats, 285
firing of, 95
humor of, 284–85
longevity of, 279
managerial tenure, 92–95,
283–85
playing career, 285
talent pool, 92–93

E

East-West Negro League, 351
Eastman, Monk, 18
Eckersley, Dennis, 190, 191, 274
Edward VII, 335
Ehmke, Howard, 63
Einstein, Albert, 239–40
Eldred, Cal, 235, 236
Elia, Lee, 186–87
Ellsworth, Dick, 118–20, 139
Elson, Bob, 305–9, 312
Elston, Don, 117, 127
Emslie, Bob, 43–44, 45
Endorsement deals, 142
English, Woody, 62, 74, 78
Enright, Jim, 320
Erbes, Phil, 254
Esposito, Sammy, 115
Essegian, Chuck, 134
Essian, Jim, 217
Evans, Billy, 89
Evans, Nat, 18

Evers, Johnny, *xi*, 357
double-play skills, 22, 49–51
Golden Era, 21, 26, 30, 32,
45, 60, 181
hack incident, 31, 50–51
Hall of Fame, 50
managerial tenure, 88
Merkle's Boner, 43, 44–45
World Series, 29, 30, 41, 42
Ex-Cub factor, *xii*
Exhibition games, 42

F

Faber, Urban "Red,"351
All-Time Chicago Team, 356
arrival of, 33
Clean Sox, 4
Golden Era, 12, 22, 33–36,
86, 89
Hall of Fame, 87
World Series, 34
Fain, Ferris, 108
Falk, Bibb, 80, 87–90
Fallon, William F., 5
Family ownership, 247–57
Fans, 23–25, 29, 76–77, 103,
192–93
Farmer, Ed, 163, 311
Farm system, 264, 272
Farrell, James T., 315–16
Faul, Bill, *xv*
Federal League, *xii*, 22–23, 33,
253, 341, 346
Feller, Bob, 94
Felsch, Hap
arrival of, 33
financial settlement, 16
game fix role of, 19
indictment of, 4
perjury charge, 15–16
playing career, 34, 36

salary, 12
suspension of, 85
Femme fatale incidents, 53–57, 74
Fernandez, Alex, 204–11, 230–32, 272, 273
Fey, Jim, 191, 213–14, 217
Finley, Charlie, 280
Finnegan, Bob, 306
First National Bank of Chicago, 251
First Regimental Armory, 40
Fisher, Eddie, 122, 123
Fisk, Carlton
  acquisition of, 163
  All-Time Chicago Team, 356, 357
  comparisons, 234
  Hall of Fame, *xiii*
  honors, 353
  playing career, 164, 197, 202, 205–8
  retirement of, 209
Fitzgerald, Ed, 270
Fitzgerald, F. Scott, 1
Fixed games, 14–15
Flaherty, John, 284
Flanagan, Pat, 305
Flannery, Tim, 190
Fletcher, Scott, 198, 199, 206
Flon, Rick, de, 351
Florida Marlins, 231
Fonseca, Lew, 91–92, 244, 285
Football, 351
Forbes Field, 304
Fordyce, Bruce, 234, 235
Forest City, 328
Forster, Terry, 158, 161
Fortune, 254
Foster, Kevin, 219, 221
Foulke, Keith, 233, 235–36
Fournier, Jacques, 286

Fox, Charlie, 187
Fox, Nellie, 351
  acquisition of, 104, 268, 298, 299
  career stats, 357
  Go-Go Sox, *xiii*, 105–12, 115, 132, 134
  Hall of Fame, *xiii*
  MVP, 116, 134, 299, 357
  trade, 122
  World Series, 116, 135, 349
Foxx, Jimmie, 63
Frailing, Ken, 175
Frain, Andy, 83, 251
Frain, Pat, 251
Franco, Julio, 210, 211, 229
Franklin, Benjamin, 18
Franks, Herman, 146, 177–78, 180, 182
Free agency, 176–79, 217, 254, 331
Freehan, Bill, 168, 170
Freese, Gene, 121, 135–36, 297
Fregosi, Jim, 167, 205, 208
French, Larry, 66, 68, 265
Fresso, Vince, 171
Frey, Jim
  acquisitions/trades, 276
  background, 276
  as broadcaster, 311
  career stats, 187, 188
  managerial tenure, 187–88, 275–76
  on Sutcliffe (Rick), 189
Frick, Ford, 73, 126
Frick (Ford C.) Award, 312
Frisch, Frank, *vii–viii*, 72, 105, 107, 323
Froelich, Ed, 289
Front office
  Cubs, 259–61, 263–66, 273–77
  White Sox, 261–62, 266–73

Fryman, Woody, 179, 361–62
Fuchs, Emil, 281
Fullerton, Hugh, 318
    career, 319
    Hall of Fame, 320
    on Jackson (Joe), 33
    on Kling (John), 30
    legacy, 322
    World Series, 16–18
Funk, Frank, 199

G

Gaetti, Gary, 223, 225
Galan, Augie, 66, 67
Gallagher, James Timothy,
        69–70, 289
    acquisitions/trades, 266
    career change, 320
    firing of, 113
    five-year plan, 266
    replacement, 105
    as sportswriter, 320
    tenure, 266
    on Wrigley Field lights, 255
Gallico, Paul, 75
Gamble, Oscar, 161
Gambling, 14–15
Gandil, Chick
    Black Sox Scandal, 5–10
    game fix role of, 19
    Golden Era, 22, 34
    indictment of, 4
    salary, 12
Garr, Ralph, 160
Garvey, Steve, 190
Gehrig, Lou, 198
    Hall of Fame, 92
    records, 346, 354, 355
    World Series, 65–66, 68, 76
Gehringer, Charlie, 67
George III, 326, 335
George V, 324

Gibson, George, 60
Gideon, Joe, 3
Giles, Warren, 126
Gill, Warren, 45
Girardi, Joe, 226
Glanville, Doug, 222
Glavine, Tom, 300
Gleason, Kid, 20, 37, 85, 88
Goat, Billy, *xv*
Goddard, Joe, 320
Go-Go Sox Era, *xiii*, 103–21,
        268, 270, 351
Golden Era, 21–38
Goldis, Al, 272
Gomez, Lefty, 65, 68, 92
Gomez, Preston, 180–81
Gonzalez, Jeremi, 222
Gonzalez, Luis, 220
Goodman, Billy, 112, 115, 135
Gordon, Joe, 68, 269
Gordon, Tom, 227
Goslin, Goose, 67
Go-Slow Sox, 121–22
Gossage, Goose, 214
Gossage, Rich, 161
Grabiner, Harry, 11, 18, 88,
        90–92, 95, 261–62
Grace, Mark, *xi*, 214–27
Graham, Frank, 71
Grange, Red, 348
Grant, Mudcat, 134
Graybeards, 225
Great Chicago Fire, 329, 344
Great Collapse, *xiii*
Great Flop, 141–45
Green, Dallas, 213
    acquisitions/trades, 185–86,
        189, 274
    apology to fans, 192–93
    contract extension, 191, 275
    after Cubs, 193
    departure of, 193
    Executive of the Year, 191

hiring of, 183–85, 273
managerial tenure, 274–75
playing career, 273–74
Greenberg, Hank, 67, 71, 114, 121, 251, 269
Greene, Willie, 226
Grego, John J., 15–16
Griffey, Ken, 360–63
Griffith, Clark, *ix*, 24–25, 27, 338–39
Grimes, Burleigh, 76, 78
Grimes, Ray, 60
Grimm, Charlie, *xi*, 357
acquisition of, 264
background, 289–90
as broadcaster, 305, 308
career of, 59–72
College of Coaches Era, 126
after Cubs, 68, 72
longevity of, 279
managerial tenure, 105, 260, 265, 288–89
meaning of baseball to, 59
playing career, 65, 289
replacement of, 81, 105
return of, 113, 117
roles of, 66
World Series, 71, 75, 77
Grimsley, Jason, 172
Grissom, Marv, 108
Grobstein, Les, 186
Gropman, Donald, 2
Grove, Lefty, 148
Grove, Orval, 93, 95
Gudat, Marvin, 54
Guillen, Ozzie, 351
acquisition of, 202
departure of, 233
playing career, 205–9, 233
Rookie of the Year, 202
Gutierrez, Ricky, 226
Gutteridge, Don, 133, 156–57, 169

Guzman, Jose, 218
Gwynn, Tony, 190

H

Haas, Mule, 92, 95, 285
Hack, Stan, 66–67, 71, 110–13
Hacker, Warren, 109
Hack incident, 31, 50–51
Hall, Donald, *x*
Hallahan, Wild Bill, 100
Hallinan, Kevin, 171
Hamilton, Milo, 306, 308, 310
Hands, Bill, 138–42, 145, 147
Hansen, Ron, 122, 169
Hargrove, Mike, 172
Harkey, Mike, 216–19
Harrelson, Ken "Hawk," 203, 207, 271, 311
Harridge, Will, 98, 99
Harris, Vic, 175
Harshman, Jack, 108, 112
Hart, James, A., 24–26, 249–50, 337–39
Hartford Blues, 291
Hartnett, Charles Leo "Gabby," *xi*, 289
All-Star Game, 100
All-Time Chicago Team, 356, 357
firing of, 69
Hall of Fame, *xiv*, 84
homer in the gloanin', *xv*, 67, 81–84, 346
humor of, 69
managerial tenure of, 287
MVP, 84
playing career, 59, 61, 66, 68
World Series, 68, 78, 84
Hart's Remnants, 25
Hassey, Ron, 203
Hatfield, Fred, 112
Hayes, Jackie, 93

Heathcote, Cliff, 61
Heisenberg, Werner, 240
Hemond, Roland, 157, 159
    acquisitions/trades, 157–58,
        161, 202, 271
    background, 271
    Executive of the Year, 199
    managerial tenure, 271
    replacement of, 202–3
Henderson, Ken, 159, 160
Hendley, Bob, 120
Hendrix, Claude, 14–15, 36
Henrich, Tommy, 68
Henry, Bill, 117
Herbert, Ray, 122
Herman, Billy
    double-play combination, 64
    Hall of Fame, *xiv*
    playing career, 65–67, 83
    World Series, 67, 77
Hernandez, Roberto, 208–9,
    230–32
Herzog, Buck, 15
Herzog, Whitey, 188
Heydler, John, 99, 292
Hibbard, Greg, 206, 218
Hickman, Jim, 145
Hicks, Tom, 11
Hill, Glenallen, 223, 225, 226
Himes, Larry, 209
    acquisitions/trades, 203–8,
        218, 272, 299–300
    background, 204, 272
    departure of, 220
    draft choices, 204
    farm reorganization, 272
    firing of, 207
    managerial tenure of, 217,
        271, 276
    player contracts, 218
    staff changes, 219
Himsl, Vedie, 118, 126–28

Hirsley, Michael, 12
Hitless Wonders, 25, 39–42,
    349, 354
Hobbie, Glen, 113, 117
Hodges, Gil, 135
Hodges, Russ, 305
Hoffman, John C., 254–55
Hoffman, Solly, 31, 41
Hofman, Fred, 44
Hogan, Marty, 308
Holcomb, Stu, 157, 159
Holland, John A., 262
Holland, John Davis, 114, 138,
    146
    acquisitions/trades, 119, 260,
        294–95
    apprenticeship, 262
    College of Coaches Era, 126,
        128
    managerial tenure, 175, 260,
        261
    nature of, 262
    playing career, 113
    rebuilding efforts, 174
    retirement of, 176, 263
Hollocher, Charlie, 36, 60
Holt, Goldie, 126
Holtzman, Ken, 138–43, 145,
    147, 179
Home run battle, 222–25
Homer in the Gloamin', *xv*, 67,
    81–84, 346
Hooton, Burt, 147, 148,
    173–76
Hoover, Herbert, 76
Horlen, Joel
    Bossard's Swamp, 169–70
    playing career, 122, 154–56,
        169
    suit give-away program, 170
Hornsby, Rogers, 35, 59, 69,
    280, 346

acquisition of, 62, 264
dismissal of, 64, 281
managerial tenure, 64
playing career, 62–64, 216,
    264–65
records, 13, 64, 367
World Series, 75
Hough, Charlie, 207
Houston Astros, 147
Howard, Bruce, 301
Howry, Bobby, 233–36
Hoyt, LaMarr
    acquisition of, 161
    Cy Young Award, 199
    playing career, 163–64,
        196–99, 201–2
    records, 366
    trade, 202
Hubbs, Ken, 118–19
Hughes, Pat, 311
Hulbert, William, 291, 317,
    330–31, 344
Hundley, Cecil, 149
Hundley, Randy
    acquisition of, 138
    catching style, 149–51
    playing career, 138–39, 142,
        144, 174
Hundley, Todd, 151 175, 227
Hunt, Marshall, 319
Hunter, Catfish, 176
Hurst, Don, 297–98

I

Illinois Sports Facility Authority,
    350
Inter-league competition, *x*, 42,
    263, 352
Iron Age, 85–96
Iron man. *See* Hundley (Randy)
Isbell, Frank, 40, 41, 354

J

Jackowski, Bill, 296
Jackson, Al, 296
Jackson, Bo, 207, 209
Jackson, Danny, 217
Jackson, Darrin, 210, 211, 229,
    311
Jackson, Larry, 119, 120, 367
Jackson, Randy, 107
Jackson, Reggie, 364
Jackson, "Shoeless Joe," *xi*, 351,
    354, 355
    acquisition of, 13, 33
    All-Time Chicago Team, 356
    childhood, 12
    confession, 2, 4, 14, 15
    court transcript, 5–10
    financial settlement, 16
    game fix role of, 19
    Golden Era, 21, 22, 33–37,
        86
    Hall of Fame campaign, 2
    honors, 353
    indictment of, 4
    lawsuit, 10–11, 15–16
    perjury charge, 15–16
    salary, 12
    statistics, 12–13
    suspension of, 85
    World Series, 34
Jacobs Field, 351
Jarvis, Pat, 145
Jenkins, Ferguson, *xi*, 346
    acquisition of, 138, 299
    All-Time Chicago Team, 356
    Hall of Fame, *xiv*
    honors, 353
    playing career, 139–42,
        145–48, 173–74
    records, 367
    trade, 175

Jensen, Jackie, 133
Jethroe, Sam, 298
John, Tommy
  Bossard's Swamp, 169–70
  deadened ball incident,
    167–68
  playing career, 123, 154–57,
    169
  suit give-away program, 170
  trade, 158
Johnson, Byron "Ban," 15, 18,
  24, 249–50, 338–39
Johnson, Charles, 207–10, 225,
  235
Johnson, Darrell, 195
Johnson, Harold, 319
Johnson, Lamar, 161, 162
Johnson, Lance, 205–6, 222,
  230
Johnson, Walter, 284–86, 288
Johnstone, Jay, 157
Jolley, Smead, *xi*, 90, 91, 243–44
Jolly Cholly. *See* Grimm (Charlie)
Jones, Fielder, 21, 25–28, 40,
  354
Jones, Sam "Toothpick," 113
Journalism, 313–23
Judson, Howard, 268
Jurges, Bill, 53–55, 64–69, 74,
  77

K

Kaat, Jim, 159, 160
Kaese, Harold, 242
Kaline, Al, 168
Kamm, Willie, 88
Kansas City Athletics, 133, 154
Kansas City Monarchs, 109, 299
Karchner, Matt, 231, 232
Karkovice, Ron, 208
Karlins, Marvin, 316
Kasey, Sen, 304

Kawano, Yosh, 260
KDKA, 304
Keane, Johnny, 294
Keegan, Bob, 108
Kell, George, 110
Kelly, Edward J., *xi*, 97
Kelly, King, 333–35, 355
Kemp, Steve, 164
Kennedy, Bob, 119–20, 129,
  177–79, 182, 294–95
Kennedy, Vern, 93
Kerr, Dick,
  Black Sox Scandal, 6
  Clean Sox, 4
  Golden Era, 12, 21, 37, 86
  salary dispute, 88
  World Series, 20
Kessinger, Don, 120, 139, 142,
  162, 175–76
Kessler, Gene, 319
Kids Can Play campaign, 234,
  236
Killebrew, Harmon, 170
Killefer, Bill, 35, 60
Kiner, Ralph, 101, 109–12, 306
King, Eric, 206
Kingman, Dave, *xv*, 179–81, 367
Kirby, James, 2–3
Kittle, Ron, 165, 197–99,
  202–3, 207
Klein, Chuck, 66, 100
Klein, Lou, 118, 120, 123,
  126–29, 137, 295
Kling, Johnny, 26, 30–32,
  40–42, 47
Kluszewski, Ted
  acquisition of, 131, 269
  career stats, 131
  playing career, 115, 133–34
  World Series, 116, 134–35,
    349
Knowles, Darold, 361
Koenig, Mark, 74, 78

Konerko, Paul, 234–36
Koosman, Jerry, 164, 273
Koufax, Sandy, 120
Kravec, Ken, 163
Kreevich, Mike, 93
Kroh, Floyd, 45
Kruk, John, 229
Krukow, Mike, 178, 181–82
Kuenster, Jack, 255
Kuenster, John, 320
Kuhel, Joe, 93, 94
Kuhn, Bowie, 199, 301
Kwietniewski, Cass, 96

L

Ladies' Day, 263–64
LaGrow, Lerrin, 161
Lakefront Park, 344–45
Lake Park, 329, 344
Lake Street Dumping Ground,
    344
Lamabe, Jack, 143, 171, 208–9,
    230
Lamp, Dennis, 164, 181, 199
Lancaster, Leo, 215
Landis, Jim
    acquisition of, 112
    playing career, 112, 115–16,
        132–34, 270
    on Veeck's trades, 121
    World Series, 135, 349
Landis, Kenesaw Mountain, 4,
    18, 69, 98, 245
Lane, Bill, 252
Lane, Frank, *xi*, 96, 98, 351
    acquisitions/trades, 104–10,
        268–69, 298–99
    background, 267–68
    death of, 269
    inagural address, 104
    with Indians, 112
    personnel shuffling, 105

resignation, 111, 269
    tenure, 104–11
    waivers, 268
Lane Era, 104–11
Lange, Bill, 283, 338
Lardner, Ring, 263, 315,
    318–20, 322
La Russa, Tony, 162–64,
    196–99, 203, 231
LaSalle Street Station, 76
Latman, Barry, 115, 121
LaValliere, Mike, 172
Law, Rudy, 164, 199
Law, Vance, 198, 199, 214
Lawing, Gene, 126
LeCarre John, 240
Lee, Bill, 66–68, 83, 367
Lee, Carlos, 234–37
Lee, Vern Thornton, 93, 94
Lefebyre, Jim, 217–19
Leiber, Hank, 69
Lemon, Bob, 161, 162
Lemon, Chet, 159, 161–62, 164
Levin, Josh, 311
Lewis, Darren, 231
Lewis, Lloyd, 315
Leyland, Jim, 231
Libertys, 248
Lieber, John, 225, 227
Liebold, Norm, 4
Life Magazine, 287
Lincoln, Abraham, 327
Lindstrom, Fred, 265
Liston, Sonny, 351
Littlewood, Tom, 97
Lloyd, Vince, 306, 308, 311
Locker, Bob, 155, 174
Locker rooms, 22–23
Lockman, Whitey, 147, 173–75,
    279
Lollar, Sherm, 108, 112,
    115–16, 132–35, 202
Lombardi, Ernie, 69

Lombardi, Vince, *viii, xiii*
Long, Bob, 202
Long, Dale, 113, 114
Lonnett, Joe, 189
Lopat, Ed, 96
Lopez, Alfonso Ramon, 54–55,
    121, 279, 351
  acquisitions/trades, 301
  All-time Chicago Team, 356,
    357. 358
  with Cleveland, 287
  deadened ball incident, 168
  fan letter, 288
  guidance of, 120, 121, 122,
    132
  honors, 288
  managerial tenure, 270,
    287–88
  playing career, 111, 285–87
  predictions of, 114–15
  replacement of, 153
  retirement of, 123, 156
  return of, 155–56
  World Series, 135
Los Angeles Angels, 101, 252,
    264
Los Angeles Coliseum, 116
Los Angeles Dodgers, 101
  1965 season, 120
  1966 season, 139
  1969 season, 143
  1981 season, 185
  1984 season, 189
  1998 season, 234
  trades with, 158, 176, 177
  World Series, 116, 134–35,
    349
Lost season, 210–11, 219–20,
    229, 273
Lotshaw, Andy, *xv*, 76
Louis, Joe, 351
Lown, Turk, 115, 133, 270
Lucas, Henry, 336

Luckman, Sid, 348
Lumpe, Jerry, 168
Lundgren, Carl, 27, 27
Luzinski, Greg, 163–64, 197, 202
Lynch, Ed, 189
  acquisitions, 220–22, 226
  on graybeards, 225
  house cleaning, 225
  managerial tenure, 220,
    276–77
  playing career of, 192
  resignation of, 226, 277
Lynn, Fred, 101
Lyons, Ted, *xi*, 244, 351
  All-Time Chicago Team, 356
  career stats, 96
  Depression Era squad, *xiii*,
    89–90, 94, 95
  Hall of Fame, *xiii*, 87, 92
  managerial tenure, 95, 96
  records, 366
  resignation of, 104

M

McAfee, George, 348
McAuliffe, Dick, 168
McCarthy, Joe, 59, 62–64, 75,
    78, 92, 96, 264
McConnell, Joe, 310
McCormick, Bernie, 97–98
McCormick, Bertrand, 185
McCormick, Moose, 44
McCraw, Tom, 157
McCullough, Clyde, 113
McDaniel, Lindy, 119
McDonald, Charles, 15
McDowell, Jack, 230
  acquisition of, 204, 272
  Cy Young Award, 209,
    273–74
  playing career, 204–11, 273–74
  records, 366

McElroy, Chuck, 217
McFayden, Danny, 287
McGinnity, Joe, 43–45
McGlothlin, Jim, 146
McGlothlen, Lynn, 180, 181
McGraw, John, 16, 35, 46–47, 98, 357–58
McGwire, Mark, *xiv*, 222–26
Mack, Connie, 26, 75, 290
  ball tampering, 168–69
  Dykes (Jimmy) and, 284, 285
  first All-Star manager, 98
  longevity of, 280
  World Series, 31, 63
McKenna, Andrew J., 183–85, 190, 274
McKenna, Joan, 185
McLain, Denny, 300–301
McMullin, Fred, 4, 12
McNamara, John, 280
McNertney, Jerry, 169
MacPhail, Andy, 220, 222, 226–27, 267, 276–77
McRae, Brian, 220–22
McVey, Cal, 330
Maddux, Greg, 192, 214–18, 276, 300, 346
Madigan, John, 193
Madlock, Bill, 175–77, 221, 359–63, 366–367
Magee, Lee, 4
Magerkurth, George, 78
Maharg, Bill, 18–19
Mailer, Norman, 188
Majestic Hotel, 243
Malone, Pat, 62–65, 76, 367
Managers, 279–92
Mancuso, Ken, 69
Mandel, Harvey, 145
Mann, Louis, 16
Mantle, Mickey, 359
Manuel, Jerry, 233–37, 273

Maranville, Rabbit, *xv*, 60, 105, 242–43, 264, 290
Marion, Marty, 108, 110–11
Maris, Roger, 222, 224, 359
Marshall, Jim, 175–77, 361–62
Martin, Billy, 280
Martin, Fred, 126, 295
Martinez, Carmelo, 190
Martinez, Dave, 229
Mathews, Wid, 105–12
Mathewson, Christy, 3, 46, 47, 315
Matthews, Gary, 188–90, 227, 274
May, Carlos, 156, 158
Mays, Carl, 36
Mays, Willie, 243
Meany, Tom, 74, 75, 286
Media coverage, 16–18
Media defamation, *xii*
Melton, Bill, 156–60, 351, 359, 363–67
Merkle, Fred, 15, 30, 43
Merkle's Boner, *xv*, 43–48
Mertes, Sandow, 24
Metro, Charlie, 118, 128–29
Michael, Gene, 191–92, 275
Michaels, Cass, 96, 104, 106, 268
Mid-afternoon games, 23
Miller, Bing, 93
Miller, Glen, 297, 301
Miller, Lawrence, 60–61
Milwaukee Brewers, 68, 72, 202, 235
Milwaukee County Stadium, 343
Milwaukee Journal, 15
Mincher, Don, 121, 135, 270, 297
Minner, Paul, 109
Minnesota Twins, 230
Minoso, Minnie, *xi*, 351
  acquisition of, 104, 106, 136, 268

All-Time Chicago Team, 356
Go-Go Sox, *xiii*, 106–11, 120–21
trading of, 112
Misel, Harvey, 198, 199
Mitchell, Fred, 14, 35–37, 60
Mitterwald, George, 175
Molloy, Paul, 316
Monday, Rick, 147, 174–77
Montono, 285
Montreal Expos, 143–44
Moore, Joe, 64
Morales, Jerry, 175, 178–79
Moran, Bugs, 172
Morandini, Mickey, 222, 223, 225
Moreland, Keith, 186, 189, 191, 274
Morgan, Mike, 218
Morris, Johnny, 348
Moryn, Walt "Moose," 113, 114
Moses, Wally, 95, 132
Moss, Les, 155–56
Mostil, Johnny, 87, 89, 90
Moyer, Jamie, 214, 215
Mueller, Bill, 227
Mullholland, Terry, 221, 223
Munzel, Edgar, 139, 268–69, 319–20
Murcer, Bobby, 177–79
Murphy, Charles, 22–23, 26, 32, 283
Murray, Dale, 362
Musburger, Brent, 155
Myers, Forrest B., 318
Myers, Randy, 219–21
Mystique, *xv*

N

Nagurski, Bronko, 348
National Association of Base Ball Players, 327

National Association of Professional Base Ball Players, 329, 343
National Football League, 99
National League, *ix*
founding of, 291
locker room decree, 22
National League of Professional Base Ball Clubs, 330–31
Navarro, Jaime, 220–21, 232–35
Neal, Charlie, 134
Neily, Harry, 319
Nettles, Graig, 170
New York Clipper, 313
New York Daily News, 75
New York Evening Mail, 17, 44
New York Giants
Merkle's Boner, 43–48
1906 season, 26, 39
1908 season, 30
1911 season, 315
1916 season, 333
1951 season, 153
1969 season, 142
1998 season, 223
player suspensions, 4
Thompson's homer, 147
trades with, 69
World Series, 334–35, 137, 349
world tour, 250
New York Herald-Tribune, 77, 304
New York Highlanders, 27
New York Journal, 286
New York Knickerbocker Base Ball Club, 326
New York Mets, 155
1967 season, 139
1969 season, 142–44, 273
1970 season, 145
1973 season, 174
1984 season, 189
1989 season, 215

1999 season, 234
trades with, 181, 222
New York Mutuals, 291
New York Times, 49, 77, 78, 313
New York World Journal, 75
New York World Telegram, 74, 75
New York Yankees, 32, 55
  All-Star Game, 100
  1927 season, 12
  1951 season, 107
  1955 season, 110
  1956 season, 111
  1957 season, 111
  1959 season, 115, 133, 134,
    287–88
  1963 season, 122
  1964 season, 122
  1973 season, 159
  1974 season, 170
  1985 season, 202
  1989 season, 193
  ownership, 280
  player salaries, 176
  success of, 107–8
  talent pool, 92
  trades with, 159, 161, 199,
    203, 266
  World Series, 65–66, 68,
    73–79, 84
Newhouser, Hal, 71
Nicholson, Bill, 71, 366, 367
Nicholson, Dave, 122
Niekro, Joe, 140–41
Night games, 3, 23, 94, 213,
  254–55
Nipper, Al, 214
Nixon, Richard, 133
North Side Ball Park, 346–47
Nye, Rich, 140

O

Oakland A's, 147, 206, 241

O'Connor, Leslie, 95, 96
O'Day, Hank, 44–45
Oddballs, *xv*
O'Dea, Ken, 69
O'Doul, Lefty, 252
Oeckers, Bryan, 197
O'Farrell, Bob, 61
Office of Strategic Services
  (OSS), 239, 240
Offield, Bud, 260
O'Hara, Johnny, 305
Old Roman. *See* Comiskey
  (Charles A.)
Onslow, Jack, 96, 104, 105
Ontiveros, Steve, 177, 179
Ordonez, Magglio, 233–37
Organic Theater, 316
Orta, Jorge, 159
Osborne, Tiny, 61
Otto, Wayne, 319
Overall, Orval, 29, 30, 32
Owen, Frank, 26, 27
Owens, Paul, 274

P

Pacific Coast League, 3, 165,
  244, 252
Paciorek, Tom, 164, 311
Pafko, Andy, 71, 105, 107, 298
Palmeiro, Rafael, 214, 215, 298
Pancake, Edith, 283
Pappas, Milt, 145–48, 173–74
Parque, Jim, 233–34, 236–37
Parrish, Larry, 362
Parsons, Bill, 365
Paskert, Dode, 297
Passeau, Claude, 69
Patterson, Corey, 227
Patterson, Floyd, 351
Paul, Gabe, 254
Paulette, Gene, 4
Peabody, Eddie, 290

Pearson, Monte, 68
Pegler, Westbrook, 78
Pepitone, Joe, 145, 146
Perez, Melido, 206
Perry, Herbert, 235
Peters, Gary, 357
   playing career, 154–56, 167,
      169
   records, 366
   Rookie of the Year, 122
Peters, Johnny, 314
Pettit, Lloyd, 308
Pfiester, Jack, 26, 29, 31, 40, 47
Philadelphia Athletics
   ball tampering, 168
   1905 season, 26
   1908 season, 12
   1911 season, 12
   1932 season, 75
   ownership, 280
   trades with, 105, 268, 298
   World Series, 31, 63
Philadelphia Pearls, 291
Philadelphia Phillies, 35, 69
   All-Star Game, 100
   ball tampering, 169
   1922 season, 61
   1969 season, 141
   1972 season, 148
   1979 season, 180
   1981 season, 184–85
   player suspensions, 4
   trades with, 117, 135, 138,
      186, 188, 217, 222, 270,
      274, 297
Philley, Dave, 1951, 106
Phillips, Adolfo, 138–41, 143
Phillips, Bubba, 115
Phillips, Dave, 171–72
Phillips, Tony, 231
Pierce, Billy, 111, 351
   acquisition of, 104, 268, 298,
      299

All-Time Chicago Team, 356
as broadcaster, 308
playing career, 104, 106–12,
   115, 121, 133, 270
records, 366
World Series, 116, 135
Piersall, Jimmy, 164, 274, 310
Pipp, Wally, 198
Pittsburgh Pirates, 89
   All-Star Game, 101
   ball tampering, 168
   1907 season, 29
   1908 season, 45
   1909 season, 30
   1921 season, 304
   1932 season, 75
   1938 season, 67, 81–82, 83
   1984 season, 189
   trades with, 60, 109, 113,
      131, 161, 199, 264
Pizarro, Juan, 121–22
Plank, Eddie, 31
Player
   contracts, 12, 232, 254, 331
   parades, 22–23
   rebellion, 146
   salaries, 11–12, 176–77, 334
   suspensions, 3–4, 85
   waivers, 268
Players Association, 101
Players' League, *xii*, 249, 336,
   345
Players' strike, 163–64, 182,
   219–21, 229
Podres, Johnny, 135
Polinsky, Bob, 161
Polo Grounds, 46–47, 295–96
Popovich, Paul, 143
Popovich, Violet, 53–55
Povich, Shirley, 79
Power, Vic, 115, 134
Powers, Francis J., 320
Prairie teams, 327

Prell, Ed, 59, 127, 319
Puckett, Kirby, 354
Pulliam, Harry, 43, 45

Q

Quinlan, Jack, 311
Quinn, Robert, 270

R

Radcliff, Rip, 93
Rader, Doug, 195–96
Radio ban, 304
Radio broadcasts, 263
Raines, Tim, 207, 208, 210
Rariden, Bill, 34
Rath, Morris, 19–20
Reagan, Ronald, 308
Redford, Robert, 56
Redmon, Harry, Sr., 3
Regan, Phil, 140, 142, 145
Reichardt, Rick, 157
Reinsdorf, Jerry, 206, 231, 233
    bat-gate incident, 171
    front office changes, 203, 207
    on Green (Dallas), 185
    longevity of, 257
    1984 club, 201
    player contracts, 231–32
    purchase of Sox, 163, 271,
        310, 350
    rebuilding Comiskey Park,
        204–5
    White Flag Trade, 232, 236
Reisinger, Grover, 170
Rent-a-player scheme, 161
Reploge, Hartley L., 5–10
Reserve clause, 254, 331
Reulbach, Ed, 26–32, 40–41, 71,
        282, 357
Reuschel, Rick, 147–48, 173–81
Reuss, Jerry, 205, 206

Reynolds, Carl, 82
Rice, Grantland, *viii*
Richards, Paul, 106–8, 160, 268,
        279
Rickey, Branch, 298
Riggleman, Jim, 220–22,
        224–25
Rigney, John, 94, 111, 251, 269
Risberg, Swede, 3–4, 12, 15–16,
        20, 34
Rivera, Jim, 108, 133–35
Roberts, Howie, 320
Roberts, Robin, 148
Robertson, Charlie, 87
Robinson, Aaron, 104, 268, 298
Robinson, Eddie, 104, 106–8,
        268
Robinson, Floyd, 121, 122
Robinson, Jackie, 101, 320, 351
Rockne, Knute, 100
Rodriguez, Alex, 11
Rodriguez, Henry, 222–26
Rogovin, Saul, 106–8, 268
Rohe, George, 28, 40–41
Rojas, Mel, 221, 222
Roller-Coaster Era, 153–65
Romano, John, 121, 122, 136
Rooney, John, 311
Roosevelt, Franklin Delano, 76
Root, Charlie, 346, 357
    called-shot incident, 73
    playing career, 61, 65–66, 84
    records, 367
    World Series, 63, 65, 77, 78,
        79
Rose, Pete, 274
Rosello, Dave, 175
Rothstein, Arnold, 1–2, 4–5,
        17–19
Rounders, 326
Rowe, Schoolboy, 67
Rowland, Clarence "Pants," 68,
        113

acquisition/trades, 265
managerial tenure, 36, 112, 260
playing career, 33–34
replacement of, 69
World Series, 35
Royko, Mike, *xv*, 220, 315
Rudolph, Don, *xv*
Ruffing, Red, 65, 68, 92
Runnels, Pete, 101
Rush, Bob, 105, 109–10, 113, 306
Russell, Ewell, 32–33
Ruth, Babe, 134, 334
    All-Star game (1933), 99, 100
    Banks (Ernie) comparison, 114
    called-shot incident, *xv*, 65–66, 73–79, 346
    exhibition tour, 240
    Polo Grounds homer, 296
    records, 135, 224, 288, 354–55
    World Series, 36
Ruth, Claire, 76
Ruthven, Dick, 191
Ryan, Quin, 305

S

Sabo, Chris, 229
Sain, Johnny, 158
St. Louis Browns, 3, 248–49, 334–35
    1881 season, 333
    1910 season, 349
    1922 season, 86
    1939 season, 350
    1952 season, 108
    1953 season, 108
    ownership, 280
    trades with, 299
St. Louis Cardinal, 35

All-Star Game, 100, 101
Broglio/Brock trade, 293–96
Gas House Gang, 72
1924 season, 64
1926 season, 62
1935 season, 66
1938 season, 84
1954 season, 108
1955 season, 111
1969 season, 143
1984 season, 188, 189
1998 season, 222
1999 season, 225
trades with, 67, 119, 176, 181, 205, 265, 299
World Series, 323
Salary arbitration, 254
Saltwell, E.R. "Salty." 176, 177
San Diego Padres
    1969 season, 142
    1972 season, 148
    1984 season, 190
    trades with, 141
San Francisco Giants, 138, 215
San Francisco Seals, 244
Sanborn, I.E. "Cy," 318
Sandberg, Ryne "Ryno," *xi*
    acquisition of, 186, 274
    All-Time Chicago Team, 356
    career stats, 222
    contract extension, 218
    Gold Glove, 216, 276
    honors, 353
    MVP, 191, 275
    playing career, 186–89, 214–22, 275–76
    records, 216, 367
    retirement of, 220
    return of, 221
    on Zimmer (Don), 216
Sanderson, Scott, 191
Santiago, Benito, 225
Santo, Ron, *xi*, 174, 176, 296,

346
  acquisition of, 118
  All-Time Chicago Team, 356
  as broadcaster, 311
  College of Coaches Era,
    118–20, 129
  playing career, 118–20,
    139–46
  trade, 175
  with White Sox, 159
Sauer, Hank, 113
  acquisition of, 105, 266
  All-Star Game, 101
  MVP, 109, 266
  playing career, 105–13
Sax, Steve, 208
Schaefer, Rudy, 153
Schalk, Ray, 351
  arrival of, 33
  career stats, 357
  Clean Sox, 4
  Hall of Fame, *xiii*, 87
  managerial tenure of, 89
  playing career, 37
Scheffing, Bob, 72, 112, 114–17
Schiraldi, Calvin, 214
Schmidt, Mike, 180
Schmitz, Johnny, 72, 105, 107
Schoendienst, Red, 101
Schueler, Ron, 209, 231, 233
  acquisitions/trades, 207, 234,
    235, 299
  credentials, 272
  front office changes, 230
  hiring of, 207
  on lost season, 211
  managerial tenure, 229,
    272–73
  player contracts, 231–32
  resignation of, 273
  White Flag Trade, 232
Schulte, "Wildfire," 30–32, 41,
    47, 366

Schumacher, Gary, 286
Scott, Jim, 33
Seattle Mariners
  1980 season, 350
  1983 season, 199
  1993 season, 209
  2000 season, 236
  trades with, 199
Seaver, Tom, 201–3, 144, 273
Seerey, Pat, 96
Segar, Charles, 50
Selee, Frank, 26, 283
Selig, Bud, 42, 156, 224, 171
Selma, Dick, 141–42
Servais, Scott, 220
Seys, John O., 263
Shaw, Bob, 115–16, 133–35,
    270
Shea Stadium, 143–44
Sheckard, Jimmy, 26, 42
Sheely, Earl, 87, 89, 90
Sheridan, John, 290
Sherry, Larry, 116, 135
Shires, Art, *xv, xi*, 90–91,
    244–45
Short, Ed, 121–22, 153, 155,
    157, 270–71, 317
Shotton, Burt, 101
Sievers, Roy, 121, 135, 297
Silver Era, 59–72
Simas, Bill, 233
Simmons, Al, 92– 93, 100, 285
Simons, Herbert F., 74–75, 320
Singleton, Chris, 234
Sinton Hotel, 16
Sirotka, Mike, 233, 234, 236
Skinner, Joel, 201, 202
Skowron, Bill, 122, 123
Slaton, Jim, 364
Slaughter, Enos, 101
Smalley, Roy, 72
Smead, Jolley, *xv*
Smith, Al, 112, 116, 121,

133–35
Smith, Bob, 294
Smith, Curt, 304–9
Smith, Dave, 217
Smith, Dwight, 214–16
Smith, Edgar, 93, 94
Smith, Frank, 28
Smith, Lee, 180–81, 190, 192,
    298, 356
Smith, Marshall, 287
Smith, Reggie, 364
Smith, Wendell, 320
Smith, Willie, 141
Snider, Duke, 101
Snyder, Cory, 207
Snyder, John, 233, 234
Society for American Baseball
    Research, 353
Soderholm, Eric, 161, 162, 198
Softball, 333
Soldier Field, 348
Sorrento, Paul, 171, 172
Sosa, Sammy, *xi*, 346
    acquisition of, 206, 218, 299
    All-time Chicago Team, 356
    background, 224
    home run battle, 222–23
    MVP, 223
    playing career, 206–8, 219–27
    records, *xiv*, 224, 367
    trade, 208, 299–300
South Side Hit Men, 161, 351
South Side Park, 336–37, 345,
    348–49
Spahn, Warren, 148
Spalding, Albert Goodwill, *xi*,
    291, 355
    as author, 317–18
    building of West Side
        Grounds, 345
    building of West Side Park,
        345

departure of, 337
    playing career, 314, 327–31,
        344
Players' League disintegration,
    336
    Union League disintegration,
        336
    world tour, 335
Spalding (A.G.) & Brothers, 331
Spalding Guide, 281
Speake, Bob, 113
Spencer, Jim, 160, 161
Sperring, Rob, 175, 362
Spink, Al, 248, 332
Spink (J.G. Taylor) Award, 320
Sporting News, The, 13, 17, 176,
    248, 265, 275, 290,
    314–15, 319–20, 332, 334
Sports Illustrated, 253
Sportsman's Park, 335
Springstead, Marty, 171
Square Sox. *See* Clean Sox
Squires, Mike, 163
Stairs, Matt, 227
Staley, Gerry, 109, 115–16,
    133–34, 270
Stallings, George, 3
Stanky, Eddie, 123, 153–55,
    170, 280
Steinbrenner, George, 192, 199,
    280
Steinfeldt, Harry, 26, 29, 40, 41,
    44
Steinhagen, Ruth Anne, 55–57
Stengel, Casey, 90, 107, 155,
    281, 286–88
Stephenson, Riggs, 62, 65, 264,
    356
Stewart, Jimmy, 94
Stirnweiss, Snuffy, 95
Stone, Steve, 159–62, 175,
    310–11

Stratton, Monty, 93, 94
Suit give-away program, 170
Sullivan, Sport, 19
Sunday, Billy, 333
Sutcliffe, Rick
  acquisition of, 189, 274, 298
  Cy Young Award, 191,
    274–75
  playing career, 190–92,
    214–17, 274–75
  records, 367
Sutter, Bruce, 188
  All-Time Chicago Team, 356
  Cy Young Award, 180
  playing career, 176, 178–81
  records, 276
  trade, 181
Sutton, Ezra, 330
Swisher, Steve, 175

T

Taft, Charles, 23, 347
Taft, William Howard, 23
Tannehill, Lee, 40
Tanner, Chuck, 157–60, 363–65
Tapani, Kevin, 221–25, 227,
    231–32
Tappe, Elvin, 118, 126–28
Tartabull, Danny, 231
Tavarez, Julian, 227
Taylor, Jack, 299
Taylor, Sammy, 127
Taylor, Tony, 117
Tebbetts, Birdie, 285
Television, 306–12
Tennant, John H., 17
Tenney, Fred, 46
Texas Rangers, 11
  1977 season, 280
  1983 season, 195–97
  1993 season, 209

1995 season, 230
  trades with, 206, 215, 299
Theater, 316
Thigpen, Bobby, 204–6, 209
39th Street Grounds, 339, 348
Thomas, Frank "The Big Hurt, "
    xi, 351, 352
  acquisition of, 204, 272
  All-Time Chicago Team, 356
  MVP, *xiv*, 209, 211
  playing career, *xiii*, 206–11,
    230–37, 273
  records, 366
Thompson, Bill, 324
Thomson, Bobby, 114, 147
Thornton, Andre, 175, 298
Thurston, Sloppy, 89
Tidrow, Dick, 197–99
Tinker, Joe, *xi*, 33, 357
  double play skills, 22, 49–51
  Golden Era, 21, 26, 32, 47
  hack incident, 31, 50–51
  Hall of Fame, 50
  longevity of, 279
  Merkle's Boner, 45
  World Series, 32, 41, 42
Tipton, Joe, 105, 268, 298
Toney, Fred, 35
Top 100 Players of the Century,
    353
Torborg, Jeff, 205, 206, 208
Torgeson, Earl, 135
Toronto Blue Jays, 210
Totten, Hal, 73, 303–5
Townball, 326
Trachsel, Steve, 219, 221, 223,
    225
Trafton, "Tornado" George, 244
Trammell, Alan, 198
Trebelhorn, Tom, 219, 220
Tribune Co., 182, 184
  front office changes, 220

player contracts, 218
purchase of Cubs, 252, 257, 274, 310
on Wrigley Field, 348
Trillo, Manny, 175
Triple Crown, 32
Trout, Dizzy, 71
Trout, Steve, 162–63, 190–91
Trucks, Virgil "Fire," 71, 108, 110, 299
Turner, Bulldog, 348
Turner, Ted, 281
23rd Street Grounds, 330, 331, 344
Two balls in play incident, *xv*, 346
Tyler, Lefty, 36

U

Union Association, *xii*, 336
Union Base-Ball Grounds, 344
Union Stock Yard, 327, 343

V

Valdes, Ismael, 226, 227
Valentin, Jose, 235
Valentine, Bobby, 193
Vandenberg, Bob, 121
Van Dyck, Dave, 172, 320
Vaughn, Hippo, 22, 35–37
Vaughn, Irving, 318, 319
Veeck, William, Jr., "Bill," 68, 255
acquisitions/trades, 120–21, 131, 135, 160, 270, 297
Caray (Harry) and, 309
in Cleveland, 262
on College of Coaches, 126
Executive of the Year, 161
gimmicks, 160, 162
Harry's diary, 18

on La Russa (Tony), 163
ownership share, 114–16, 251–52, 257, 269
rent-a-player scheme, 161
re-purchase, 160, 271
sale of Sox, 121, 350, 163, 270
Wrigley Field scoreboard, 347
Veeck, William, Sr., xi, 36, 61, 64
acquisitions/trades, 264, 265
All-Star game proposal, 99
career change, 320
contributions, 263, 264
Cubs Park improvements, 60
Cubs restructure/resurgence, 62
death of, 66, 265
fixed games, 14
firing of Hornsby (Rogers), 64
on radio broadcasts, 305
as sportswriter, 318, 319
tenure, 263
Ventura, Robin
acquisition of, 204, 272
departure of, 234
Gold Glove, 273
playing career, 206–9, 230–33, 271
Vidmer, Richard, 77
Vukovich, John, 191, 193, 275

W

Wagner, Leon, 101
Waitkus, Eddie, 55–57, 72
Waldorf Astoria Hotel, 361
Walker, Dixie, 93
Walker, Greg, 165, 198–99, 204–5
Walker, Harold, 265
Walker, Verlon "Rube," 126, 295
Wallis, Joe, 362
Walls, Lee, 114

Walsh, Ed, *xi*, 32
  All-Time Chicago Team, 356
  Golden Era, 21, 22, 27–28,
    40, 241, 316, 354
  Hall of Fame, *xiii*
  honors, 353
  managerial tenure, 88
  records, 367
  World Series, 27–28, 41
Walton, Jerome, 215, 216, 276
Waner, Lloyd, 82
Waner, Paul, 82
Ward, Arch, 97–100
Ward, Geoffrey C., *x*
Ward, John Montgomery, 336
Ward, Pete, 122, 154, 169
Ward, Tom, 98
Warneke, Lou, 64–66, 141, 357,
  367
Warner Hotel, 6
Washington, Claudell, 162
Washington Nationals, 328
Washington Post, 79
Washington Senators, 25, 133,
  297
WBKB-TV, 307
Weaver, Buck, 4, 12, 85, 33
Weber, Charles, 265
Weber, James, 66, 68, 69
Weeghman, Charles, 36, 253
  contributions, 22, 23–24
  purchase of Cubs, 346, 347
  spending spree, 35
  tenure, 23–24, 33
Weeghman park, 346
Weimer, Jack, 26
Weis, Al, 155
Wells, Don, 306
Wendell, Turk, 221–22
Wert, Don, 168
West, Jim, 308
West Side Grounds, 23, 27, 29,
  337, 345–47

West Side Park, 334–36, 345
WFLD, 308
WGN, 304, 307–10
Whales Park, 346
White, Bill, 294
White, Doc, 26–28, 32, 41, 315,
  349, 357, 366
White Flag Trade, 232, 236
White, Jim, 330
White, Rondell, 227
Whitehead, John, 1935, 93
White Sox
  All-Star Game, 100
  Allyn brothers ownership, 257
  beginnings, 339
  Black Sox Scandal, *xvi*,
    xii–xiii, 1–20
  City Series, 42
  Comiskey family ownership of,
    249–52
  Depression Era squad, *xiii*
  exhibition games, 42, 285
  farm system, 233, 251
  front office, 261–62, 266–73
  Golden Era, *xiii*, 12, 24,
    26–28, 32–40, 316,
    349–50, 354
  Go-Go Sox Era, *xiii*, 21,
    110–12, 114–15, 268, 270
  Go-Slow Sox, 121–22
  Hall of Fame, *xiii*
  Hitless Wonders, 25, 39–42
  home games in Milwaukee,
    155, 156
  individual achievements, *xiv*
  inter-league play, 42
  Iron Age, 85–96
  Lane Era, 96, 104–11,
    268–69
  major league status, *ix*, 24
  media defamation, *xii*
  name change, 24
  nicknames, *xii*

1960s, 121–23, 136, 167–68
1980s, 201–6
1990s, *xiii*, 201, 206–11,
   229–35, 273–74, 348
player raids, 24–25
player salaries, 12
Reinsdorf (Jerry) ownership,
   257
Roller-Coaster Era, 153–65,
   169, 350
2000, *xiii*, 235–37
Veeck (Bill) ownership, 257
Winning Ugly, *xiii*, 195–200
World Series, *xi–xiii*, 21,
   27–28, 34–42, 68, 85–87,
   116, 134–35, 346, 349
world tour, 250
White Stocking Park, 344
White Stockings, *ix*, 250
   1800s, 331, 337–38
   nicknames, 337, 338
   original, 329
   player raids, 330
   semi-pro status, 330
   World Series, 334–35
   world tour, 335
Whitlow, Robert, 119, 120,
   259–61
Wilhelm, Hoyt, 122, 145, 155
Wilkins, Rick, 219, 220
Will, Bob, 295
Williams, Biart, 40
Williams, Billy, 346
   All-Time Chicago Team, 356
   Hall of Fame, *xiv*
   playing career, 118–20,
      139–42, 145–48, 174
   records, 366–67
   Rookie of the Year, 118
   trade, 175
Williams, Claude "Lefty," 2,
   4–12, 19–20, 33–37, 86
Williams, Cy, 297

Williams, Dick, 280
Williams, Joe, 74–75
Williams, Kenny, 273
Williams, Mitch "Wild Thing,"
   215–17, 276
Williams, Ted, 199, 242
Williams, Walt "No Neck," 156
Wills, Maury, 116
Wilson, Bert, 306, 307, 311
Wilson, Hack, *xi*, 289, 321
   acquisition of, 264
   All-Time Chicago Team, 356
   playing career, 61–63, 264
   records, *xiv*, 366, 367
   trade, 64
Wilson, Jim, 69, 111
Wilson, Joe, 307
Wilson, Owen "Chief," 282
Winning Ugly, 351
WMAQ, 303, 304
Woltz, Larry, 319
Wood, Kerry, *xi, xiv*, 223, 225,
   227, 277
Wood, Wilbur, 156–59, 351,
   357, 366
World Series
   first, 334–35
   1903, 25, 250
   1906, *xi, xiii*, 22, 25, 29,
      40–42, 71, 346, 349
   1907, *xiii*, 23, 346
   1908, *xii, xiii*, 21, 23, 346
   1917, *xiii*, 21, 34–35, 68, 349
   1918, 349
   1919, *xii–xiii*, 13, 16–18,
      85–87, 250, 349
   1929, 63
   1932, 65–66, 73–79
   1934, 323
   1935, 67, 68
   1938, 84
   1945, 71
   1954, 137

1959, 116, 134–35, 349
1969, 144
radio broadcasts, 304
Wortham, Tex, 1979, 163
Wright, Bill, 94, 104
Wright, George, 328
Wright, Harry, *vii*, 328, 329
Wright, Taft, 93, 94
Wrigley, Bill, 125
  death of, 257
  financial woes, 181–82
  sale of Cubs, 252, 257
Wrigley, Helen, 263
Wrigley, Philip K., 66, 320
  acquisitions/trades, 265
  All-Star game proposal, 99
  apology to fans, 103
  Broglio/Brock trade, 295
  College of Coaches, 118–19,
    125–29, 280
  death of, 181, 253, 257
  as fan, 255–56
  housecleaning by, 113
  integration, 109–10
  loyalty of, 146, 147
  on 1969 team, 144–45
  night baseball, 254–55
  as pioneer, 254–55
  player salaries, 67, 176–77
  rebuilding efforts, 174, 175
  reclusiveness, 253–54, 256
  staff changes, 64, 68–70, 105,
    112, 117, 137–38
  testimony before Congress,
    247, 254
Wrigley, William, Jr., *xi*, 23, 36,
    61, 320
  acquisitions, 62
  background, 252–53
  behavior of, 252
  Cubs Park improvements, 60
  death of, 253, 265
  as fan, 63

farm system, 264
firing of McCarthy (Joe),
    63–64
hiring of first general manager,
    263
majority ownership, 247, 253
on radio broadcasts, 305
Wrigley Field, *xii*, 23
  All-Star Game, 100, 101
  alterations, 341–42
  architect, 349
  assets, 348
  attendance, 87, 103, 141–42,
    179, 180, 202, 213, 215,
    224
  building of, 22
  Chicago Bears at, 347–48
  flexibility of, 342
  improvements, 68, 264
  legendary events, 347
  lights, 254–55, 342
  move to, 346
  night games, 213
  prior name, 347
  renovations, 62
  scoreboard, 347
  temporary bleachers, 76
World Series, 63, 68
Wrigley (Wm.) Co., 252
WSNS, 308
Wynn, Early, *xi*
  acquisition of, 112
  as broadcaster, 311
  Cy Young award, 115
  playing career, 112, 115–16,
    121, 133–34, 270
  records, 366
  World Series, 116, 135
Wyse, Hank, 266

Y

Yankee Stadium, 65, 170, 236

York, Rudy, 71
Young, Don, 141, 143, 226
Young, Eric, 226
Young, Pep, 82

Z

Zernial, Gus, *xi*, 104, 106
Zim's Boner, 34
Zimmer, Don, *xi*, 198
   College of Coaches Era, 127,
     128

longevity of, 280
managerial tenure, 214, 276
on 1989 club, 215
replacement of, 217
on Sandberg (Ryne), 216–17
Zimmerman, Heinie, *xi*, 4
   All-Time Chicago Team, 356
   Golden Era, 32
   records, 366
   suspension of, 4
   World Series, 31, 34
Zisk, Richie, 161
Zuleta, Julio, 227